Fodor's

EXPLORING

GERMANY

FODOR'S TRAVEL PUBLICATIONS, INC.

NEW YORK • TORONTO • LONDON • SYDNEY • AUCKLAND

WWW.FODORS.COM/

Copyright © 1996 by The Automobile Association
Maps copyright © 1996 by The Automobile Association

All rights reserved under International and Pan-American Copyright Conventions. Distributed by Random House, Inc., New York. No maps, illustrations, or other portions of this book may be reproduced in any form without written permission from the publishers.

Published in the United States by Fodor's Travel Publication, Inc.
Published in the United Kingdom by AA Publishing.

Fodor's and Fodor's Exploring Guides are trademarks of Fodor's Travel Publications, Inc.

ISBN 0–679–03207–X
Third Edition

Fodor's Exploring Germany

Authors: **John Ardagh, Lindsay Hunt, Michael Ivory, Michael Kallenbach, Stephen Locke, Tim Locke, Colin and Fleur Speakman**
Revision verifier: **John Ardagh**
Additional writing and research by: **Tony Evans, Audrey Horne**
Cover Design: **Louise Fili, Fabrizio la Rocca**
Front Cover Silhouette: **Kevin Galvin**

Special Sales
Fodor's Travel Publications are available at special discounts for bulk purchases (100 copies or more) for sales promotions or premiums. Special editions, including personalized covers, excerpts of existing guides, and corporate imprints, can be created in large quantities for special needs. For more information, contact your local bookseller or write to Special Markets, Fodor's Travel Publications, 201 East 50th Street, New York, NY 10022. Inquiries from Canada should be directed to your local Canadian bookseller or sent to Random House of Canada, Ltd., Marketing Department, 2775 Matheson Blvd. East, Mississauga, Ontario L4W 4P7.

Printed and bound in Italy by Printer Trento srl
10 9 8 7 6 5 4

Bad Wimpfen, on the River Neckar north of Heilbronn, makes the most of its attractive architecture

About this book

This book is divided into three principal sections.

The first part of the book discusses aspects of life today and in the past. The second part covers places to visit, including drives and walks. The Focus on... features, also in this section, look at subjects in greater detail. The final part is the Travel Facts chapter, which includes both practical day-to-day information for the traveler, and the Hotels and Restaurants section, a selective list of accommodations and places to eat.

Some of the places described in this book have been given a special rating:

 Do not miss

 Highly recommended

 See if you can

General Contents

CONTENTS

CONTENTS

Features

Walks

Drives

My Germany

by Professor Werner Niefer, former Chairman, Mercedes-Benz Corporation

It's an exciting, interesting time in Germany today, as two completely different states—separated for 40 years—grow together again. A great deal is being accomplished, as everyone wants Germany to maintain its strong economic role despite its new size. Germany is one of the most densely populated regions on earth, with more cars per 1,000 inhabitants than anywhere else in Europe—but the image of an overdeveloped countryside packed with concrete industrial plants and lined with traffic routes is false. Only 7 percent of the country's land area goes to community and industrial development; only 5 percent is devoted to transportation, although Germany is certainly the main axis of travel from the European north to the south and, since the opening of eastern Germany, from west to east as well. The rest of the land area is countryside, and it could hardly be more varied—from flat, sparsely populated North Friesland with its islands to the picture-book landscapes and high mountains of the Alps. Since the peaceful revolution in the former GDR and the reunification of the two states, our country has grown by about a third. We West Germans marvel at how time has stood still in eastern Germany. We are fascinated with cobblestone streets and endless tree-lined alleys—and have to overlook the bad, hopelessly overtaxed infrastructure, reminiscent of western Germany 40 years ago.

I must admit that for me, my Germany is the southwest—Baden-Württemberg, the heart of Europe, where the car was born and where still today the most fascinating cars are manufactured. My Germany is also the rough landscape of the Schwäbischen Alb, the hills and deep valleys of the Black Forest, Lake Constance with its friendly shores and historical cities, the hills and mountains of the Allgäu and the steep peaks of the Allgäu Alps—all unique in their variety and beauty.

Naturally these areas attract tourists, but for the residents, the variety of landscapes, historical background and cultural richness, the ever-changing views, are never dull. May these areas remain the insiders' vacation gem—not to be missed on any account.

Bavarian forest scenery

My Germany

by Praxedes Leitner

Since unification, Germany has almost doubled in size. Now, we former West Germans have the chance to discover the five *Länder* (states) that East Germany comprised, as unknown to us as to any visitor from another country. For a West Berliner, once living in the "island in the Communist sea," going east now is as simple as crossing a bridge.

Well, I'm ready at the wheel of my car to discover the area around Berlin, and what do I find? Everyone else in the city has the same idea—it's bumper-to-bumper traffic. A little patience, though, and soon I'm looking at lush meadows and fields dotted with brown and white cows, rolling hills scattered with wildflowers. There are endless romantic roads—though the East Germans were never known for building good roads, and some roads are still badly potholed. The houses look outdated, shabby and uninviting. The people seem to be introspective—they're not exactly used to tourists—but, soon, people begin to appear on the sidewalks, realizing that tourists have strong Deutschmarks in their pockets and are willing to spend them. Local residents have erected colorful homemade stalls offering fruit and vegetables—produce grown on their small plots of land. Feeling hungry, I find an *Imbiss* (snacks) stand taking advantage of the free market economy. The owner is somewhat reserved...should I feel guilty? Am I disturbing his peace and quiet?

It is odd being a tourist in your own country, enjoying atmosphere and surroundings that haven't changed in 40 years, but soon I've totally overcome any hesitation I had about exploring this part of Germany. I make plans to spend a weekend at the Baltic Sea, rent a kayak in the Spreewald for a couple of days, tour the Elbsandsteingebirge near Dresden and Meissen, to travel through the Saale Valley. And I must keep some time for a winter skiing trip to the Erzgebirge.

Why don't you try to find some of the hidden treasures of eastern Germany, and then maybe we could swap stories?

■ **For centuries, Germany did not exist as one country. The peoples who make up the German nation lived where they live today, but the country consisted largely of small, independent units. The differences between the peoples were—and still are—great. Asked to sum up Germany as a country, some foreigners simply claim that it still doesn't exist ...■**

First there's the language. Throughout the provinces, a vast variety of words is used to describe the most common objects. More than mere dialect, this reflects the local nature of German thinking. Many youngsters leaving home to visit another part of Germany have to abandon the vernacular and use Hochdeutsch, the nation's lingua franca, to communicate. Traveling out of one's region can be like going on a trip abroad.

As with language, so with loyalties. Germans talk lovingly of their *Heimat*, or local area. This emotional attachment is felt by Germans of all ages. The alleged German lust for power doesn't tally with this world where the small unit is the most important—the club, the choir, the *Stammtisch* (the regulars' table in a bar, labeled as such and respected).

How, then, to explain the determination of the eastern Länder to join with the west and form an even bigger national unit? The nation-state is a compromise. Easterners have stressed, since

❏ During the national debate in 1991 about whether the united Germany's seat of government should return to Berlin from Bonn, Bavarians often spoke out against this idea, saying that the entire country believed Munich to be the secret capital of Germany. ❏

GERMANY

0	50	100	150 km
0		50	100 miles

The tourist's Germany: an Augsburg café

unification, that they feel more attached to their surroundings than to some bureaucracy in Bonn or Berlin. The general attitude is that there has to be a bureaucracy—vital in a truly world-class nation—but let it get on with its business and leave individual parts of the alliance that is Germany in peace. That is the measure of the new Germany, which has grown from an understanding of the errors of the old Germany. The emphasis on home, hearth, and locality is natural in a nation for which dogmatic imperialism is a bitter memory.

Food

■ **Sausage, sauerkraut, beer, coffee and enormous cakes come to mind as typical German fare. And, yes...sausages come in hundreds of varieties, while cabbage *is* consumed quite frequently, along with large quantities of potatoes. These stereotypical images are, as you might expect, only a small part of the picture. The reality is much more varied and adventurous ...■**

There are some staple menu items: *Kaffee und Kuchen*—coffee and cake—is a favorite afternoon snack, with rich cakes, usually topped with mounds of whipped cream. Beer is found in a variety of forms, from Pilsner to Berlin's *Weisse*, a beer with a sweet syrup added to it. Local wine is a welcome addition to a hearty German meal.

Quality and variety Visitors are often surprised at how well prepared German food is—and at its variety. A visit to the food halls in Berlin's giant KaDeWe department store or the elegant Alois Dallmayr store in Munich will bear this out.

❑ In KaDeWe's seventh-floor food hall, with its special high-speed elevator that stops nowhere else, there are over a thousand varieties of German sausage—overwhelming to the uninitiated sausage buyer! ❑

German cooking is reputedly heavy, but the country's restaurant scene has recently been invaded by *neue deutsche Küche*—nouvelle cuisine German style—featuring creative and tasty dishes using traditional German ingredients.

Eating through the day For most Germans, breakfast may include a boiled egg, granola and yogurt, but more probably bread with cheese, jam and/or cold meats. Lunch, the main meal of the day, could include a juicy *Schnitzel* (cutlet)—usually pork—roasted potatoes and a salad.

Dinner is often a cold and lighter meal of bread, a larger variety of meats and cheeses than at breakfast, and, in colder weather, perhaps a soup or small stew. A popular stew is a combination of lentils and sausage. German desserts are almost always fruit- or cream-based dishes.

The amount of bread consumed by most Germans will astound visitors, and the variety and amount of textured, heavy, dark brown breads in the bakery is amazing. Try them all and decide which you like most.

Bread is an important ingredient in German cuisine

■ **The homeland of Bach, Beethoven, Brahms, Wagner and Stockhausen, among many other of the world's musical geniuses, Germany has a reputation for nurturing musicians and composers—a tradition centuries old that survives today. Visitors will find a wealth of musical events, from the historic and classical to modern, up-to-the-minute rock ...■**

Among the joys of a trip to Germany are evenings at the Berlin Philharmonic, the Staatsoper of east Berlin, the Hamburg Opera and Munich's National Theater (home of the Bavarian State Opera), which offer some of the best orchestral sounds and operatic productions to be heard and seen anywhere in the world.

14

❑ The Berlin Philharmonic—the best orchestra in the country and one of the best in the world—has Claudio Abbado as its chief conductor. ❑

A brief history The German love of music and traditional folk songs can be traced back to pre-Christian tribal times. By the end of the 15th century, with the widespread use of the newly developed organ in churches, national interest and support for classical music had blossomed. In the 16th and 17th centuries, with the Reformation and the flowering of the Lutheran chorale, musical excellence was associated with churches. At this time vocalists, choristers, organists, instrumentalists, and their directors worked as professionally paid musicians.

By the 18th century, court patronage was an important source of employment for musicians. German Baroque music began to flower in such geniuses as Handel, Telemann, and Bach. At the same time, musical theater was developing in Vienna, and the German singspiel became the rage. At the peak of the singspiel's popularity, Mozart wrote

Above: Ludwig Van Beethoven
Top: the Munich Oktoberfest

his last opera, *The Magic Flute*, and German opera came of age. Beethoven produced his major romantic symphonies and his only opera, *Fidelio*, soon after this time.

Romanticism was in the air in Germany in the 19th century. After Beethoven came Schumann and Mendelssohn, then Brahms, Liszt, and Wagner, who transformed German national folk tales into powerful Romantic operas.

German music suffered a setback in the mid-20th century, under Nazism, when all "Jewish" music was banned. However, since the war the avant-garde—headed by Karlheinz Stockhausen—has pioneered new musical forms.

The music scene today The numerous choirs founded earlier in Germany are still the springboard for much of the country's musical talent.

Thanks to the nation's generous tax system, which includes a levy for churches, choirs are found in many small communities. At city, state, and national levels, huge subsidies for the performing arts and symphony orchestras help keep standards extremely high, and the cost of tickets for performances exceptionally low. Thus classical music is enjoyed by a greater segment of society in Germany than almost anywhere else, though this has the drawback that tickets are much more difficult to come by.

Visitors are always advised to plan ahead and reserve seats well in advance. However, as in most major cities, the concierge in the bigger hotels invariably has his own excellent contacts and will generally be able to meet your last-minute wishes—encouraged, of course, by a generous tip.

During the 1950s, jazz—totally suppressed by the Third Reich—was effectively a copy of the American scene. By the 1960s foreign jazz musicians had lost their appeal to German youth, and the embryonic rock groups flourishing in Britain,

most notably the Beatles, were invited to play in new clubs in Hamburg, Hannover, and West Berlin. Their popularity quickly spawned imitators such as the Rattles, who enjoyed great domestic success. Their lack of confidence and rock tradition, however, meant that any songs destined for foreign markets were sung in English.

Particularly popular was the heavier, more introspective end of the rock spectrum, and artists such as Amon Duul and Tangerine Dream soon released albums—rarely singles—with huge sales, the latter conquering the international market. This "progressive" music gave rise to the technically sophisticated and influential Kraftwerk, a band with a more definable German identity.

The varied jazz scene now includes a host of imaginative German musicians. Many record on the ECM label, an adventurous company that promotes contemporary music.

Music in all forms flourishes in Germany. Below: jazz in Hamburg; top: the Berlin Philharmonic Orchestra

■ **Health in Germany is a national obsession. Foreigners living in the country remark at how often they are told by Germans that certain foods, certain activities and many prescribed drugs are "not good for you." But the German view of health is not usually negative. Good health is seen as an attainable goal, and Germans tend to take a positive, active approach to staying healthy ...■**

Even a dentist will try to talk you out of having an injection of anesthetic during a filling because of its poisonous content. Germans, it seems, prefer to endure the pain!

With doctors and pharmacists prescribing homeopathic drugs, and people cycling to work on specially designated pathways during the week or enjoying long hikes in the woods and forests during weekends, it is no wonder that the average life expectancy in Germany is one of the highest in Europe.

The spa The best place to study this pursuit of good health is at the *Kurort*, or spa town. Spas are dotted all over Germany, from seaside towns to the Bavarian Alps. Usually, they have a giant bathhouse where anyone can take the healing waters.

In most other countries in Europe, spa towns have become relics of the 19th century, but German spas are

Baden-Baden (below and top): a popular spa in the southwest

❑ Until recently German medical students were required, as part of their qualifying studies, to take a course in *Balneologie*, the science of taking the waters. ❑

kept alive by the nation's long-standing tradition of allowing its citizens six-week vacations, in addition to normal sick days, etc.; employees are expected to use some of this time to rest and recuperate. A generous medical insurance scheme allows doctors to prescribe mostly free spa treatments for a variety of ailments, so people are often able to extend their stays with sick leave. Besides the baths, today's modern spa resorts offer such amenities as golf, tennis, horse racing, casinos, boating, and skiing—something for every taste.

A typical spa treatment might include a mud bath or hydrotherapy, saunas and steam treatments, all followed by a wrap in warm blankets and a compulsory rest. A word of warning: baths in Germany are often not segregated by sex, so visitors who are uncomfortable with nudity should inquire beforehand to find out whether or not the facilities are suitable for them.

A trip to some of the large bathing and swimming centers in spa resorts can be a treat for all family members. Amenities often include wave pools, pools with currents, lap pools, and whirlpools. These giant complexes provide enormous fun whatever the weather, as they often have adjoining outdoor bathing areas.

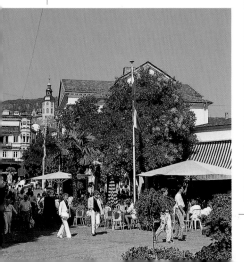

The sporting life Although most visitors will be able to participate in the sports of their choice when visiting Germany, the three national favorites seem currently to be football, skiing, and tennis. While many German children are often allowed to take inexpensive skiing vacations through schools, church groups, and other youth organizations, the nation's craze for tennis seems to stem from the recent surge in world-famous champions such as Steffi Graf, Boris Becker, and Michael Stich.

Lothar Matthäus in action during the 1990 World Cup

Soccer, as in nearly all European countries, is the national sport, and locally sponsored teams are found all over the country. Soccer's popularity surged even more in 1990, the dramatic year in which Germany saw unification—and won the World Cup.

Skiing is one of the three national favorite sports and has become widely popular

❏ The German airline Lufthansa tried to ban smoking on domestic flights, but this caused such an angry response from the tobacco industry that the airline quickly caved in and changed its mind. Given that the longest domestic flight lasts less than two hours, this was rather faint-hearted of Lufthansa. ❏

The smoking paradox While so many Germans are interested in good health and fitness, it may seem ironic that so many are also regular smokers. The no-smoking lobby has no great influence, and a campaign to ban smoking in public places has had little effect. Cinemas depend heavily on cigarette advertising.

However, more and more restaurants now have no-smoking sections and surveys indicate that young people now smoke much less than their elders, and are more aware of the harmful effects.

■ **The Federal Republic of Germany came into being in 1949 and has proved remarkably durable, being responsible for bringing the West German people from a state of near ruin to their present prosperous condition. It has seen the collapse of the Communist system in the former GDR, has absorbed that state, and is now struggling to bring equal prosperity and democracy to the whole of Germany** ...■

18

The German political structure is based on its constitution—the *Grundgesetz* (basic law), which includes human-rights guarantees. It is often used as an excuse for inactivity by German politicians, although it has been amended more than 30 times.

The Bundestag The German parliament has two chambers. The Bundestag, the lower chamber, carries more weight in decision making. It is directly elected to a four-year term, though the government can call an election earlier if necessary after referring to the federal constitutional court (see below).

At the time of writing, the parties represented in the Bundestag are the Christian Democratic Union, the conservative party led by Chancellor Helmut Kohl; the Christian Social Union; the Free Democratic Party, a liberal party; the Social Democratic Party, former rulers under the past leadership of ex-Chancellors Willy Brandt and Helmut Schmidt; the Greens; and the Party of Democratic Socialism, made up of the revamped Communists of eastern Germany. The current government is a coalition of the Christian Democratic Union and Free Democratic party.

The Bundesrat The upper house represents all 16 German Länder. Delegates are chosen by the Länder and always include state prime ministers. Under the Grundgesetz, the Bundesrat approves all laws that affect the states. Leadership of the Bundesrat is currently in the hands of the Social Democrats.

Top jobs The German chancellor, the leading figure in German politics, is not directly elected but holds the office as leader of the majority party in the Bundestag. The post of federal president is mostly ceremonial; the president is elected for a five-year term of office.

The constitutional court Germany's judicial system is led by the *Bundesverfassungsgericht* (constitutional court), which has two chambers, one dealing with individual liberties, the other with political issues. Each court contains eight judges, elected by the Bundestag and Bundesrat.

In 1994 the court ruled that Germany had the right to use troops abroad, for U.N. or other Missions, exactly like other NATO members, but Parliament had to approve in each case.

The Bundestag in Bonn

❏ Guest workers—the *Gastarbeiter*—mainly from Turkey but also from southern Europe, were encouraged to come and work in Germany during the boom years. Many have settled down with their families but are now unemployed. The Government has been encouraging some to return home. ❏

Extremists out In Germany, the system of proportional representation allows every voter two votes, one for a constituency candidate and another for a political party. Any political party is excluded from the Bundestag if it polls less than 5 percent of a party list vote—effectively keeping out extremist groups.

The economic miracle The rapid development of the economy after near total collapse at the end of World War II—the *Wirtschaftswunder*—transformed West Germany and gave its citizens some of the highest living standards in the European Union (E.U.).

This was despite strong bureaucratic controls that seemed to discourage private enterprise, minimal emphasis on customer service, and relatively little use of high-tech equipment (although much of Europe's advanced technology is produced in Germany).

Economic success was helped along by America's Marshall Plan and other aid programs. However, it was probably due above all to the Germans' hard work and discipline, and their desire to forget the past and rebuild their country.

Slowdown With the absorption of 17 million people from the former GDR and the world recession in the early 1990s, the miracle began to fade. As the economy stagnated, unemployment climbed—particularly in eastern Germany as it moved from a "command" to a market economy. By 1995 this problem remained, even though recession had ended and the German economy was the strongest in the E.U.

Where the decisions are made: the Bundestag, or lower chamber

The Bundesbank Central to the German economy, the bank controls interest rates—and so inflation. The bank, an independent body, often opposes the economic policies of the federal government.

19

■ **The West Germans have for many years been in the forefront of the environmental or "Green" movement. "Green" politics have been much more central to events in Germany than, for example, in Britain where the issues have been largely peripheral. The term "environmentally friendly" was invented here in the mouthful *umweltfreundlich*. An aversion to atomic power provided the motivating force for 10 years of student and youth activism. Habits that have become second nature to environment-conscious people—such as the separation of glass, paper and other waste for recycling—began here ...■**

Legacy of pollution In the new Germany the political environment holds sway over the natural environment. In the GDR, heavy industry was seen as the economic savior: its legacy of smoke, fumes, and rivers streaked with chemicals suggests the opposite. After unification, the stream from east to west of Trabant cars, with their billowing exhaust fumes, added insult to injury.

Then there is Bitterfeld, described by ecologists as a chemical time bomb. For years, the 60,000 inhabitants lived in the shadow of two huge plants making herbicides, pesticides, and paints. Since unification they have closed, but local rivers remained victims of years of industrial sewage. A coal-burning power plant in Cottbus reportedly emitted more sulfur dioxide than all the power plants in Norway and Denmark combined.

Tackling the problem Authorities in the new Germany are having to tackle this sort of ecological mess. The pre-unification Bonn administration maintained a careful environment program, largely due to the growing influence of the Green Party. No such receptiveness to public opinion prevailed in the GDR. Now the Bonn Government has been spending billions of DM on a vast clean-up operation in the east, with some success. Most of the old polluting factories have been closed down or renovated.

Public concern Some view the German interest in environmental issues with cynicism. The fact that the German student lobby, vocal on a whole range of issues since 1968, seems to shout loudest makes suspicious observers doubt the extent of the concern. But a look at the age range of those involved in demonstrations shows that environmental issues affect Germans on many levels and in many ways.

❑ West Germans are particularly avid ecologists: they recycle 59 percent of their wastepaper and reprocess 71 percent of their glass bottles and about 70 percent of their tires. ❑

The question of acid rain and its effects on the German forests bears this out. For many Germans, their woodland is not just a set of surroundings, or even an economic resource. The forests are a refuge for recuperation; they are a place of leisure and—with more than 30 percent of the country still occupied by woodland—an almost mythical retreat to the roots of the nation.

This explains the horror that gripped communities, notably in the south, around the Schwarzwald (Black Forest), when it became clear that *der Wald stirbt*—"the forest is dying." Rain had once been an essential vital force for the wood, enabling it to survive, but the mixture of polluting agents inflicted by factories, power plants and cars turned the rain into an acid cocktail. Add to this the recent hurricane-style winds and it is easy to see why Germans are so concerned their woods should be protected. But there is a paradox here.

The car is king The logical solution would be for the Germans to limit use of their cars, but this would go against another tenet in modern German life, which demands that citizens should drive as fast, powerfully and, in the end, as damagingly as they like. *"Freie Fahrt für freie Bürger"* (A Free Path for Free Citizens) is the cry of the car industry, and of many Germans. At least, all new cars must now carry catalytic convertors.

Hope for the future Western conservationists have rediscovered a forgotten landscape in the Lower Oder Valley National Park, near the Polish border. The River Oder flows through the middle, with Poland on one bank and Germany on the other. Several projects are being set up to conserve the diverse flora and fauna that have been discovered, including ospreys, sea eagles, and beavers.

Film-Casino
Odeonplatz 8-10, 8 München 22

abc-FILMTHEATER
MÜNCHEN · HERZOGSTRASSE

Gültig auf allen Plätzen

Preis mit Steuer siehe Anschlag an der Kas.
Nach Beginn der Vorstellung kein Anspruch
auf zusammenhängende Plätze GEWA-Dru

■ **The German film industry does not operate on the Hollywood scale and has not achieved the same worldwide success. Nevertheless, film is a respected art form. It enjoyed a golden creative age in the 1970s and 1980s, but in the 1990s has again been in the doldrums, producing very few notable films ...■**

Directors rule In Germany, it is the directors, rather than the actors, who get the accolades. Some, such as Rainer Werner Fassbinder, have deliberately cultivated their own protégés (though Hanna Schygulla has become a star in her own right). Fassbinder's determination to investigate controversial sexual and social themes—coupled with his own controversial life and death—did much to develop his high profile as a public figure. Wim Wenders has attracted interest for his serious, poetic, emotional visions of apparently well-known landscapes. An acclaimed example of this is *Der Himmel über Berlin* (*Wings of Desire*), in which modern Berlin is viewed through the eyes of two invisible angels, listening to the thoughts of anxious city dwellers. In a sense, this sums up the "*Neues Deutsches Kino*" (New German Cinema), which promotes the validity of emotions in the face of modern reason.

International success These directors have earned a lasting reputation. Volker Schlöndorff, with his adaptations of such literary works as Günter Grass's *Die Blechtrommel* (*Tin Drum*), has extended this type of

❑ In 1962 the Oberhausen Manifesto announced the birth of the "new German feature film." Among its signatories was Edgar Reitz, who in 1984 gained international renown for the TV series *Heimat*. ❑

film on an international scale. It is often the quirky rather than the characteristic that gets the most prominence abroad. Werner Herzog is known for his remake of *Nosferatu* and his exotic South American–based works *Aguirre, Wrath of God* and *Fitzcarraldo*. His vision of desperate individuals, underdogs at the mercy of nature and fate, is personal and poetic, and Herzog could hardly be regarded as part of a German "trend." Margarethe von Trotta is one highly respected director who has broached contemporary themes (the role of women, the importance of the family) in such films as *The German Sisters*.

A scene from Der Himmel über Berlin (Wings of Desire)

Top People

■ **Some aspects of German culture, such as classical music, are internationally known; others are largely confined within the country's borders. Open any German television magazine, read about the trials and tribulations of the country's media stars, and marvel—you won't have heard of most of them ...■**

Our unfamiliarity with Thomas Gottschalk and "Blocky" Fuchsenberger (game-show idols in their own land) goes with the comparatively unusual choice of Germany as a vacation destination.

The famous in sports (Boris Becker, top) and in politics (Helmut Schmidt, above left, and Helmut Kohl)

Political giants The figures who make an impression abroad do so for weightier reasons. Willy Brandt, former chancellor, mayor of Berlin and Nobel Peace Prize winner, stood out, until his death in 1992, as a great European statesman, committed as much to a fair policy toward the Developing World as to untangling domestic problems. His successor as chancellor, Helmut Schmidt, has to a lesser extent taken on a similar role (as well as being a talented concert pianist).

Helmut Kohl, arguably less charismatic than Brandt, has been around at the right time, pressed home his advantage and grasped the mood of the nation. He seems clumsy (German magazines have seemed obsessed with his battle to control his wildly fluctuating weight, invoking improbable comparisons

with Elizabeth Taylor) but has held on. Never a model of elegance, he has acquired an air of solidity—and aroused adulation when he visited his new Länder in the old German Democratic Republic. For those citizens, in that country and at that time, he *was* unification. He was duly re-elected in 1994.

Royalty watching The weekly newsmagazines—*Bunte*, *Stern*, *Quick*—dote on anyone royal and regularly tell readers far more about the personal lives of the rich and regal than any palace-conscious editor could in Britain. As substitutes for the missing German royalty, tennis stars Boris Becker and Steffi Graf have played an important role. It's not so much the game, but having home-grown stars of indisputable world class. Becker's personal fortunes are paraded for every German to enjoy. In royal terms, it's perhaps more Grimaldi (Monaco) than Windsor (Britain), but until kaisers and princes return to Germany (and they won't), this is how Boris and Steffi serve their nation.

■ **The first identifiable permanent settlers in the area that is now Germany were Celtic tribes in the 8th century BC; the Rhineland was a key area of production in their industrial society. But new forces were developing in Europe. The Roman Empire was expanding, and Germanic peoples were on the move from Scandinavia ...■**

Germanic tribes moved to lands east of the Rhine and north of the Black Sea, and their invasions and periodic uprisings created instability within the Roman Empire. Roman attempts to push across the Rhine failed to establish permanent occupation. These ended in AD 9; after reaching the Elbe the Romans were pushed back by German tribes under the leadership of Arminius, who destroyed three legions.

Charlemagne's coronation as Holy Roman Emperor marked a new era

Rise of the Franks By the time of Constantine, when the empire's capital shifted to Byzantium in the east, Roman rule was beginning to break down. After the introduction of Christianity by Emperor Constantine, the Roman Empire disintegrated and the area that is now Germany was overrun by the Franks. When Charlemagne was crowned Holy Roman Emperor in 800, Frankish influence stretched across most of Europe. Civil war followed Charlemagne's death; the Treaty of Verdun in 843 split the empire into a Latin western section, and a Germanic eastern part led by Ludwig the German. Ludwig's appointment marked the emergence of a German identity.

The Saxon ascendancy In the 10th century, the area came under the rule of the Saxons. Otto the Great was faced with invading Magyars from the east and a growing threat from duchies and principalities inside the eastern empire. After defeating the Magyars in 955, Otto strengthened his ties to the papacy, which led to church dominance over a large part of the country. In 962, he was crowned Holy Roman Emperor.

The power of the princes The influence of powerful dynastic German families increased steadily. By the 13th century, the Holy Roman Emperor had little power against feudal princes. Many began to push eastward, conquering Poland and setting up German communities in areas now in Russia and Romania. In 1356, the law regulating the election of an emperor (the Golden Bull) was introduced, based on the votes of four noble and three ecclesiastical electors, excluding the papacy. In the 15th century, the Habsburgs were elected Holy Roman Emperors, and they retained the title until it was abolished some 400 years later.

Germany in 1608, from Geographiae Universae tum veteris, tum narae absolutissimum opus *by Giovanni Magini (Köln)*

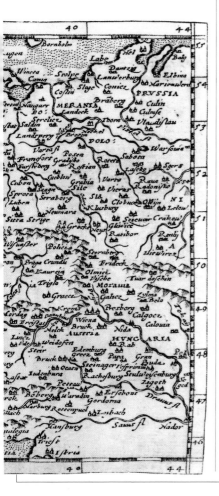

■ **In the 16th century Germany was suffering under a greedy and powerful aristocracy that appropriated land and held the oppressed peasantry in serfdom. This, alongside an equally grasping and cynical church trading in "indulgences," led to the religious upheaval of the Reformation in the 16th century ...■**

Discontent with the church authorities increased. Martin Luther led accusations over corruption, nailing his "95 theses," an attack against papal abuses, to the door of Wittenberg church in 1517. Luther was excommunicated, but politically powerful German princes were able to protect him from sentence of death.

Century of conflict After publication of Luther's translation of the Bible, the oppressed in Germany were ready to revolt. The Peasants' Rebellion of 1524–5 brought destruction of church properties but was put down by princely armies. The period of the Reformation and Counter-Reformation created more than a century of strife between Catholics and Protestants, and by the early 17th century, Europe was embroiled in the Thirty Years' War. Many battles were fought on German lands, bringing extensive destruction. Negotiations to end the war began in 1643, culminating in the Peace of Westphalia in 1648. The treaty ended the conflict, reduced the status of Holy Roman Emperor and began the decline of the House of Habsburg, while giving power to more than 300 principalities and other territories.

❏ In the 16th century, German mercenaries led the way in high fashion. The style of "slashing" clothes—cutting slits in the material and pulling the lining through for display—started with battlefield booty used to patch clothes and found its way to the French and English courts. ❏

The rise of Brandenburg-Prussia
By the end of the 17th century, a power in the area of Brandenburg-Prussia emerged. The Hohenzollern family, who held the Electorate of Brandenburg, defied the laws of the Holy Roman Empire and assumed the title of kings of Prussia. Frederick William, the Great Elector, was the first; the dynasty consolidated itself in the early 18th century. Under Frederick the Great, the third Hohenzollern king, Prussia rose to be one of the dominant European powers in the middle of that century. Despite liberal laws at home, Frederick asserted Prussia's military authority and, after going to battle with Austria over Silesia, engaged in the Seven Years' War (1756–63). Frederick annexed much of Poland and established Prussia as a counter power to Austria. Prussia's power was tested during the Napoleonic Wars of the early 19th century, but in the Battle of Waterloo in 1815 Napoleon was defeated by the armies of Britain, Hannover, and Prussia. The Congress of Vienna, which met that same year and created the Deutscher Bund (German Confederation), established Prussian dominance among some 40 states in the German world, alongside Austria.

German unification Now Germany began to experience the pains of the industrial revolution. Economic reforms and customs unions were introduced to ease the strain caused by the many protective borders in the German region. Also, a wage-earning class as well as a bourgeoisie emerged. Uprisings in 1848 demonstrated how serious the demands for the dissolution of an

older political order in Germany were becoming. In 1862, Prussia's Wilhelm I chose Otto von Bismarck as his chancellor. Within a decade Bismarck united Germany under Prussian leadership. After a war with Denmark over Schleswig-Holstein in 1864, and the Bohemian War with Austria in 1866, all the German states north of the River Main were united.

To gain the support of German southern states (Bavaria, Baden and Württemberg), Bismarck provoked a war with France; after the Franco-Prussian War ended in 1871, Germany was united as the Second Reich, with King Wilhelm of Prussia as kaiser.

Below: the Rüdesheim Niederwald Monument celebrates German unification in 1871

Above: the Peasants' Rebellion, 1524–5. Below: Bismarck

Bismarck then embarked on a number of liberal domestic reforms, as well as creating alliances with Austria and Russia.

World War I France sought revenge for 1871 and, together with Russia, feared the strength of the German army. Britain for its part was worried by the threatening expansion of the German navy. These three powers, therefore, stood against the alliance of Germany and Austria in 1914, when World War I broke out over Habsburg claims in the Balkans. Germany's defeat came in 1918, hastened by the entry of the United States into the war the year before.

■ **Germany's humiliating defeat in World War I was followed in 1919 by the founding of the Weimar Republic, based on a democratic constitution. That same year, Germany's new leaders were forced to sign the Treaty of Versailles, marking a radical shift in the European balance of power. It called for enormous war reparations as well as the confiscation of and withdrawal from territories that Germany had controlled, in some cases, for centuries ...■**

Unemployment and inflation hit Europe after World War I, and in almost every country political movements on the extreme left and right began to gather strength and make themselves heard.

The Treaty of Versailles, finally signed and set out in "The Golden Book," May 1919

The rise of the Nazis During the 1920s and early 1930s, Germany suffered galloping inflation. Due to the lack of central political strength in Germany, elections in 1930 allowed extremist parties to gain prominence, most noticeably the Nazi Party, led by Adolf Hitler. This attracted the unemployed and destitute, and industrialists and other wealthy groups who saw the party's authoritarian policies as a return to the order that the country had known under the last kaiser.

Adolf Hitler gained more power and was made chancellor by the republic's president, Paul von Hindenburg, in January 1933. On February 27, 1933, the Reichstag, the nation's parliament building, was set on fire, an incident orchestrated by the Nazis. Hindenburg declared a state of emergency.

The road to war The Nazi Party became the only legal party in the country, and Hitler became president as well as chancellor. Democracy was suppressed under Dr. Joseph Goebbels's propaganda ministry. Many horrors occurred during Hitler's Third Reich. Jews were persecuted and murdered. The government and education systems were perverted. Many of the nation's most talented people— many of Jewish origin—emigrated, and gradually the terms of the Treaty of Versailles were nullified. Hitler's plan for Europe became well understood, but the West was not ready to stand up to him until September 1, 1939, when Germany invaded Poland. Two days later, Britain and France declared war.

World War II and its aftermath The war and the vicious activities of Nazis against Jews, Slavs, and others are well documented.

At first the war went well for the Nazis, but their invasion of Russia in 1941 proved a turning point. Defeats in North Africa and at Stalingrad followed in 1942 and 1943. A German resistance movement developed among the top army

❏ The Nazi extermination program involved the murder of an estimated 6 million Jews. Other groups that fell victim to the "Final Solution" were Slavs, Gypsies, homosexuals, and mentally ill and mentally and physically handicapped people.

leadership and attempts were made on Hitler's life. Germany was totally defeated, and in 1945 Hitler committed suicide.

The legacy of the Third Reich and World War II will be a burden to Germany for decades to come. Six million Jews murdered in concentration camps cannot nor should not be forgotten by the world. Those leaders held responsible were put on trial for war crimes and crimes against humanity.

The victorious Allies divided Germany into four occupied zones under Soviet, U.S., British, and French control. Two separate political systems emerged; in May 1949 the territories occupied by the British, Americans, and French were combined to form the Federal Republic of Germany. Four months later, the Russians created the German Democratic Republic. The two Germanys rivaled each other for more than 40 years, each trying to rebuild a nation out of the ruins and rubble of World War II. They came to represent the cold-war division of Europe, formalized by the erection of the Berlin Wall in 1961.

The years of division Throughout the cold-war period, West Germany's economy became Europe's strongest. More modestly, East Germany's industriousness made it the most prosperous and productive country in Comecon, the Eastern bloc's economic alliance.

By the 1970s, many Germans accepted the division, though they still hoped that Germany would be reunited. Unofficial recognition of the division developed in the Ostpolitik policies of Willy Brandt, when he became chancellor from 1969. Nevertheless, West German political parties, while attempting to work with the leaders of the GDR on some economic and social programs, still insisted that unification was the ultimate aim. By the mid-1980s, however, many West Germans had all but dismissed the idea.

Adolf Hitler at the Nazis' Parteitag *in Nürnberg, 1933.*
Top: a Nazi parade

■ **On November 9, 1989, the momentous decision to open up the Berlin Wall was made. East Germans had spent days and nights peacefully demonstrating for political rights. The communist East German regime no longer had the steadfast military support of its closest ally, the former Soviet Union. The government of the GDR finally gave way and opened up points on the wall, allowing its citizens to flood over into West Germany ...■**

Some had never seen the west in their lifetime, but most had conjured up a picture in their minds from television programs that had been beamed across the barbed wire.

One Germany Within months, a new democratically elected federal government had been set up, with the task of uniting East and West Germany. At first, people thought the process would take several years, but the government moved quickly to merge the two economies, providing East Germans with Deutschmarks on July 1, 1990. East Germany's economy began to deteriorate as a result of the inability of its industries to compete with western production standards. The Federal Republic's ruling coalition was compelled to move quickly and absorb the territory of the former East Germany into the republic much faster than had been expected. On October 3, 1990, after more than four decades of division following Germany's defeat in World War II, a dream came true for many Germans—the country was finally reunited.

After euphoria The political leaders in east and west called on the nation to work together and to avoid treating the former East Germans as second-class citizens. Sadly, the wall still exists in many people's minds. Those from the east continue to complain that their country was simply annexed by the west, and accuse the West Germans of arrogance, while West Germans are

angry that their taxes have been increased to pay for reunification (despite repeated assurances by Chancellor Helmut Kohl that this would not happen).

In the early 1990s, high unemployment, especially in eastern Germany, led to a wave of resentment against immigrants. Many East Germans, unused to people of color, reacted with a xenophobia bred of fear and ignorance, and racist incidents grew. This mood was exploited by groups of neo-Nazi thugs both in east and west, who attacked and killed a number of Turks. Germany's politicians were at first slow to react, and in view of Germany's past, fears grew abroad of a revival of Nazism.

But in fact the neo-Nazis are only a tiny minority, and most Germans abhor the violence. The killers of five Turks near Köln in 1993 were finally tried and jailed in 1995. Even so, social unrest seems likely to continue in Germany until the economy is stabilized.

Return to Berlin With unification, the federal government was faced with the important question: should the seat of government remain in Bonn, the former capital of western Germany, or return to Berlin, the historical seat of the German government? Parliament was besieged with concerns about the costs, and fears that a return to Berlin could rekindle old German militaristic attitudes about German leadership in Europe.

Finally, Parliament voted narrowly

in favor of a return to Berlin, despite the heavy costs, and this was set to take place in stages before the year 2000. In the meantime, infrastructure developments—roads, telephones, electricity, and economic integration of the east—have become the main focus of the federal government's policy. Special federal taxes have been introduced to pay for the very costly work.

The European goal Since the Federal Republic of Germany (West Germany) was founded in 1949, German national policy has passionately supported European integration. At first through common agricultural and trade policies, and now through economic and political integration, German politicians have used the banner of the European Union as a standard for the next generation. This policy is often at odds with the other European countries, particularly Britain—and some opponents fear German dominance of the Union. Others argue that tight European integration is needed to curb a rise of German nationalism. But though Germans want a politically unified Europe, many remain dubious about merging their strong Deutschmark into a single currency, in the planned development of European monetary union that is official government policy.

Top right: souvenir pieces of the Wall go on sale.
Below: the Brandenburg Gate, an accessible meeting point once again

■ A strong tradition of stories and poetry undoubtedly existed in the German language long before written literature. The one tantalizing glimpse of this that was written down is the "Hildebrandslied" (The Lay of Hildebrand), a 9th-century fragment of an alliterative heroic poem. Otherwise, the earliest German manuscripts were of a religious nature, written and preserved as part of the Christian monastic tradition of learning ...■

By the 12th century, literature had passed from the monasteries to the courts. German versions of French romances, such as the tale of Tristan and Isolde and the Arthurian stories, were written; in about 1200, tales of the hero Siegfried took form in the anonymous *Nibelungenlied*. *Minnesang* (lyrical love songs) also flourished in the 12th century.

The literary renaissance Martin Luther's translation of the Bible (1534) is generally regarded as the first great modern German work of literature, but it was not until the 18th century that German writings—notably those of Johann von Goethe and Friedrich von Schiller—reached a level comparable with that of the Middle Ages. A meeting between Herder and Goethe led to the Sturm und Drang (Storm and Stress) movement. Weimar, where Goethe

❑ Philosopher and mathematician Gottfried von Leibniz (1646–1716) is remembered for the development of differential calculus, for which his notation is still used. His ideas of expressing "all truth" in terms of simple statements using symbols was a forerunner of modern mathematical logic. ❑

and Schiller spent much of their lives, became synonymous with their writings—Schiller's poetry and many dramas, and Goethe's dramas (notably *Faust*), novels, poetry, and philosophical works.

From Romanticism to naturalism The German Romantic movement started around 1790. It had a profound effect throughout Europe, and Romantic ideas dominated

❑ Georg Wilhelm Friedrich Hegel (1770–1831) put forward the theory that history, which he called the *Weltgeist* (world spirit), was a developing process of "consciousness of freedom," from the "Oriental" through the "Greek" to the "Christian–German" period. He saw the process paralleled in three stages of awareness, from "awareness of objects" through "awareness of self" to "awareness of reason." ❑

Luther, father of the Reformation

❏ The philosopher Immanuel Kant (1724–1804) greatly influenced the 18th-century Weimar literary school with his emphasis on moral duty and esthetics. ❏

German literature up to the mid-19th century, with "folk" poetry and tales (such as those of the Brothers Grimm) being an important element.

Transition The poet and political radical Heinrich Heine marks a transition from Romanticism to realism. Contemporary life became the theme of writers at the end of the 19th century, as in the stories of Gottfried Keller and Theodor Storm, and the plays of Gerhart Hauptmann.

The 20th century At the turn of the century there was a reaction to naturalism in the Nietzsche-inspired poetry of Richard Dehmel and the aestheticism of Stefan George.

The greatest German poet of the 20th century was undoubtedly Czech-born Rainer Maria Rilke, whose intense poetic world was spun almost entirely out of his own psyche. Another Czech-born 20th-century giant was Franz Kafka, whose novels shed a grotesque and often absurd light on human experiences. The novelist Thomas Mann explored the contrast between solid bourgeois insensitivity and the fragile world of the artist.

In 1947 Gruppe 47, a group of politically left-wing writers, was formed. Some of its members have gained international status, including Heinrich Böll (winner of the Nobel Prize for Literature in 1972) and Günter Grass, best known for *The Tin Drum*.

Martin Heidegger (1889–1976) espoused a philosophy that was a form of early existentialism. His ideas had great influence in Germany in the first half of this century.

Notable among writers of the former GDR are the innovative dramatist Bertolt Brecht, who died in East Berlin in 1956, and the novelist Christa Wolf.

❏ The reputation of Friedrich Wilhelm Nietzsche (1844–1900) has suffered as a result of Nazi enthusiasm for his philosophy. His concept of the *Übermensch* (superman) is to blame for this, though he himself in no way connected it with the Aryan myth. For Nietzsche the basic motive of human action was the will to have power (he despised Christianity for its morality based on humility). He saw the super-man as one who succeeds in overcoming himself. ❏

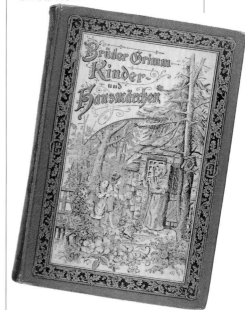

The cover of Hansel and Gretel *by the Brothers Grimm, 1892*

■ The first architectural style to emerge in medieval Germany—the Romanesque— owed much to the traditions of Rome. The Rhineland has relics of Roman buildings— notably at Trier, where the great Porta Nigra, a gateway in the Roman city walls, still stands. The Roman basilica (meeting hall) inspired many Romanesque churches and cathedrals ...■

Romanesque and Gothic Fine cathedrals arose during the 11th to 15th centuries: Romanesque Speyer, Mainz, and Worms, then the soaring Gothic splendors of Bamberg, Cologne, Ulm, and Freiburg. Sculpture in stone and wood was used to complement architecture. Painting, often done anonymously, can be seen in altarpiece panels and manuscript illuminations.

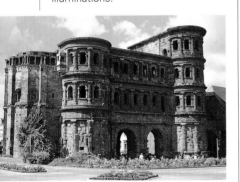

The Roman Porta Nigra, Trier

❏ The sculptor Tilman Riemenschneider—the "Master of Würzburg"—bridged the Gothic and Renaissance in Germany. He was one of the first German sculptors not to use gilding or color. ❏

Renaissance In the late 15th to early 17th centuries, architecture took a backseat as the influence of the church waned and the wealthy middle classes asserted themselves. Many notable buildings show Italian

❏ The rococo style — a kind of ultra-baroque—emerged in Germany in the mid-18th century. A French invention, it is characterized by dainty and irregular "Louis Quinze" motifs. Sanssouci Palace at Potsdam and Cuvillié's Amalienburg in Munich are examples. ❏

influence. Some of the great names of German art belong to this time, including the Renaissance painter, draftsman and engraver Albrecht Dürer and the mystical painter Matthias Grünewald. In this period Lucas Cranach the Elder painted the portraits of the leaders of the Reformation, and the two Holbeins, Elder and Younger, were prominent.

Baroque and neoclassical The 17th and 18th centuries arguably produced very few distinguished German artists, but saw a brilliant age of Baroque architecture by Lukas von Hildebrandt, Balthasar Neumann, Andreas Schlüter and others. During the Age of Enlightenment, Frederick the Great employed Georg Wenzeslaus von Knobelsdorff to help design official buildings for Berlin, and the Prussian capital continued its prominence as an architectural center into the 19th century, as the neoclassicism of Karl Friedrich Schinkel made its mark.

Romanticism As in music and literature, the trend toward Romanticism is seen in art and architecture in the 19th century. Otto Runge and Caspar David Friedrich,

Rathaus detail, Lemgo

era inspired powerful works.

After World War I, the Bauhaus (literally, Building House) movement developed. Its founder in Weimar, Walter Gropius, envisaged cooperation between art and industry, and the name Bauhaus became synonymous with austere functionalism. Nazi hostility led to its dissolution in 1933; members of the movement settled in other countries and continued to influence architectural developments.

The contemporary scene Today, German painters are again prominent figures in the international art world. The current German movement, influenced by the flourishing avant-

Above: The Garden Café, *by Ludwig Kirchner (1880–1938) Top:* People by the Pool, *by August Macke (1887–1914)*

who worked in Dresden, were the finest of the German Romantic painters. In architecture, Romanticism is found to an almost absurd degree in castles built for King Ludwig II of Bavaria: the Baroque-style Linderhof, the mini-Versailles of Herrenchiemsee and the "Disneyland" Neuschwanstein.

The modern age At the end of the last century, many German painters adopted the Impressionist style of France, and painters such as Max Liebermann had strong support from the emerging German bourgeoisie. Jugendstil, the German form of Art Nouveau, was emerging. By the beginning of the 20th century, the Expressionist school was in full swing with the founding in Dresden and Munich of Die Brücke (The Bridge) and later Der Blaue Reiter (The Blue Rider) groups. This historic

garde interpretations of social and cultural life in a prosperous modern society, has been referred to as Neo-Expressionism. Postwar Germany's best-known artists include Georg Baselitz and the sculptor Joseph Beuys.

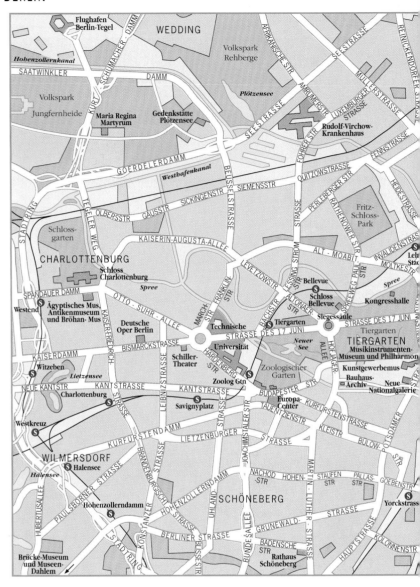

Since the Berlin Wall began to crumble on that extraordinary night in November 1989, the city's two halves have slowly and painfully attempted to fuse. Berlin is now just as fascinating for a visitor as it ever was in the midst of the cold war. The minor thrill of crossing Checkpoint Charlie (and wondering if you would ever return) has vanished, and you can now drive unhindered across the Glienicke Bridge (where once only spies set foot), but Berlin remains a compelling city. As it prepares to regain its former status as the capital of a united Germany, Berlin is perhaps a litmus test for relations between East and West. Berlin has always been a place on the fringe, bursting with avant-

Map

BORNHOLMER STRASSE

WISBYER STR

BADSTR

Gesundbrunnen

Schönhauser Allee

Gethsemanes-Kirche

Prenzlauer Allee

Humboldthain

Planetarium

BRUNNENSTRASSE

SCHÖNHAUSER ALLEE

DIMITROFFSTRASSE

BERNAUER STRASSE

PRENZLAUER BERG

Nordbahnhof

INVALIDENSTRASSE

GREIFSWALDER STR

CHAUSSEESTRASSE

Naturkunde-museum

WILHELM-PIECK-STRASSE

Volkspark Friedrichshain

Charité

Museumsinsel: Neues-Museum, Pergamonmus, Nationalgalerie, Bode-Museum, Altes Museum

ROSENTHALER STR

MOLLSTRASSE

LUISENSTRASSE

Friedrich-str

Hackescher Markt

Alexanderplatz

KARL-MARX-ALLEE

Reichstag

FRIEDRICHSTRASSE

MITTE

Berliner Dom

KARL-LIEBKNECHT-STR

Fernsehturm

ALEXANDERSTR

Branden-burger Tor

UNTER DEN LINDEN

Nikolai-viertel

ANDREASSTR

Unter den Linden

Staatsoper

St-Hedwigs-Kath

GRUNER STR

STRALAUER STR

Jannowitzbrücke

Berlin Hauptbahnhof

WILHELM STR

Potsdamer Platz

Französischer Dom, Schauspielhaus, Deutscher Dom

MÜHLEN DAMM

HOLZMARKTSTR

Märkisches Museum

LEIPZIGER STR

POTSDAMER PLATZ

Haus am Checkpoint Charlie

HEINESTR

KÖPENICKER STRASSE

Saats-ibliothek

SCHÖNEBERGER STR

LINDENSTRASSE

ORANIENSTRASSE

artin-Gropius-au Berlinische Galerie

FRIEDRICHSTRASSE

Anhalter

WILHELMSTRASSE

KREUZBERG

SKALITZER STRASSE

GITSCHINER STR

WIENER STRASSE

Museum für verkehr und Technik

MEHRINGDAMM

BLUCHER-STR

BAERWALDSTR

URBANSTRASSE

KOTTBUSSER DAMM

Landwehrkanal

YORCKSTRASSE

GNEISENAUSTR

HASENHEIDE

Viktoria-park

BERLIN

Tempelhof Luftbrückendenkmal

0   500   1000 metres

DUDENSTR

COLUMBIADAMM

Flughafen Tempelhof

garde ideas and sometimes subversive culture. Its reputation for decadence, even vice, is not unfounded—mostly a legacy from the Weimar years of the 1920s. It's a city of youth, and a cosmopolitan one. In the late 1960s and 1970s, young people flocked here to study on government grants, or to avoid military service, from which Berliners were exempt. A large number of foreigners have settled here—many of them guest workers. This has enriched Berlin's culture, but has sometimes led to racial tension.

Berlin is vast in area—Munich, Frankfurt, and Hamburg could all fit within it. Its population is 3.5 million, but huge tracts of the city consist of forests,

BERLIN

Turkish workers
More Turks live in Berlin than in any other city outside Turkey. Many arrived originally as Gastarbeiter, to do the jobs that few Berliners wanted to do. Now many of them are second- and third-generation citizens who want their fair share of the city's resources. A high proportion live in Kreuzberg.

Fabrics at the Turkish market, Maybachufer

lakes, even farmland, contrasting oddly with the intense urbanization of other areas. The west, all but razed by the Allies during Hitler's last stand in 1945, is almost entirely modern. Frequently meretricious and ill-conceived, the best of postwar West Berlin is a tour de force, studded with startling examples of art, architecture, and design. East Berlin, also badly mauled by the bombs, has been reconstructed in two bizarrely conflicting styles: drab, Stalinist functionalism on one hand and a painstakingly accurate reproduction of grandiose monuments on the other. Two former working-class districts with some intact (or carefully renovated) architecture give a more realistic picture of prewar Berlin: Kreuzberg in the west and Prenzlauer Berg in the east both display a volatile mixture of bohemian lifestyles and "alternative" culture.

Berlin gives visitors a sense of double vision. Most cultural venues are duplicated on the other side of the city (two national galleries, two Egyptian museums, etc.), with sometimes an extra one added for good measure (*three* symphony orchestras, universities, etc.). The city has about 60 museums, some world-class.

The former No Man's Land astride the Wall in the very heart of the city, empty and sinister, is now at last being rebuilt to a grandiose plan, to prepare for the return of the German parliament and government in 1999. New ministries and a new Chancellor's office are being built. The Potsdamer Platz—once a wasteland—is now the largest building site in Europe and a massive new complex of offices, shops and housing is being erected and a tunnel for traffic is being carved out beneath the Tiergarten park. However, the mental scars of the city's long division will take longer to heal than the physical ones; attitudes and lifestyle in east and west remain quite different, and suspicions linger.

▶▶ Ägyptisches (Egyptian) Museum

Schlossstrasse 70
This collection is housed in an officers' barracks and the Old Royal Stables opposite the Charlottenburg Palace. The star exhibit is a bust of Nefertiti; other fine pieces include smiling mummies, a carving of the priest Tenti and his wife holding hands, a flying scarab, and a strange blue hedgehog. The 2,000-year-old Kalabscha Gate was a gift from the Egyptian government in 1973. *Open*: Monday–Friday, 9–5; Saturday and Sunday, 4–5.

▶▶ Alexanderplatz

Before World War II, "Alex" was the hub of the Mitte district, the historic core of old Berlin. After the war, many of its buildings were replaced by truly ghastly architecture. The Alexander-Haus and Berolina-Haus are examples of an earlier "objective" style, dating from the late 1920s. Since the wall came down, the square's antiseptic dreariness has been exchanged for a patina of graffiti and litter, though street musicians and artists add a human touch. One focal point in the square is the Weltzeituhr (world clock) which gives the times in various cities around the world. The high office buildings on the north side are due to be pulled down and replaced with something more attractive.

The dome of the Protestant Cathedral beside the river Spree

Queen Nefertiti
Queen Nefertiti was the wife of the unorthodox Pharaoh Akhenaton, who ruled Egypt from 1375 to 1358 BC. The famous limestone bust in the Ägyptisches Museum shows her as a remarkably beautiful woman by today's Western standards (best seen in profile), but the first thing you notice is that she has only one eye. Some historians believe Nefertiti may have suffered from a cataract, a common disease in ancient Egypt. The bust was unearthed by a German archeologist in 1912, during excavations of Akhenaton's royal capital. Toward the end of World War II it was removed from the Neues-Museum on Museumsinsel to keep it out of Soviet hands. Other Egyptian antiquities are housed in the Bode-Museum in eastern Berlin.

The square has several times seen revolutionary happenings, including the pro-democracy rallies of 1989. The history of the square is depicted in eight panels in a pedestrian underpass near the Hotel Stadt Berlin. The Fernsehturm (see panel) now dwarfs Berlin's second-oldest parish church, the Marienkirche, restored in 1950. Its best feature is a dance of death fresco near the organ.

Southwest of Alexanderplatz is the Rotes Rathaus (Red Town Hall), so named for its bricks, not its politics! A 243-foot tower dominates this neo-Renaissance building, decorated by 36 lively terra-cotta reliefs depicting Berlin's history. Near its entrance is the bronze Neptunbrunnen (Neptune Fountain).

► Bauhaus-Archiv

Klingelhöferstrasse 13
This distinctive building beside the Landwehrkanal holds a variety of exhibits showing how widely the Bauhaus movement influenced 20th-century design, from architecture to typography. Plans and models of Mies van der Rohe's boxlike buildings, period coffee services and desk lamps, paintings by Kandinsky and Klee, and Marcel Breuer's famously uncomfortable-looking chair are all on display. Computerized information (in English) summarizes the ideas and achievements of the Bauhaus artists. (See also **Dessau**, page 135.)
Open: daily except Tuesday 11–5.

► Berliner Dom

Museumsinsel
The Protestant cathedral (Dom) is one of the landmarks of eastern Berlin. It was built at the turn of the century by Julius Carl Raschdorff, in heavy neo-Baroque surmounted by an imposing dome. Massive restoration has recently been completed. Inside are tombs of the Hohenzollerns and the Imperial Staircase leading to the parish church, where an exhibition is housed.
Open: Monday–Saturday, 10–5:30; Sunday, 12–6. Admission charge to some parts of the cathedral.

Brandenburger Tor from the east side

Döblin's novel

Alfred Döblin drew on his experiences as a doctor in one of Berlin's lowlife districts for his novel *Berlin Alexanderplatz*. A pioneer stream-of-consciousness novel, it tells the grim story of an ex-convict released from prison after being wrongly convicted of murdering a prostitute. Trying to build a new life in the Berlin of the 1920s, he winds up in a lunatic asylum, then, eventually, in a bottom-of-the-heap job as a porter.

Quadriga Chariot

Sculptor Gottfried Schadow's *Quadriga*, the four-horse chariot that crowns the Brandenburger Tor, was recast in copper after the original was destroyed in World War II. It was vandalized at the end of 1989 as crowds marked the peaceful revolution in East Germany. The *Quadriga* was fit again by August 1991—just in time for the gate's 200th anniversary.

▶▶ **Berlin-Museum**
Lindenstrasse 14
Due to re-open in 1998 as a major museum of Jewish history in Berlin.

▶ **Berlinische Galerie**
Stresemannstrasse 110
This museum of modern art, photography, and architecture is housed in the famous Martin-Gropius-Bau, its exhibits enhanced by special exhibitions.
Open: daily except Monday, 10–8.

▶▶▶ **Brandenburger Tor**
After the erection of the Berlin Wall, the Brandenburg Gate—stranded in No Man's Land—symbolized the division of Germany. Modeled on the Propylaea (entrance gate) to the Acropolis in Athens, it was built in 1788–91 as a triumphal arch for Friedrich Wilhelm II of Prussia by Langhans the Elder. Six tall Doric columns, front and back, form five passages. Under the Prussian empire, the gate made a spectacular theater for military parades. Draped in swastikas, it also became a symbol of Nazi Germany. Hitler displayed his arrogance by driving through the wide middle archway.

Brücke-Museum
Bussardsteig 9
This tiny museum in the leafy Berlin suburb of Dahlem is difficult to get to, but worth it for those interested in 20th-century German art. Opened in 1967, it was built specifically for the work of Die Brücke (The Bridge), a group of Expressionist painters which included Emil Nolde, Ernst Ludwig Kirchner, and Karl Schmidt-Rottluff.
Open: daily except Tuesday, 11–5.

▶▶ **Charlottenburg Museums**
Antikenmuseum (*Schlossstrasse 1*) An excellent display of antiquities containing objects of great esthetic appeal as well as scholarly interest. Contents include Roman bronzes and Etruscan vases, Minoan carvings and Greek helmets. Downstairs is a treasure trove of

Roman silver: the Hildesheim collection, dating from the time of Caesar Augustus.

Open: Monday–Thursday, 9–5; Saturday and Sunday, 10–5. Admission charge.

Bröhan Museum (*Schlossstrasse 1a*) This museum, next to the Antikenmuseum, houses a collection of art-nouveau and art-deco *objets d'art*: ceramics and glass, silver, paintings and furniture. The top floor (coffee services, cigarette cases, cutlery, etc.) is worth the climb.

Open: daily except Monday, 10AM–6PM (until 8 on Thursday). Admission charge.

Museum für Vor- und Frühgeschichte (*Langhans [West] Wing, Schloss Charlottenburg, Spandauer bau*) Excellently organized material from early Paleolithic cultures through the Bronze and Iron ages. Though depleted after World War II, the collection of Schliemann's Trojan finds is still remarkable. There are other Trojan finds in the Bode-Museum (see page 42).

Open: Monday–Thursday, 9–5; Saturday and Sunday, 10–5. Admission charge.

►► Haus am Checkpoint Charlie

Friedrichstrasse 44

The hut where East German border guards kept watch was moved to the Deutsches Historisches Museum (on the west side of the wall) in 1990. The "House at Checkpoint Charlie" stands near the former crossing point. It gives a history of the wall and of Berlin in video form with photographs and biographies of those who tried to escape to the west.

Open: daily 9–10. Admission charge.

►► Kunstgewerbemuseum

Matthäikirchsstrasse 10

The Applied Art Museum stands in the new Kemperplatz (Culture Forum) of buildings. Inside is a host of beautiful objects from all over Europe: silver, gold, bronze, glass, jewelry, porcelain, furniture, textiles and much more, dating from medieval times to the present.

Open: Tuesday–Friday, 9–5; Saturday and Sunday, 10–5. Admission charge.

►►► Kurfürstendamm

The famous Kurfürstendamm (Elector's Causeway) dates to the 16th century, when it was a bridleway by which the Prussian kings reached their hunting lodges in the Grunewald. It became a favored address for Berlin's jet set and was remodeled in 1871 by Bismarck, who'd been impressed by the Champs Elysées. In World War II virtually all its great houses were destroyed and its 2¼-mile length became a parade of bars and shops. The most striking landmark is the ruined tower of the Kaiser Wilhelm Gedächtniskirche (memorial church), bombed in 1943 but left as a reminder of the war. Inside is an exhibition with references to such cities as Coventry (in England), which suffered similarly. A modern glass-and-concrete church stands alongside. Nearby is the tall, black plate-glass slab, the Europa-Center (see page 46), surmounted by a whirling Mercedes logo. The area at this top end of the Ku'damm is seedy at night, a haunt of homeless youngsters and loitering prostitutes.

Die Brüke artists
The eight-year association of the artists who called themselves Die Brücke (The Bridge) was unusually coherent. Four young artists, Kirchner, Heckel, Schmidt-Rottluff, and Bleyl, founded the group in Dresden in 1905. They wanted to get away from the dull, imitative German painting of the 19th century, and painted in a crude style using distortion and clashing colors in order to express emotions rather than verisimilitude—hence the name of this school of art: Expressionism.

Rabies threat
The huge areas of woodland in the Grunewald and around the River Havel make up a fascinating nature reserve. Before the wall came down, West Berlin was largely protected from the danger of rabies, so prevalent among East European wildlife. With the demolition of the wall this is no longer the case; infected foxes and, even more alarmingly, wolves have managed to swim the River Oder from Poland and now colonize Berlin's forests.

BERLIN

►►► Museen-Dahlem
Arnimallee 23–27

Dahlem, home of the Free University and a residential area, is known for its important group of museums. The **Gemäldegalerie** (Picture Gallery) houses a huge range of European paintings from the Middle Ages to the end of the 18th century. The German section includes works by Dürer, Altdorfer, Cranach, and Holbein the Younger. The Dutch section has works by Rembrandt and Bosch. There is also a fine collection of Islamic art. In the **Skulpturengalerie** (Sculpture Gallery) is work by the 15th-century master wood-carver Riemenschneider. The **Museum für Indische Kunst** (Museum of Indian Art) has one of Europe's largest collections, with bronzes, wood carving and early Sanskrit manuscripts. The **Museum für Völkerkunde** (Ethnographic Museum), near the main complex, covers cultures from around the world. *Open*: daily except Monday, 9–5; Saturday and Sunday, 10–5. Admission charge. (All Dahlem museums.)

The Museum für Verkehr und Technik includes old German warplanes from World War I

►►► Museumsinsel

Friedrich Wilhelm IV of Prussia in 1841 designated Museumsinsel (Museum Island) "an open space for art and science." This complex of museums—including Berlin's oldest, the Altes—stands on an island in the River Spree. The first building you will notice here is the ruined Neues-Museum (there are plans to restore the complex to its prewar grandeur). If you only have time to visit one museum, make it the Pergamon.

The **Altes Museum►**, on Lustgarten, was built in 1824–30 by Schinkel, Friedrich Wilhelm III's architect, to look like a Greek temple. Completely destroyed during World War II, it was rebuilt in 1966 and houses the National Gallery's 20th-century collection and the Kupferstichkabinett (print cabinet), which contains illustrations by Botticelli for Dante's *Divina Commedia*. *Open*: Tuesday–Sunday 10–8.

The **Bode-Museum►►**, formerly the Kaiser Friedrich Museum, was the final addition to Museumsinsel. It was renamed in 1956 after its founder, Wilhelm von Bode, and includes the Ägyptisches (Egyptian) Museum. The Bode also houses the Museum für Ur- und

The Reichstag

Frühgeschichte (museum of pre- and early history), notable for antiquities unearthed by Heinrich Schliemann at the site of ancient Troy, and the Münzkabinett, one of the world's largest coin collections.
Open: Wednesday–Sunday, 9–5.

Three great wonders of the ancient world are housed in the **Pergamonmuseum►►►**, which had to be constructed around them. The colossal Pergamon Altar, after which the museum is named, is a temple of Zeus and Athena from Asia Minor (ancient Pergamon is now Bergama in Turkey) dating from about 180–160 BC. Marble steps ascend to a wide colonnade; gods and giants writhe in complex friezes around the plinths. Next is the huge Roman Market Gate from Miletus. Third is the most startling exhibit of all—Nebuchadnezzar's Ishtar Gate and Processional Way from Babylon, with lions striding towering walls of azure tiles. Upstairs is the Pergamon's Islamic collection. Don't miss the Mshatta Gate from Jordan, smothered with carvings, and the paneled Aleppo Room.
Open: daily 9–5. Only major exhibits are open on Monday and Tuesday. Admission charge.

►► Neue Nationalgalerie
Potsdamer Strasse 50
The glass-and-steel New National Gallery was designed by Mies van der Rohe and completed in 1968. The collection of paintings, drawings, and sculpture from the 19th and 20th centuries has works by Kokoschka, Klee, Picasso, Beckmann, von Menzel, Corot, and Courbet.
Open: Tuesday–Friday, 9–5; Saturday and Sunday, 10–5. Admission charge.

►► Reichstag
Platz der Republik
The original parliament building was damaged in the notorious fire of 1933 and then by bombs in World War II. The dedication, *"Dem deutsche Volk"* (To the German People), is visible on the façade. The building has been re-designed internally by Sir Norman Foster, ready for use as the German Parliament in 1999.

Nikolaiviertel
This area southwest of Alexanderplatz and centered on Berlin's oldest recorded building, the 13th-century Nikolaikirche, is a creation of the postwar planners of East Berlin. Destroyed in 1944, it is now a renovated quarter with restaurants and shops, masquerading as medieval Berlin. Some buildings are replicas of originals; others, modern in style, were designed to blend with the surroundings.

43

Music Museum
A bright and cheerful museum, the Musikinstrumenten-Museum (Museum of Musical Instruments), at Tiergartenstrasse 1, is right next door to the Philharmonie (Philharmonic Hall). It features instruments and their manufacture from the 16th century to the present day, from an ancient set of bagpipes to synthesizers. There are occasional demonstrations of instruments and special tours at 11 on Saturday mornings.
(*Open*: Tuesday–Friday, 9–5; Saturday and Sunday, 10–5. Admission charge.)

The head of a dying warrior at the former Zeughaus

▶▶ **Sachsenhausen**

Strasse der Nationen, Oranienburg (take S-Bahn to Oranienburg).

Sachsenhausen Concentration Camp has recently been opened as a memorial after 45 years in East German hands. Visitors wander around the camp in increasing horror. First you see the boot-testing track, where prisoners were forced to run on different surfaces carrying heavy weights until they dropped (at which point they would be shot where they lay); then the accommodation blocks, the cell blocks in which prisoners languished in darkness for months until they died; and the "hospital" where the most perverse and horrific experiments would be carried out on inmates. The displays consist mostly of photographs and information boards charting the somber history of the place.

Open: daily except Monday. Admission free.

▶▶ **Schloss Charlottenburg**

Luisenplatz

This vast palace began life in 1695 as a modest home for Sophie-Charlotte, wife of the future Friedrich I of Prussia. Eventually it became a grand baroque summer residence for the Prussian kings. The rococo-style Neuer Flügel (New—or Knobelsdorff—Wing) was built for Frederick the Great.

The gardens were first laid out in 1697 in the French style, but were transformed into an English-style garden in the early 19th century. Be sure to see the Schinkel Pavilion, the Mausoleum and the Belvedere, with its fine collection of porcelain (Meissen and Berlin's homegrown KPM, or Königliche Porzellan Manufaktur). Note the Iron Cross on Frederick's dinner plates.

Open: Tuesday–Friday, 9–5; Saturday and Sunday, 10–5. Admission charge.

▶▶▶ **Unter den Linden**

Berlin's famous thoroughfare—the name means "under the lime trees"—was once a royal mall. Frederick the Great's bronze equestrian statue, backed by the Brandenburger Tor, looks down on the swirling traffic from the center of his great avenue. The statue was turned around by the former communist authorities so that Frederick appears to ride eastward, rather than bearing down on the Brandenburger Tor. The "Linden" runs from the Brandenburg Gate to the river. If you follow it east you will reach, on the left, the neoclassical palace of the **Humboldt University** building. The former **Zeughaus**▶▶ (Arsenal), is situated near the eastern end, and houses the Deutsches Historisches Museum (open daily except Wednesday). The great baroque sculptor Andreas Schlüter designed and cast the 22 heads of dying warriors in the inner courtyard; they represent particularly outstanding examples of German monumental sculpture.

Other buildings to look for as you continue your stroll include Schinkel's neoclassical **Neue Wache** (New Guardhouse), the restored baroque **Alte Bibliothek**, and the **Deutsche Staatsoper** a splendid example of neoclassical architecture, which is home to the opera house.

Excursion

▶▶▶ Potsdam

Public transportation and organized bus tours allow easy access to Potsdam. Its main claim to fame is **Schloss Sanssouci**▶▶, summer home of Frederick the Great of Prussia, whose aim was to indulge in cultural pursuits *sans souci*—"without care." This example of German architecture is arguably the finest example of rococo in Europe. Below it are broad south-facing terraces where Frederick planted vines: their rows of green-framed protective glass screens are a curious sight. In 1945 the town's **Cecilienhof**▶—an English-looking, 1916 mock-Tudor building—hosted the Potsdam Conference, when Churchill (and then Attlee), Truman, and Stalin met to decide Germany's future. Part of the building is now a hotel; some rooms can be visited.
Open: daily, 9–5, but closed the second and fourth Monday of each month.

The ostentatious **Neues Palais** (New Palace) is open once more. Look for the huge Marble Hall and, beneath it, a fine indoor grotto encrusted with shells and minerals. In the park is the 18th-century **Chinesisches Teehaus** (Chinese Teahouse). Additionally there is the restored 18th-century theater, and the lovely **Belvedere**, shelled by the Russians in 1945 but restored in time for Potsdam's 1,000th anniversary, in 1993.
Open: as for Schloss Sanssouci.
In the town Try to see the fine classical **Nikolaikirche** (St. Nicholas Church) by Schinkel and Persius, restored after war damage, and the 18th-century **Holländisches Viertel** (Dutch Quarter).

Potsdam: Frederick the Great's rococo summer palace is surprisingly small and intimate

Shopping

Weekend itinerary

Saturday
Morning: Ku'damm. Investigate the old quarters either side of the Ku'damm, such as around Savignyplatz or the Jewish quarter on Fasanenstrasse. Stop for coffee at Leysieffer's, diagonally opposite the Kempinski Hotel. Visit Kaiser Wilhelm Gedächtniskirche. On to KaDeWe for lunch on the 7th floor.
Afternoon: Neue National-galerie in Tiergarten, perhaps also Kunstgewerbemuseum or Musikinstrumenten-Museum; take a stroll round the restored area of Nikolaiviertel, then a short walk to Potsdamerplatz. Take in the Brandenburger Tor and the Reichstag before walking down Unter den Linden. Take a break at the Opern Café next door to the Staatsoper.
Evening: (try to) get tickets for the Staatsoper (Unter den Linden). Dine at one of several typical Berlin restaurants within walking distance.

Sunday
Morning: The Zoo (Budapesterstrasse), followed by lunch at Café Einstein (Kurfürstenstrasse 58).
Afternoon: Walk through Tiergarten to open-air market on Strasse des 17 Juni (crafts, antiques, porcelain, and silver). Refreshments at the Berlin Pavilion, next to Tiergarten subway station.

There is only one store that is an absolute must—the famous **KaDeWe** (Kaufhaus des Westens—Store of the West), said to be Europe's largest department store. Its food hall is arguably more sumptuous than that of Harrods in London. Don't waste much time in other departments, but head for the *Feinschmecker Etage* (gourmet floor)—an express elevator takes you nonstop to the 7th floor.

Not far from the KaDeWe, on Tauentzienstrasse, is the **Europa-Center**. Although it has more than 70 shops and restaurants, there is little of startling interest to the tourist. Shop owners have the reputation of being abrupt and unfriendly; you may want to give it a miss.

For fashion, the area to frequent is the Kurfürstendamm and its side streets, particularly Uhlandstrasse and Fasanenstrasse, where exclusive (and expensive) shops sell the latest creations of Berlin's top designers. Fashion of yesteryear is also a Berlin specialty, in the form of stylish secondhand clothing on sale in flea markets and in many other shops in the Kreuzberg, Schöneberg, Charlottenburg and Prenzlauer Berg districts. Around Savignyplatz are a wealth of antiques and specialized shops

Elegant Friedrichstrasse, the prewar shopping mecca of the well-heeled, is again developing into an exciting area for shoppers, with new stores (including a branch of France's Galeries Layfette) opening all the time. The same applies to the revived old center of Spandau, a select residential suburb. Rather than the inevitable bear, you might choose Berlin porcelain as a souvenir of your visit; attractive, if pricey, it is available from the Ku'damm showroom. If you prefer the "opposition," try the Meissen showroom on Unter den Linden.

Markets Lovers of markets are well served in Berlin, where local markets abound. For bric-a-brac, **Trödelmarkt** in Prenzlauer Berg can produce a bargain, as can the **Nollendorf flea market**, under cover in the old Nollendorf S-Bahn (not Tuesday), or the colorful weekend **Strasse des 17 Juni flea market**. For a glimpse of the Orient, visit the **Turkish market** on Maybachufer, in Neukölln (Tuesday and Friday afternoons).

Food and Drink

Where to eat German food is frequently somewhat heavy, but with a degree of Austrian influence and a dash of German creativity, a new generation of chefs have come up with *neue Deutsche Küche*—Germany's version of *nouvelle cuisine* (not cheap). Highly recommended is **Trio** at Klausenerplatz 14 (closed Wednesdays and Thursdays); The **Spree-Atken** in Charlottenburg offers music from old Berlin and six-course meals. If money is no object, the **Bamberger Reiter**, Regensburgerstrasse 7, is your best bet. At the **Opernpalais unter der Linden**, Fridericus specializes in a variety of fish dishes. **Die Alte Pumpe**, Lützowstrasse, 42 Schonberg, with an enormous restored water pump as centerpiece, is a three-story restaurant with traditional Berlin specialties, and a superb array of sweet and savory pancakes. Also recommended, its splendid Sunday breakfast, "Pumpenfrühstück." The **Mövenpick** (Europa-Center) is a Swiss restaurant divided into many themed sections, all differently decorated, so you could have *Schnitzel mit Rösti* in one bit, *Kaffee und Kuchen* here, pizza or pasta there, beers and drinks elsewhere. Well run and friendly, it sells all its sumptuous cakes at half price after 7 PM.

In an unsung but appealing part of the city, **Martin Gropius Kneipe** (Martin-Gropius Bau, Stresemannstrasse 110) is a most handsome building, now devoted to exhibitions: art, Jewish life, and so forth. The attractive white-painted café with baroque music and health foods is a welcome change from the meat-based dishes of most Berlin restaurants—good *Apfelstrudel*, too.

Alter Dorfkrug Lubars (Alt Lubars 8, 1000–Berlin 28), miles from the center, is a little oasis out among fields. The restaurant looks like something Bavarian, and makes a very nice (if touristy) lunchtime venue on sunny days. **Cafe Einstein** (Kurfürstenstrasse 58) is a popular (and crowded) re-creation of Viennese coffeehouse culture, with gardens at the back.

The department store **KaDeWe** has a number of counters where you can enjoy a typical Berliner lunch that won't break the bank. **Restaurant Hardtke** in Meinekestrasse offers traditional if robust food with wurst and various cuts of meat for those with very healthy appetites. Try their homemade sausages or Eisbein, or their amazing selection of fresh meats.

47

The Ku'damm's famous Café Kranzler

Week's itinerary

Monday
Morning: Ku'damm and Kaiser Wilhelm Gedächtniskirche; explore side-street shops.
Afternoon: Bus tour to Potsdam (but check opening times).

Tuesday
Morning: Dahlem museums, lunch in museum café.
Afternoon: Finish Dahlem museums or wander around Dahlem village and its small church.

Wednesday
Morning: Zoo; Neue Nationalgalerie; Musikinstrumenten-Museum; Kunstgewerbemuseum.
Afternoon: Martin-Gropius-Bau (Stresemannstrasse, Kreuzberg, tea at café/restaurant), and walk along the Schöneberger Ufer.

Thursday
Morning: Schloss Charlottenburg; walk through the extensive gardens at the back of the castle.
Afternoon: Ägyptisches Museum and Bröhan Museum.

Friday
Morning: Tour the Reichstag; Brandenburger Tor; Alexanderplatz; Nikolaiviertel.
Afternoon: Shopping/leisure or, if stamina allows, Museumsinsel.

Saturday
Morning: Coffee on the Ku'damm, then on to the open-air market at Winterfelderplatz.
Afternoon: Walk in the Tiergarten; market on Strasse des 17 Juni.

Sunday
Morning: Breakfast at Savignyplatz; visit to an art gallery or museum (e.g., Bauhaus-Archiv).
Afternoon: Walk around Englischer Garten, part of the grounds of the Schloss Bellevue; alternatively, look out at Berlin from the train window on the S-Bahn line to Sachsenhausen, getting off for a wander.

Like New York, Berlin is a city that never sleeps, and certainly not at night. The nightlife only starts in the early hours of the morning, so if you're someone who needs a good night's rest, you'll probably miss out on the more exciting (if seedier) aspects of the city. (Despite its lively feel, Berlin can also be surprisingly quiet at night.)

Nothing ever gets going before midnight at least, and while prowling around the discos at 11 PM will get you an entrance ticket, once inside you'll find you're the only one there. Young Germans living in Hamburg or Munich often come to Berlin for a weekend of clubbing; there are no laws for closing hours, and many bars and discos stay open until 6 AM. You might consider the **Friedrichstadt Palast** (Friedrichstrasse 107), highly recommended for all sorts of night shows and revues.

For night bars, discos and cabarets, the liveliest youth scene is now in the Scheunenviertel ("barn quarter") in the east, near the finely restored New Synagogue: very trendy is the Tacheles counter culture center, also the Franz Club and Variété Chamäleon.

The Ku'damm—equivalent to London's Oxford Street and just as touristy—is by day a fashionable shopping street; by night it is the haunt of prostitutes. In Kreuzberg, Berlin's answer to Manhattan's East Village, there are a variety of leather bars, discos, and strip joints, making up the city's "alternative" scene.

Cabaret, folk music, and dance clubs are scattered throughout the city. For jazz lovers, the **Quasimodo Club** on Kantstrasse near the Bahnhof Zoo is a must. Magazines such as *Checkpoint* (published monthly in English), *Berlin-Program*, *Tip*, and *Zitty* (published, on alternate weeks), provide details on what's on where and what's in vogue. On a different level, there are three opera houses, four symphony orchestras and enough cabaret and theater to keep you occupied for months on end. In the summer, the **Waldbühne**, the city's open-air arena in the shadow of the Olympic stadium, plays host to classical concerts and performances by international pop stars.

T-shirts for sale

Accommodations

There are some ambitious hotel projects in the east, notably the palatial Grand just off Friedrichstrasse, and the luxury Hilton in the shell of the old Dom hotel in Mohrenstrasse. West Berlin, however, remains the most convenient and lively place to stay, with a greater choice of nightlife and restaurants when darkness falls. Until the wrangles over land ownership between east and west are settled, there is unlikely to be much investment in the east, leaving the west's hotels in this increasingly popular city with a captive market of regular business visitors, a booming conference trade, and a growing number of tourists. Berlin hotels have become very expensive since the Wall fell. Increasingly, tourists find themselves using small pensions and bed-and-breakfast accommodations, or staying some distance out of town. Since public transportation is so efficient, the last is quite feasible if you have the time and don't mind quiet evenings or traveling to the center at night; there are several peaceful hotels in the Grunewald area near the Wannsee.

Bedrooms debugged
Following the collapse of the Communist regime, many hard-currency hotels were closed for several days so that corridor cameras could be taken out, bedrooms debugged and secret-police rooms converted to hotel use.

Where the rich and famous go
The best place to observe the rich and famous is at the Deutsche Oper on Bismarckstrasse—spend the intervals celebrity-spotting in the bars. Between January and March the fashionable world takes to the dance floor in balls, including the Press Ball, usually attended by the chancellor and foreign minister. The most sought-after and elegant ball is organized by the wealthy business community. The top shopping spot is along the western end of the Ku'damm, while top people dine at the Grand Slam restaurant in Zehlendorf or in the heart of the Grunewald at the Landhaus Bott.

49

Housefronts and terrace cafés give style to the mighty Ku'damm boulevard

Other options for budget travelers are a number of youth hostels and hotels designed with students in mind. The tourist office provides a list of these free of charge. Accommodations are basic, possibly without a private bath or shower, but civilized. There's one on a side-street near Schöneberg Town Hall off Martin-Luther Strasse, another toward the Wilmersdorf end of the Ku'damm. Or for a modest charge you can stay with a private family: tourist offices have lists and will make bookings.

If you like more idiosyncratic accommodations, try a pension or small hotel on or just off the Ku'damm in the older houses that escaped RAF bombs. These are often family-run, with characterful rooms, some retaining original art deco or Jugendstil (art nouveau) features. There are several in Wielandstrasse, others in Meinikestrasse. Most hotels, however, lie clustered around the Europa-Center, and are a bit dull. Though generally in good condition, with most facilities and sparklingly clean, they now look quite passé.

If you are a non smoker it's as well to note that a surprising number of "health-conscious" Germans smoke (see page 17), and hotel bedrooms may smell of stale tobacco. Ask for nonsmoking rooms, if they are available.

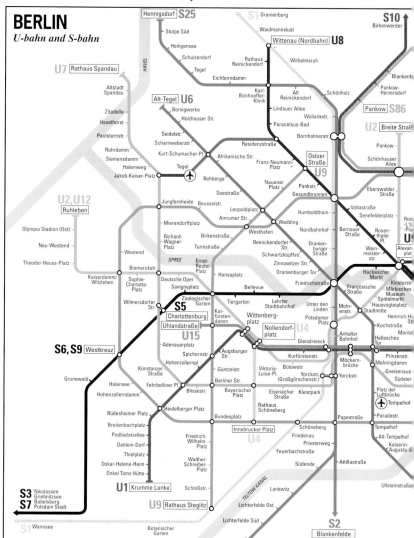

The trains may not be new, but are fast and frequent

Berlin's public transportation system is highly efficient; there are few areas you cannot reach. Compared with many European cities, traffic congestion is low; buses are thus able to move at a reasonable speed and keep to timetables. Since reunification the city's twin transportation networks (formerly impeded by the Wall) have been merged, and many of the old subway lines and stations reopened. Berlin has an underground rail U-Bahn system (11 lines, excellent for the central areas), an S-Bahn system (10 lines) serving more outlying areas, and a conventional rail network for the distant suburbs. An excellent bus system operates throughout the city, with night services too. There are some ferries, and the east has a few trams. This network is now being

S8 Bernau
S85 Buch

U-Bahn	S-Bahn	Airport bus
U1	S1	109
U2	S2 & 25	128
U4	S3,5,6, 7 & 9	
U5	S45 & 46	○ Interchange station
U6	S8, 85 & 86	
U7	S10	
U8	S75	Hönow U5 Terminating station and Line number
U9		
U12 (night only)		
U15 (peak only)		

S75
Wartenberg

Ahrensfelde S7

Louis-Lewin Str.

U5
Hönow

Mehrower Allee
Hellersdorf

Hohenschönhausen
Raoul-Wallenberg-Str.
Cottbusser Platz

Prenzlauer Allee
Gehrenseestr.
Grottkauer Str.

Greifswalder Straße
Marzahn
Kaulsdorf-Nord

Landsberger Allee
Poelchaustr.

Storkower Str.
Wuhletal
S5 Strausberg Nord

Springpfuhl
Biesdorf

Elsterwerdaer Platz

Freidrichsfelde Ost
Biesdorf-Süd

Straus-berger Platz
Rathaus Friedrichshain
Frankfurter Allee
Tierpark
Friedrichsfelde

hillingstr. Weberwiese Samariterstr.
Magdalenen-straße
Lichtenberg

U15 U1 S75
Nöldnerplatz

nnowitzbrücke
Warschauer Str.

Hauptbahnhof
Ostkreuz

S86

ottbusser
Schlesisches Tor
Rummelsburg

or
Görlitzer Bahnhof
Treptower Park
Betriebsbahnhof-Rummelsburg
Karlshorst

Schönleinstr.
Plänterwald
Wuhlheide
Köpenick

Sonnenallee
Hirschgarten

Rathaus Neukölln
Karl-Marx-Str.
Baumschulen-weg
Friedrichshagen
Rahnsdorf

ermannplatz
Köllnische Heide
Schöneweide
Wilhelms-hagen

Boddinstraße
Neukölln
Erkner S3

Grenzallee
Oberspree

ermannstr.

8
Blaschkoallee
Spindlersfeld S10

Parchimer Allee

Britz-Süd

Johannisthaler Chaussee
S6 Königs Wusterhausen

Westphalweg
Lipschitzallee
S8
S46 Grünau

Wutzkyallee

Zwickauer Damm
S9
S45 Flughafen Schönefeld ✈
S85

Alt-Mariendorf
Rudow U7

U6

improved. Standard fares operate for buses, U-Bahn and S-Bahn (cheaper for short hops, or *Kurzstrecke*, and children). Tickets are valid for two hours and can be used on any system within that time. Before your journey you must validate each ticket by punching it into a machine to stamp the time. For most visitors planning to explore Berlin extensively, it is well worth buying a "Welcome Card": this gives free travel on public transport for three days, plus reductions on entry to many museums, theaters, and tours.

Ask for details of inclusive or family tickets at main transport offices (the companies serving the two halves of the city are BVG and BVB), for example outside Zoo Station or at Alexanderplatz S-Bahn.

Bus No. 100

One bus route of particular interest to visitors is Bus No. 100, from outside the tourist office past many of Berlin's main sights to Alexanderplatz. With a pass, you can hop on and off as you like and see much of the city. Several companies offer city bus tours and excursions to Potsdam or Dresden; in summer boats ply the lakes and canals. Private cars are as unwelcome in central Berlin as in most major cities.

Tourist offices

There is a local Verkehrsamt (tourist office) in the Europa-Center, with its entrance on Budapesterstrasse (tel: 262–6031), which is near to the main train station and KaDeWe. Amerika Haus and the British Council are both located nearby, on Hardenbergerstrasse, if you want to inquire about English-language events in town. The local tourist offices are open from 8 AM until 11 PM.

51

Official red-starred caps of the old GDR are now collectors' items

THE NORTHWEST

0   20   40   60   80 km

0   20   40 miles

Nordfriesische Inseln

Sylt

Kampen
Keitum
Westerland
Nolde-Museum

Schloss
Glücksburg

Niebüll   Leck

Flensburg

Föhr

Amrum

Bredstedt

Treene

A7

Halligen

Silberstedt
Dannewerk

Pellworm
Nordstrand

Husum

N o r d s e e

Eiderstedt

Friedrichstadt

Eider

St.Peter-
Ording

Tönning

Heide

Helgoland

A23

NordOstsee-Kanal

Büsum

Meldorf

Wilster

Itzeh

D e u t s c h e

B u c h t

Helgoländer
Bucht

Brunsbüttel

Glückstadt

Cuxhaven

Otterndorf

Eib

Ostfriesische Inseln

Wangerooge

Langeoog

Norderney

Spiekeroog

Hemmoor

Bederkesa

Stade

Juist

Baltrum

Esens

Wattenmeer

Bremerhaven

Alte

Borkum

Memmert

Norden

Wittmund

Jever

Bremervörde

Greetsiel

Jade-

Kanal

Wilhelmshaven

Ems

Aurich

Schloss
Gödens

A27

Oste

Emden

Wiesmoor

Varel

Brake

Osterholz-
Scharmbeck

Zeven

A1

A28

Westerstede

Elsfleth

Tarmstedt

Leer

Bad Zwischenahn

Rastede

Weser

Worpswede

Weener

Ems

Barssel

Hunte

Hamme

Papenburg

Kanal

Oldenburg

Delmenhorst

Rotenbu
Wümm

Kusten-

Aue

Ganderkesee

BREMEN

Friesoythe

Grossenkneten

Weyhe

Achim

A27

NL

Werlte

Wildeshausen

Syke

Verden

A31

Sögel

Emstek

Bassum

Haren

Cloppenburg

Visbek

Twistringen

Löningen

Hase

Vechta

Barnstorf

Sulingen

Rethe
Rodewal

Meppen

Haselünne

Quakenbrück

A1

Lohne

Hunte

Barenburg

Nienburg

Vecht

Emlichheim

Bersenbrück

Steinfeld

Diepholz

Aue

Uelsen

Neuenhaus

Lingen

Freren

Fürstenau

Damme

Wagenfeld

Uchte

Steinhuder
Meer

Nordhorn

Bramsche

Rahden

Weser

Dortmund-Ems

Recke
Hörstel

Ibbenbüren

Mittellandkanal

Levern

Espelkamp

Stadthagen

Bad Bentheim

Rheine

Ems

Kanal

Tecklenburg

Osnabrück

Hase

Wiehengebirge

Lübbecke

Bückeburg

A2

Gronau

Ochtrup

Lengerich

Melle

Enger

Minden

Spring

A30

Rinteln

Fischbec

Ahaus

Burgsteinfurt

Bad
Iburg

Teutoburger Wald

Herford

Hameln

A1

Ostbevern

BIELEFELD

Bad Salzuflen

Weser

Lemgo

Bad
Pyrm

MÜNSTER

Telgte

Lage

Coesfeld

Ems

Detmold

A31

Warendorf

Gütersloh

52

DK

Kappeln

eswig

Eckernförde
Strande

Altenholz • Laboe

Heiligenhafen

Puttgarden

Febmarn

Febmarnbelt

Kieler Bucht

Kiel

Freilichtmuseum

Lütjenburg

Oldenburg

Mecklenburger Bucht

endsburg

Preetz

Holsteinische Schweiz

Bordesholm

Plön

Eutin

Neustadt

Lübecker Bucht

Norton

Neumünster

Ahrensbök

Stör

Bad Segeberg

A1

Travemünde

Wismar

A7

Bad Oldesloe

Lübeck

Grevesmühlen

mshorn

Ahrensburg

Ratzeburg

Schweriner See

Jetersen

Trittau

Lauenburgische Seen

Mölln

Schwerin

a n d

✈ **HAMBURG**

Friedrichsruh

Wittenburg

chude

Geesthacht

Elbe

Hagenow

Stde

Wandsbek

Winsen

Lauenburg

Boizenburg

Ludwigslust

Buchholz

Bardowick

Lübtheen

Lüneburg

Lüneburger

Undeloh

Egestorf

Hitzacker

Dömitz

Döhle

Elbe

Schneverdingen

Bad Bevensen

Dannenberg

Jetze

Heide

Ebstorf

Soltau

Munster

Uelzen

Clenze

Fallingbostel

Fassberg

Suhlendorf

Wieren

Salzwedel

Bergen

Elbe-Seiten-Kanal

Belsen ■

Eschede

Wittingen

Beetzendorf

Winsen

Knesebeck

Garssen

Gardelegen

Celle

Fubse

Kloster Weinhausen

Langenhagen

Uetze

Gifhorn

Burgdorf

Oker

Wolfsburg

Mittellandkanal

HANNOVER

Lehre

A2

Haldensleben

Peine ■

Königslutter

A7

BRAUNSCHWEIG

Helmstedt

Nordstemmen

A39

Wolfenbüttel

Hildesheim

Schöningen

Elze

Hornburg

Bode

Saltzgitter

A395

Alfeld

Egelen

Leine

Goslar ■

Halberstadt

A24

Elbe

NORTHWEST GERMANY

Katharinenkirche (St. Catherine's Church) in Braunschweig

The Guelph princes
The powerful Welfen (Guelph) family were a thorn in the side of the imperial family, challenging their power and policy. Heinrich der Löwe (Henry the Lion) was a powerful imperial prince, but was forced to retire to Brunswick by his cousin the emperor—a close childhood friend who became a rival in adulthood.

The northwest includes the two great seaports of **Hamburg** and **Bremen**, each a semiautonomous *Land* (state) on its own, as well as the whole of the *Land* of Schleswig-Holstein and nearly all of the *Niedersachsen* (Lower Saxony). The area lacks the scenic wonders of the south, but it has its own quiet beauties, such as the **Lüneburg Heath**, and many historic and picturesque towns with buildings of mellow red brick, half-timbers and stepped gables.

Some areas carry on the Hanseatic merchant tradition (see page 75); others are influenced by the great princely houses of the past, such as the Guelphs and Brunswicks. The farms on the rolling plains tend to be large, rich, and modern. **Schleswig**, long fought over between Germany and Denmark, did not become part of Prussia until 1864, and still has some Danish character. In 1945 the two former dukedoms of Schleswig and Holstein merged to form one *Land* with its capital at **Kiel** (but **Lübeck** is much the more interesting town). The coastlines of the two *Länder* are very different; the Baltic coast is gently pastoral, cut by low fjords and backed by wooded hills, while the North Sea coast is more flat and stark, buffeted by winds and storms that erode the coast. Major vacation resorts include the offshore island of **Sylt**.

Lower Saxony is misleadingly named, for its Saxon tribes emigrated in the Dark Ages and today it has no connection with true Saxony around Leipzig (see page 148). It has handsome old towns, such as **Celle**, **Lüneburg**, and **Stade**, and modern industry, mostly around **Hannover**, its capital. In coastal area **Friesland**, which extends up into Schleswig, people keep their own culture and dialect, and their own dour temperament.

▶ **Braunschweig (Brunswick)**
A historic city with royal connections: in the 12th century it was the seat of Germany's most powerful ruler, the Guelph prince Henry the Lion. A bronze statue of a lion (his symbol), still standing in the Bergplatz, was erected in his day (1166). Later (1753–1918) the dukes of Brunswick lived here. The city was heavily bombed and then rebuilt. Today it is mainly industrial (trucks, machinery, etc.) but some fine buildings survive—notably the half-timbered Gothic and Renaissance houses on the Altstadtmarkt, and Henry's Romanesque cathedral. The latter contains his gift of a big seven-branch candelabra, the splendid Imervard Crucifix (1150), and the tomb of Henry and his English wife, Mathilda. The Herzog Anton Ulrich Museum has paintings by Rembrandt, Rubens, Cranach, etc.

▶▶ **Bremen**
Germany's largest port after Hamburg is a fascinating old Hanseatic city with a quirky, individualistic personality. Like its bigger rival, it has a long history of independence and so today is a *Land* on its own. Its people are maritime, outward-looking and liberal-minded. Its port expanded in the 19th century as a center for coffee and cotton imports. Although it is 40 miles upstream from the mouth of the Weser, it can take oceangoing ships and still handles much of the German intake of raw materials (it is well worth making the trip). Sadly,

like Hamburg, the port is today in trouble. Its shipyards have declined and, despite the arrival of new modern industries (notably aerospace and electronics), many people are out of work. The new university began life in the 1970s, in a blaze of radical leftism. It has now grown milder but remains interestingly innovative.

Despite being a northern city, Bremen is full of colorful outdoor life—markets, street musicians, festivals. In the Marktplatz► (Market Square) you might find men in sailors' dress singing sea chantys, or see a man in top hat and tails sweeping rubbish from the cathedral steps (it's a local custom that a man still unwed on his 30th birthday must do this, then marry the first girl who kisses him). The buildings are varied—tall mansions in Weser Renaissance style (see page 119), newer Jugendstil villas with oddly shaped gables, even a windmill on a grassy hill made from part of the old ramparts that enclose the Altstadt (Old Town).

Rebuilt after the bombing, much of the Altstadt is traffic-free and best toured on foot. The twin-towered cathedral is a Romanesque/Gothic mix and has a 13th-century bronze font. The arcaded Rathaus►► (town hall), also Gothic, with a rich Renaissance façade, has a noble banqueting hall. Its *Ratskeller* (cellar restaurant) serves no French wines, only German (a custom kept from Napoleonic days), and has 17th-century cubicles for private parties (a woman and a man dining alone must keep the door open). Outside stand two famous statues. One, built in 1404 as a symbol of independence, is a 33-foot figure of Charlemagne's nephew, Roland. The other is modern: a bronze pyramid of a cock on a cat on a dog on a donkey, depicting a Grimm's folktale.

The Böttcherstrasse►, leading off the Marktplatz, is a Jugendstil alleyway designed in the 1920s by the offbeat Worpswede (see page 77) architect Bernhard Hoetger. Its gabled houses form a shopping arcade with

In the stately Markplatz is the statue of the Knight Roland (1404) bearing the sword of justice

55

The Renaissance façade of the majestic Rathaus. Inside is a sumptuous Guildhall

Heligoland
In the North Sea, 56 miles northwest of Bremerhaven, Heligoland is an unspectacular small sandstone island. Its strategic position, however, commanding the sea-lanes to the North Sea ports, made it a valuable possession. Germany eventually gained possession in 1890 by swapping it with Britain for the island of Zanzibar.

stylish boutiques. There are also two small museums, one of medieval art, one devoted to the Worpswede painter Paula Modersohn-Becker. The nearby Schnoor district is a "village" of narrow streets lined with old fishermen's cottages. It is now very touristy, full of crafts shops, cafés and boutiques, but still engaging.

The main museums are outside the Altstadt. The large **Focke Museum▶** gives a wonderful idea of Bremen's history, with maps, paintings, photos, model ships and much else. The Überseemuseum is devoted to Asian and African ethnography. The excellent Kunsthalle's varied paintings range from Cranach and Altdorfer via Brueghel and Delacroix to the Worpswede school.

▶ Bremerhaven

This big workaday port, 40 miles downstream from Bremen at the mouth of the Weser, was created in 1827 as Bremen's deep-sea port. It is still busy, but the Columbuskaje (quay), where ocean liners used to berth, is now used only by ferries and cruise ships. This is also Germany's leading fishing port and has interesting museums: an aquarium and fishing museum, an outdoor museum with 17th-century peasant houses, and the Deutsches Schiffahrtsmuseum, a big museum of maritime history with models of old boats and harbors, plus a genuine Hanseatic trading vessel of 1380, found in Bremen harbor in 1962.

▶▶ Celle

This is a stately old town, one of north Germany's finest, with a princely history. It has a neat, gridlike Altstadt of 16th- to 18th-century red and white gabled, half-timbered houses, some with upper floors quaintly overhanging. In the Celle region, orchids are grown and horses are bred. The parade of stallions through Celle in early autumn is well worth seeing.

The Lüneburg branch of the Guelph dynasty, vaguely related to the British royal family, ruled here from 1378 to 1705. Their handsome white **Schloss▶**, enclosed by a swan-filled moat, has a 17th-century theater that is still used for staging classic plays. The lovely vaulted 15th-century chapel has rich Renaissance decor, while the state rooms are Italian baroque. Nearby, note the biblical quotes on the decorated façade of the Lateinschule (1602), a former college, and the trompe-l'oeil façade of the old gray Rathaus (1579). Every day at 7:30 AM and 6:30 PM the town's bugler mounts the 235 steps of the Gothic Stadtkirche to blow his horn.

Southeast of Celle is a true marvel—the big 13th-century Cistercian abbey of **Wienhausen**, warmly evocative of medieval times. Since the Reformation it has been a kind of retirement home for elderly lay Protestant women, who will escort you around. The stunning medieval tapestries are on display only around Whitsun (late May), but you can see the 14th-century murals in the chapel, and other curiosities—above all the tiny museum containing 15th-century scissors, knives, nail files, spectacles, notebooks, etc., all found under the chapel floorboards in 1953 and supposed to have been hidden or dropped there by the nuns before the Reformation!

Celle's town crest derives from the mighty Guelph princes who ruled the town from 1378 to 1705

The harbor at Emden, from the viewing deck of the Rathaus tower

Working windmills
The Grossefehn area is known for its five handsome 19th-century windmills. Two have recently been restored to working order and are again grinding corn. This brings in some money, but the main purpose is to attract tourists. The friendly owner of the Dutch-type mill at Spezterfehn will show visitors around on the weekends and take them up to the gallery to inspect the metal sails. The other restored mill is at Bagland. These are the only working windmills left in the region.

Emden

Emden is situated on the Ems estuary and is a herring-fishing center and industrial port for the Ruhr via the Ems-Dortmund canal. The Landesmuseum has displays of weapons and of local history. The windy Friesland plain around here is mainly dull, but **Greetsiel** is a pretty, if touristy, fishing village. To the east is the quiet and attractive **Grossefehn** area, where wooden bridges span canals.

► Flensburg

Set on a fjord by the Danish border, this handsome old port was long part of Denmark and still has a Danish look and ambience. Its fine buildings include the 15th-century Gothic Nikolaikirche and the 16th-century Nordertor (north gate). For local history visit the Städtisches Museum. Flensburg used to be a wealthy merchant center based on Caribbean sugar imports. The trade still continues, and rum is still made here.

Out on an islet in the fjord to the northeast is majestic, white-walled **Glücksburg Castle►**, a northern Renaissance jewel. It contains mementos of its former owners, relatives of the Danish royal family, as well as Gobelin tapestries and a richly decorated banqueting hall. A pretty coastal route leads east to the old port of **Kappeln**, where strange long wooden fences in the water are still used to catch herring. It was from here in the 5th and 6th centuries that the Angles, who gave their name to England, went colonizing under their leaders Hengist and Horsa.

West of Flensburg, near the Danish border north of Niebüll, is the former **home of Emil Nolde►**, the Expressionist artist. It is now a museum of his colorful, anguished work—powerful, but maybe not to all tastes.

Emil Nolde
Although he joined the Nazis in 1920, the painter Emil Hanse (called Emil Nolde after his birthplace) was forced into internal exile by the Third Reich. His intense Expressionistic style of painting was considered degenerate by the Nazis.

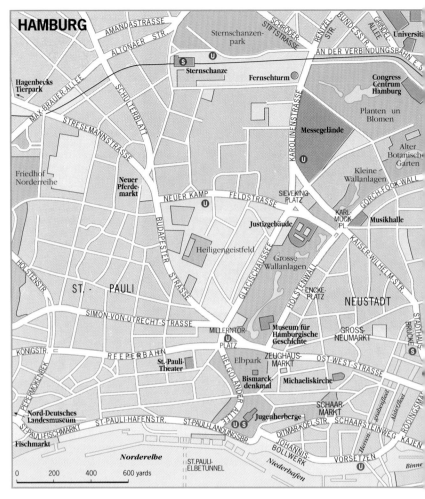

HAMBURG

▶▶▶ Hamburg

Germany's second-largest city and major port is the proud heir of a great merchant-seafaring tradition dating from Hanseatic days. A cultured as well as an industrial city (it has probably the best opera in Germany), Hamburg is an unusually spacious and civilized place that delights nearly all its visitors. For centuries it was a Free Imperial City and today is a *Land* on its own, an autonomous city-state; its most famous son in postwar times is ex-Chancellor Helmut Schmidt, a former city senator. His Socialist party (S.P.D.) has ruled this city almost without a break since the war.

Set by the broad Elbe some 63 miles upstream from the sea, it's a town of water—the river, the huge port, the many canals (it has more bridges than any other world city, 2,195 against Venice's 400), and the big and beautiful Alster Lake, at its very heart. As it was never a royal or episcopal town but a merchant one, it has few grand or distinguished buildings compared with, say, Munich. Overall, though, it is pleasingly harmonious and

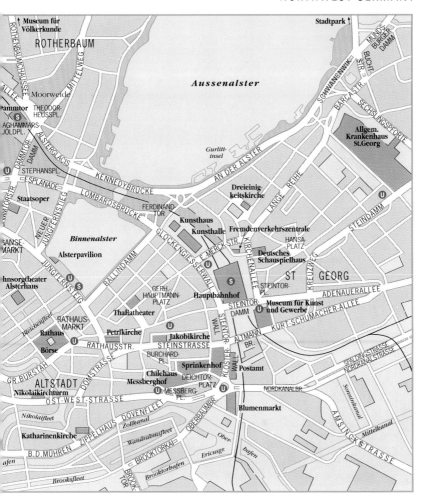

after massive wartime destruction has been tactfully rebuilt, mostly in local redbrick style, avoiding the concrete harshness of so many German towns. There are no skyscrapers to spoil the elegant skyline of green-copper spires by the Alster. In the suburbs are charming Jugendstil wrought-iron balconies, parks and gardens, even old timbered farmsteads and leafy lanes within the city's wide borders. Some streets retain odd names, such as Ole Hoop.

The people, often tall, lean and blond, have real style in their own Nordic way; some men wear the local blue sailors' caps that Helmut Schmidt favors. They are cautious and reserved, not exuberant like Bavarians but direct, businesslike, and very polite to visitors. Theirs is a tolerant, liberal spirit, cosmopolitan and Anglophile. Hamburg has been called the most English of German towns, still proud of the historic trade links; as the old saying goes, "When it rains in London, Hamburgers open their umbrellas."

Hamburg has long been a major commercial center.

Media capital
Since World War II, Hamburg has been the press and media capital of Germany. The national TV news programs are edited here, as are most of the big weekly magazines, such as *Der Speigel* and *Stern*. These days a few national daily newspapers (such as *Die Welt*) are shifting back to Berlin, but Hamburg is still home to the weekly *Die Zeit*, intellectual symbol of the city's liberal, free-thinking tradition.

First established as a port in 1189, then a leader of the Hanseatic League, it created Germany's first stock exchange in 1558 and was a Free Imperial City from 1618. Wrecked by a huge fire in 1842, it was then rebuilt on the spacious scale it still enjoys. Its major growth came in the late 19th century, due to sea trade with America. Later, this free-thinking town was less welcoming to Hitler than other towns were, and the Nazis never held major rallies there—but it was to suffer badly from British RAF fire raids in 1943.

Since the war, although it has shared in the economic miracle it has ceased to be Germany's richest city, overtaken by others as German industry has shifted to the south. This huge port has suffered as a result of Rotterdam's better situation for the Atlantic trade. The once-mighty shipyards, such as Blohm und Voss, have been forced to contract, close or diversify, like so many others in Europe. Although new modern industry has arrived, notably in electronics (Philips, etc.) and aeronautics (huge Lufthansa repair yards, MBB factories working on Airbus, etc.), unemployment remains high. After 1945 Hamburg was cut off from its natural markets in the GDR and Poland, but today it is eagerly reclaiming them, and its prospects have improved.

Despite the decline of the old merchant firms, there is still much wealth in Hamburg. With its musical tradition—it's the hometown of Brahms, and the first German opera house opened here in 1677—there's a

The city of Hamburg, viewed from the harbor

The free port
Hamburg's wealth is based on trade and commerce. One important source of earnings is the *Freihafen* (free port), which is a customs-exempt area where goods can be stored in transit or processed for re-export without incurring duty.

wealth of culture here as well. Since World War II Hamburg opera and ballet have been as good as any in Germany, the former under the great Rolf Libermann (now retired), the latter under John Neumeier. Theater has shone under Peter Zadek and Michael Bogdanov. Since its merchant rulers were less concerned with collecting art treasures than were the aristocrats of south Germany, Hamburg has few major art museums. But it is a key German center for modern popular music: many big record companies are here.

The port and city center With annual traffic of some 60 million metric tons, this is Europe's fourth-biggest port, taking vessels of up to 110,000 tons. Its terminals can load or unload rapidly, using few workers. This has put many dockers out of work, but it suits the owners of the containers, as port dues are high.

A guided **boat tour of the port►** (starting from the Landungsbrücken in the suburb of St. Pauli) is a good way to start a city visit. You'll be shown the 42 miles of

quays, the 2½-mile Kohlbrand bridge (1975), and the protective walls built after the 1962 floods, which caused 350 deaths. Near the eastern side of the port, Speicherstadt is an impressive group of high gabled brick warehouses by canals. Built in the 1880s, they are still used for storing spices, tobacco, etc.

Nearby is what remains of the Altstadt after the 1842 and 1943 fires. Here St. Catherine's Church is Gothic with a baroque tower; St. Nicholas's, with its slim spire, has been left partly in ruins as a war memorial. Attractive gabled warehouses line the Nikolai fleet canal, and many of the 17th-century merchants' houses off the narrow Deichstrasse are now atmospheric restaurants. To the west, the baroque church of St. Michael, large and stately, has a famous tall green tower (with a good view from its platform). The nearby **Krameramts-wohnungen▶**, an alley of 17th-century almshouses, is a most picturesque surviving corner of old Hamburg.

Glance at the high-pedestaled statue of an arrogant Bismarck with sword and spiked helmet, in a park by St. Pauli. Move on to the dullish Hamburg history museum, which has photos and models of city and port, and a large model railroad. Farther along the broad inner ringway you'll come to the rebuilt Opera House, then to an area of new shopping arcades, wonderfully stylish and luxurious, with startling window displays—Hanse Viertel and Galleria are the best. The massive Rathaus, with its heavy, lavish interiors, was built in 1897 in the neo-Renaissance style and seems symbolic of the city's proud heyday. The broad square and the canal beside it are attractive; so are St. Jacob's late Gothic hall-church, and St. Peter's with its high 14th-century tower. Beyond

A boat tour around the harbor at Hamburg offers interesting views

Hamburg's massive neo-Renaissance Rathaus is still the seat of the city's government, the Senate

Local beer
Hamburg beer is known for being cold, with a good head (like its citizens, some would say)—and it's also strong. A specialty of the harbor district is *Lütt um Lütt*, beer fortified with schnapps—not a drink for the fainthearted.

Flowers that bloom in the Planten und Blomen flower park

the ringway looms the glass-vaulted roof of the Hauptbahnhof (station), next to the Museum für Kunst und Gewerbe (arts and crafts), which has Renaissance furniture, Jugendstil ornaments, etc., and even offers authentic Japanese tea ceremonies in a real teahouse. The **Kunsthalle►**, the city's main art museum, offers a huge but confusingly presented array, from north German primitives via European masters to the Romantic Caspar David Friedrich, and Dix and Klee.

Alster and the north side The **Aussenalster►**, the larger outer lake, is a lovely shimmering focus of the city's life, much used for recreation. Against a setting of spires, handsome villas and weeping willows, sails glide and Hamburgers stride the shore paths with their dogs. There are outdoor cafés for summer; in winter the lake often freezes so hard that, despite police warnings, stalls selling *Glühwein* (mulled wine) are set up on the ice.

The upmarket residential district of Harvestehude, on the lake's west side, contains the charming village of Pöseldorf, a mini-Chelsea of bistros and bars frequented by media folk and the trendy set. At the Museum für Völkerkunde (ethnology) do not miss the Javanese shadow puppets among the displays of Developing World folk art brought to Hamburg by past explorers. Nearby is the huge university, actually quite recent (1919); farther on are the attractive Planten und Blomen flower park, the Botanical Garden (illuminated fountains play on summer nights), and the 889-foot TV tower (with a fine view from its top). To the north, the big Hagenbeck Zoo was the pioneer of the civilized trend of letting zoo animals live outdoors in some freedom.

St. Pauli and Altona The suburb of St. Pauli, a former fishing village, is best known for its garish main street, the notorious Reeperbahn▶, which has thrice changed its tone. It began in the 19th century as a fairly respectable amusement district for the new transatlantic passenger trade, full of terrace cafés with live orchestras; the sailors' brothels were in side alleys. After the war, as the liner age waned, it slid downmarket into sex and voyeurism for tourists and businessmen. Today, due in part to AIDS, the Reeperbahn is moving back to "decency"—the biggest brothel has closed, chic restaurants are opening—but if you wish you can still spot the women in the pink-lit windows of the Herbertstrasse, and St. Pauli has a new Museum of Erotic Art, with some 500 works on show. The Star Club, where the Beatles first won fame, is no more.

On the quayside below, the traditional St. Pauli Fischmarkt (fish market) is held every Sunday from 5 to 10 AM. It is now mainly a flea-cum-food market, but does sell some fish. Go afterward to the exuberant Fischerhaus restaurant for a Hamburg breakfast of eel-and-plum soup, herring and beer.

The big suburb of Altona, Danish until 1864, still feels like a separate town. It has white patrician houses and a fine view of the river from the Altonaer Balkon (Altona Balcony). Its **Nord-Deutsches Landesmuseum▶**, rebuilt after a recent fire, is Hamburg's nicest museum, with splendid old ships' figureheads and fishing boats, local costumes, rural interiors, and paintings of Schleswig scenes. Beyond Altona, you can stroll under trees by the river at idyllic Övelgönne, where some old boats now form a "museum harbor." Visit the neoclassical Villa Jenisch (with superbly furnished interiors) and the Ernst-Barlach Haus (works by the sculptor), both in a pretty park. Finally you reach the former fishing village of Blankenese, an enchanting little place, with steep alleys and good riverside bars.

The fish market
All life meets at St. Pauli's Fischmarkt between 5 and 10 every Sunday morning. Revelers partying into the small hours mix with market workers digging into a hearty breakfast in the bars and restaurants, and early, morning shoppers buying fish, fruit and vegetables or browsing in the flea market.

63

Some girlie "live-shows" still survive along the once-so-garish Reeperbahn

Royal culture
Hannover's golden age began in the mid-17th century when a branch of the House of Brunswick built a royal palace. Under the ambitious Elector Ernst August and his cultured wife, Princess Sophie, the city saw a flowering of the arts. Handel gave concerts and the philospher Gottfried Leibnitz was court librarian for 40 years.

Perhaps the finest baroque gardens in Germany, the ornate Herrenhausen gardens contain a fountain with Europe's highest jet

▶▶　　**Hannover**

A dynamic and prosperous commercial city, Hannover is the home of automobile and audiovisual industries, as well as of Europe's leading annual trade fair and the major world Expo 2000. It is also a place of great historic importance, with much worth seeing. It was the princely seat of the House of Brunswick from the 17th century, and the House of Hanover inherited the British throne in 1714 through a Stuart connection. Hannover became a kingdom itself until its absorption by Prussia in 1866. Its people, with a reputation for being somewhat reserved, speak the most precise and (to a foreigner's ear) accentless German.

The modern central area, around the broad Kröpcke square and the imposing opera house, is affluent and spacious. From here you can stroll through the rebuilt but picturesque Altstadt, full of interest; the half-timbered Ballhof (1650), now a theater; the historical museum, with old maps and four state coaches; the busy taverns of the narrow Krämerstrasse; the high gabled façade of the 15th-century Altes Rathaus; and the Gothic Marktkirche with its superb stained glass. On the banks of the little River Leine, opposite the neoclassical Leineschloss (now housing the Landtag), are three insouciant pop-art sculptures, the "Nanas" (meaning "wench" in French), by the French artist Niki de St.-Phalle: these rotund multi colored oddities caused a local outcry when they were first put up, but are now easily accepted in a city with many outdoor sculptures. The Gothic Aegidienkirche with its blue tower has been deliberately kept half-ruined after the bombing, as a memorial—like Berlin's Gedächtniskirche.

The grandiose neo-Gothic Neues Rathaus (1913), across the ringway, has scale models of what the city was like before the bombing. The adjacent **Kestner Museum▶**, covered in an odd honeycomb of concrete, contains Greco-Roman antiquities and much medieval art. Farther on, close to the Maschsee (an artificial lake used for water sports), are two other major museums: the **Landesmuseum**▶ (paintings of many periods, notably German late 19th century) and the Sprengel Museum, excellent for modern art (e.g., Klee, Picasso, lots of Germans such as Dix and Beckmann, and the Hannover-born surrealist Kurt Schwitters).

In the western suburbs are the famous and masterly baroque **Herrenhausen**▶▶, the former royal gardens of the Brunswicks. The main one, the Grosser Garten, is formal and French, with a maze, statues, and fountains which are sometimes lit up (one jet rises 269 feet). This is a wonderful setting for the concerts and plays performed here in summer. The Georgengarten contains a museum devoted to the hugely popular cartoonist and poet Wilhelm Busch (1832–1908). The smaller botanical Berggarten has a wealth of interesting tropical plants and flowers. Nearby was the royal palace of the House of

The British throne
The electors of Hannover became heirs to the British throne through a strategic marriage to the royal house of Stuart. From 1714 the elector also ruled in London. However, in 1837, with the accession of Queen Victoria, Hannover passed from the British royal family, as the original German title could not be inherited by a woman.

The Michaeliskirche, one of Hildesheim's two restored Romanesque churches, dates from the 11th century

Hannover, largely destroyed in the war. But the royal mausoleum, containing the tomb of George I, survives.

▶▶ Hildesheim

Apart from the 15th-century Templarhaus, few of the many old buildings of this distinguished town survived the war. Some have been well restored, notably the Gothic Rathaus and two Romanesque churches: the Michaeliskirche and the **cathedral**▶, where the artwork include an 11th-century carved bronze column, with biblical scenes. Legend has it that the celebrated rose tree in its cloister dates from AD 815. After a 1945 air raid it began to flower again, adding to the local belief in its miraculous powers.

HOLSTEINISCHE SCHWEIZ

KIEL, Raisdorf, Selenter See, Selent, Panker, Grosser Binnensee, Hohwacht, Giekau, Lütjenburg, Hohwachter Bucht, Oldenburg in Holstein, Blekendorf, Wangels, Hansühn, Wagrien, Muscheln, Kossau, Högsdorf, Preetz, Lehmkuhlen, Tresdorfersee, Dannau, Bungsberg 168m, Lensahn, Postsee, Lanker See, Lebrade, Holsteinische, Kirchnüchel, Schönwalde, Cismar, Trammer See, Schluensee, Malente, Keller see, Sielbeck, Sagau, Kleine Plöner See, Bebler See, Dieksee, Gremsmühlen, Kasseedorf, Ascheberg, Plön, Grömitz, Stolpe, Stolper See, Grosser Plöner See, Bösdorf, Altenkrempe, Schashagen, Dersau, Schweiz, Eutin, Beldauer See, A21, Bosau, Klenzau, Bujendorf, Neustadt in Holstein, Damsdorf, Stocksee, Hutzfeld, Barkau, A1, Lübecker Bucht, Bornhöved, Seedorf, Glasau, Gleschendorf, Scharbeutz, Trappenkamp, Berlin, Ahrensbök, Blunk, Garbek, Gnissau, Sarkwitz, Timmendorfer Strand, Wensin, Curau, Hemmelsdorfer See, Travemünde, Klein Rönnau, Wardersee, Pronstorf, Ratekau, Wahlstedt, Pötenitzer Wiek, Bad Segeberg, Bad Schwartau, Dassower See, Stockelsdorf, LÜBECK, Trave

0 5 10 km
0 5 miles

► Holsteinische Schweiz

This is a gentle region of woods and low hills good for walking, and of pretty lakes good for sailing and swimming. Its nickname, Holstein Switzerland, was given it locally in the last century to attract tourism, but it's a misnomer, for none of the hills rises above 551 feet. You can tour the lakes by excursion boat from Plön, an old town with a big white baroque hilltop castle that formerly housed a Prussian army college. At Eutin, a pleasant town of 18th-century brick buildings, there's another baroque castle, with a moat and bronze cupola. In summer, its pink courtyard hosts the operas of Carl Maria von Weber (1786–1826), born in Eutin. Malente, nearby, is a delightful little lakeside resort where water galas are held. Best of the nearby Baltic seaside resorts is Hohwacht.

► Husum

This graceful old North Sea fishing port and market town is close to a region of polders. The history of these reclaimed tracts of land and the age-old battle against sea and storm is well recorded in the Nissenhaus Museum. Another museum is in the home of Theodor Storm (1817–88), a suitably named poet and novelist whose work movingly evokes the life of this strange, flat, melancholy region.

Friedrichstadt, to the south, was built in the 17th century by Dutch Protestant refugees. It's a picturesque little Dutch-looking town of stepped gables, canals, and cobbled streets. On the long peninsula to the west is St. Peter Ordning, a resort with good sandy beaches, known for its sulfur cures.

▶ Jever

This brewery town is known for its pilsner beer and for its delightful pink **hunting Schloss**▶ set in a moated park. This once belonged to the Russian czars, hence the portraits of Catherine the Great, alongside local costumes, toys, furniture, etc., in its interesting museum. On the wall of the café by its gates is an old *Glockenspiel* (musical clock) where figurines of Catherine and others do an hourly dance. In the Marktplatz, note the superb Renaissance sarcophagus with marble statues, situated in the belfry next to a modern church.

▶ Kiel

At the head of a broad fjord, always lively with shipping, stands Schleswig-Holstein's capital, formerly the leading German naval base. Badly bombed in World War II, it has been gracelessly rebuilt and has few notable buildings except for the restored Jugendstil Rathaus (1911), with a 348-foot-tower. Shipping is still a major activity. The 63-

The polders
Northwest of Husum, around Bredstedt, you can explore some of the polders—areas of low-lying land reclaimed from the sea—known here as *Köge* (singular *Koog*); typical examples are St. Cecilien and Sonke-Nissen. The people tend to be taciturn and dour, due maybe to the incessant howling winds. They live in houses with flat green tin roofs and breed sheep, which sometimes even graze on the seaward side of the dikes.

The Olympiahafen (harbor) at Kiel

mile **Kiel Canal**, which links the Baltic with the North Sea, is the world's busiest, with 50,000 ships a year—ahead of Panama or Suez. There's a fine sea walk along the Hindenburgufer (quay) to the Holtenau locks, where the passage of ships between canal and sound is an impressive sight. At **Laboe**, the high brick tower shaped like a ship's stern is Germany's main naval war memorial (climb to its roof for a fine view). The museum inside includes a model of the 1916 Battle of Jutland.

To the southwest, at Molfsee, the Schleswig-Holsteinisches **Freilichtmuseum**▶ is one of the best of the new German outdoor museums of rural life. About 60 old buildings, half-timbered and redbrick in the regional style—including three windmills, a watermill, a 16th-century vicarage, and an 18th-century manor (note its 1817 school timetable)—are set in a pleasant park; bakers, carvers, and potters work here and sell their products.

Kiel regatta
Kiel is a mecca for water-sports enthusiasts. Since 1882 the Kieler Wache (sailing regatta) has been an annual event (in late June, early July). Kiel has also been the water-sports center for two Olympics—1936 (Berlin) and 1972 (Munich).

Thomas Mann

Thomas Mann's family left Lübeck for Munich in 1891, when Thomas was 16 years old. He recorded his youth in his masterly novel *Buddenbrooks* (1901), which first made him famous. It gives a vividly detailed picture of the city's upper-crust society and is a poignant study of human frailty. Its central characters were based on real people and this did not please Lübeck. Mann had won the Nobel Prize for Literature in 1929.

Detail of architecture in the Altstadt (Old Town) area of Lübeck

▶▶▶ Lübeck

This Baltic river port and onetime leader of the Hanseatic League is a stately old city with tremendous local pride and a lovely relaxed, civilized ambience. Although the city was badly bombed and then had to be rebuilt, its main streets still evoke its wealthy merchant heyday. Here you will see those high zigzag gabled façades often mistakenly thought of as Dutch, though in fact the old builders of Lübeck invented this style, which the Dutch later copied. Some old houses also have the unusual Lübeck brickwork which uses alternating strips of red unglazed and black glazed brick. Behind the brick street fronts you'll find many small houses amid greenery, for this is secretly a very verdant city, full of enclosed gardens.

In the Middle Ages this "Queen of the Hanse" was the main business center of northern Europe, and Germany's largest town after Köln (Cologne). Later it lost ground to Bremen and Hamburg, but it still handles a lot of cargo, and has some big industries. Its position on the old GDR border was once a handicap, but today it is reforging links with its natural Mecklenburg hinterland.

Some of the old merchant families still flourish today. One leading family was the Manns, wealthy grain dealers, who produced two great writers, Thomas and Heinrich (see panel, left). The family's old home, where they lived from 1841 to 1891, was the model for Thomas Mann's novel *Buddenbrooks*, at Mengstrasse 4, has been rebuilt since the bombing and now houses a museum of the Manns' life and work.

Lübeck's medieval center lies between two arms of the River Trave and is best visited on foot. The grander quarter, with fine old houses, is west of the central Breitstrasse; the artisan quarter is to the east. To make a circular tour, enter by the **Holstentor▶**, an imposing red twin-towered gateway housing a museum of history. Here by the river are some 16th- to 17th-century gabled warehouses, used to store salt in transit from the Lüneburg mines to Sweden. Crossing the river, you can visit the Gothic Petrikirche and the beautiful Music Academy, converted from 22 merchant homes (concerts are often held here). In the narrow street oddly named Kolk, the marionette theater and puppet

Ratzeburg and Mölln
South of Lübeck are two charming old towns. Ratzeburg, on a lake, has a tall redbrick Romanesque cathedral on its outskirts. Mölln, with its 14th-century Rathaus, is where the folk hero Till Eulenspiegel is said to have died of the plague in 1350. Touching the thumb of his statue (in the market) is supposed to bring good luck. Before reunification Ratzeburg was the archetypal frontier town. Until recently the eastern shore of the lake near the town (which is built on an island) was fenced off, forming the border between West and East Germany.

museum have a splendid and intriguing collection of exotic oriental puppets.

To the southeast, the double-towered cathedral (1173) is Romanesque with a Gothic chancel; the nearby St. Annen museum contains relics of old Lübeck. Just to the north, in an area of mewslike alleys, are two fine 17th-century almshouses, Fucthtingshof and Glandorpshof, built for the widows of merchants and craftsmen and still used as homes for the elderly. On the 14th-century façade of the Katharinenkirche (now a museum) are fine modern statues, three of them by Barlach. The nearby Behnhaus and Drägerhaus are elegant houses, now small museums showing Mann souvenirs and paintings by Munch.

The Heiligen-Geist-Hospital, built in the 13th century as an old people's home, has a superb vaulted Gothic chapel with old frescoes. In the Gothic Jakobkirche are 17th-century organ lofts. Just opposite, the tall step-gabled Haus der Fischergesellschaft, a Renaissance mansion built for the Fishermen's Guild, today serves as a tavern, very popular with tourists, but atmospheric. The lofty Marienkirche, with the highest brick nave in the world, was the main church of the merchant rulers. Badly bombed, it has been skillfully restored to its original style.

The handsome Gothic/Renaissance **Rathaus►** should be seen for its council chamber and the memorial to eight citizens shot as anti-Nazis.

Finally, pay a visit to the famous Niederegger marzipan store, which sells this local delicacy in every bizarre size and shape conceivable.

►► Lüneburg

This is a distinguished old town with handsome redbrick buildings in the local style. In the Middle Ages it grew prosperous from its salt deposits, which were sold to Scandinavia and the Baltic towns. Lining the broad street called Am Sande are tall houses with oddly shaped stepped gables; some, as in Holland, still have the iron bars near the roof that were used for pulling up furniture. The big yellowish **Rathaus►** (13th to 16th century) has a superbly ornate interior: a Renaissance council chamber with detailed wood carvings, and a Gothic Fürstensaal (princes' chamber) with lamps made from stags' antlers. Close by is the highly picturesque **Wasserviertel►**, the old river port, with a gabled Renaissance brewery, a half-timbered millhouse by the water, and an 18th-century crane.

At **Ebstorf**, to the south, little remains of its 14th-century Benedictine abbey save a Gothic gallery and cloister. Its main attraction is a copy of a 13th-century map of the world: the original was destroyed in the war.

Lüneburg's large and elegant Rathaus has a sumptuous interior. In the council chamber are delicate wood sculptures by Albert Von Soest (1566)

▶▶ Lüneburger Heide (Lüneburg Heath)

The famous Lüneburger Heide, not flat but gently undulating, is a large and subtly beautiful area stretching from the Elbe down to the River Aller, near Celle. It is best visited in August or September, when the juniper shrubs are in leaf and the vast tracts of heather are in bloom—but in any season this varied landscape has its charms. You'll find low valleys, marshy ponds, pastures full of sheep, and forests rich in game. In the three big nature reserves cars must stay on the main road, but you can rent a horse and cart, horse, or bicycle and go meandering down quiet, clearly signposted paths. In some places, cross-country skiing is possible in winter. The sheep that browse on the juniper and heather yield a delicious fragrant mutton, known as *Heidschnucken*, that finds its way onto many local menus.

The main nature reserve is just west of the Hannover-Hamburg Autobahn and has several entry points. Among them are Undeloh to the north and Döhle to the east, two pretty villages reachable by car. From either you can hike or ride to the Wilseder Berg, a 554-foot hill that offers a wide view of the heath—even as far as the spires of Hamburg on a clear day (with binoculars). The rolling heathland is covered with oaks, pines, birches, red-berried junipers, and above all with heather. Here and there are large, thatched, smelly sheepfolds where the animals spend the night.

Heather is omnipresent. The villages have stalls selling heather bouquets (in season) and kitschy heather ornaments of all kinds. At Egestorf, a picturesque village east of Undeloh, heather is used to decorate the altar of the Protestant Heidekirche, an odd half-timbered structure that—from the outside—looks less like a

Belsen Camp
The former Belsen concentration camp is next to a big British army barracks southwest of Bergen. Here 50,000 Nazi victims died, 30,000 of them Jewish, as the camp's museum relates in stark detail. You can also see the heather-covered mounds on the site of the mass graves, and the obelisk in honor of the victims. Near here, on May 4, 1945, large sections of the German armed forces surrendered to Montgomery, beginning the process that led to their final unconditional surrender three days later. The area has since been a major British army base, within NATO, though this is now being much reduced.

church than a dwelling. Several churches in the area have curious-looking wooden belfries.

The glories of the Heide were extolled sentimentally in poetry by Hermann Löns, whose memorial tomb stands alone in an area of cairns and ancient chamber tombs near Fallingbostel, southwest of Soltau. Farther west is the huge **Vogelpark Walsrode▶** (bird sanctuary), where parrots, flamingos, cranes, and ostriches are among the huge variety of species of birds from the world over that live and fly freely here. There's a playground for children at the sanctuary.

The huge Lüneburg Heath has wide expanses of birch and pine, as well as its famous heather (Heide) and juniper bushes

▶ **Minden**

This busy junction town on the Weser has a huge *Schachtschleuse* (lock), 280 feet long, that links the river with the Mittelland canal; a small museum describes the lock's workings and the Weser area. The cathedral has a Romanesque façade and a striking 11th-century crucifix. At the Porta Westfalica, a scenic spot to the south, the River Weser has forced its way between two wooded hills. On each stands an unlovely memorial: a tower dedicated to Wilhelm I, and a statue of Bismarck.

▶▶ **Nordfriesische Inseln (North Friesian Islands)**

This low-lying archipelago off the west coast of Schleswig is popular with vacationers. There are hotels on Amrum and Fohr—islands served by ferry—but the biggest and by far the best-known island is Sylt▶▶, a long strip of land linked to the mainland by a causeway that bears a railway but no road. Cars must board the train shuttle at Niebüll, and fares are high. Sylt is a legend in Germany for showy jet-set tourism. Its windy but bracing climate has made it a fashionable resort since the 19th century; Thomas Mann and Marlene Dietrich used to vacation here. Today its heyday is past, but Sylt remains a haunt of senior tycoons, politicians, editors and others seeking privacy. Sylt's history far predates tourism: witness the 12th-century church at Keitum, and the Altfriesisches Haus, an old farmhouse that is now a museum of local lore and history.

The remorseless wind from the North Sea whips the clouds into odd shapes, causing shifting patterns of light, and this lends Sylt a special beauty. The North Sea coast has high dunes in the form of reddish cliffs, above a long and broad sandy beach. Coastal erosion is a serious problem, but Sylt is a paradise for bathing and surfing, as well as for cycling, riding and jogging, and it attracts huge numbers of sport lovers and health freaks from all social classes—almost all of them Germans. Sylt has nine separate resorts. Westerland is the biggest, but not the trendiest. Of the others, Keitum is the prettiest, a showpiece full of boutiques, galleries, and thatched cottages. The trendiest is Kampern, where bars and nightclubs try to keep alive the glory of the sixties. One short street, Stron Wai, is known as Whisky Strasse, its neat modern thatched villas bizarrely constructed into bistros and boutiques. Kupferkanne, a former wartime bunker on the cliffs, is a popular disco and bistro, with a lovely garden café.

▶ **Oldenburg**

A modern, spacious town with a new university and a river port linked to the North Sea by a tributary of the Weser, Oldenburg is also the market center of a rich farming region noted for horse and cattle breeding. In the small Altstadt, agreeably closed to traffic, some handsome older buildings remain, notably the Gothic Lambertikirche and the 15th-century Lappan tower. The nearby Schlossgarten has splendid trees. Of the three museums, the Augusteum has paintings from the Worpswede colony; the Landesmuseum, in the former ducal palace, contains works by Tischbein and interesting reconstructed farmhouse interiors; and the natural history museum has displays of 2,400-year-old corpses that were preserved over the centuries in nearby peat bogs.

Bad Zwischenahn▶, to the west, is one of the most fashionable of North German spas and a large summer resort, beside a big lake much used for water sports. The Johanniskirche is an exceptionally lovely church, with charming paintings on its wooden gallery, 16th-century frescoes on its wooden ceiling, and a fine painted altar. The well-kept lakeside gardens contain, curiously, an outdoor **rural museum**▶ with a real windmill, old cottages and a superbly restored 17th-century redbrick farmhouse from the plain nearby: humans and animals used to live together in its one huge room. At Ocholt village, to the west, is the picturesque old Howieker water mill.

▶ Osnabrück

Today heavily industrial, producing paper, textiles and metalwork, this town of 150,000 people is also strongly historical, a bishopric since 785. Here, and in Münster, the 1648 Peace of Westphalia was negotiated—in a room in the Rathaus now called the Friedenssaal (peace hall). The room bears portraits of the signatories of the peace treaty. The town has three fine old churches but is mostly modern. Curiously, its daily paper, the *Osnabrücker Nachrichten*, is renowned in Germany for its high-level political interviews and scoops from Bonn.

Peace of Westphalia
The Treaty of Osnabrück (1648) was part of the Peace of Westphalia, which ended the civil war of religion, the Thirty Years' War. Among the treaty's provisions was one that the bishopric of Osnabrück should be administered alternately by a Catholic bishop and a Protestant appointed by the Guelph family.

Beside this modern fountain in Osnabrück is a satiric new sculpture (of bishop and townsfolk) in a style common in German towns today

The Friesians
The Friesians first settled in the Netherlands and on Germany's west coast in prehistoric times, driving out their Celtic predecessors. They were eventually conquered and converted to Christianity by Charlemagne.

Open-air museums
Northwest Germany, like other areas, has a number of open-air museums (*Frerlichtmuseen*) of rural life. Old farmhouses and other buildings have been collected and reassembled, complete with old furniture and farm implements. It is an artificial trend, maybe, but better than letting a whole heritage vanish. And it is a key aspect of modern Germany's new concern with tradition and ecology.

► **Ostfriesische Inseln (East Friesian Islands)**
This is the eastern half of a long string of offshore islands that extends into Holland. Not surprisingly, this part of Friesland is quite like Holland, with windmills, dikes, and black-and-white Friesian cows.

The seven German islands, all inhabited and reachable by ferry, are popular for summer vacations, thanks to their bracing climate and broad sandy beaches backed by high dunes. Langeoog has an important bird sanctuary; the old church on Spiekeroog has mementos of the Spanish Armada; and Borkum and Juist are lively family resorts, good for horseback riding and sailing.

The most populous island and biggest resort is Norderney, 7½ miles long. It is reached by regular ferries from Norddeich, which will take cars; to discourage motorists, auto fares are set high, so for a short stay it might be best to park at Norddeich and travel by foot or taxi on the island. Norderney is not a fashionable resort, but it has an elegant-looking casino and lots of amenities. The little Fischerhaus museum gives details of the history and folklore of the island, which has been a resort since 1797. The town and hotels are at its western end; the rest is rolling dune, much of it covered with wild grass. The interior has the feel of desolate moorland, with the sea out of sight behind the dunes, but the long sandy beaches are excellent. The insistent wind is a problem, as in other North Sea resorts; the beaches are neatly dotted with big hooded wicker chairs that give protection. As on Sylt, coastal erosion is a menace, and breakwaters are being built to check it.

►► **Schleswig**
Starting life as a Viking trade center, this attractive old seaport stands at the head of the Schlei, a long, low fjord filled with small boats. Just to the south is a new museum of Viking culture and history, the **Haithabu**. The town's towering redbrick Gothic cathedral contains the beautiful Bordesholm Altar (1521); in the nearby Holm district you'll find little streets of old fishermen's cottages, a bit too neatly restored.

Continued on page 76

In the Schleswig region, many cottages are whitewashed—in contrast to the red-brick and half-timbering so common in north Germany

The Hanseatic League

■ **At a time when Germany had yet to become a single political unit, its cities and merchant groups, benefiting from lively international trade, formed a wealthy and influential sector of medieval society. When these groups joined together they became an impressive force. The Hanseatic League was a union of 150 mainly north German towns, and the most powerful economic and political power of the region ...■**

Having started in the mid-14th century as a loose association for the protection of German tradesmen, the league created a single market that covered all trade between the North and Baltic seas, a market that it fully controlled under the leadership of the town of Lübeck.

Top: The league's ships
Above: Danzig in the 16th century

Member cities followed the decisions of the Hansetag, the league's representative assembly. Any breaches of these decisions by a city would bring on the process of *Verhansung*, the boycott of the city by all others. No trade would take place with the boycotted city, nor could it use the league's common facilities abroad until it was brought

back into line. By using such measures, the league managed to influence the economic and political development of each city as it wished. But this defect in the system—a loss of individual sovereignty—was compensated for by the enormous advantages of membership: no customs duties, common protection against competition, harmonized units of measurement, to name but a few. The parallels with the modern European Union and its Single Market, together with the possibility of introducing a single currency, are remarkable.

By 1370 the league was so strong it could afford to wage war against Denmark in order to gain free access to the Baltic Sea. However, with the development in the 16th century of nation-states such as Sweden and Russia, the influence of the Hanseatic League began to wane; by the time of the Thirty Years' War (1618–48), its useful life had ended.

Lübeck (above) and Danzig were both chief cities within the league

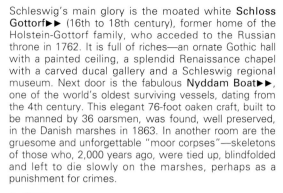

Schleswig's main glory is the moated white **Schloss Gottorf**►► (16th to 18th century), former home of the Holstein-Gottorf family, who acceded to the Russian throne in 1762. It is full of riches—an ornate Gothic hall with a painted ceiling, a splendid Renaissance chapel with a carved ducal gallery and a Schleswig regional museum. Next door is the fabulous **Nyddam Boat**►►, one of the world's oldest surviving vessels, dating from the 4th century. This elegant 76-foot oaken craft, built to be manned by 36 oarsmen, was found, well preserved, in the Danish marshes in 1863. In another room are the gruesome and unforgettable "moor corpses"—skeletons of those who, 2,000 years ago, were tied up, blindfolded and left to die slowly on the marshes, perhaps as a punishment for crimes.

Viking settlement
Close to Schleswig, the 8th- to 9th-century Viking settlement of Haithabu was a major trading center. Trade in Scandinavian furs and marine ivory and slaves from east of the Baltic passed through the settlement on the way to Western Europe and Arab territories.

► Stade
This is a carefully restored old Hanseatic port near the Elbe west of Hamburg. An unusual wooden crane, formerly used for unloading grain, stands by the narrow curving harbor, bordered with handsome old houses; best is the white-and-pink Renaissance one, number 23. Upstream is the Altes Land, a picturesque, pastoral district of cherry and apple orchards, best seen at blossom time. The old brick farmhouses, many thatched and timbered, are lovely, too.

► Visbek
Down a woodland path near this village south of Oldenburg are some strange megaliths that Stone Age man created from granite boulders left by the Ice Age. One long double line of stones, forming a funeral chamber with adjacent sacrificial table, is known as the Visbeker Bräutigam (bridegroom). Similar but smaller is the Visbeker Braut (bride).

To the west, at Cloppenburg, the **Niedersächsiches Freilichtmuseum**► is one of the best of the many museums of traditional rural life, so popular in Germany today. In a big park, farmhouses and other old buildings from all over the *Land* have been rebuilt and arranged to look like a real old village. There's a tiny school, a church, a manor, live ducks and sheep in a pen, plus an old pub.

►► Wolfenbüttel
A dignified old town, for three centuries this was the residence of the dukes of Brunswick. Chief relic of that time is the great white Schloss, with a fine Renaissance tower and baroque additions. Handsome old half-timbered houses line the Stadtmarkt and Holzmarkt.

The Herzog-August-Bibliothek, where the 6 million volumes include precious medieval illuminated manuscripts, was Europe's leading library in the 17th century. Its librarian from 1770 to 1781 was the playwright Lessing, whose home next door is now a museum of his life and work.

► Wolfsburg
The principal factory of the Volkswagen car company is located here, founded by Hitler in 1938 to produce the "people's car." Today the firm employs 45,000 people in this town of 130,000—a true "company town." The

factory pioneered industrial robots; you can go on a guided tour to watch these orange creatures perform precise balletic steps as they assemble Golfs and Jettas.

►► Worpswede

An intriguing village north of Bremen, Worpswede will fascinate art lovers. In the 1880s it was colonized by a group of gifted young artists and writers from Berlin and Munich, who were drawn by the melancholy beauty of the moorlands. When they left, the odd houses they built began to crumble; these have now been restored, and Worpswede is trendily touristic. The **museum►** has works by the Worpswede artists, whose ideas were close to the Pre-Raphaelites: Fritz Mackensen, Otto Modersohn, Paula Modersohn-Becker (the best), and the eccentric Romantic Heinrich Vogeler are represented. The architect Bernhard Hoetger has left several offbeat buildings and sculptures, such as the Villa Mackensen, and the Kaffee Worpswede with its funny statuette of a grinning bonze—an Oriental Buddhist priest.

The picturesque old harbor of Stade is no longer in use. A museum tells the town's remarkable history

RHINELAND

NL

78

B

L

F

Ochtrup
Tecklenburg
A30
Bad Iburg
Enger
Herford
Bad Salzuflen
Lage

Gronau
Burgsteinfurt

Ahaus

Teutoburger Wald
A1

BIELEFELD

Anholt

Haus Hülshoff
Coesfeld
Telgte
Ems

Gütersloh

Emmerich
Kleve
Kalkar
A3
Bocholt
A31
Dülmen
Lüdinghausen
Wiedenbrück
Dreinsteinfurt
A33
Paderborn

Xanten
Wesel
Dorsten
A43
Lippe
Recklinghausen
Ahlen
Hamm
A2
Lippe
Lippstadt
Wewelsburg

A57
Gelsenkirchen
Castrop-Rauxel
West Falen
Soest
Bad Sassendorf
A44

Moers
Herne
Unna

DUISBURG
Mülheim
BOCHUM
DORTMUND

A40
Krefeld
ESSEN
Hagen
Iserlohn
Arnsberg
Brilon

Velbert
Hohenlimburg
Meschede

Neuss
DÜSSELDORF
WUPPERTAL
Sauerland

Mönchengladbach
A46
Remscheid
Lüdenscheid
Oberkirchen
Winterberg
841m Kahler Asten

Zons
Benrath
Solingen
Schmallenberg

Linnich
A61
Leverkusen
A1
Bergisches Land
Bad Berleburg
Frankenberg

Altenberger Dom
Bergisch Gladbach
Krombach
Rothaargebirge

A44
Jülich
KÖLN
A4
Kreuztal
Lützel
Eder

A4
Düren
Brühl
Siegburg
Krottorf
Freudenberg
Siegen

Aachen
Marburg

Rur-Stausee
BONN
Königswinter
Drachenfels
Altenkirchen
A45
Dillenburg

Kommern
A1
Euskirchen
Sieg
Hachenburg
Herborn

Monschau
Schleiden
Bad Münstereifel
Linz
Westerwald
Wetzlar
Gießen

Dahlem
Altenahr
A61
Neuwied
Montabaur
Braunfels
Weilburg
Münzenberg

Adenau
747m
Andernach
Limburg
Runkel
Friedberg

Prüm
Nürburgring
691m
Mayen
Koblenz
Bad Ems
Balduinstein

Dasburg
Daun
A48
Schaumburg
Taunus
880m
A5

Karden
Treis
Boppard
Goarshausen
Königstein

Kyllburg
Cochem
St Goar
FRANKFURT AM MAIN

Bitburg
A1/A48
Beilstein
Oberwesel
Wiesbaden
Mainz
A3

Irrel
Kröv
Zell
Bacharach
Assmannshausen

Bernkastel-Kues
Enkirch
Simmern
Bingen
Rüdesheim
A60
Rüsselsheim
Darmstadt

Neumagen-Dhron
Kirchberg
Kirche Ravengiersburg
A61
A63

Morbach
Bad Kreuznach
Oppenheim

Trier
Igel
Hunsrück
Nabe
Bad Münster
Altenbamberg
Zwingenberg
Heppenheim
A67

Saarburg
Birkenfeld
Idar-Oberstein
Meisenheim
Worms
A61

Serrig
Nonnweiler
Offenbach-Hundheim
Weinheim

Mennig
A62
Frankenthal
Ludwigshafen
MANNHEIM

Mettlach
Tholey
St. Wendel
A6
Neckar

Merzig
Oftweiler
Kaiserslautern
Heidelberg

Saarland
Neunkirchen
Homburg
Deidesheim
Speyer

Saarlouis
Saarbrücken
A8
Zweibrücken
Pfälzer Wald
Kalmit 673m
Edenkoben
Annweiler
Neustadt
A6

Pirmasens
Landau
A5

Dahn
Rhein
Bruchsal

Bad Bergzabern

Karlsruhe
Maulbronn
A8
Ettlingen

Rastatt
Pforzheim

0   20   40   60   80 km
0 10 20 30 40 50 miles

This westernmost part of Germany focuses on the mighty Rhine and its tributaries, some of them scenic rivers in their own right—the Mosel, Lahn and Ahr. Other tributaries—the Saar and above all the Ruhr—have given their name to great industrial conurbations.

This is a region of contrasts. The Ruhr cities, comparatively new, have their own identity and high cultural status, but none compares with the richness of 2,000-year-old Köln (Cologne), one of the great cities of Europe. Sophisticated Düsseldorf is the capital of the Land of Nordrhein-Westfalen, relaxed Mainz of the Land of Rheinland Pfalz, while Bonn will soon lose most, but not all, of its role as Germany's capital.

To the west, the Eifel and the Hunsrück have some of Germany's loneliest and most rugged landscapes. To the southeast, the Palatinate wears a kindlier air, perhaps due to the warm red sandstone from which many of its buildings are made. Beyond the deep trench of the Rhine Gorge are farther uplands, of which the most extensive is the Sauerland, its rivers and woods a haven for the crowded populations of nearby cities.

To the north, the hills give way to the rich agricultural countryside of the North German Plain, where riverside poplars take the place of beech and spruce forests.

The region's vineyards are the world's northernmost, with delightful wine villages and cheerful cellars and taverns. Life is taken less seriously here than in other parts of Germany, particularly in the Catholic cities of Köln (Cologne) and Mainz, where exuberance knows no bounds during the pre-Lenten carnival period. This was the most Romanized part of Germany, with the Rhine forming the frontier of the empire for centuries. Potent reminders of the Roman presence exist in Trier, with the greatest concentration of Roman monuments north of the Alps. French influence has been felt constantly, as successive kings, revolutionaries, emperors, and republican governments all sought to push France's frontier eastward. The Saarland was only definitively returned to Germany in the late 1950s.

Today, no other part of Germany is so intimately tied to its neighbors across the unguarded frontiers, in links aptly symbolized by the joint administration of nature parks along the Belgian and Luxembourg borders.

THE RHINELAND

Rüdesheim, seen from the Niederwald Monument

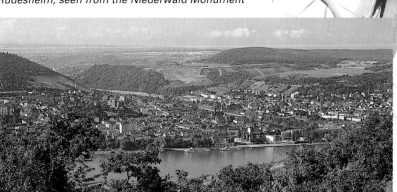

Hottest spa
The spa in Aachen's suburb of Burtscheid, with a water temperature of 168°F, is the hottest in Central Europe.

Aachen's splendid Rathaus is built on the site of Charlemagne's palace, of which two towers survive

►► **Aachen**

Germany's westernmost city, the country's gateway to many visitors from Great Britain and Belgium, Aachen deserves more than passing attention.

The city limits extend to the frontiers of both Belgium and Holland; a popular excursion is to the Dreiländereck, the wooded hills where the three countries meet. In the late 9th century, Aachen's location attracted Charlemagne (Karl der Grosse, or Charles the Great), who built a fine palace here from which to rule the Frankish Empire, which extended over most of Western Europe. Aachen's hot springs may have influenced the emperor's choice; he was a notable bather. Though Aachen is still a spa town, with a good reputation in the treatment of rheumatism and similar afflictions, empire and palace have long since crumbled away, save for the Imperial Chapel. But what a chapel!

Forming the centerpiece of the city's *Dom* (cathedral), Charlemagne's octagonal chapel►►► is one of the key monuments of early Christian Europe. It has a two-story arcaded gallery and is embellished with marble brought from Italy. The huge 12th-century chandelier hanging from its dome is one of the many treasures that make the cathedral such a storehouse of ecclesiastical art. In the light and airy 14th-century Gothic chancel is the Ambo, an extraordinarily ornate pulpit, as well as the gorgeous altar front known as the Pala d'Oro and the golden shrine containing Charlemagne's mortal remains. In the gallery is the imposing stone throne on which some 30 German kings were crowned. An incomparable array of precious objects—crucifixes, chasubles, and reliquaries—fills the Schatzkammer►► (cathedral treasury).

The first German city to be taken by the Americans in late 1944, Aachen sustained severe damage, but enough of the Altstadt remains to remind us that this is an ancient and lived-in place. Appropriately for a spa town, water features prominently in the townscape; the lighthearted Puppenbrunnen (Dolls' Fountain) has figures with movable limbs, while the thermal springs themselves are housed in neoclassical pavilions designed by the great Prussian architect Schinkel. Dominating the marketplace is the fortresslike Rathaus; its splendid Kaisersaal (Kaiser's Hall) is decorated with 19th-century paintings of episodes in Charlemagne's career and also houses reproductions of the crown jewels (the Habsburgs made off with the originals to Vienna).

Museums The city's museums are varied; the Suermondt-Ludwig-Museum has old masters as well as a medley of medieval sculpture, while the Sammlung Ludwig specializes in more modern work. The Couven Museum has well-appointed interiors showing how the comfortable classes lived in the 18th and 19th century. More unusual is the Internationales Zeitungsmuseum (International Newspaper Museum), commemorating Paul Julius von Reuter's early days, when his news service depended on carrier pigeons; the intriguing displays reveal how the news has been reported—or misreported—over the years.

► **Bocholt**

This cotton town close to the Dutch border is graced by two architectural landmarks. Dedicated to St. George, the late Gothic hall church has a spectacular west window and a high altar with a fine 15th-century depiction of the Crucifixion by a Cologne master. The gabled and arcaded Renaissance Rathaus is one of the best preserved of its kind in the country.

Wasserburg Anholt stands right on the frontier with Holland, 10 miles west of the town. The origins of this moated stronghold go back to the 13th century, when the squat tower known as the Dicker Turm was built. The castle now houses the local museum.

►► **Bonn**

For centuries, Bonn languished in pleasant provincial obscurity on the west bank of the Rhine at the point where the great river flows past the Seven Mountains into the flatlands around Cologne. In 1949, the committee assembled here to draft the constitution of the new West German state decided that the city should be made the capital of the Federal Republic. Far from the East German border and with no metropolitan pretensions of its own that might upset more obvious candidates, such as Frankfurt, Bonn had the advantage of being a short ferry ride across the Rhine from the Königswinter home of Konrad Adenauer, the elderly but immensely shrewd chancellor of the newborn state.

Express trains were persuaded to stop in Bonn, rather than steaming straight through, and an influx of civil servants and diplomats helped double the population. The notion that one day Berlin would resume its rightful place as the nation's capital inhibited grandiloquent government building; parliament was housed in a teachers' college, the chancellor in the 19th-century Villa

Aachen's little squares are full of outdoor cafés and statue fountains— one fountain is made of bronze dolls

Beethoven's Bonn
Bonn's most famous son, Ludwig van Beethoven (1770–1827), left the place at the age of 22 for Vienna, never to return. He is commemorated in Bonn by a statue, the Beethovenhalle (a modern concert hall) and an annual international festival. His birthplace contains an exemplary display of memorabilia, including, most poignantly, the ear trumpets that failed to breach the barrier of the composer's advancing deafness.

Hammerschmidt. By the 1970s, hopes for reunification were fading, and lumpy modern "official" buildings began to transform the townscape. Today, with the Government set to move to Berlin by 1999, Bonn will soon lose most of its functions as capital. But eight ministries will remain there indefinitely, including the key Ministry of Defense.

Look for the spectacular complexes housing the City Art Museum and the National Art and Exhibition Center, the latter's 16 rusty columns symbolizing the German *Länder*. The government quarter extends southward from the city center, 2,000 years ago the site of a Roman fort defending the Rhine crossing. Much damaged in the last war, Bonn's old core still contains plenty of evidence of its long past. Prehistoric, Roman, and Frankish remains are in the Landesmuseum, where the star exhibit is the skull of Neanderthal Man, found near Düsseldorf in 1856 (see panel page 83). The late Romanesque/early Gothic *Münster* (minster), with its immensely tall central tower, airy interior and splendid cloisters, is one of the finest of many such churches in the Rhineland. The prince-bishops of Cologne preferred to reside in backwater Bonn rather than among the more rowdy citizens of their cathedral city; their contributions to the urban scene include the pink rococo Rathaus, as well as the Residenz and the Poppelsdorfer Schloss, both part of the university.

Its setting is one of Bonn's great assets (its humid climate less so). The vast new Rheinauen Park links the city to the river and gives fine views of Drachenfels peak and the Seven Mountains (see page 100). Southward lies the old spa of Bad Godesberg, with a pleasant riverside promenade, while the terrace of the Godesburg, the ruined castle high above the town, offers a fine panorama.

► **Düsseldorf**

Capital of Nordrhein-Westfalen, Germany's most populous *Land*, money-conscious Düsseldorf is the showcase in which the country's wealth is dazzlingly displayed. The city's skyline is dominated less by its numerous old churches than by such monuments of modern commerce as the coldly elegant Thyssen skyscraper. As well as the headquarters of many of the great Ruhr industrial concerns, Düsseldorf has also attracted numerous Japanese firms, which have made it the base of their overseas operations; the city's Japanese community is the largest in Europe.

Private affluence is balanced by a strong sense of civic pride dating back to the city's rule by its electors, the most notable of whom was Johann Wilhelm (1679–1716). Known affectionately as Jan Wellem, he laid out the spacious new districts beyond the Altstadt and attracted artists to the city; he is commemorated by a statue in front of the Renaissance Rathaus. Modern Düsseldorf is well endowed with parks, gardens and landscaped pedestrian areas, which make it possible to stroll across the city without encountering traffic.

Theater, music, opera and cabaret all thrive here, and the city's galleries are outstanding; the collection of Paul Klee paintings in the Kunstsammlung Nordrhein-Westfalen is the biggest in the country.

Excursions

Schloss Benrath, a sumptuous rococo palace in a fine park, is a favorite local outing. It was built in the mid-18th century by a French architect for one of Jan Wellem's successors.

The **River Wupper** snakes through a steep-sided valley to the east of Düsseldorf. Wuppertal is a string of industrial towns that form a linear city. Birthplace of Freidrich Engels, the city has an outstanding collection of 19th- and 20th-century German and French art in the Von der Heydt Museum, and is the home of Germany's leading modern dance company, created and run by the great Pina Bausch.

Wuppertal is also known for its unique Schwebebahn, the overhead railway that has stitched its disparate communities together since 1901. Downstream, the valley is crossed by a more conventional railway line, carried 351 feet above the river on the Müngstenerbrücke, Europe's highest railway bridge. This links the timber-framed and slate-roofed town of Remscheid with Solingen, where the Klingen-museum displays every possible kind of cutlery, a traditional center of steel production. Farther downstream still, high above the river, is the spectacularly sited castle of Burg an der Wupper, housing the local history museum.

►► The Eifel

Bounded by the Rhine, the Mosel, and the country's border with Belgium and Luxembourg, the rugged Eifel is the northwesternmost of Germany's upland massifs. In spite of its proximity to great centers of population, its sweeping heights, vast forests and deep valleys offer endless opportunities for escaping the crowds.

The area's core is formed by the Hohe Eifel, composed of ancient volcanoes. Its highest point is the Hohe Acht, a basalt peak of 2,450 feet. The hills are pitted with strange circular lakes known as *Maare*, formed by violent volcanic explosions that also left other curiosities in the shape of "bombs," like the one near the little spa town

Brahms to Beuys
Writers, artists and musicians have long been associated with Düsseldorf. The poet Heine was born here. Brahms, Mendelssohn and Schumann all found the atmosphere congenial, as did (in his own way) the ex-Messerschmitt pilot and postwar *enfant terrible* Josef Beuys (*d.*1986), whose felt-and-fat sculptures won international attention, if not always approval.

Lively Altstadt
Düsseldorf brews an unusual beer, "Alt," not unlike a pale ale, consumed in large quantities in the Altstadt. Echoes of the days when the city was no more than a riverside fishing village can still be picked up among the many bars, pubs, restaurants and discos, which virtually guarantee a memorable night out.

Neanderthal Man
The valley of the little Düssel River was a favorite retreat of the poet Joachim Neander, who gave it his name. The site of the cave where the skeletal remains of Neanderthal Man were found in 1856 is marked by a plaque. The skull is now in the Landesmuseum in Bonn, but there is a small museum at the cave with displays on life 60,000 years ago.

Düsseldorf's Königsallee, known as the "Kö," is lined with some of Europe's most stylish cafés

THE RHINELAND

The Ahr Valley, home of some of Germany's best red wines

Bad Neuenahr
While ancient Ahrweiler has kept its town wall, with towers and gates, the spa town of Bad Neuenahr is a 19th-century creation, dating from the discovery of medicinal springs here in 1852. Parks and gardens provide a manicured setting for visitors taking their cure. On the Silberberg hill, a patrician Roman villa now houses the Museum Roemervilla.

Open-air museum
In a wooded setting on the edge of Mechernich-Kommern, the Rheinisches Freilichtmuseum (Rhineland Open-Air Museum) is an extensive collection of carefully re-erected traditional buildings of the countryside, including wind and water mills and workshops, as well as cottages and farmsteads.

of Daun. Perhaps the loneliest part of the Eifel is the Schnee-Eifel, to the west, where cross-border nature parks merge with the Belgian and Luxembourg Ardennes. To the north is a "Lake District," formed by the damming of the Rur and Erft rivers, and very popular with vacationers from across the Dutch and Belgian borders. More popular still is the pretty valley of the River Ahr, descending eastward through a series of picturesque wine villages to the Rhine.

An entire vacation could easily be spent in these attractive uplands, particularly by lovers of fresh air and exercise. Some of the Eifel's characteristic landscapes and little towns can be visited as an alternative to the autobahn on the way southeast.

Monschau► Overlooked by its medieval castle, and generally agreed to be the prettiest place in the Eifel, Monschau winds along the steep-sided valley of the River Rur. Among its black-and-white houses stands the grand redbrick residence known as the Rotes Haus; its interior is evocative of the comfortable lifestyle of its 18th-century proprietor, a dealer in the cloth for which the town was famous.

Bad Münstereifel With its walls still enclosing an intricate web of cobbled streets and alleyways, this is one of Germany's best-preserved medieval small towns. The River Erft chatters alongside the main street, while the castle stands guard over one side of the valley, the buildings of the town's renowned spa on the other. The best townscape is to be seen in the Orchheimer Strasse, where the high-gabled and intriguingly carved Windeckhaus forms a perfect composition with its neighbors.

On the lonely plateau to the east of the town is a great surprise—the utterly unmedieval structure of the Eifelsberg radio telescope, the largest in the world.

The country road to the east drops down into the romantic valley of the River Ahr, a delightful miniature version of the Rhine Gorge.

Altenahr A pretty little place, dominated by its castle ruin and with many inviting wine cellars, Altenahr marks the western end of Germany's northernmost wine-growing area. Sheltered by the Hohe Eifel, the slaty slopes rising precipitously from the twisting river provide excellent growing conditions for vines. The local Spätburgunder, a "velvety, noble wine," is considered by many to be easily the best of the country's otherwise rather undistinguished reds.

Maria Laach▶ This splendid Benedictine abbey stands in what was once a remote setting beside the largest of all the volcanic lakes in the Eifel, the Laacher See. Founded in 1093, the great six-towered abbey church is one of the grandest and most harmonious Romanesque buildings in Germany. After the dissolution of the country's monasteries in 1802, the abbey's numerous art treasures disappeared, leaving the interior looking rather bare but still very dignified.

Schloss Bürresheim
The castle, southwest of Maria Laach, owes its exceptionally picturesque appearance to successive waves of building and rebuilding from the 12th to the 19th century. The interior, unusually for Germany, is well furnished, and there is an attractive formal garden with high hedges.

THE RHINELAND

Crazy carnival
Of German pre-Lenten carnivals, the biggest and most boisterous is Cologne's and it fits well with the city's spirit of fun-loving whimsy. First a Carnival Prince is elected along with his two henchmen, the Peasant and the Virgin (she has always been a man, save under the Nazis who hated transvestism). They "rule" the city during the *Tolle Tage* (Crazy Days). On Thursday vengeful women cut off the tie of any male (very Freudian?). Sunday is devoted to satiric floats, and on Monday a million people line the route for the main parade, full of pirouetting majorettes. *Karneval* is one merry booze-up of local pub parties and street parties, when adultery is not grounds for divorce.

▶ **Kleve (Cleves)**
The last substantial place on the west bank of the Rhine before the Dutch border, Kleve is an ancient ducal residence whose *Oberstadt* (upper town) is built on the low hills rising over the floodplain of the great river. To the southwest is the vast forest tract known as the Reichswald, the scene of bitter fighting as the Allied armies prepared to cross the Rhine early in 1945. To the northeast stretch watery flatlands where the Rhine once wandered at will before being confined behind its present high embankments.

The medieval counts of Kleve eventually rose to the rank of duke, though their bid for even more enhanced status by marrying into the English royal family came to nothing (see panel). Though virtually destroyed in World War II, the town is still marked by their castle, the Schwanenburg, and by the fine parks and gardens they laid out.

Excursions
Emmerich, 5 miles east, is reached from Kleve by the country's longest suspension bridge. The brick-built port of Emmerich makes its living from the river, and celebrates this long-standing connection in its Rheinmuseum.

Kalkar, 7½ miles southeast, was famous in the late Middle Ages for its talented wood-carvers. This small town boasts a brick church with an astonishing array of fine altarpieces, as well as a number of houses with stepped gables and a 15th-century Rathaus.

Xanten, 17 miles southeast, was rebuilt after its near-destruction in early 1945. This is a neat little town that has conserved stretches of medieval fortifications (including the picturesque Kleve Gate) and a cathedral crammed with splendid artwork. The town lies between two Roman settlements, civilian Colonia Trojana to the north and military Castra Vetera to the south. The civilian town is now an archeological park, with thorough reconstructions of fortifications and buildings that attempt to bring the days of Roman occupation back to life.

▶▶▶ **Köln (Cologne)**
With the twin spires of its glorious cathedral visible far away across the surrounding plain, this is one of Germany's great metropolitan cities, a center of culture and learning as well as industry and commerce.

First founded by the Romans in 33 BC, "Colonia" achieved city status under Emperor Claudius in AD 40. Its importance at this time is reflected in the superb Dionysus Mosaic forming the centerpiece of the splendid modern Römisch-Germanisches Museum in the city's heart. By the Middle Ages, Cologne had become the largest city in Germany, with no fewer than 150 churches. The Altstadt is consequently huge, extending to the semicircular Ring, a boulevard laid out along the line of fortifications demolished in the 19th century but still punctuated at intervals by the surviving city gates (Eigelstein Tor, Hahnentor, St. Severin's Tor).

The city suffered the RAF's first 1,000-bomber raid in 1942, and in the course of the war nine-tenths of the buildings in the center of town were destroyed; their replacements may not always be of the highest architectural quality, but planners' retention of the ancient street pattern has helped maintain something of the spirit of the city's 2,000 years of history. Konrad Adenauer, later to be Germany's Chancellor, was the city's mayor in 1917–33. Another distinguished son of Cologne in this century was the novelist Heinrich Böll, who spent most of his life and set many of his books here. His satiric humor and Catholic humanism were typical of the Rhineland.

Cologne's atmosphere is that of a city-state, its strong local patriotism expressed in its own

Eau de Cologne
In the 18th century an Italian resident distilled an astringent liquid from flower blossoms. Intended originally as an aphrodisiac, the famous Kölnisch Wasser (Cologne water, or eau de Cologne) is more commonly used as toilet water.

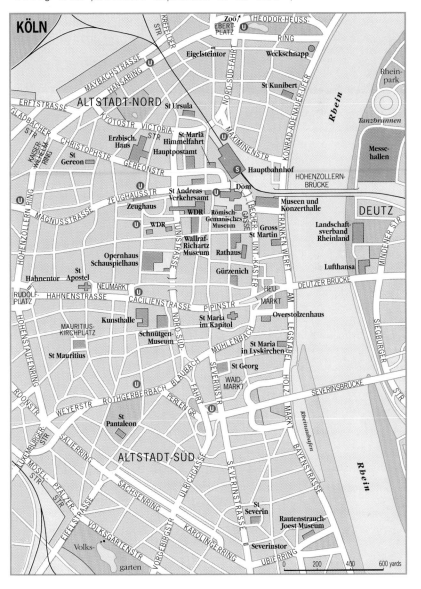

KÖLN

The River Rhine and the Cologne cathedral

impenetrable *Kölsch* (dialect). Its sociable people seem smaller and swarthier than the German norm, their enjoyment of wisecracking best exemplified by the potbellied waiters serving the distinctive bitter beer (also called Kölsch) in the numerous pubs and beer halls. Local liking for a good time reaches its peak during Karneval.

Most visitors probably get their first glimpse of Cologne from the hall of the main train station, whose high windows frame the clifflike side of the cathedral. Walk out along the railway bridge (Höhenzollernbrücke) to savor the city's silhouette rising over the bustle of traffic on and alongside the Rhine.

The **Dom**►►► (cathedral) is one of the world's great Gothic structures. Begun in the 13th century, it was completed only in the 19th, still in faithful accord with the intentions of its medieval architects, whose original drawings had miraculously survived. Externally its sheer mass is relieved by the lacelike delicacy of its masonry, while the vast interior contains such incomparable works of art as the majestic golden shrine of the Magi, the 9th-century Gero Crucifix, the glorious 15th-century Cologne School altarpiece painted by Stefan Lochner, and superb stained glass. A stiff climb up the south tower is rewarded by a fine panorama over the city center.

The well-designed pedestrian spaces characteristic of so many German cities invite exploration. Southeast of the Dom is the **Romisch-Germanisches Museum**►, with its wonderful collection of Roman art found locally (notably the Dionysus Mosaic) as well as items such as toys and clothes that illustrate daily Roman Life. Nearby is a modern complex housing the Philharmonie, the central concert hall, as well as the **Wallraf-Richartz and Ludwig museums**►, with their major collections of German and international art. Not to be missed are the exquisite late medieval paintings of the Cologne School or the array of works by such early 20th-century masters as Dix, Beckmann,

St . Ursula
Daughter of a 4th-century British king, the virginal St. Ursula is reputed to have been murdered in Cologne by rampaging Huns, along with 11,000 other Christian maidens. This spectacular end led to her beatification and commemoration in the city's coat of arms, as well as in the church that bears her name.

Kirchner, and Barlach. This is also a good place to ponder the Americana of the postwar Pop Artists—Roy Lichtenstein and Andy Warhol.

Straying southward is the Hohe Strasse, the city's main shopping street. Other streets and passageways lead Rhineward into the core of the Altstadt, centered on the Alter Markt and the 14th-century Gothic Rathaus, with its Renaissance loggia. Before the completion of the Dom, the distinctive four-turreted tower of the Romanesque church of Gross St. Martin dominated the skyline; completed in 1172, this is one of the city's several **pre-Gothic churches►** (a grouping unique in Europe), each with its own special features. St. Pantaleon, from the 10th century, is the oldest; St. Gereon is the most spectacular, with a superb delicately ribbed, 10-sided tower, the Decagon; while St. Maria im Kapitol is richly furnished, with remarkable 11th-century carved doors. The best place to see religious art and furnishings is in the deconsecrated church housing the Schnütgen Museum; the squeamish should avoid the exquisitely carved *memento mori* (corpses in the last stages of decay).

Cologne continues to be a churchy place. Many striking places of worship have been built this century, notably St. Gertrud, north of the Ring, or Neu St. Alban, to the west, with a dimly lit, highly atmospheric interior. Nearby is the Fernmeldeturm (telecommunications tower), 794 feet high, offering a vast panorama. The large and remarkably new Imhoff-Stollwerck Museum, entirely devoted to the history of the production of chocolate, stands on an island in the Rhine. On the far bank, reached by cable car, is the Rheinpark; its centerpiece is the Tanzbrunnen, a vast fountain above a canopied dance floor.

Excursion

Altenberger Dom is about 10 miles northeast of Cologne among the lush woodlands of the hilly countryside known as the Bergisches Länd. This is no cathedral but a former Cistercian monastery, one of the finest examples of Gothic architecture in Germany, restored in the last century. Unusually, it is worshipped in by both Catholics and Protestants.

Night train
"The Express feels its way and pushes the darkness along.... Then suddenly the ground roars like a sea: we are flying, suspended, royally through air seized from the night, high above the current.... Rushing like torches."—Ernst Stadler, *Journey over the Rhine Bridge at Cologne by Night.*

89

Schloss Augustusburg
Brühl, 9 miles southwest of Cologne, has Germany's largest theme park, Phantasieland, as well as the pleasure gardens from an earlier time that surround Schloss Augustusburg, the sumptuous rococo palace of the archbishops of Cologne. Often used for state receptions (and consequently liable to be closed to the public), this echo of Bavarian lightheartedness has an incredibly ornate staircase by the great south German architect Balthasar Neumann.

Cafés in Cologne

Goethe's love
Germany's greatest writer came to Wetzlar as a young man to attend a session of the Imperial Courts. He fell, passionately, for a local girl, Charlotte Buff, already betrothed to another man, who subsequently killed himself. The experience of this tragedy was distilled by Goethe into *The Sorrows of Young Werther*, a key work of German Romanticism. Charlotte's house (Lottehaus) is now a museum devoted to the sad affair, with much personal and literary memorabilia.

► **Lahn Valley**

Rising in the Rothaargebirge nature park (see page 102) and flowing for much of its length through a wooded gorge, the River Lahn winds past picturesquely sited castles, ruined like Balduinstein or romantically rebuilt like Schaumburg and Braunfels, before joining the Rhine near Koblenz. The valley can be explored by car—but also along riverside foot and bike paths, by steamer, canoe and raft, or by railroad, which often hugs the river more closely than the road.

Each of the Lahn towns has a highly individual character. The classic spa town of **Bad Ems** was the favored resort of Kaiser Wilhelm I; his statue stands in the immaculate riverside gardens. As well as haughty hotels, aristocratic Ems has a casino, an onion-domed Russian Orthodox church, and a cable-hauled railway to hoist health seekers up to the modern spa installations on the heights above the narrow valley.

Both **Nassau** and **Diez**, the latter with a high-walled castle, are associated with the Orange-Nassau dynasty.

Limburg►, in a more open part of the valley, has won prizes for careful conservation work, and the results can be enjoyed among the picturesque timber-framed houses of the medieval center. Alleyways lead up to Limburg's cathedral, on a rocky spur overlooking the river. With its exterior repainted in the bright orange and white livery of medieval times, the cathedral is a fine example of the transition from Romanesque to Gothic. The cool interior has unique 12th-century paintings, while the Diocesan Museum and Treasury house ecclesiastical art objects.

The biggest castle along the Lahn was once the medieval Burg at **Runkel**; its rugged walls still rise imposingly over the old village with its bridge and weir. The stronghold at **Weilburg** is different altogether—an elegant Renaissance residence constructed by the

Top: the tranquil spa town of Bad Ems
Left: a quiet street in Limburg

counts of Nassau. Ornate interiors are complemented by terraced gardens stepping down to the river, which almost encircles the spur on which the castle and its dependent little baroque town are built. Boat traffic can take a shortcut through the promontory via a 770-foot tunnel, the longest of its kind in Germany.

Wetzlar's industries make an array of products, of which Leica cameras may be the most famous. But this is a historic town, too, for over 100 years the seat of the law courts of the Holy Roman Empire. Towering over the old houses that step down to the seven-arched bridge over the Lahn is the unfinished cathedral, a strange amalgam of Romanesque and Gothic.

► Mainz

Seat of the government of Rheinland-Pfalz, 2,000-year-old Mainz is endowed with most of the good things to be expected of a lively provincial capital: a cathedral, an archbishop's palace, an ancient university, museums, an attractive Altstadt. Its position on the banks of the Rhine and its exceptionally mild climate may explain its cheerful atmosphere; its great pre-Lenten Karneval is second only to Cologne's for high spirits, and there are more jollifications—like Johannisnacht in March and a big wine festival in August/September.

The great red sandstone cathedral, with its six towers, looms over the largely pedestrianized city center. Essentially Romanesque, though with many later additions, it has a spacious interior containing the splendid tombs of its powerful prince-bishops. The Diocesan Museum off the Gothic cloisters houses some of the wonderfully sensitive sculpture of the mysterious medieval mason the Master of Naumburg.

A short walk from the cathedral, the banks of the Rhine hold a medley of public buildings ancient and modern, including the exuberant Renaissance-baroque Schloss housing the Römisch-Germanisches Zentralmuseum. There are more spectacular Roman artifacts in the Landesmuseum nearby. Start a stroll "inland," through the Altstadt with its half-timbered houses and wine taverns, at the Marktbrunnen, the delightful Renaissance fountain. Perhaps the outstanding work of modern art in Mainz is to be found in the Stefanskirche; the church's **stained glass►**, glowing with visionary intensity, is the work of the great Russian Jewish artist Marc Chagall, who took as his theme "Reconciliation."

►► Marburg

With half-timbered houses clustering around the castle high above the River Lahn, a great **church►** dedicated to St. Elisabeth, and a venerable university, Marburg seems to represent the very essence of medieval Germany.

The focal point of Marburg's Altstadt, particularly in university term time, is the Marktplatz, with its late-Gothic Rathaus and St. George fountain. In this part of town, the steep streets are supplemented by stairways. One leads up to the Schloss, the residence of Elisabeth's descendants, the Landgraves. Built from about 1260 on, it has a three-story Rittersaal (Knights' Hall) and houses part of the outstanding collections of the Universitätsmuseum (University Museum).

A window by Chagall in Stefanskirche, Mainz

Gutenberg, printer
A native of Mainz, Johannes Gutenberg revolutionized communications by elaborating the idea of printing using movable metal type, rendering the painstaking work of the medieval scribe obsolete at a stroke. Between 1452 and 1455 he printed some 200 Bibles, one of which can be seen in the fascinating Gutenberg Museum. Housed in the Renaissance mansion known as the Römischer Kaiser, the museum includes a replica of his original workshop with an operating press. Hounded by a grasping partner, Gutenberg made no money from his extraordinary achievements, though in later life he was elevated to the petty nobility and given a pension by the elector of Nassau.

▶ ▶ ▶   **Mosel (Moselle) Valley**

Rising high up in France's Vosges Mountains, the Mosel forms the boundary between Germany and Luxembourg before reaching the ancient city of Trier. From here to its confluence with the Rhine at Koblenz, the river cuts through the Hunsrück and Eifel uplands in a series of extraordinary loops and bends. Every square yard of steep slope able to catch the sun is completely covered with a forest of poles to hold the vines steady in the rather slaty soil. The wines that are yielded are delicate, sometimes with a touch of sharpness that nicely matches the elegant green bottles in which they are presented.

It was the Romans who brought the vine to this northeastern extremity of their empire. A replica of the famous Roman Wine Ship (the original is in the Landesmuseum in Trier) stands in the Peterskapelle in Neumagen, the town where it was found. Downstream is the charming double town of **Bernkastel-Kues▶**, renowned for its Doktor vineyard. Colorful Renaissance houses line the sloping market square with its fountain, while the odd-shaped Spitzgiebelhaus nearby comes straight out of a picture book. Among the vines above the town stand the ruins of Landshut castle. On the far bank, Kues has a Gothic almshouse still serving its original purpose; in the chapel is a fine 15th-century altarpiece.

Another double town spanning the river is the resort of **Traben-Trarbach**, not particularly attractive, but a useful urban center. In the square at **Zell** is a curious statue of a black grimacing cat, subject of a local legend (*Schwarz Katz* is one local wine). Fortified **Beilstein** is dominated by the massive ruined castle once owned by Metternich. **Cochem**'s picturesque setting, with its romantically rebuilt castle crowning a vine-clad knoll, has inevitably made it one of the most-visited places along the river. Equally popular is **Burg Eltz▶**, a short distance up a deeply wooded side valley. This is one of Germany's dream castles, its sheer walls rising spectacularly through the trees and capped by steep-

The river Mosel at Zell, a charming wine-town whose round tower was part of its medieval defenses

The Mosel
The 320-mile Mosel River rises in eastern France. For 21 miles it forms the border between Luxembourg and Germany; it then travels 150 miles in Germany, ending in the Rhine at Koblenz.

Cochem, with its romantic castle overlooking the Mosel River

pitched slate roofs and an array of turrets. The interior is relatively intimate—a succession of small courtyards with half-timbered façades. A tour includes the hall of banners, the "treasure chamber," and a fascinating collection of old weapons.

More castles follow, one at **Thurant** and two at **Kobern-Gondorf,** before the river flows beneath the great autobahn bridge that marks the approach to Koblenz and the river's junction with the Rhine.

► **Münster**

The historic capital of Westphalia, Münster is a prosperous university city, proud of its strongly Catholic identity in an otherwise largely Protestant province. Its splendidly varied architectural heritage suffered badly in World War II, but local pride has expressed itself in loving restoration and reconstruction.

The bustle on the Domplatz (Cathedral Square) is presided over by the handsome, twin-towered **cathedral►,** built in the early 13th century in the transitional style between Romanesque and Gothic. The interior is richly endowed with statuary, tombs, and altars, and has a remarkable astronomical clock of 1540, with automata that bestir themselves daily at noon for the benefit of the assembled crowds. The foundations of the present building's 8th-century predecessor can be seen in the cloisters; beyond is the treasury, which numbers among its precious objects an 11th-century jewel-studded reliquary of St. Paul.

As well as the cathedral, Münster has other remarkable churches, including the 14th-century Überwasserkirche, with an elaborately decorated tower, and the Gothic Lambertikirche. The three cages hanging from the latter's tower once held the corpses of leading Anabaptists who unwisely overthrew church rule and proclaimed the millennium. This rash act precipitated the massacre of the townsfolk and the Anabaptists' own execution by mercenaries in the pay of the bishop. From the Lambertikirche, the city's main thoroughfare, the

MOSEL VALLEY

KOBLENZ
Rhein
Neuwied
Lahnstein
A61
Winningen
Ochtendung
Kobern-Gondorf
A48
Thurant
Polch
Brodenbach
Münstermaifeld
Ehrenburg
Bischofstein
Burgen
Elzbach
Burg Eltz
Karden
Treis
Lahr
Mosel
Wildburg
Winneburg
Bruttig
Cochem
Beilstein
Burg Cochem
Metternich
Nehren
Bremm
Alf
Bullay
Zell
Marienburg
Burg
Pünderich
Alf
Arras
Enkirch
Kröv
Traben-
Trarbach
Ürzig
Zeltingen
Bernkastel-
Wehlen
Kues
Wittlich
Landshut
Lieser
Piesport
Klausen
Neumagen
Dhron
A1/A48
Trittenheim
Mosel
Schweich
Mehring
A1
Kenn
0   10 km
0   5 miles
TRIER

Pfälzer Wald (Palatinate Forest)

The splendid forestland of this upland country, much of it protected as a nature park, forms the most extensive area of continuous woodland in the whole of Germany. To the east rises the Haardt, a high ridge that then falls steeply to the vineyards lining the Weinstrasse (see page 107). To the south, linking with the Vosges Mountains in Alsace, are the sandstone hills of the Wasgau, weirdly weathered into castle-crowned cones, cliffs, and spikes.

With its timber-framed houses and millstream, the little town of Annweiler is a good center for exploring the southern part of the forest. Within easy reach is a clutch of castles. Overlooking the town itself is 11th-century Trifels, where Richard the Lion-Hearted was imprisoned in 1193. Splendid views from the chapel tower include the lesser castles of Anebos and Scharfenberg. To the southwest is Berwartstein, typifying the 19th-century Romantic view of what a crag-top castle should look like. Nearby Drachenfels, now a ruin, had no need of walls, so sheer were its natural defenses. Dahn is the best place to investigate the effects of wind and weather on the soft local sandstone. Eroded into strange shapes, it formed the building material for Dahn's three castles, all of them erected within the same perimeter wall.

Prinzipalmarkt, is lined with the arcaded and gabled Renaissance town houses (mostly rebuilt) of prosperous merchants. At the far end is the superb Rathaus, with a wonderful paneled chamber—the Friedenssaal (Hall of Peace); this is where the Peace of Westphalia was signed in 1648, bringing to an end the disastrous Thirty Years' War.

Less flamboyant than its south German equivalent, the baroque style evolved by the local architect Johann Schlaun resulted in a number of notable buildings, such as the aristocratic mansion called the Erbdrostenhof, the unusual circular Clemenskirche, and, above all, the huge palace of the prince-bishops (1767–73), now the main building of the university.

Two museums merit mention. Medieval sculpture and old masters feature in the Landesmuseum. Rural Westphalia has been re-created on the banks of the Aasee, the city's big recreational lake, at the Mühlenhof museum—one of the longest established of Germany's open-air museums, with a fascinating collection of old buildings, water mills, windmills, timber-framed farmsteads, and more.

The agriculturally rich and rather damp area around Münster—the **Münsterland▶**—is famous for its country houses, most of them moated. Ranging from the grandiose "Westphalian Versailles" at Nordkirchen to the more homey Haus Rüschhaus just outside Münster, these delightful *Wasserburgen* (water castles) could hold your interest for days. Start at the 700-year-old Burg Vischering (near Lüddenhausen), which conveniently houses an informative Münsterland museum. Rüschhaus was from 1826 to 1846 the home of the great poetess Annette von Droste-Hülshoff, who was born nearby at the lovely **Hülshoff water-castle▶**. Its Renaissance and neo-Gothic buildings are on two tiny islands, within a moat where swans glide.

Nahe Valley and the Hunsrück

The idyllic valley of the River Nahe runs northeastward through a series of gorges to join the Rhine at **Bingen**. The products of the picturesque vineyards along its course are reckoned by some to combine the best qualities of German wine, full-flavored yet fresh. Farther north is the rugged Hunsrück, a high plateau of upland farms and extensive forests of beech and spruce. Quaint old houses stand on the bridge at **Bad Kreuznach**, a good starting point for a tour of the Nahe. This pleasant spa town comes complete with casino and strange timber structures known as "salinas" in which brine is vaporized for the benefit of health seekers.

Bad Münster is another spa, located south of Bad Kreuznach on the B48. It is overlooked by the lofty castle called the Ebernburg. To the west of Bad Münster on the riverside road, and shouldering the river aside, is the mighty cliff known as the **Rotenfels**. Vines flourish in the narrow strip of soil at its base, as they do on the slopes around the attractive villages that succeed one another upstream.

At **Odernheim** the valley of the River Glan leads to medieval **Meisenheim**, which has an array of picturesque old houses and a fine stone church. The road along the

Nahe valley can then be rejoined if you wish, near the abbey ruins at Disibodenberg.

Beyond the health resort of **Sobernheim**, the village of **Monzingen** has particularly fine half-timbered houses, among them the Altes Haus of 1589. Off the main valley to the north the castle ruin of **Dhaun** affords a splendid panoramic viewpoint, while **Kirn** is dominated by another ruin, the **Kyrburg**.

The steep rock face at the jewelry town of **Idar-Oberstein** is also crowned with fragments of old fortress, but the real curiosity here is the Gothic church set spectacularly into the cliff itself and reached via 214 steep steps from the town's market square. Much is made of Idar-Oberstein's long history of mining, cutting and polishing precious stones of all kinds; after visiting the Heimatmuseum (local history museum), the **Edelsteinmuseum▶** (Museum of Precious Stones) and the Steinkaulenberg mine, you should know more about gemology than most!

A half-hour drive north from Idar-Oberstein will bring you onto the Hunsrück Höhenstrasse. This fine highway was built in the interwar period to relieve unemployment and help open up this inhospitable area, then one of Germany's poorest and most isolated regions. More prosperous today, the Hunsrück is still a lonely place, drawing city dwellers in search of rural peace and quiet.

The Nahe river flows along the southern side of the Hunsrück plateau. Here Edgar Reitz, born nearby, at Morbach, set and filmed his masterly 15-hour epic Heimat *(1984), the saga of a local family from 1919 to 1982*

95

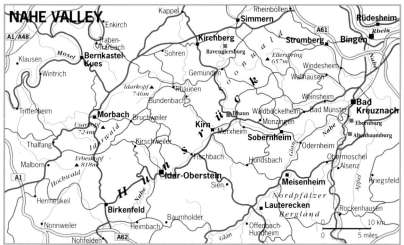

NAHE VALLEY

From the Niederwald memorial high above the Rhine , a chairlift (top) leads down to Rüdesheim, where the tourist-filled Drosselgasse (above) is lined with 18th-century taverns

▶▶▶ Rheintal (The Rhine Valley)

The Rhine invariably conjures up a string of clichés: a rocky gorge with a robber baron's castle clinging to each crag, vineyards growing precariously on the steep slopes, passengers waving at each other from the decks of white steamers, unbridled merriment in the cobbled streets of cheerful wine villages. Accurate enough, like all clichés, yet really only applicable to the Rhine Gorge, the relatively short Bingen–Koblenz stretch of the 825-mile river. A mountain torrent near its source in the Swiss Alps, and still pretty untamed at the great falls near Schaffhausen, the Rhine is for most of its length the watery equivalent of a many-laned highway, a traffic artery tying together the canal and river systems of most of Europe. Below Lake Constance the river forms most of the boundary between Germany and Switzerland, turning north at Basel to flow across the broad plain between the French Vosges Mountains and the Black Forest. Its erratic past, when it wandered freely over its floodplain, means that most cities are built on one bank only, or even a fair distance away, like Strasbourg and Karlsruhe. Fed from the east by its tributaries the Main and Neckar, the Rhine near Mainz is up to 2,666 feet wide, a dimension it attains again only well below its gorge. Downstream from Bonn the river matures, carrying the heavy traffic of the industrial Ruhr region across the flatlands linking northwest Germany and Holland to its ocean outlet at Rotterdam's Europoort.

Places of interest along the river (L = left bank, looking downstream; R = right bank) are described below from south to north (i.e., downstream), from Wiesbaden to Bonn.

Below Wiesbaden and Mainz the vines of the **Rheingau** (R) extend to the very top of the high south-facing slopes. Sheltered from the north by the wooded Taunus hills, this is one of Germany's most renowned wine regions. It has its own scenic highway, the Rheingau-Riesling-Route, which hops up and down among the slopes taking in such pretty places as Kiedrich, with a Gothic church full of fine furnishings. Eberbach Abbey has a splendid collection of winepresses, Johannisberg Castle a panoramic view. The Rheingau's "capital" is Rüdesheim; the tavern-lined

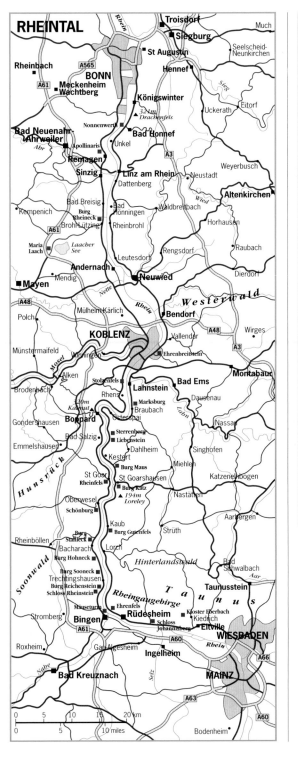

RHEINTAL

Travel options

There are many ways of getting acquainted with the Rhine Valley's spectacular landscape. Even the hurried traveler should consider leaving the autobahn and driving along one of the riverside roads. Until a new high-speed railroad line is built between Cologne and Frankfurt, expresses will continue to wend their way through the gorge, giving you the chance to view it in armchair comfort—but given the frequency of tunnels, it's especially dangerous to lean out the window. Drivers with time to spare can try the signposted scenic routes on either bank (Rheingoldstrasse on the left bank, Lorelei-Burgenstrasse on the right), which link minor roads together to give some of the best views down into the gorge. There's a high-level route for ramblers, too, the Rheinhöhenweg, while cyclists can ride along sections of the old towpath. Remember that there are no bridges between Koblenz and Bingen, though there are plenty of ferries (some for foot passengers only). Perhaps the most relaxing and time-efficient mode of transportation is to go one way by boat (possibly downstream) and return by train (combined tickets available; see the helpful leaflet in English published by German Rhine Line).

THE RHINELAND

Lorelei rock
A particularly rugged section of the gorge leads to the high Lorelei rock, around which the river makes one of its more tortured twists. This legendary haunt of troglodytic dwarfs may be the place where the treasure of the Nibelungs lies buried, but it is known above all as the place from which a flaxen-haired temptress (the Lorelei herself) lures sailors to a watery grave with her seductive song (definitive version by the Romantic poet Heine). The danger to shipping is real enough: the river is forced by the rock to squeeze itself through a gap only a third of its normal width, and here it reaches its greatest depth of 65 feet.

Drosselgasse alleyway does its best to contain the high tide of tourists washing up from the landing stage. Genuine picturesqueness fights it out with the tackiness of take-out joints and tawdry souvenir shops. High above the town stands the Niederwald memorial. Its massive figure of Germania celebrating the German unification that followed victory over the French in 1871 is in better shape than the crumbling remains of Ehrenfeld castle nearby.

At the railway town of **Bingen** (L) the Rhine narrows and turns north to enter the gorge. This turbulent section is known as the Binger Loch (Bingen Hole) and still presents some difficulties to navigation, though the reefs of hard quartzite that once gave rise to dangerous rapids have long since been blown up.

A succession of strongholds now follows (L): Rheinstein, Reichenstein, Sooneck. Tiny fiefdoms, good defensive sites and the chance of extorting tolls from traffic on the river help explain the building of so many castles. Many now stand in ruins, while most others were overzealously restored in the 19th-century rush to re-create a more than medieval Middle Ages, a mania that went to the lengths of embellishing railroad tunnels with turrets and battlements.

Boppard, a large and very lively resort, especially at wine-festival time, has outdoor dancing in many of its Rhineside cafés

Mouse Tower
Standing guard in the stream at Bingen is the 13th-century Mouse Tower. Legend has it that this is where Bishop Hatto of Mainz was eaten alive by mice in just retribution for a variety of misdeeds (hoarding grain in time of famine, burning bands of beggars to death...).

Attractive, slate-roofed **Bacharach** (L) has its fortress, too, Burg Stahleck, now a youth hostel. Towers and ramparts still protect this attractive little town; its main enemy is now the railroad trains roaring past on its embankment. It's touristy, to be sure, but there's lots to see along its cobbled streets and around the pretty marketplace.

Kaub (R) is overlooked by Gutenfels Castle, where the lords continued to exact tribute from passing traffic until well into the 19th century. Their instrument for doing so was the 14th-century Pfalz, the extraordinary white toll-castle standing shiplike amid the stream. **Oberwesel** (L) is dominated by verticals—the Ochsenturm near the waterfront, the red tower and slate steeple of the Liebfrauenkirche (Church of Our Lady), and the keeps and ramparts of Burg Schönburg high above.

St. Goar (L) is overlooked by **Rheinfels▶**, a city-sized castle that French Revolutionaries did their best to demolish, without quite succeeding. Burg Katz (Cat Castle) above **St. Goarshausen** (R) can't match Rheinfels for sheer size; it was built in the late 14th

century by the count of Katzenelnbogen to outface his territorial rival, the bishop of Trier, whose fortress downstream the count disdainfully nicknamed Burg Maus (Mouse Tower; see panel page 98). Beyond are two more castles, Sterrenberg and Liebenstein (R), named "the Warring Brothers" after a 14th-century family feud.

As befits its origins—it was founded by the Romans—**Boppard** (L) is the most substantial place along the gorge, with two fine churches, remains of Roman and medieval defenses, and a Heimatmuseum in the Archbishop's Castle. The town turns an attractive face to the Rhine; its long promenade dates from the 19th century, when it first became popular as a place of retirement and refined tourism. Hotels abound, together with taverns dispensing the produce of the big Bopparder Hamm vineyard. Boppard is a good starting point for river trips and for excursions inland as well; a branch railway winds up through the woods to the rugged Hunsrück region (see page 95), or there is a chairlift up to the famous Vierseenblick viewpoint.

Old-fashioned **Rhens** (L) and **Braubach** (R) are both worth a visit. High above the latter is the imposing silhouette of **Marksburg►**, the only medieval castle to have escaped ruin or wholesale restoration, and consequently able to give a truly authentic feel of life along the medieval Rhine. **Stolzenfels** (L), opposite Marksburg, is one of the more thoroughgoing efforts at making a ruined castle better than new.

The city of **Koblenz►** has made the most of its position at the confluence of the Rhine and Mosel since Roman times. Four-fifths flattened in World War II, the town is still worth a stroll, starting perhaps at the Deutsches Eck, the promontory between the rivers. A massive masonry plinth once carried a statue of Kaiser Wilhelm I, now controversially awaiting reinstatement. The riverside promenades enfold the old town, with its

Burg Stahleck, a typical Rhine castle, stands above the quaint old wine town of Bacharach, its narrow streets lined with wine bars and craft shops in half-timbered houses

THE RHINELAND

Koblenz, where the Rhine and the Mosel meet

two fine twin-towered churches, Romanesque St. Kastor and the Liebfrauenkirche. Crowning the heights on the far side of the Rhine is the vast fortress of Ehrenbreitstein, an impressive setting for the August fireworks extravaganza "The Rhine in Flames."

Between Koblenz and Bonn the riverside scenery remains varied and interesting. Attractive towns include **Andernach** (L), Roman and medieval; and **Linz** (R), whose Schloss contains two unusual museums, one of musical instruments, the other of medieval tortures. **Sinzig** (L), has a perfect example of a Rhineland Romanesque church. High above **Remagen** (famous for its bridge—see panel) stands a virtual scale model of Cologne Cathedral, the pilgrimage church dedicated to St. Apollinaris.

Downstream, the river divides to flow past Nonnenwörth (Nuns Island), overlooked by the ruins of **Rolandsbogen** (L)—supposedly built by the paladin Roland to give him an occasional glimpse of his fiancée, who turned nun on the (false) news of his death. It commands a fine panorama of the old volcanic hills on the far bank, collectively called the Siebengebirge (Seven Mountains). These myth-encrusted heights have long furnished the stuff of fairy tales and legends, the most potent story (see panel) being that of the dragon that met its end at the hands of Siegfried on the "castled crag of **Drachenfels**"▶ (Byron)—today Europe's most popular summit, climbed by 3 million visitors every year (on foot or by rack railway). Walkers can try to escape the crowds among the lovely woodlands of these miniature mountains with their 30-odd (not seven) peaks, many of them topped by castle ruins. At their base lie the riverside resorts of **Bad Honnef** and **Königswinter**, the latter with the **Konrad Adenauer Museum**▶. This is housed in the former residence of federal Germany's first and doughtiest chancellor, whose liking for his home ground seems to have influenced the choice of Bonn—just downstream—as the country's provisional capital.

■ **Germany's 11 main wine-growing areas follow the valleys of the Rhine and its tributaries the Mosel, Main, Nahe, and Neckar; the former GDR has some little-known vineyards around Naumburg and Dresden. The mild climate and 2,000 years' expertise (the Romans introduced the vine to these parts) mean that these vineyards—farther north than any other major vineyard—yield some of the world's greatest (and most expensive) wines ...■**

Most German wine is light, largely from the white-wine-producing Riesling, Müller-Thurgau, and Silvaner grapes, but about one-eighth of the total production is red, little known abroad but much appreciated at home.

Wine production has created some spectacular landscapes. The need to capture as much sunshine as possible explains the remarkable terracing on the steep sides of the valleys, where even the most inaccessible south- or west-facing slope is cultivated. Good conditions for the vine favor fruit production, too, and some wine-producing areas (Pfalz, Main, Baden) are glorious with blossoms in spring. Wines are always best tasted where they are made, but nowhere more so than in Germany, particularly at vintage and festival times.

New tastes German wines are traditionally sweet, but the recent hankering after a more "sophisticated" taste has encouraged a range of *trocken* (dry) or *halb-trocken* (medium-dry) wines. Categorization and labeling are strictly regulated, producing useful information about the area of origin and standard of a particular bottle. A *Deutscher Tafelwein* (German table wine) is a pleasant, unpretentious product from one of five main areas. A *Qualitätswein* (quality wine), of a higher standard, must be characteristic of both grape type and one of the 11 main regions. A *Qualitätswein mit Prädikat* (quality wine with distinctive features) has special attributes: the grapes must be fully mature and the wine have a certain percentage of alcohol without added sugar. All wines within this category (beginning with those designated *Kabinett*) come from one district. The very best wines are those made with ripe and overripe grapes, selected specially, either in the vineyard (*Spätlese, Auslese*) or in the vat room (*Beerenauslese, Trockenbeerenauslese*). Trockenberrenauslese is the summit of German wine culture, made from raisinlike grapes affected by the mold unappetizingly known as "noble rot" and picked as autumn expires. A rarity is *Eiswein* (ice wine), based on the intensely sweet liquor yielded by grapes frozen by the first frosts of winter. *Sekt* (sparkling wine), the best made as carefully as any champagne, should undoubtedly be tried.

Only a fraction of Germany's wines are produced by the red grape

THE RHINELAND

Sauerland and Rothaargebirge

Little known abroad, these green hills make a wonderful playground for the cities of the Rhine and Ruhr. Consisting of forested ridges broken by sometimes gorgelike valleys, the area is an important water-gathering ground, with many reservoirs providing endless opportunities for water-sports fans. Outdoor life isn't confined to one season: the chief resort, Winterberg, has probably the best winter-sports facilities north of the Alps. The hills are attractive rather than spectacular, the more or less continuous forest cover making for a certain monotony. The most comprehensive view is from the bare summit of the Kahler Asten (2,758 feet) in the Rothaargebirge (Redhead Heights), the easternmost of the four nature parks making up the area. With abundant ores and minerals beneath the surface, wood for fuel and rushing streams for power, the valleys attracted metalworkers long before the Ruhr was industrialized. Some spots have the dismal air of a workplace past its prime, but elsewhere the long-standing industrial tradition has been turned to advantage, with good examples of industrial archeology. The building tradition is a distinctive one, with many fine old timber-framed and whitewashed houses under steep slate roofs making a harmonious picture against the invariably green background. Few places could be described as particularly picturesque, but there are sturdy upland villages around the Kahler Asten (Nordenau, Oberkirchen, Grafschaft...), and most of the towns have some features of interest—such as Altena, dominated by its massive castle.

▶ The Ruhr

Named after the river running along its southern boundary to join the Rhine near Duisburg, Germany's "Kohlenpott," or Black Country, is still Europe's greatest industrial agglomeration, though coal and steel are no longer as important as they once were. Population, though still an impressive 5.5 million, has declined—spread over a combination of varied settlements ranging from such great cities as **Essen** and **Dortmund** to picturesque riverside places like **Kettwig** and **Herdecke**.

The Ruhr was never a continuously urbanized area, and sensible planning has ensured that the whole conurbation is now interspersed with green spaces threaded by footpaths and cycleways that connect city centers with splendid new parks (like Essen's Grugapark) and with the open countryside.

It is still industry that characterizes the scene, and most visitors are here for business rather than pleasure. Urban pleasures are plentiful, however, and should not be neglected. Each city proclaims its own identity and boasts an enviable array of cultural facilities. Galleries abound, foremost among them the **Museum Folkwang▶** in Essen, with superb collections of 19th- and 20th-century painting, and the Ruhrland Museum with its dour souvenirs of the life of 19th-century miners and steelworkers. **Recklinghausen** has a rarity, a museum devoted almost entirely to icons. **Bochum**'s modern, wedge-shaped Städtisches Schauspielhaus (City Theater) enjoys an international reputation for its classical and avant-garde productions. At Hagen is a remarkable open-air museum, the Westfälishes Freilichtmuseum, devoted not to rural life but to the early technology of the region.

Bochum's **Bergbaumuseum▶** (Mining Museum), with its excellent displays and its 1½ miles of underground galleries, is outstanding, and the city also has an Eisenbahnmuseum (Railway Museum). Industrial history can be enjoyed in the open air, too—notably in the Muttental, near **Witten**, where the Bergbauhistorischer Rundwanderweg (Mining Heritage Trail) features horse-operated pithead gear as well as the chapel where the miners gathered to pray and be counted before descending into the perilous depths.

With the digging of coal went the drinking of beer, and brews evolved to slake the miners' thirst taste just as good today, with a more distinctive character than their Bavarian counterparts. Some, like Dortmunder Union, travel the world, while others of no less quality remain a local secret (willingly shared with visitors!).

▶ Saarland

Like the Mosel, the Saar rises in the Vosges Mountains in France, joining the larger river just above **Trier**. It has given its name to Germany's second smallest *Land*. Long disputed between Germany and France, and still with a Gallic air about it, the Saarland and its capital, **Saarbrücken**, look to the future rather than back to their grimy past of rust-belt industries based on coal and steel. Thus, while Saarbrücken makes the most of its definitely limited architectural heritage (18th-century Schloss and Rathaus), it promotes itself as a business and cultural center, and cultivates a "green" image. It

celebrates this—and the healing of old rifts—in the Deutsch-Französischer Garten (Franco-German Park).

Industry extends downriver to **Saarlouis**, founded by Louis XIV as one of the fortresses consolidating his hold on France's eastern frontier; the town's market square still has the air of a parade ground.

Below **Merzig** the valley narrows and begins to run through a wild, spectacular defile. **Mettlach** is an important center of the ceramics industry, part of which occupies the palacelike buildings of the 18th-century Benedictine abbey. The viewpoint at **Cloef** overlooks the great loop in the river—the Saarschleife. Downstream from **Serrig**, scrub and woodland give way to vines, and from here onward the valley takes on an attractive Mosel-like character: vineyards climb the steep slopes, yielding lively wines that are dispensed in the taverns of such villages as Ayl and Ockfen, Wavern and Wiltingen. Center of this little wine region is 1,000-year-old **Saarburg**, with a castle and a stream dropping precipitously past houses and vineyards.

The countryside between the Saar and the Mosel was favored by the Romans. Among the 50 or so villas that have been excavated, the one at **Nennig** (12 miles west of Mettlach, overlooking the Mosel and the Luxembourg border) has the largest mosaic floor north of the Alps with scenes of the hunt and of the gladiators.

Other extensive Roman remains, with reconstructions of original buildings, can be seen in the **Römisches Freilichtmuseum Schwarzenacker**, a big open-air museum near Homburg east of Saarbrücken. To the north, **Ottweiler** has a carefully conserved Altstadt and St. Wendel, a three-towered church, while near **Nonnweiler** is the Hunnenring, the spectacular remains of a Celtic fortified settlement. A world away from the industries of the southern Saarland are the vast woodlands of the **Hochwald**, rich in deer and wild boar.

Modern industrial Saarbrücken, by the French border, has not only a Franco-German Park but a bilingual Franco-German Lycée/Gymnasium— a practical example of the new entente

The rural Ruhr
The Ruhr is not only industrial but idyllically rural too, at least on its southern side. Here disused mineheads and steelworks have been cleared away, to give the river valley back to nature. Close to Bochum's factories you'll find winding country lanes, glens where deer graze, and the romantic crag-top castle of Blankenstein. There are new pleasure-marinas, and old villages with quaint cobbled paths and streams.

Drive **Route north from steelmaking Siegen to medieval Soest**

The old core of Siegen, with its Schloss, sits on a spur of land overlooking the River Sieg. Rubens was born here, and there are several of his paintings in the castle's Siegerland museum.

To the northwest Freudenberg's black-and-white houses step harmoniously up the hill. Beyond Olpe is the largest of the region's lakes, the Biggesee. The landscape varies from rocky (at Attendorn) to industrial (around Rönkhausen) to grandiose (in the Lenne Mountains).

To the west of the Sorpe dam is the Luisenhütte, Germany's oldest blast furnace, dating from 1732. Arnsberg, an ancient center of administration, rises in tiers over the River Ruhr. Like the Sorpe and Eder dams, the Möhne dam was attacked by the RAF in 1943. After five attempts, the masonry wall of the dam, 113 feet thick at its base, was breached, flooding a vast area and disrupting water supplies to the armament industries of the Ruhr. Long since repaired, the dam holds back a 6-mile lake for the pleasure of water-sports enthusiasts (north shore) and birds (south shore).

Soest is approached from the south across the Kassel–Ruhr Autobahn.

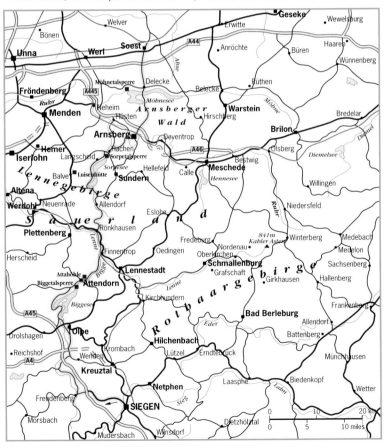

Bertelsmann
In decentralized Germany, many institutions are scattered in various cities. Thus the world's largest publishing firm, Bertelsmann, has its headquarters in modest Gütersloh—a true company town, swarming with editors and printers. The Bertelsmann world empire embraces other publishing giants such as Doubleday, a Berlin daily newspaper, a leading magazine group, and a book club with 6.5 million members.

In Soest, many red-roofed and half-timbered houses line the streets within the ramparts

►► Soest

In the Middle Ages Soest was the most important city in Westphalia, making good use of its position on the Hellweg (the ancient highway running right across northern Germany) to trade with Novgorod and Milan, Bruges and London. Having escaped the industrialization that befell Dortmund, its old rival, Soest still wears an attractive medieval air.

Near the baroque Rathaus stands a sturdy pair of Romanesque churches, each with an impressive westwork, topped, in the case of the St. Patrokli-Münster, by a formidable tower. The Petrikirche has frescoes attributed to a local master of medieval times, Konrad von Soest, who also painted the altar in the nearby chapel dedicated to St. Nicholas.

Reflected in the waters of the pretty little lake—the Grosser Teich—are the twin spires of the Gothic Wiesenkirche (Our Lady of the Meadows). The stained glass of the splendidly light interior includes a depiction of the Last Supper with typical Westphalian refreshments on the table—ham, beer, and pumpernickel, along with some Steinhäger, the local schnapps. On rising ground nearby is St. Maria zur Höhe (Our Lady of the Heights), with original Romanesque paintings.

Soest's attractive ambience seems to have drawn artists; works by two local men, Heinrich Aldegrever (a follower of Dürer) and Wilhelm Morgner (a contemporary of the Expressionist Emil Nolde), are shown in the modern Wilhelm-Morgner Haus. The municipal museum is in the 16th-century Burghof, next to a town house dating back to the 12th century. To the south, the river Möhne, a tributary of the Ruhr, has been broadened to form the Möhnesee, whose dam is famous: in 1943 a squadron of RAF Lancasters—the "Dambusters"—successfully bombed it in a bid to disrupt the Ruhr industry's water supply, and 125 factories were wrecked by the flooding.

Roman city
First established by the Celtic Treveri peoples, Trier was called Augusta Treverorum in 15 BC, becoming one of the most important Roman cities north of the Alps. With a population of 80,000—close to today's total—it flourished as an imperial residence and capital of the western part of the empire. Emperor Constantine made it Germany's first bishopric. By the Middle Ages, Trier's prince-bishops were powerful rulers. But the city's most influential son was Karl Marx: the house where he was born in 1818 is now a fascinating museum of his life and work.

Modern Trier, once the Roman Empire's northern capital

▶▶▶ Trier

Trier, situated among the vineyards of the Mosel Valley close to the Luxembourg border, is probably the oldest city in Germany. Its heritage of buildings spanning two millennia makes it irresistible for visitors.

Start exploring Trier's compact center at the massive **Porta Nigra▶▶**, the biggest and best-preserved Roman gateway in Europe, so named for the blackened appearance of the huge blocks of limestone from which it is made. Its ingenious construction as well as its sheer scale foiled all attacks by besieging armies. In the Middle Ages it was converted into a church in honor of St. Simeon; the nearby monastery bearing his name has a unique, delightful courtyard with two-story cloisters.

The traffic-free Simeonsstrasse leads to the Hauptmarkt, with an ornate Renaissance fountain as its focal point. On the rise to the east is the huge **cathedral▶**, begun by Constantine but predominantly Romanesque with a baroquified interior.

Part of Constantine's great imperial palace, the brick Konstantinsbasilika survives as an awesome and austere Protestant church; apart from the Pantheon in Rome, it is the biggest enclosed space to survive from the days of antiquity. Next door, in total contrast, is the lighthearted strawberry-and-vanilla façade of the rococo Prince-Bishop's Palace; its formal garden extends south to Trier's third great Roman monument, the **Kaiserthermen▶** (Imperial Baths). In a better state of preservation are some of the Roman artifacts in the Landesmuseum, among them the famous stone Wine Ship with its grinning oarsman.

Trier's further delights include a 20,000-seat Roman amphitheater, the piers of a bridge over the Mosel, the **Bischöfliches** (Episcopal) **Museum▶**, the medieval interior of St. Matthias Church, St. Paulin Church by Balthasar Neumann, and modern Karl Marx Haus.

The Weinstrasse

■ **At the foot of the Haardt Mountains, forming the eastern rim of the vast Palatinate Forest, lies a cheerful, sun-drenched countryside that produced fine wines for the Romans. Today the delightful wine towns and villages of the Rheinpfalz are linked by one of Germany's best-known touring routes, the Deutsche Weinstrasse, or Wine Road. Some 50 miles long, it links Bockenheim in the north to the border with Alsace in the south ...■**

Pfalz wines are made from a variety of grapes; the whites span the whole quality range from everyday table wines to the most exquisite Trockenbeerenauslese. Reds are produced, too, from the Portugieser grape, but account for only one-tenth of total production. No one should miss tasting the wines offered in traditional vintners' houses opening off cobbled village streets.

Every place along the route has something special to offer: charming half-timbered or mellow red sandstone houses; the remains of medieval fortifications; a ruined castle on a hill... The landscape gives continual pleasure, too, with ever-changing views of hills and broad plains. The benevolent climate means that not only vines but other southern plants thrive, such as fig, almond and chestnut trees, tobacco, and maize. Kallstadt is proud of its local specialty, *Saumagen* (sow's belly in wine—give it a try!). Bad Dürkheim celebrates the vintage with Germany's biggest wine festival, the Wurstmarkt. Deidesheim has one of the best arrays of restaurants and inns, including the oldest tavern in the Palatinate. Medieval Neustadt, with its viticultural institute, is the region's miniature metropolis, while nearby Hambach Castle is where Germany's black-red-gold tricolor was raised by patriots for the first time in 1832. There are stunning panoramas from the Kalmit summit (2,207 feet), a short way into the hills, or from Bavarian King Ludwig I's summer residence, Schloss Ludwigshohe. The fantastic turrets and ramparts of another castle, Madenburg, loom over Eschbach. Beyond the resort of Bad Bergzabern, the route's terminus is marked by the huge Weintor gateway.

Weinstrasse vineyards

CENTRAL GERMANY

The Germans tend to keep the charms of Central Germany to themselves. Only a handful of towns, such as **Hameln** (Hamelin), with its Pied Piper fable and spectacular Weser Renaissance houses (see page 119), are on the international tourist circuit. Although it has none of the drama of the Alps, it can be rewarding making your own discoveries in the numerous attractive small towns and rolling, forested uplands. **Hessen** (Hesse), crossed by the River Main and with **Frankfurt** as its chief city, was used by the Americans as an administrative center after World War II, and it is very much the center of Germany. It did, however, exist long before the Americans came along, although it was fragmented along geographic and religious lines. In 1866 Hesse was

Alsfeld's town square, with the Rathaus in the background

incorporated in the Kingdom of Prussia, and five years later became part of the Greater German Reich.

While Frankfurt, the banking capital of Germany, remains the heart of the country's economic wealth, other towns, notably **Kassel** in north Hesse, generate enormous wealth from industrial output. Not far away from the urban landscapes of the 20th century are reminders of slower-moving times in such old towns as **Marburg** and **Alsfeld**.

For lovers of the countryside, the **Vogelsberg**, a plateau created by a volcanic eruption approximately 30 million years ago, is a little-developed area of hills and forests. But best of all, this is the land of the Brothers Grimm, whose often chilling and disturbing tales evoke a landscape of forests, rivers, lakes and castles. The region stretches from **Göttingen** up into the **Weserbergland**, whose green hills (which rise to a height of some 1,640 feet) flank the Weser, one of the loveliest rivers in Germany. It is difficult to imagine this region 500 years ago, when it was the center of battle and generals made it their meeting point to discuss strategy. **Hanau**, near Frankfurt, where the Grimm brothers were born, is about two hours from Göttingen, and it's from here that the **Deutsche Märchenstrasse** (Fairy Tale Road) begins, continuing on to the coastal town of **Bremerhaven**. The **Harz Mountains** comprise the highest ground in the region; once they were harshly divided by the East–West German border, now they offer good opportunities for discovering the lesser-known Germany.

This door is typical of the ornate architecture of Alsfeld, a key center of folk tradition

▶▶ Alsfeld

Set amid the rolling, wooded Vögelsberg hills, Alsfeld is a picturesque old town with some fine half-timbered Renaissance buildings. It is set on the upper course of the River Schwalm, where the folk traditions inspired the Grimm brothers. At summer festivals the girls still wear the local red folk costumes. Outside the Walpurgiskirche is a fountain with a figure of a goose girl in the style of costume worn by Little Red Riding Hood.

In the Marktplatz the tiny, quaint 1516 *Rathaus* (town hall) stands above arcades where markets were once held. Opposite is the Renaissance-style Hochzeithaus, built for weddings, as its name implies. Fine examples of baroque architecture can be seen in the Rittergasse, notably the Neurath Haus at number 3 and the Minnigerode Haus at number 5. In Hersfelderstrasse, numbers 10 and 12 are among Germany's oldest half-timbered buildings.

▌ Bielefeld

This big industrial town has manufactured linen since the 16th century. Today it is also a center for engineering, electronics, and food-processing. Of the two museums of interest, the Kunsthalle has some German Expressionist works (Beckmann, etc.), and sculptures by Rodin, Moore, and others; the Bauernhaus Museum is devoted to traditional farm life.

Herford, an old Hanseatic town nearby, has a late Romanesque Münster and a number of Gothic churches; of these, the Johanniskirche has notable 17th-century woodwork and stained-glass windows.

▶ ▌ Darmstadt

This otherwise dullish industrial town is best known as the heartland of the Jugendstil (art nouveau) movement of the early 1900s. An artists' colony was established on the low hill of Mathildenhöhe, and their **Jugendstil buildings▶** still stand there (see panel): the Ernst-Ludwig-Haus, with its Adam and Eve figures on the portal; the Behrens Haus; and the Hochzeitturm (wedding tower), designed for the wedding of Grand Duke Ernst Ludwig in 1905. The spectacular Russian Orthodox chapel with its gilded domes dates from the 1890s. A collection of Jugendstil artifacts is displayed in the Landesmuseum near the reconstructed 18th-century Schloss. The rococo Prinz Georg Palais holds a notable collection of porcelain given by members of various European royal families.

▶ ▌ Detmold

Until 1918 this town was capital of the principality of Lippe, and it still has a strong sense of its own identity. Its noble 16th-century castle has Brussels tapestries and souvenirs of the family of Prince Bernhard of the Netherlands, whose seat was here. There are British Army barracks in the town, nicknamed "Little London."

To the south is the Teutoburger Wald, a long, narrow range of wooded hills with two interesting sights on its crest. One is the Hermannsdenkmal, an 85-foot green-copper statue of Arminius, the local chieftain who in about AD 9 rallied the Germanic tribes to oppose Rome's rule and defeated its legions near this spot.

Jugendstil
Darmstadt was a center of the Jugendstil—German art nouveau. The style began as quite floral and naturalistic, but after the 1900s it took on an increasingly abstract form. The architect Peter Behrens, who built a house for himself in the Mathildenhöhe, was an exponent of the late Jugendstil.

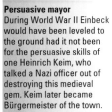

Duderstadt, a small town right beside the former GDR border, has over 500 half-timbered buildings. This one is the town hall

111

Erected under Bismarck, the memorial became a focus for German nationalism; the Nazis sometimes held rallies here.

The **Externsteine►** nearby is a cluster of high rocks in strange, toothy shapes, once used as a place of worship by pagan tribes, later by Christians. Carved on one rock is a 12th-century bas-relief depicting the Descent from the Cross. Also hewn from the rock are a tomb and a pulpit. The summer solstice used to be celebrated here, as the sun rose between the rocks. For a closer view you can climb up new stairways carved into the rock. On the plain below is a large ornithological park, as well as the Westfälisches Freilichtsmuseum, an open-air museum with nearly 100 reassembled farm buildings from the region.

Persuasive mayor
During World War II Einbeck would have been leveled to the ground had it not been for the persuasive skills of one Heinrich Keim, who talked a Nazi officer out of destroying this medieval gem. Keim later became Bürgermeister of the town.

► Duderstadt

Only 13 miles east of the university town of Göttingen, Duderstadt has a successful blend of Renaissance and Gothic architecture, which can be seen both on Hinterstrasse and in the Rathaus. The Westertorturm (gate tower) is notable for its curiously twisted narrow roof.

The town contains two worthwhile churches: the Gothic St. Cyriakuskirche, decorated in ostentatious baroque style, and St. Servatiuskirche, refurbished in the art nouveau manner after a fire in 1915.

► Einbeck

A small town (pop. 29,000), Einbeck was known in the Middle Ages for its beer. There were no fewer than 700 breweries then, but only one survives, producing a well-known strong beer. Around the cobbled Marktplatz and in the Tidexerstrasse are half-timbered Gothic and Renaissance houses. In the Stiftskirche St. Alexandri is the oldest choir stall in Germany (1288).

CENTRAL GERMANY

►► Frankfurt-am-Main

A proud history
Barbarossa and other early German kings were elected in Frankfurt, and from 1562 to 1806 the Holy Roman Emperors were crowned here Goethe, born in the city, called it "Germany's secret capital" (perhaps it still is?), and the first pan-German parliament met here in 1848–9. The city began to mint its own money in the 16th century; then in the 19th century local financiers, such as Rothschild, made it into a key world center of banking. After 1945 it was proposed as the new federal capital, but Adenauer insisted on Bonn—a pity, very many people think. Today, together with Hannover, it is Germany's major trade-fair venue, and it has the country's leading international airport. Industry includes machine tools and chemicals.

Europe's tallest office building (833 feet) rises up in the heart of downtown Frankfurt (pop. 627,000), a city that is the home of the mighty Bundesbank and has branches of some 390 world banks. It is Germany's well-established financial capital, and its battalions of skyscrapers near the River Main have lent it the nickname "Mainhattan." Its image of a dull, heartless moneymaking place is far from the whole truth: there's a great deal for the tourist to see, including some of Germany's best museums. Because the city is rich, it has the money to spend on culture, such as high-class opera, and at its annual Book Fair—the world's largest—literature and commerce join hands. Many other international trade fairs are also held in Frankfurt.

Frankfurt has a metropolitan, outward-looking ambience, largely due to all the high-profile international activity. It is also a city of tensions, with relatively high levels of crime and drug abuse and a large immigrant population, 22 percent of the total. Politically, it is polarized: Green and left-wing protest has habitually been sharper here than in other cities (except Berlin), maybe because these militants react against the banks' assertive capitalism. Today—ironically—this city of bankers is ruled by an S.P.D./Green coalition: one of its councillors is Danny Cohn Bendit, once a May '68 rebel and now a Green.

One local hotbed of Leftism has been the famous university (45,000 students), where radical philosophers such as Habermas and Adorno once propounded new ideas. This city of money is also a lively center of the alternative avant-garde, with many fringe theaters:

Excursion boats pass Frankfurt cathedral

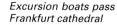

controversial film director Rainer Werner Fassbinder once worked here.

Frankfurt is a major publishing center and has two of Germany's leading dailies, the conservative *Frankfurter Allgemeine* and the more liberal *Rundschau*. In short, this is no mean city.

The main sights are central, and many can be toured on foot. Near the Messegelände (exhibition center) and the central station is the financial district, where the 24-story Deutsche Bank building with its gleaming gray-blue glass façade is the most graceful of the city's skyscrapers (the Bundesbank itself is out in the suburbs). Much of this central area was gracelessly

rebuilt after wartime bombing (witness Zeil, the hideous main shopping mall), but some older buildings have been well restored, notably the big neoclassical opera house (though operas are now staged elsewhere). The imposing 15th-century Eschenheimer Turm is one of the 42 towers that used to encircle the city; nearby is the Börse (stock exchange) and the 18th-century *Hauptwache* (guard room). The Goethehaus, the handsome family home where the poet was born and brought up, has been well restored after wartime damage and now houses a museum of memorabilia.

Frankfurt before the bombing had the biggest medieval Altstadt in Germany. Little now survives save for a carefully restored sector around the cathedral and the Römerberg, a cobbled square lined with fine half-timbered houses that used to be the city's focus for festivals and royal ceremonies. Here the **Römer►**, a group of 15th-century houses that once formed the Rathaus, has a Renaissance stairway leading to the stately Kaisersaal. Across the square is the tiny Gothic Nikolaikirche and the History Museum, which includes scale models of how the Altstadt used to look and photos of what the Allied bombers did. Just to the east is a fascinating hodgepodge zone where new modernistic buildings have purposely been put up next to ancient ones. The new glass-walled Kultur-Schirn, an arts center, gives onto the ruins of a Carolingian palace and of a Roman bath (around AD 100) beside St.

113

The opera house (left), built in the 1880s, is now used for conventions, while operas are staged in the city theater. The high Gothic cathedral (below) is a local landmark, even if dwarfed by some of the skyscrapers

CENTRAL GERMANY

Once the setting for royal ceremonies: Frankfurt's cobbled square, Römerberg

Goethe the great
Born in Frankfurt-am-Main in 1749, Goethe is undoubtedly Germany's greatest literary figure—and a lifelong lover of women. The young Johann reluctantly studied law in Leipzig, where he met his first love, Kätchen Schönkopf. He continued his law studies in Strasbourg, where he had another love affair and met the German writer and thinker Herder. With Herder's help, Goethe became part of the Sturm und Drang (Storm and Stress) movement. In 1771 he returned to Frankfurt and became a newspaper critic.

Bartholomew's Cathedral▶, with its lofty Gothic tower (the view from the top is splendid). The emperors were crowned in this austere-looking reddish church, which has interesting medieval murals and choir stalls. In the adjacent Wahlkapelle the Holy Roman Empire's seven electors would choose their king, and the cathedral's little museum displays the adornments they wore. The 15th-century St. Leonard's Church has impressive stained glass.

Down by the river, on Untermainkai, the remarkable new **Jewish Museum**▶ expounds the history of the city's once so influential Jewish community. The Nazi period is dealt with very discreetly. There are books from the Rothschild library, and details of Jewish life. Just across the river are six other excellent museums, some quite new. From west to east they are: (1) the Liebieg museum of sculpture, ranging from ancient Egypt to the baroque; (2) the important **Stadel Museum of art**▶, with a large if somewhat muddled collection containing works by, among others, Holbein and Cranach, Tintoretto and Rembrandt, Renoir and Monet, the rich array of German painting including, suitably, Tischbein's memorable portrait of Goethe sitting pensively near Rome; there are pleasing works by the German impressionist Max Liebermann. Other Germans on display include Thoma, Beckmann, Kirchner, and Nolde; (3) the Postal Museum, with details of stamps, mail coaches, and telephones; (4) the Cinema Museum, mostly technical and scientific, with not much about individual films; (5) the Museum of Ethnography, with objects from native tribes; (6) the Museum of Applied Art, displaying a striking collection of glass, porcelain, Jugendstil furniture, a good Asian and Islamic section, and more, all in a lovely new building: (7) the Deutsche Arkitectur Museum, the only one of its kind in Germany.

This south side of the Main is Sachsenhausen, a residential area with some 16th- and 17th-century houses and a lot of cider bars and other evening entertainment. At the eastern end, near the Alte Brücke, one group of narrow streets is now full of discos, bars and cheap restaurants, which look amusing but have grown tacky, and many are full of exuberant U.S. soldiers at the weekend. Back north of the river, Frankfurt's large zoo▶ has lovely rare fish and a special section on nocturnal creatures. Dead or extinct animals, such as dinosaurs, can be studied in the Senckenberg natural history museum, which is near the university and the large Grüneburg Park, containing botanical and tropical gardens.

Two towns near Frankfurt are well worth a visit. Offenbach, Germany's chief leather-making center, has a big museum devoted to the subject. Höchst, home of the giant Hoechst chemicals firm, has a charming undamaged Altstadt and several fine old buildings. One is the Justiniuskirche of Carolingian origin; another is the baroque Bolongaro palace, former home of Italian snuff makers. Hochst was a famous porcelain-producing center in the 18th century; this industry is now being revived (methods are on display at the Dalberghaus).

Powerful cider
Frankfurters cross the river to let their hair down in the cider houses of Sachsenhausen. *Apfelwein* is the local specialty, but if you're not used to this cider the first quaff could take your breath away—it's dry, almost vinegary, and very strong.

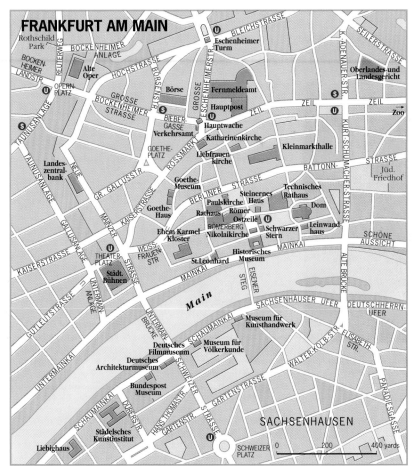

FRANKFURT AM MAIN

Rothschild Park
BOCKENHEIMER ANLAGE
BOCKENHEIMER LANDSTR.
REUTERWEG
Alte Oper
HOCHSTRASSE
OPERN-PLATZ
GROSSE BOCKENHEIMER STRASSE
BORSENSTR.
Börse
BIEBER-GASSE
Verkehrsamt
TAUNUSANLAGE
NEUE
Landes-zentral-bank
GR. GALLUSSTR.
GOETHE-PLATZ
ROSSMARKT
Goethe-Museum
GOETHE-STRASSE
BERLINER STRASSE
Goethe-Haus
MAINZER STRASSE
KAISERSTRASSE
WEISS FRAUEN STR.
THEATER-PLATZ
Städt. Bühnen
UNTERMAIN ANLAGE
KAISERSTRASSE
GUTLEUTSTRASSE
GALLUSANLAGE
TAUNUSANLAGE
ESCHENHEIMER STR.
Eschenheimer Turm
BLEICHSTRASSE
Fernmeldeamt
GROSSE
Hauptpost
ZEIL
Hauptwache
Katharinenkirche
Liebfrauen-kirche
Kleinmarkthalle
BATTONN-STRASSE
Steinernes Haus
Technisches Rathaus
Paulskirche
Rathaus
Römer
Dom
Ostzeile
RÖMERBERG
Nikolaikirche
Schwarzer Stern
Leinwand-haus
Ehem. Karmel Kloster
Historisches Museum
St. Leonhard
MAINKAI
EISENER STEG
UNTERMAIN BRÜCKE
Main
SACHSENHAUSER UFER
ALTE BRÜCKE
SCHÖNE AUSSICHT
DEUTSCHHERRN-UFER
Museum für Kunsthandwerk
SCHAUMAINKAI
Deutsches Filmmuseum
Museum für Völkerkunde
Deutsches Architekturmuseum
SCHWEIZER STRASSE
Bundespost Museum
DÜRERSTR.
HANS THOMASTR.
GARTENSTRASSE
Städelsches Kunstinstitut
Liebighaus
SCHAUMAINKAI
UNTERMAINKAI
GARTENSTRASSE
SCHWEIZER PLATZ
SACHSENHAUSEN
WALTER-KOLB-STR.
ELISABETH STR.
PARADIESGASSE
K. ADENAUER-STR.
SEILERSTRASSE
Oberlandes-und Landesgericht
KURT-SCHUMACHER-STRASSE
ZEIL
Zoo
Jüd. Friedhof
Fernmeldeamt
Verkehrsamt
Dom

0   200   400 yards

Schloss Fasanerie
If you haven't yet had your fill of baroque, visit Schloss Fasanerie (guided tours April to October, closed Mondays), built for the 18th-century prince-bishops of Fulda. Its sumptuous décor and size are almost over-powering, but the park offers a relaxing respite. Near the town is the Kirche auf dem Petersberg (Petersberg Church), built on a 1,312-foot-high rock and visible from afar.

The tall 14th-century Adolpsturm overlooks the old streets of the "dual" town of Friedberg

▶ Friedberg

There are a few Jewish bathhouses remaining in Germany, and Friedberg has one of them. The Judenbad here is a particularly fine example of this type of ritual bathing place for women. Built in the 13th century, it descends 82 feet below ground level—reached by 74 steps. The Burg (Imperial Town) was built by the emperor Frederick Barbarossa in 1180 and today remains a district community, as it was in medieval times. The separation of church and state is apparent, with the other main part of town being focused on the Stadtkirche, dating from the 13th and 14th centuries.

▶▶ Fulda

Ever since the 8th century, Fulda has been one of the most important centers for Catholic religious instruction in Germany. It all began when a Benedictine abbey was founded here by St. Boniface, an English missionary to the pagan Germanic tribes. The abbey became a famous center for culture and learning throughout the Christian world.

Today the town contains a variety of architectural styles, above all a wealth of baroque, a style that extends to the huge palace (now a museum) and even the former police station. The main *Dom* (cathedral) was rebuilt by Johann Dientzenhofer (one of a family of architects much in demand) at the beginning of the 18th century, having been inspired by Italian baroque architecture; in fact, he worked from a model copy of St. Peter's in Rome. The Michaelskirche is one of the oldest churches in Germany, with a crypt dating from 822.

The Hanauisches Amtshaus at **Steinau**, about 15 miles southwest of Fulda, was the boyhood home of the Brothers Grimm; a puppet theater re-enacts their fairy tales, and the much-fortified Schloss (open daily except Christmas and Mondays) contains a monument to the Grimms.

▶ Gelnhausen

This town is said to have been founded by Emperor Frederick Barbarossa in 1170 (it is sometimes called Barbarossa Stadt). It stands on a slope of the Kinzig Valley (close to the Naturpark Hessischer Spessart, good walking country with its forested hills). The town was built as a military foundation and is still partly surrounded by fortifications. The Marienkirche (St. Mary's) is a multitowered Romanesque church that looks over Gelnhausen from above. The best feature of the interior is the chancel, with its high altar and a shrine depicting the Madonna with four saints. The unusual choir stalls are ornately decorated, and there are two well-preserved tapestries. Barbarossa's castle, the Kaiserpfalz, stands ruined on an island in the River Kinzig (open daily except Monday).

Büdingen, about 6 miles north of Gelnhausen, possesses an intact town wall dating from the 15th and 16th centuries, distinguished by squat towers and pierced by elaborate Gothic gateways. Guided tours of the Schloss (Tuesday–Sunday, 11:30–4, March to October) take you over a still-inhabited 12th- to 17th-century building ranged around a courtyard.

Many of the older houses in Goslar are half-timbered, like these lining a stream in the heart of town

▶▶ Goslar

One of the loveliest towns in north Germany, Goslar is also a winter-sports resort, popular with Berliners. It was a seat of the Salian emperors in the 11th century, then a Free Imperial City. In the Middle Ages it became a center of silver and lead mining. Merchants began to pour in, lead and silver were increasingly mined and refined, and this led to a building boom around the 16th century, the peak of Goslar's prosperity. This explains its legacy of fine buildings from different epochs—Gothic, Renaissance, baroque. Many are half-timbered or of stone, rather than the usual north German red brick. The mines, in the hills south of the town, ultimately went bankrupt and the last one closed in 1992. By the 19th century, Goslar was prospering again under Prussian domination.

The Altstadt is full of interest. The traffic-free, cobbled Marktplatz, surrounded by dignified stone and half-timbered houses with elaborate slate roofs, has a quaint chiming clock (modern) on the treasurer's building, which performs four times a day—at 9AM, noon, 3PM and 6PM—with scenes outlining the mining history of the town dating back to the Middle Ages. In the old arcaded Rathaus, a fine Gothic building, the **Huldigungssaal**▶▶ is covered from floor to ceiling with splendid colored frescoes from around 1500; it also holds the Goslar Gospel (1230). Across the square, the 15th-century Kaiserworth, once a guildhouse, is now a hotel: on one corner gable is a impudent statue of a boy ejecting a coin from his backside (symbolic of Goslar's former right to mint coins). The square also has a fountain with two large bronze basins surmounted by an imperial eagle. Many of the houses in the streets off the square are half-timbered (*Fachwerkhäuser*). The Siemenshaus (Schreiberstrasse 12, daily guided tours by arrangement) was built in 1693 by Hans Siemens, an ancestor of the Berlin industrialist who created the Siemens empire. The Goslarer Museum (Königstrasse 1) contains a detailed outline of the artistic and cultural history of the Harz region, and models of the town. The Mönchehaus (Mönchestrasse 3) contains a modest collection of modern art. The terrace by the Bismark statue near the station offers a good view of the town and its encircling hills.

CENTRAL GERMANY

Friedland camp
At Friedland, near the former GDR border south of Göttingen, there used to be a large transit camp for political refugees arriving not from the GDR but from other east European countries. Here they stayed while their papers were processed, before moving on to a new life in some West German town.

The Gänselieselbrunnen *at Göttingen (top right) and (below) the door of the city's 16th-century pharmacy*

▶ Göttingen

Göttingen is first and foremost a university town. The university, named after its founder, the elector of Hannover, who was also George II, king of Great Britain and Ireland, has given the town a hallowed reputation as a leading place of learning. The university has produced several Nobel Prize winners, and is the headquarters of the Max Planck-Institut, which groups some 50 high-level scientific research bodies all over Germany. Max Planck, creator of the quantum theory in physics, spent his final years in the town and is buried here.

The 30,000 university students bring added life and color to the town, which prides itself on its Gothic churches and neoclassical buildings, such as the Aula, or Great Hall, scattered about the campus. The students have made the town hall area and its Ratskeller the hub of activity. Even during vacations you will find throngs of young people milling about. Nightlife is always interesting. A famous music festival devoted to Handel is held in June. There is a tradition for students to visit the *Gänselieselbrunnen* ("Goose Lizzie's fountain") in the center of town in front of the Rathaus, once they've completed their examinations, and to give the bronze statue a kiss.

The Vierkirchenblick (viewpoint of four churches) is a memorable sight. Stand at the southeast corner of the Markt and you will see, to the east, the 15th-century St. Albanus; to the south, St. Michael; to the west, the two octagonal towers of the Johanniskirche; and to the north, St. Jakobi, the tallest, which stands at 236 feet. In the old quarter of the town, there are half-timbered houses to be seen; one dating from 1563, northeast of the Markt, houses the old pharmacy and is also elaborately and attractively decorated.

▶▶ **Hameln (Hamelin)**

There is more to Hameln than just the legend of a man in a strange costume and a plague of rats. There are many attractive half-timbered buildings left, despite severe damage done during the 1618–48 Thirty Years' War (World War II fortunately had less impact).

The town is a treasure house of immaculately restored buildings in the so-called Weser Renaissance style of the 16th and 17th centuries. Typically this makes use of scroll decorations and pinnacles on gables, carved-stone banding and large bay windows. The **Rattenfängerhaus▶** (Rat Catcher's House), at Osterstrasse 28, dates back to 1603 and is a good example. Its carved stonework is embellished with busts and heads, and there is an inscription about the Pied Piper on the side; the house was actually built for a councillor. The Hochzeitshaus (Wedding House), at Osterstrasse 2, was built between 1610 and 1617 and was used for burghers' weddings. You will easily recognize it, since today it is the town hall and library. On the side facing the Marktplatz, the Pied Piper clock features mechanical figures, which appear three times a day—at 1:05, 3:35 and 5:35PM.

A stroll through the streets will reveal other beautiful old buildings. Two in Osterstrasse house the Museum Hameln (open daily except Monday), with a collection of religious art, local history, and Pied Piper lore.

Excursion

Hämelschenburg, about 7 miles south of Hameln, is a magnificent example of the Weser Renaissance style. The castle (guided tours April to October, closed Mondays) was built between 1588 and 1618 in a horseshoe shape.

North of Hameln is **Fischbeck** (5 miles), where there is a convent dating from the 10th century. The church is 12th-century and has a fine Romanesque crypt.

Wartime sorrow
The poet Max Herrmann Neisse used the story of the Pied Piper to express the sorrow of the wartime evacuation of children: "So dead are squares and gardens now like Hameln after the rat catcher's revenge: the children have all left us, a mother's heart is trembling under every roof."

"Rat pastries"

Pied Piper play
Thanks to the Pied Piper legend, immortalized by Goethe and then in verse by the English poet Robert Browning, Hameln has become famous far beyond Germany. Every Sunday afternoon from mid-May to mid-September, between noon and 12:30, a Pied Piper play is performed on the terrace of the Hochzeitshaus.

Local children play the part of rats, lured away by the Piper's music

The brothers Grimm

Northern Hessen, around Kassel, is the heartland of the folk tales collected by Jacob and Wilhelm Grimm. Born near Frankfurt, they spent their early caeers (1805–30) as court librarians at Kassel, where they concieved a passion for folklore and spent many years collecting their material orally from country people. Jacob was the scholar, Wilhelm the poet who put the tales into readable form. After their death, other writers tried to make the tales less frightening to small children.

Harz witches

The Harz is famed for its witch legends. The eve of May 1 is believed to be the Walpurgisnacht, the night of the witches' sabbath on the Brocken (3,746 feet), the highest mountain in the region; this occasion features as an episode in Goethe's *Faust*.

There is a strange mixture of the comic and the tragic in German folklore—the piper of Hameln who charmed the rats away, then, because he was not properly paid, took the children with him, too; Tannhäuser, the knight who abandoned his vows and went into a strange mountain to spend the rest of his days in the company of Venus. The most celebrated mountain in Germany is the Kyffhauser, east of Göttingen, where the emperor Frederick Barbarossa slumbers in a hidden cavern, radiant with gold and jewels. His great red beard has grown almost three times around the stone table at which he sits. A shepherd once strayed into the cavern and spoke to the emperor, who told him that he must remain there until the ravens cease to fly around the peak outside.

Traditionally, the 16th-century Dr. Johann Faust, a mountebank who traveled throughout Germany but who is particularly associated with the city of Erfurt, sold his soul to the devil in return for knowledge of science and alchemy, and died with his neck being wrung by an archdemon. The devil was, however, outwitted at Cologne, for the great cathedral was built there supposedly according to a plan drafted by him as a lure to gain the soul of the architect. The clever architect came to a rendezvous carrying a crucifix, which kept the devil at bay while he snatched the document.

In many parts of the country there are traditions of the *Wilde Jagd* (wild hunt), a ghostly cavalry crashing through the forests to the accompaniment of trumpets and shouts. This is a survival of the cult of the great Teutonic deity Odin.

The transfer from paganism to Christianity, too, is represented in various legends, such as that of the Drachenfels, a mountain near Bonn, where a wicked fire-breathing dragon tried to seize a beautiful Christian maiden but was hurled by the girl's prayers into the river below.

The Rhine is the most venerable of European rivers. According to legend, a treasure trove lies hidden in it; the secret was known only to the last two Nibelung heroes, who refused to divulge it despite torture and death. When the sun shines on the Rhine, the reflection of this treasure can be seen, but none of it can be found. Old lore also tells of Charlemagne, who was especially

Figures from folklore:
*Red Riding Hood
(opposite page); the
Valiant Tailor and
Giant (left); and the
Goose Girl (above)*

121

partial to a castle that he had at Ingelheim. When he
noticed that the snow melted quickly on the hills of
Rüdesheim, west of Mainz, he established fine
vineyards there, and now his spirit can be seen on
spring nights, blessing the vines. A predilection for wine
was also shown by the 14th-century emperor Wenzel,
who once feasted in a beautiful meadow at Rhens,
south of Koblenz, and was so impressed with a cask of
fiery wine from Bacharach that he sold his realm for it.

At Bingen, in the 10th century, lived Hatto, a bishop
who was so rapacious that in time of famine he refused
food to the starving multitude. By divine punishment his
palace was infested with mice. To escape the pests, he
retired to a tower in the Rhine, but he was pursued
there by the mice and devoured by them. More
fortunate was a prisoner in Frankfurt long ago, who was
offered his freedom if he could hit a weathercock on a
tower in the wall of that city with nine consecutive shots
from his musket. He succeeded, leaving holes in the
weathercock in the perfect shape of the figure 9.

At Darmstadt, a story is told of a poor and inept knight
stopping to pray at a roadside statue of the Virgin Mary.
He fell into a faint, and while he remained there, the
Virgin took on his appearance and won the laurels at a
great tournament.

A fine deed was performed by the women of
Weisberg, north of Stuttgart, whose town was besieged
during the civil wars of the 12th century. They begged to
be allowed to depart in safety with whatever they could
carry with them. This request was granted, and they
walked unmolested through the enemy lines, each lady
carrying her husband on her back!

Brocken sorcery
Goethe in Faust describes
the sorcery associated with
the Brocken in folklore: "And
when we sail around the top,
first skim the ground, then fill
it up, that all the Brocken
height may be smothered in
swarms of witchery."

HARZ

Langelsheim   Vienenburg   Badersleben

Osterwieck

GOSLAR   Oker

Seesen   *O b e r*   Bad   Heudeber   Gröningen

Harzburg   Halberstadt   Wegeleben

Lautenthal   Hahnenklee   Ilsenburg   Derenburg   Harsleben

Bockswiese   *h*   Wernigerode

Wildemann   *a r z*

Bad Grund   Torfhaus   Brocken   1142m

Clausthal-   Altenau   Elbingerode   Blankenburg   Quedlinburg

Zellerfeld   Oderteich   Thale

Riefenbeek   Schierke   Rappbode-   Bad   Gernrode

Stausee   Suderode

Osterode   Sankt Andreasberg   Braunlage   Ellend   Ballenstedt

Sieber   Tanne   Hasselfelde   Friedrichsbrunn

Hohegeiss   Harzgerode

Herzberg   Zorge   Benneckenstein   Stiege

Giebold...   Bad   Güntersberge

Lauterberg   Walkenried   *600m*   *U n t e r h a r z*   Wippra

Bad Sachsa   Ellrich   Stolberg   Wippra

Morungen

Duderstadt   *Helme*   Nordhausen   Rottleberode

Sangerhausen

Silver lining
The Harz region has a strong mining tradition associated with gold and silver, and for this reason the mountains were once known as the "Treasury of the Emperors." Clausthal-Zellerfeld was a busy mining town until the last mine closed in 1931. Its Oberharzer Museum (Museum of the Upper Harz—closed on Mondays) has displays of tools and explanations of some unusual local mining methods. The local church was built of wood in the 17th century. Amazingly, since its interior furnishings are also all wooden, it has escaped destruction by fire. At Sankt Andreasberg, the *Silberbergwerk* (silver mine) known as Grube Samson (the Samson pit) arranges guided tours (daily except mid-November to mid-December). The mine was in operation from 1521 to 1910. It was reopened in 1951 as a museum.

►► **Harz**

Straddling the old East–West German border, the Harz Mountains, the highest land in northern and central Germany, are a rewarding area for exploration. Summits rise to over 3,280 feet, and although the "Little Switzerland" nickname may be an exaggeration, it contrasts strikingly with the surrounding plains.

On the west side, hotels are efficiently run, restaurants and cafés plentiful, buildings well restored and neat pine forests crossed by well-signposted paths and skiing routes. In the east, everything is catching up fast, and now there is virtually little difference between the two.

The neat spa town of Bad Harzburg

The Harz region comprises two distinct areas—the **Oberharz** (Upper Harz) in the west, containing vast areas of delightful forests and valleys suitable for long refreshing walks, and the **Unterharz** (Lower Harz) in the east, which has more open land scattered with beech forests. The Brocken was situated just east of the boundary between the former German Democratic Republic and the Federal Republic. It is still possible to spot the old border posts where East German guards once stood on the lookout for those trying to escape to the west. It is already difficult to discover where the border once was.

Because it is relatively easy to get to the Harz from a number of large German cities, it has become a popular tourist destination, in both summer and winter. An unpredictable climate, often damp and cold, does not deter the visitors who come for the walking, skiing, and spas. They follow in the footsteps of 19th-century Romantics, who saw the Harz Mountains as the epitome of poetic, myth-steeped landscape.

Since reunification, you can visit this very attractive area without constraint. **Wernigerode▶**, a well-preserved 14th-century town with its very beautiful Rathaus and other half-timbered houses with ornate façades, is packed every weekend, even when the weather is not good. An enormous amount of careful renovation has been achieved in a short time, and more will follow. **Stolberg** also has some superb streets of half-timbered houses. **Quedlinburg▶** with its UNESCO World Heritage status has a superb collection of timber-framed buildings. The spa and health resort of **Bad Harzburg**, a short drive from Goslar, is a good base from which to explore the Harz region.

The highest point of the Harz, the **Brocken▶** (3,746 feet), was in the old forbidden zone close to the border, but now it can be visited again, either on foot or by Brockenbahn to the scene that features in Goethe's *Faust*. You can go up by cable car to the Hexentanzplatz in the lovely **Bode** Valley south of Thale, or visit the giant caves at **Rübeland** with their stalagmites and stalactites, which are also worth exploring.

The Romerkalle waterfall, in the Harz, lies close to the high rocky cliffs of the Bode gorge

123

Walk **From Bad Harzburg (about 12 miles)**

Starting point: Train station at Bad Harzburg. Head for the large parking lot at the cable car. Look for signs to Papenberg (7F, red triangle), then Ahrendsberger Weg to Brockenblick (17K, yellow triangle). From Eiserner Weg to the B4 road to Bastesiedlung, pass along Grenzweg and Kaiserweg (35E, blue dot inside triangle) to Molkenhaus (11A, blue cross) and then return to the parking lot.

Walk **Goslar to Altenau (about 18 miles)**

Starting point: Goslar (50A, blue point)—Bad Harzburg—Panenberg—then look for 71F, red triangle to Ahrendsberger footpath—Salzsteig—Ahrendsberg (17M, green point)—Kalbetal—Kellwassertal—Schwarzenberg—Schultal—and finally Altenau. Take a knapsack with refreshments. It is possible to stay overnight at Altenau (several youth hostels, reasonable pensions, and hotels).

Wilhelmshöhe park

From the rear of Schloss Hohenlohe there's a fine view over the Wilhelmshöhe Schlosspark, as splendid a Romantic landscape park as any in Europe, begun soon after 1700. It is crowned by a vast Hercules statue (copy of the Farnese Hercules in Naples) atop a towering 230-foot gray granite monument. Below it are waterfalls and fountains (activated on certain days in summer) and some charming 18th-century follies—Pluto's Grotto, Devil's Bridge, baroque temples, and the startling gray-pinnacled castle of Löwenburg, which may look medieval but is pure Romantic fake.

Schloss Wilhelmsthal

Just north of Kassel, the pretty rococo Schloss Wilhelmsthal is worth a visit: its ornate interior, designed by Cuvilliés, contains Tischbein portraits of ladies.

▶ **Kassel**

Badly bombed in 1943 and rebuilt in a dull style, the principal city of north Hesse is today an industrial center for engineering, chemicals, etc., and has little charm (its Altstadt has vanished). But its setting amid wooded hills is pleasant, and it is worth visiting for the extravagantly Romantic **Wilhelmshöhe park**▶▶ and for its excellent museums.

The *Landgraves* (counts) of Hesse developed Kassel in the 17th and 18th centuries, creating the great park and encouraging industry. They were avid art collectors—a tradition kept alive today with the famous avant-garde and multimedia Dokumenta exhibition, held every five years since 1955 (next in 2000). One of its patrons was the late Joseph Beuys, who planted 7,000 oak trees in Kassel as an action sculpture. In the town center is the Dokumenta's main venue, the opera house and the curiously shaped Ottoneum, Germany's oldest theater (1606). Best of the nearby museums is the Landesmuseum (early astronomical and scientific instruments, prehistory and an unusual display of wallpapers dating from the 16th century). A small museum nearby is devoted to the Brothers Grimm, who lived and worked in Kassel. The Neue Galerie has 19th- and 20th-century paintings, few of them notable, but there are some attractive canvases by Tischbein, who was born near Kassel.

In the western suburbs is the pink granite **Schloss Hohenlohe,** where the Westphalian king Jerome Bonaparte held lavish court (1807–13). The Schloss contains a large and excellent **museum**▶▶, notable less for its Egyptian, Greek, and Roman antiquities than for its excellent paintings, especially Italian, Flemish, and Dutch (note Teniers's *Peasants' Dance*). Napoleon III was interned here in 1870: as he passed through Aachen the crowd jeered, "*Ab nach Kassel!*"—the origin of today's German phrase, which means "Off we go!"

Kassel's Hesse Museum

*Market day at
Lemgo's Marktplatz,
where old buildings
recall its proud
Hanseatic past*

125

▶▶ Lemgo

One of the best-preserved towns in northern and central
Germany and formerly a member of the Hanseatic
League, Lemgo was once known as the Leipzig of
Westphalia because of its printing presses (Leipzig was
the publishing capital of Germany). In the 15th and 16th
centuries trade with Flanders and England brought wealth
to Lemgo; today signs of this early prosperity are much in
evidence, particularly as the town escaped damage in
World War II. The unusual old Rathaus consists of eight
adjacent buildings dating from different periods. You'll
find many half-timbered houses with a rich variety of
façades in Breitestrasse, the town's main street. At
number 19 there is the **Hexenbürgermeisterhaus▶**
(House of the Witches' Mayor), completed in 1568, a
famous example of the Weser Renaissance style with
characteristic oriel windows. The house gets its name
from Hermann Cothmann, who sentenced 90 women to
death for witchcraft when he was mayor of Lemgo,
from 1666 to 1681. It houses a Heimatmuseum (local
history museum), with a display relating to law and
punishment as they were applied to witchcraft,
including a macabre display of instruments of torture.

The Marienkirche is a Gothic hall church with a
Renaissance organ still in excellent shape, both in sound
and appearance. Take advantage of any concert being
performed in the church. The 13th-century
Nickolaikirche, with its two dissimilar towers, shows
both Romanesque and Gothic work.

▶▶ Münden (Hannoversch Münden)

A delightful old town of narrow streets and black-and-
white half-timbered houses, Münden stands, in the
words of a well-known poem, "where Werra and Fulda
kiss each other," for these rivers meet here, and the
Weserstein, a monumental stone, marks the spot.

Fine Rembrandts
The Staatliche
Kunstsammlungen in Kassel
has an outstanding
collection of paintings by
Rembrandt. The gallery
once boasted 17 canvases
by the artist, but the origins
of six of these are now in
dispute. An undisputed
masterpiece is *Jacob Blessing
the Sons of Joseph,* a late work
of remarkable tenderness.

Dr. Eisenbart
Münden's most famous son, Johann Andreas Eisenbart, was an 18th-century doctor with allegedly miraculous powers. A costume play commemorating his life is performed outdoors on Sundays from mid-May to the end of August.

Scrollwork, pyramids and statues adorn Münden's Rathaus (right), in a town rich in old half-timbered houses

The bridge over the Werra behind the Schloss dates from no later than the 14th century. In the Marktplatz are buildings in Weser Renaissance style, including the very handsome gabled Rathaus. The St. Blasiuskirche is a Gothic hall church with a late-14th-century bronze font

► Münzenberg

You can visit Schloss Münzenberg, about 19 miles north of Frankfurt-am-Main, all year round. (Open Tuesday–Sunday, 10–noon, 2–6 April–October, 10–noon, 2–4 November–March). You will be able to visit the grounds and the fortifications and living quarters. The latter are heavily decorated in the Romanesque style, especially apparent in the windows and the gallery. There is a keep at each end of the complex. The well-maintained grounds are pleasant for a leisurely stroll, and there is a magnificent view from the top of the east tower, which takes in the low-lying Welterau, a region between two upland massifs, the Taunus and the Vogelberg.

Paderborn

This ancient Westphalian town (pop. 123,000) is an active commercial and industrial center. It entered history in 799, when Charlemagne had an important meeting here with Pope Leo III, reaching an agreement that led the following year to the creation of the Holy Roman Empire. The site of the palace where the meeting took place came to light during the rebuilding of the city after World War II. Paderborn's main landmark is its **cathedral▶**, which dates mainly from the 13th century: its Romanesque tower has become the city's emblem. The Bartolomäuskapelle (St. Bartholomew's Chapel), a separate structure north of the cathedral, was Germany's first hall church (11th century). On the exterior of the cathedral, note the Paradiesportal, a 13th-century porch on the south side. Another porch, the Brautportal, bears sculpted scenes from the life of Christ. Just below the church of the Abdinghof monastery are more than 200 warm springs, the source of the little River Pader.

▶ Taunus

Densely clothed in forests, the rolling hills of the Taunus are Germany's richest region of mineral springs. This has resulted in the opening up of several famous spas. The region's proximity to Wiesbaden, Mainz, and Frankfurt-am-Main has helped in its development. There are several good roads giving easy access to the peaks, of which the highest is the **Grosser Feldberg**, an important telecommunications center at 2,886 feet. You can drive near the summit, then climb the tower on top (167 steps) for a grand view, as far as Frankfurt to the south and Westerwald to the north.

The little town of **Königstein im Taunus** is situated on a height well away from the main slope. Its most interesting feature is Burg Königstein, a mighty ruined castle with 16th-century bastions and 17th-century projecting defenses. Built around 1200, it was finally destroyed in 1796.

Bad Homburg▶, in the foothills of the Taunus, used to be one of Europe's most fashionable spas, visited by the kaiser, the prince of Wales, and others (Dostoevsky set *The Gambler* here). Today it has moved somewhat downmarket, but the big Kurpark is still attractive, with a Russian chapel and a Thai temple, gifts from former royal visitors from those lands. In the center are the medicinal springs and lawns and walks. The stately white high-towered 17th-century Schloss was the residence of the Landgraves of Hesse-Homburg and subsequently summer palace of the kings of Prussia. Concerts take place in the Schlosskirche.

North of Bad Homburg, amid pleasant forests, is the *in situ* reconstruction of **Saalburg Roman Camp▶** (open daily), originally guarding the adjacent Limes fortifications, which demarcated the northern extent of Roman occupation (still visible, to varying degrees). Just outside the village of Neu Anspach is the **Freilicht Museum Hessenpark** (open daily except Monday, March to November), with reconstructed Hessian buildings, including a functioning bakery, and workshops that produce crafts.

Paderborn's massive 13th-century cathedral exemplifies, in its interior, the transition from Romanesque to Gothic

127

Right and below: Burg Waldeck has a Witches' Tower, with three prison cells. It stands above the Eder Dam, which was blown up by a four-ton RAF bomb in 1943, causing severe flooding

► Waldeck

Thanks largely to the spa resort of Bad Wildungen, the Waldeck region, just southwest of Kassel, has become one of the most popular tourist areas of central Germany. The countryside is attractive, with dense forests and gentle hills cut through by the course of the River Eder. The most spectacular feature of the locality is the great lake formed behind the Edertalsperre (Eder Dam).

The waters of **Bad Wildungen** are used mainly to treat kidney and gallbladder complaints, and problems of hypertension and metabolism. Peaceful walks cross the Kurpark to the Georg Viktor spring. The Evangelische Stadtkirche (Protestant church), famed for its altarpiece of 1403 by Konrad von Soest, has a 14th-century tower that overlooks the rest of the town. Farther east, the fortified town of **Fritzlar** occupies a site above the River

Eder. Dom St. Petri, founded by St. Boniface in 724, is essentially late Romanesque with baroque additions; the huge crypts are the main feature of the cathedral, predating its reconstruction in 1180. The Marktplatz is also interesting, containing an appealing range of half-timbered buildings.

In the town of **Waldeck** itself, part of the castle of the Waldeck princes (Burg Waldeck) is now a hotel, and down in the vaults is a museum established as a tribute to the House of Waldeck. One of Germany's largest feudal castles, **Burg Waldeck►** was built in the late 12th century and was much added to in subsequent centuries. It was abandoned by the House of Waldeck in the 17th century. The view from the castle terrace is particularly impressive. Below the castle is the Eder Dam with its artificial lake, surrounded by wooded shores.

About an hour's drive away is **Korbach**, with its many old timber houses. The town was formed after two fortified settlements, Altstadt and Neustadt (Old Town and New Town), amalgamated. North of Korbach is **Arolsen**, its regular plan very much the creation of the Waldeck princes who lived here. Their baroque-styled Schloss, which hosts concerts and theater evenings, is at the eastern end of the main street. Built between 1714 and 1724, the palace was inspired by Versailles; some of the rooms were not decorated until 1811.

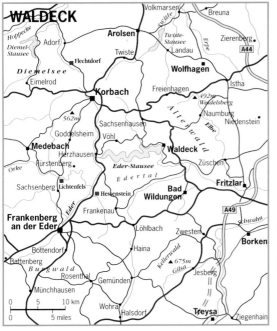

*A view from
Waldeck's castle
toward Eder Dam*

Weserbergland

▶▶ Weserbergland

The Weserbergland is a region of green hills lining both banks of the River Weser. This is one of Germany's most picturesque river valleys, and it is well worth taking four or five days to follow the river's course north. You can either take the passenger boats that glide downstream, or drive along one of two roads: either the Wesertalstrasse (Weser Valley Road) or, on the other side of the river, the B80, called the Deutsche Märchenstrasse (Fairy Tale Road) because it was the route the Brothers Grimm took when they gathered their famous fairy tales. The towns and villages along the way are characterized by the Weser Renaissance style of architecture.

A recommendable route starts at the old town of **Münden** (see page 125), founded in 1170 by Henry the Lion. From there, go through the beautiful Kaufunger Wald, a forest south of Münden, part of which is a nature park, and on to **Mollenfelde**, with its unique Europäisches Brotmuseum (European Bread Museum), where you can trace the history of bread from ancient Egyptian days to the present. Now go north to the romantic 14th-century **Schloss Sababurg**, where the Brothers Grimm used to attend hunting parties. It is said to have been the model for the castle in *The Sleeping Beauty*, and is now a hotel. The nearby zoo, with bears, penguins, etc., is Germany's oldest (1571). Farther on, **Bad Karlshafen** is a beautiful white town, founded in 1699 for French Huguenot settlers, while **Höxter▶** has a townscape of elaborately painted and carved facades, and a magnificent Renaissance alabaster pulpit in the twin-towered Kilianikirche. The Dechanei (Deanery) and Rathaus are two of the most eye-catching buildings, and busy Westerbachstrasse is perhaps the finest street. Nearby, at **Corvey,** you can see the Imperial Abbey (822), with a rare example of an original Carolingian west end. It was in the abbey (now converted to secular use) that the poet Hoffmann von Fallersleben composed the German national anthem.

Continuing north, the Rathaus at **Bodenwerder▶**was once the home of Baron Münchhausen, famous for tall stories about his unbelievable feats (he did actually live, but his true exploits were somewhat tamer than the tales). The building houses a small museum commemorating him. At **Hämelschenburg**, you can visit the splendid Weser Renaissance castle (1588–1610), while the nearby town of **Hameln** is famous for its story of the Pied Piper (see page 119). At the Porta Westfalica, the Weser breaks through the mountains into the north German lowlands and continues north through Bremen and Bremerhaven (see pages 54–6) before flowing into the North Sea.

►   **Wiesbaden**

The capital of Hesse and an important spa, Wiesbaden lies between the Rheingau wine region and the Taunus Mountains. The Romans first used its healing waters and built a forum: one arch now survives from their time. The spa's 26 hot springs have long attracted visitors; today it is popular with jet-setters, artists, and businesspeople, and there is a distinct whiff of wealth. There are countless literary and musical associations. Goethe came here, as did the Russian writers Turgenev and Dostoevsky. Brahms, Wagner, and Robert and Clara Schumann were also visitors.

Wiesbaden hosts a series of annual events, ranging from horse-riding competitions to wine tastings. In May an important festival attracts top foreign theater companies.

Other sights in the town include the Stadtschloss, which became a royal castle in 1866 but which is used today as the seat of the Hesse state parliament. There is an old town hall; and the Städtisches Museum (town museum) contains many marvelous paintings including those by, among others, the Expressionist artist Alexei von Jawlensky, who worked with the Russian artist Kandinsky in Munich and later settled in Wiesbaden, where he died in 1941.

Taking the cure
Wiesbaden's Neoclassical Kurhaus was built in 1906. It houses the Spielbank casino (note the portico with six Ionic columns).
Many thermal baths are located inside hotels, but two can be visited without an overnight stay: the Kaiser Friedrich Bad in Langgasse and the Thermalbad Wiesbaden in Leibniz-strasse. Be warned that saunas in Germany are often unisex, so if you are not used to this, check with the facility beforehand. Make an appointment for a massage in advance if possible, since the masseurs often tend to be booked up.

Wiesbaden's stately Kurhaus, today housing a concert hall, casino, and congress center, has an amazing interior dating from 1907—a mix of neo-byzantine, neo-classical, neo-baroque and art nouveau

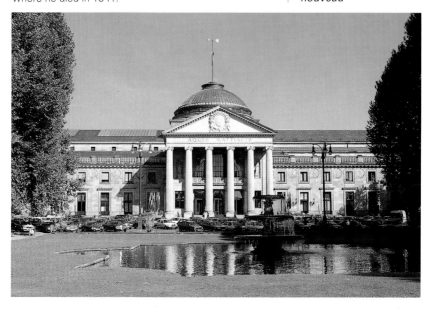

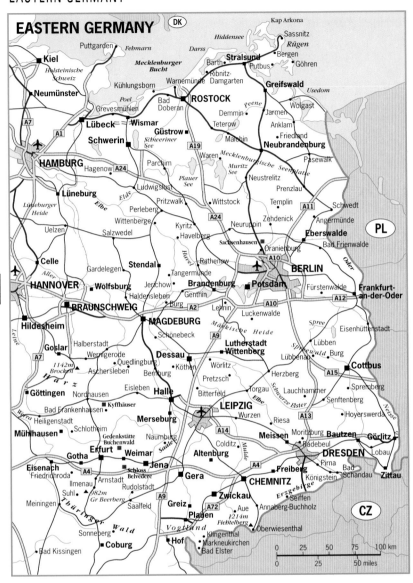

Eastern Germany was not easy for the tourist, in the days when it was the German Democratic Republic (GDR). Visitors were hedged about with visas and customs checks, and controlled on where they could go. But all that has changed totally since the Berlin Wall fell. The east, now fully part of Germany, can be toured freely and is mostly well equipped for tourism.

It richly rewards a visit. It has the great city of Dresden, horribly bombed but still full of culture and history; and its rival, Leipzig, equally interesting. And there are many fine historic smaller towns, such as Schwerin and Stralsund, Quedlinburg and Erfurt. Weimar, home of Goethe, Schiller and Herder, is a major world literary center, at the heart of Germany. The region has many superb museums and fine old palaces and castles, notably the Wartburg at Eisenach, where Martin Luther translated the Bible. In fact, the east produced many of Germany's leading writers, thinkers and musicians—Dürer, Holbein, Bach, Handel, and Wagner were all born or lived here.

In the south is some beautiful scenery, hilly and wooded—the Thüringer Wald, the Harz mountains, and the Erzgebirge where skiing is popular. The north is more flat, but not without charm—such as the great woods, lakes and rivers of the Spreewald and Mecklenburg, and the wide beaches of the Baltic.

The region is being transformed by new investment, everywhere to see—big new factories, shops, and office blocks. The stench of pollution has largely gone, and the ugly old "Trabi" cars have been mostly replaced by Opels or Volkswagens. In many ways the east now looks much like the west: yet below the surface lay differences. Many people are poorer than in the west, and whereas town centers have been renovated, in many suburbs you will still find dereliction and neglect.

This need not trouble the tourist. Nearly all the roads are now up to western standards, and new gas stations are plentiful. As for hotels, there are many large new modern ones, or well-renovated older ones, in the more expensive brackets. Good medium-priced hotels are still less frequent but family pensions are appearing. And you can always find rooms in private homes, at low prices: these can be booked through a tourist office. Restaurants of all kinds are now plentiful, but food is seldom as good as in the west. Lots of lively bars, pubs, and cabarets have sprung up in the towns.

Lastly, a word on language. Russian used to be easterners' main language, and though English is now widely taught, it is less commonly spoken than in the west, at least by older people. But easterners do tend to be friendly to visitors—especially once they realize you are not a west German.

Woodlands of Vogtland (see page 166)

EASTERN GERMANY

134

► Bernburg

Bernburg is interesting mainly for its huge Renaissance castle, with buildings of different styles and ages grouped around a large irregular courtyard; on one side, steep wooded slopes extend down to the River Saale and the lower town. Bernburg also boasts, in both the lower and upper towns, well-kept town walls and streets of 16th- to 18th-century town houses. The outskirts, though, are rundown and industrial.

There is another Renaissance palace situated at **Köthen**, 12 miles to the east. J. S. Bach worked for six years as *Kapellmeister* in the Ludwigsban part of the town; there is a small museum dedicated to him here. Köthen also has some fine aristocratic houses dotted around the town center.

In the other direction, 12 miles west of Bernburg, **Aschersleben** clusters below the 262-foot tower of St. Stephen's, a fine 15th-century Gothic hall church. There are several attractive burghers' houses in the ancient town center.

► ► Brandenburg

Brandenburg is surrounded by numerous attractive lakes along and around the River Havel, an area popular for excursions known as Havelland and famous for its birdlife—reed warblers, marsh harriers, bitterns, storks, herons, and cranes are to be observed in abundance.

Both town and *Land* take their name from the castle known as the Brandenburg, first mentioned in AD 948. It took 200 years before this seemingly impregnable fortress was finally overcome by a warrior prince with the delightful name of Albrecht the Bear. Both the old and new towns remained separate members of the Hanseatic League until 1518, and only joined together in 1715. Huguenot settlers increased the town's prosperity, and in the 20th century it became a major industrial center, consequently heavily bombed during World War II.

Brandenburg's cathedral took seven centuries to complete. It has a 14th-century Bohemian altar, a 13th-century Saxon crucifix, and countless valuable manuscripts. The town hall (1480) has a 16-foot figure of Roland, a symbol of civic rights, dating from 1474.

Bernburg, south of Magdeburg, has an imposing Renaissance castle and 15th-century ramparts

▶▶ **Colditz**

The old town of Colditz, on the River Mulde in central Saxony, has a picturesque town center with an attractive town hall, marketplace and 13th-century parish church. The ancient castle on a hill overlooking the town achieved notoriety during World War II as a formidable prisoner-of-war camp, from where a number of British officers made well-publicized escapes. Since the war the castle has been a hospital but is now being transformed into a museum and a luxury hotel. Mementos of escapees are kept in the town museum, including some false German uniforms, photographic material, and an illicit printing press.

Dessau

Dessau is world-famous among architects and designers as the home of the Bauhaus movement (see panel). The building from which it gets its name was built by Walter Gropius in 1925–6 and still stands—restored in 1977 to something like its former glory—in a suburban avenue 1¼ miles northwest of the center. There are occasional

Above: the White Bridge at Dessau
Top right: Colditz castle

performances and lectures held here. There are also examples of Bauhaus architecture on the outskirts, including a 300-dwelling housing project at Dessau-Törten to the south, but they are hard to find and the buildings themselves are not well preserved. From another era, the neo-classical Schloss Georgium (1780) survives, in a lovely park.

Much of the city center—also famous as the site of the Junkers aircraft factory—was destroyed in the war and has been rebuilt in blocky modern style.

For light relief, make for the baroque castle at **Mosigkau** (5 miles southwest). A guided tour will take you around a fine collection of furniture, porcelain and Dutch paintings; or head for **Wörlizter Park** (10 miles east), modeled in the 18th century on English landscape gardens, dotted with picturesque buildings and crisscrossed with canals and lakes.

The Bauhaus
The Bauhaus movement was founded by the German architect Walter Gropius in Weimar in 1919. His school of art (which moved to Dessau in 1925) became an experimental laboratory for architects, engineers, painters, sculptors, and designers. Gropius's central idea was to bring together esthetics with the needs of an industrial civilization. The function of an object should control the design of its structure. Thus the courses at the Bauhaus school were directed at the creation of forms suitable for mass production.

Semper Opera House, Dresden, recently restored

1945 air raid
On February 13–14, 1945, in the most intensive air raid of the war in Europe, over 2,000 Allied bombers attacked Dresden in three giant waves. In the vast inferno, at least 35,000 civilians were killed, and the city was 60 percent destroyed. The aim was to break German morale. But many critics, even among the Allies, have since argued that so cruel a raid, so near the war's end, on a town of little strategic value, was simply not justified.

▶▶▶ **Dresden**

Dresden used to be one of the loveliest cities of central Europe—"Florence on the Elbe," it was called. It has never quite recovered from the great air raid of 1945 (see panel) and many of its fine baroque buildings still wear a stunned, blackened look. In the 1950s and '60s, much of the city was rebuilt in a blocky, Stalinist style, impressive in its scale and self-confidence, but not much fun to explore. Even today, many of the outlying areas are grimy and derelict.

For all this, Dresden is not to be missed. Enough of its enormous cultural heritage remains, providing plenty of worthwhile sights and famous works of art. Most of them date back to the city's heyday as capital of Saxony, especially to the reign of the aptly named Augustus the Strong in the late 17th and early 18th centuries. Even at the height of the cold war, considerable efforts were made by the East German authorities to restore the most important of those monuments that were not smashed to pieces. Since unification, this process has accelerated. Encouraged by Dresden's revived status as capital of the state of Saxony, western investors have poured money into building projects, which have begun to transform the center and give the city a renewed claim to its old reputation for culture, commerce and gracious living. Germany's second-largest bank, the Dresdner, is again proudly present in the city where it was born in 1872.

What to see The Brühlsche Terrasse, a gracious, elevated terrace on the south bank of the Elbe, and known locally as "Europe's balcony," lies at the heart of the historic part of Dresden, surrounded by gaunt, dignified buildings in a range of styles. Immediately behind it, the stark, windowless remains of the 18th-century Stadtschloss▶ are a reminder of the reconstruction work yet to be done—the castle is due to

be reopened for Dresden's 800th anniversary in 2006. The neighboring **Frauenkirche** (Church of Our Lady)▶ is Germany's largest baroque and Protestant church. Ever since 1944 it was kept as a ruin, in memory of the horrors of the bombing: but now at last it is to be expensively rebuilt in its old style. The **Hofkirche** (royal cathedral), which was built in 1739–55 in Italian baroque style contains a fine mid-18th-century organ by Silbermann.

Facing the cathedral across the square stands the **Semper Opera House▶▶**, built by Gottfried Semper in 1838–41 and subject to a huge restoration program by the German Democratic Republic. It was eventually reopened in 1985, to reveal a very high standard of comfort and facilities as well as painstaking attention to period detail.

A few steps away is Dresden's most famous sight, the **Zwinger▶▶▶** (keep), a complex of baroque-style pavilions grouped around a graceful, relaxed courtyard. It gets its name from the ancient fortifications that used to

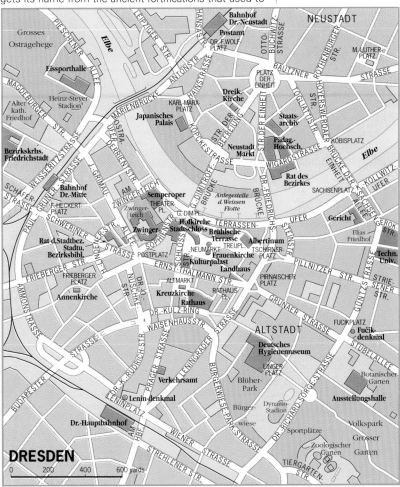

DRESDEN REGION

Map showing Dresden region with locations including Meissen, Coswig, Radebeul, Radeberg, Bischofswerda, Neukirch, Dresdener Heide, Arnsdorf, Stolpen, Lausitzer Bergland, Wilsdruff, A4, Nossen, Siebenlehn, Mohorn, Tharandt, Freita, Heidenau, Hohnstein, Neustadt, CZ, Kurort Hartha, Dohna, Pirna, Stadt Wehlen, Bad Schandau, Sebnitz, Klingenberg, Kreischa, Königstein, Krippen, Hinterhermsdorf, FREIBERG, Dippoldiswalde, Reinhardtsgrimma, Berggiesshübel, Liebstadt, Bad Gottleuba, Rosenthal, Schmilka, Branderbisdorf, Glashütte, Elbsandsteingebirge, 10 km, 5 miles

Detail from the Zwinger

occupy the site: the buildings themselves date from 1711 to 1728 but have been added to and altered over the years. They contain a treasure house of museums (some closed Mondays, some Thursdays), including a world-famous porcelain collection and museums of science and zoology. Now that restoration work has been completed, the Gemäldegalerie Alter Meister (Gallery of Old Masters) has returned from its temporary home in the **Albertinum►►►** (see below) to the Semperbau at the Zwinger (open Tuesday–Sunday). The collection includes Raphael's *Sistine Madonna*, Giorgione's *Sleeping Venus*, and works by Canaletto (many of them scenes painted on his visits to Dresden), Rembrandt, Vermeer, and Titian.

Behind the Zwinger you will find the **Langer Gang** (long passage), a 16th-century arcade with Italian-style white pillars. On the outside, it bears a huge 19th-century porcelain frieze depicting Saxon princes. Nearby are two more museums, of geology and transport.

Back by the Brühlsche Terrasse stands one of Dresden's most important galleries, the **Albertinum**, a 16th-century building that once served as an arsenal and which currently contains one of the world's most impressive art collections. One part of the building houses the Gemäldegalerie Neuer Meister (Gallery of New Masters, closed Thursdays), which includes pictures by Dix, Liebermann, and several French Impressionists. Another, the Grünes Gewölbe (Green Vault, also closed Thursdays), contains the royal collection of silver, gold and jewelry, as well as the star of the show, *The Court of Delhi on the Birthday of the Great Mogul*, a set of 132 gold, enamel, and bejeweled painted figures. Further exhibitions include one of the most valuable sculpture collections to be found outside Italy, as well as over 200,000 coins, medals, notes, and royal seals.

Farther away from the river, the scene becomes bleaker, marked by big blocks and wide open spaces. One of these, the **Altmarkt** (old market), was the bustling center of a great city before it was razed in 1945; it has now recovered some of its bustle, but the charm will be harder to restore. In its southeast corner stands the **Kreuzkirche** (Church of the Holy Cross), which dates back to 1764–92 and is the oldest church

The river Elbe at Dresden, heavily polluted in GDR days, has now been cleaned up

within the line of the city walls. It is home to Dresden's famous choir, the Kreuzchor, which performs here most Saturday afternoons. To the south of the Altmarkt, you can continue along modern, pedestrianized **Prager Strasse**, along which stand the city's larger restaurants and hotels.

There's a little more of the flavor of prewar Dresden across the Elbe in **Dresden-Neustadt**, which has many imposing 19th-century buildings and centers on a car-free main boulevard, the Hauptstrasse.

Excursions The best bet is to take a paddle steamer (the **Weisse Flotte** steamers leave from the landing platforms by Terrassenufer) along the Elbe to some of the worthwhile destinations just outside Dresden. One option is the old town of **Meissen** (see page 152).

A very pleasant alternative is to go upstream to **Schloss Pillnitz►** (6 miles southeast), a charmingly relaxed grouping of summer palaces built in Chinese style and dating from 1723; it's set in a beautiful wooded section of the Elbe Valley and is surrounded by a small park. Farther upstream is **Pirna** (12 miles from Dresden), an ancient market town straddling the river. Its market square boasts fine medieval houses, and the Marienkirche (St. Mary's Church) is one of the finest late Gothic hall churches in Saxony. Pirna is known as the gateway to Saxon Switzerland (Sächsische Schweiz; see pages 155–6).

The **Dresdener Heide** (Dresden Heath) starts on the northeastern edge of town and is easily reached by public transportation. It's a relaxed area of open woodland, crossed with well-marked paths.

The Grosser Garten
The Grosser Garten (or Volkspark), a large 17th-century park about 1 mile southeast of the center of Dresden, includes a baroque pleasure palace and the city's zoo. Running through the park is the Parkeisenbahn, an enormous model railroad with five stations and 3½ miles of track. The Deutsches Hygiene Museum, built for the 2nd International Hygiene Exhibition (held in Dresden in 1930), is best known for its glass models of a woman, a cow, and a horse (open Saturday to Thursday).

Property claims

Eisenach's big department store, Schwager, is back in the hands of its Schwager family owners. It was expropriated by the GDR in 1950, and they fled west: now they have reclaimed it, and it booms. But of the east's million or so property claims, few have been solved so easily: some are by Jewish former owners, dating from Nazi times. This huge and complex property problem has deterred investors and hampered renovation. If, in a street of neatly restored houses, one remains decrepit, it may be that the lawyers can't decide who owns it.

▶▶ Eisenach

Despite its small size, this city nestling in wooded hills at the northwest end of the Thüringer Wald has an enormous importance in the history of German civilization. This is because of its position at the foot of the Wartburg▶▶, a spectacular hilltop castle dating back to the 11th century. It became an early center for music and poetry, hosting the traditional *Sängerkrieg*, a competition for singer-poets, in the early 13th century— subsequently immortalized by Richard Wagner in his opera *Tannhäuser*. Wartburg was also famous as the residence of Martin Luther when he was preparing the first German-language translation of the Bible. It is a stiff climb to the top from the town, or you can go up by shuttle bus, or children can ride up by donkey. You can drive to the top, but the parking lot there gets full early, and is not free. A free ticket will get you into the castle's inner courtyard and up the South Tower for a spectacular view; you must then pay if you want a guided tour of the interior (avoid long waits by reserving a fixed time), taking in Luther's study, the castle's art collection and various halls, including the enormous Festsaal (banqueting hall) decorated with murals by Moritz von Schwind in the 19th century.

Back down in the town, a major point of interest is the J. S. Bach house, commemorating the birthplace of Eisenach's most famous son. As well as a collection of music and instruments, and a very pretty garden, the museum offers short recitals on some of the keyboard instruments. Nearby is the 15th-century house, prettily restored, where Luther stayed as a student: it too is now a museum, with details of his translation of the Bible. In a different vein, Eisenach also has an automobile museum, housed in a small pavilion close to the center. This contains examples of Wartburg cars, produced at Eisenach in GDR days in a huge factory with 8,000 workers. It is now run by Opel.

One of Eisenach's attractions is its big squares surrounded by graceful houses: in the center of the largest (the Markt) stands St. George's Church, which has an unusual galleried interior decorated with murals.

Old Wartburg models in Eisenach's car museum: GDR citizens often had to wait 10 years to buy one

An old street of
medieval Erfurt,
neatly restored
under the new
regime

►► Erfurt

The capital and largest town of Thüringia, Erfurt has distinct charm despite some less attractive development. But at its core lies an extensive and, for the most part, well-preserved medieval town, crowned by its imposing cathedral and neighboring St. Severin's. The church's pointed spires loom over the large, irregularly shaped Domplatz (cathedral square), which is used for fun-fairs and markets of all sorts.

The **cathedral►**, reached up a flight of 70 steps from the square, dates back to the mid-12th century and was built in the form of a Romanesque basilica, though it gained a Gothic choir in the mid-14th century. It contains some fine works of art, including a Romanesque altar, carved wooden stalls, and 14th- to 15th-century stained glass. The largest bell in eastern Germany, the "Gloriosa," hangs in the middle tower. The 14th-century St. Severin's boasts some of Germany's finest early Gothic architecture and a splendid 15th-century font.

Down in the town, there's a wealth of fine buildings and streets to see. Some of the ancient houses are still in poor shape, but many others have now been renovated, especially around the two pedestrianized main squares, the Anger and the Fischmarkt. Close by is the fascinating **Krämerbrücke►** (Shopkeepers' bridge), an extremely pretty bridge over the wide and shallow River Gera. Lined with tall, narrow half-timbered houses, it is the only bridge of its kind north of the Alps.

Thüringian rivalries
Thüringia, calling itself "Germany's green heart," is known for its lovely scenery, its sausages, and its historic cities of culture. Long a maze of separate little kingdoms and duchies, it is now a united *Land* (state). But the rivalries continue. Weimar, the former capital, resents the new capital, Erfurt, till recently part of Prussia.

Many antiques shops fill the St. Andreas quarter of old Erfurt

Lignite pollution
Lignite used to provide 83 percent of the GDR's electricity, and much of the open-cast mining of this "brown coal" was done in the Erzgebirge hills, where millions of tons of dust were scattered and the giant craters resembled a bomb site. Many of the mines have now been closed, and the blighted landscape is being replanted with grass and trees.

Nowadays, humbler trades in the narrow cobbled street that passes between the houses have given way to antiques shops. A few streets away is the restored 13th-century Augustiner church and monastery which once included Martin Luther among its novices.

A couple of miles southwest of the center, the 15th-century (but much altered) Cyriaksburg castle stands in leafy grounds, part of which are given over to a large permanent museum and exhibition devoted to all forms of gardening and horticulture—a long-established Thüringian local industry.

► **Erzgebirge**
The Erzgebirge is a range of mountains stretching for 88 miles along the Czech frontier from the Vogtland (see page 166) to Saxon Switzerland (see pages 155–6). It includes the highest point in eastern Germany, the Fichtelberg (3,982 feet).

The western part of the range is characterized by steep-sided valleys and thick forests, dotted with villages and small industrial towns; the eastern part, to the east of the River Flöha, consists mainly of high plateaus and is more open in appearance. The whole area gets its name (*Erz* means ore) from the mineral ores that have been mined here since the 12th century, starting with silver, tin, and lignite. The area was one of the main vacation spots of the old GDR, despite the pollution caused by open-cast lignite mining. This has now mostly ended, and foreign as well as local tourists now come for the good skiing, hiking, and walking.

As successive mines became exhausted, local inhabitants turned their hands to a variety of crafts, and the area is well known for its toy-making industry.

What to see Annaberg-Buchholz is the largest town in the area and has a spectacular hall church, the biggest in Saxony, dating from 1499–1525, with a fine main portal and several beautiful altars. The nearby town of **Frohnau** (1¼ miles west) has an unusual industrial museum, Frohnauer Hammer (open all year, closed Monday, October to April), which was originally (1436) a corn mill but which was then converted to a silver and iron forge in 1621. To the south, **Ober-Wiesenthal** is a winter-sports resort at the foot of the Fichtelberg; the 3,982-foot summit can be reached by cable car for a fine panoramic view.

In the eastern part of the Erzgebirge, **Seiffen►** has been the center of the Saxon toy industry since the 18th century. This remains active today, turning out hand-carved Christmas pyramids, wooden nutcracker figures in local costume, and much else. You can watch the craftsmen at work, and see details of the industry and exhibits detailing its significance to social history, in the large Spielzeugmuseum (Toy Museum, open daily) which shows many of the traditional items made in the area. The Freilichtmuseum (Open Air Museum, closed

Monday, April to October on the Deutscheinsiedel road out of town, shows furniture and exhibits on the folk history of the region.

► ► Görlitz

Görlitz is a large and extremely ancient city which once spread across both banks of the River Neisse but which, following World War II, found itself straddling the German–Polish border.

The German part of town contains most of the old center, which—though shabby in parts—has many crooked, narrow streets spectacularly rich in medieval buildings, both secular and religious. The most interesting examples are grouped around the part-arcaded Untermarkt (lower market square), which has a notably fine collection of Renaissance and baroque town houses; keep a lookout particularly for the house at no. 22, which has an unusual portal.

Görlitz on the Polish border, known for its optical and mechanical industries, has a fortified 14th-century gateway close to its upper market place

*The town hall clock
in Görlitz*

In nearby Neissestrasse, house no. 29 (the "Biblische-Haus") dates from 1570 and bears bas-relief scenes from the Old and New Testaments. The Rathaus (town hall) is in an unusual mixture of styles, dating mostly from the 14th and 16th centuries.

▶ Gotha

The center of Gotha is dominated by the 360-room 17th-century baroque castle of Friedenstein, which stands on a hill above the main square. Ranged around a large, square courtyard, the massive white-painted, arcaded buildings incorporate a museum of local history and cartography, a theater, and a library. The town's other highlight is the long, narrow Hauptmarkt (market square), which stretches down the hill. At the top of the square is a group of restored Renaissance buildings, and the neo-Renaissance red-and-white town hall. A local firm used to publish the famous *Almanach de Gotha*, a guide to Germany's nobility.

Excursion

Friedrichroda is a small, relaxed resort on the edge of the Thüringian Forest: a 10-mile ride on the narrow-gauge Waldbahn (forest train) takes you through the fields and backyards of this pretty and unspoiled area.

▶ Greifswald and Usedom

Greifswald lies on the eastern side of Mecklenburg-Vorpommern, not far from the Greifswalder Bodden, a shallow, virtually tideless bay of the Baltic. In the 13th century, monks founded this settlement near their coastal monastery of Eldena. In 1278 the town became part of the Hanseatic League. In 1648, after the Thirty Years' War, Greifswald was granted to Sweden, only to return to Germany in 1815 under Prussian rule.

Greifswald has fine buildings, notably an originally Gothic town hall (rebuilt in the 18th century after a fire), the 13th-century Marienkirche, half-timbered St. Spiritus Hospital, and town houses with elegant gabled façades. The painter Caspar David Friedrich was born here in 1774 and spent much of his life here. His evocative paintings of coastal seascapes and the ruins of Eldena Monastery provide a record of the landscape as it was early in the last century. Some of his best work can be seen in the Charlottenburg Palace in Berlin.

Usedom Not far from Greifswald, across the straits of the Peene Strom, lies Usedom, a strangely shaped island that straddles the Polish–German border. Wollin, the eastern part of the island, is Polish territory. There are excellent beaches, with small seaside resorts at Bansin, Heringsdorf, Ahlbeck, and Zinnowitz (the last overlooked by a castle), and attractive inland lakes such as the Gothenesee and the Schmollensee. Eighty-five percent of the surface area of Usedom, predominantly meadowland, woods, bays, and dunes, is protected landscape, much of it nature reserve. The area enjoys considerable peace and tranquillity. In clear weather there are views to the southeast tip of Rügen, while the border crossing at Ahlbeck brings neighboring Poland's Swinemünde within easy access.

Peenemünde
Peenemünde, on the northern extremity of Usedom, was the unlikely place where, during World War II, the physicist Werner von Braun developed and tested the notorious V1 and V2 rockets. This high technology was put to better use in postwar times when von Braun, now part of the U.S. space research team, helped to develop rockets for the U.S. space program and the successful first flight to the moon.

145

Greifswald is a handsome old university town on a flat plain close to the Baltic

Leftish sculptors
Heiligenstadt was the home of the great 16th-century sculptor and wood-carver Tilman Riemenschneider, whose works can be seen today in Franconia. He was imprisoned for backing the Peasants' Revolt. In our own century, the radical humanist sculptor Ernst Barlach suffered under the Nazis. He came from Güstrow (near Rostock), where some of his work is on view.

Halle's Rathaus, itself no beauty, presides over an old town of fine buildings with a great musical and intellectual tradition

► **Halle**

Now a major industrial and cultural center, Halle is one of eastern Germany's oldest cities and was the birthplace of the composer Handel (see opposite). Another more recent son of Halle is the former German Foreign Minister, Hans Dietrich Genscher, who did much in 1990 to persuade the Russians to accept German unification. Halle's wealth came originally from the mining of salt. The city's Halloren and Saline Museum brings much of that past to life. Halle's most striking landmark is the four-towered, 16th-century church of Unser Lieben Frauen in the market square. Nearby is the Roter Turm (Red Tower), which became a symbol to the people of Halle of their struggle against feudal domination. The Moritzburg, now the city's art gallery, is a late 15th-century Gothic fortress, built as a stronghold for the powerful archbishops of Magdeburg against insurrection. In the Alta Markt is a fountain of a boy with a donkey, the town's historic symbol.

► **Heiligenstadt**

A small, quiet resort on the River Leine, Heiligenstadt boasts a long, partly pedestrianized main street dominated by the parish church of St. Martin. The town center was partly destroyed by fire in 1759, but several half-timbered and Renaissance houses survive from earlier times, among them the 15th-century Mainzer house and the baroque Rathaus.

Set at the center of the hilly and part-forested Eichsfeld region, Heiligenstadt has long been popular as a place for recuperation.

Handel

■ **Georg Friedrich Handel was born in 1685 (the same year as J. S. Bach) in the city of Halle, where his statue now surveys the market square. His complete mastery of composition is evident from the fact that he wrote 46 operas, over 30 oratorios and a large number of cantatas, concerti grossi, pieces of sacred music, and various other instrumental and vocal works ...■**

Against the wishes of his father, a noted barber-surgeon, Handel became organist at Halle Cathedral at the age of 17, while studying law. In 1706 he left for four years in Italy, where he became known as a virtuoso harpsichordist and violinist, earning himself the title of *il caro Sassone* ("the dear Saxon"). He also wrote his first operas—including *Almira*—in the Italian style.

Despite making a poor impression (he was always in London) on the elector of Hannover, to whose court he had been appointed Kapellmeister in 1710, Handel followed his master when the elector succeeded Queen Anne to the English throne as

George I in 1714. The *Water Music* may even have been written to appease his patron. If this was the composer's aim, he was certainly successful, since, on his succession to the monarchy, George I doubled Handel's pension.

In London Handel busied himself in the composition of more operas, with mixed fortunes. This patchy operatic success caused him to experiment with a new musical form, the oratorio. In this new area success was immediate and undoubted: Handel conducted no fewer than 15 separate oratorio concerts in 1735 alone. In 1737 he suffered a stroke; nevertheless, the next five years saw him complete many of his finest works, including *Saul* (1739), *Israel in Egypt* (1739), and *Messiah* (1742). His health continued to deteriorate and in 1759 he died; he is buried in Poet's Corner in London's Westminster Abbey.

147

Right: Georg Friedrich Handel, master of the oratorio

Above: Handel's house in Halle, where the composer was born in 1685

Old and new architecture in Jena

148

Jena

The vast modern housing complex of Lobeda, which marches along the valley connecting the center of Jena with the highway, makes a sad introduction to this ancient university town, famous also for its optical industry started by Carl Zeiss in the mid-19th century. Zeiss's name and work are commemorated in the planetarium (the world's oldest working one), located in the botanic garden just north of the center; the city also has an optical museum.

Jena has illustrious associations with some of the greatest figures in German culture: Hegel and Schiller taught at the university, and Goethe was a frequent visitor to the city.

One end of the enormous market square, lined by the 14th-century town hall and Gothic St. Michael's Church, has some charm, but with most of the rest of the center rebuilt in monumental modern style, topped by a 26-story cylindrical university building, the city is heavily dependent on its past glories.

▶▶▶ Leipzig

Founded by Slavic settlers in the 7th and 8th centuries, by the 10th century Urbs Libzi, or the town by the lime trees, had become a German stronghold and a flourishing center where the great east–west and north–south trade routes intersected on the Thüringian-Saxon plain. Today Leipzig is Saxony's largest city, a major industrial, shopping, cultural and administrative center with 550,000 inhabitants, renowned for its long associations with trade, science, humanism, music and publishing, as well as for its twice-yearly trade fair.

Leipzig's university was founded in 1409. Martin Luther preached here many times and disputed passionately with his opponents. Books were printed for the first time in Leipzig in 1481, laying the foundations for the city's long publishing tradition. Music was first printed in Leipzig in 1754. Johann Sebastian Bach worked as cantor and director of music at the Thomaskirche for the last 27 years of his life until his death in the city in 1750. A bronze plaque in the church marks his grave. Richard Wagner was born in the city in 1813, but later had to flee

Museums and memorials
There's a lot to see in Leipzig. The former Imperial Court of Justice, where Hitler set the phoney Reichstag fire trial, now holds a museum noted for its Dutch and German paintings (Cranach, Friedrich, etc.). You can see the farmhouse, now a museum, where Schiller wrote his *Ode to Freedom*. Or inspect the huge, hideous Massacre of the People Memorial, completed in 1913 to mark the 1813 battle at Leipzig where the Prussians and allies defeated Napoleon—and 100,000 perished.

Instant art: a street artist produces a portrait to order in Leipzig, where there are long-established links with many branches of the arts

The Nikolaikirche
Protest against the 40-year-long Communist dictatorship in East Germany came to a head in the late 1980s in Leipzig in regular prayers for peace at the Nikolaikirche, led by Neues Forum—New Forum—an alliance of Christian and liberal-democratic protesters. Candles were lit and carried by thousands of people of the city as a potent symbol of peaceful protest, which helped to bring about the downfall of the hated Honecker regime. Prominent among dissidents was the celebrated Leipzig conductor Kurt Masur. The Nikolaikirche, built between the 13th and 16th centuries, has an inspiring 18th-century interior that symbolizes hope—elegant white columns soaring upward and bursting into delicate green palm fronds at their apex, crowned by a ceiling in shades of pink and green, complemented by stately white pews.

for his life for supporting radical views. The world-famous Leipzig Gewandhaus orchestra is based in the city at the Neues Gewandhaus concert hall.

Much of the city center is now traffic-free, with fine old squares, gardens, courtyards and shopping arcades opening out of the central pedestrianized areas. Despite some brutal rebuilding of office blocks, apartments and the university in modern concrete, many superb buildings remain. The richly decorated railway station is one of the most impressive in Germany. The **Old Town Hall▶** houses the Alte Börse, the old Stock Exchange, built between 1678 and 1687 and one of the city's loveliest baroque buildings, newly restored. Many other fine baroque façades can be seen in the city center, for example in the Katherinenstrasse.

Goethe in Leipzig
Goethe studied law in Leipzig as a young man, and set a scene of *Faust* in Auerbach's Cellar, still to be found in the Madlerpassage, where Mephistopheles is made to ride out on a barrel of wine. Goethe was also one of the celebrated visitors to the famous coffeehouse called the Kaffeebaum, in the Kleine Fleischergasse.

Modern sculptures adorn Leipzig's trendy new central shopping area

The medieval monastery of Our Lady in Magdeburg, a harmonious Romanesque ensemble

The Magdeburg hemispheres
A 17th-century experiment by Magdeburg's scientific mayor, the physicist Otto von Guericke (1602–86), who wanted to prove the strength of atmospheric pressure (the force exerted by the air around us), has ensured that Magdeburg's fame has spread worldwide. Von Guericke put together two metal hemispheres and removed the air from inside them, to form a vacuum. When 16 horses (eight tied to each hemisphere) failed to pull them apart, this conclusively proved his thesis.

▶ **Magdeburg**

As early as AD 968, this archbishop's seat was the center of the church's mission to Christianize the Slavic population. The city's original constitution of the same date became known as the Magdeburg Laws, and was used as a model for the establishment of numerous other towns in eastern Germany. Magdeburg's 13th-century **cathedral**▶▶ is the oldest great Gothic religious building in Germany, and its scale is a testimony to the power and influence of the city in the middle ages. Superb statues of the Wise and Foolish Virgins stand by the Paradise Doorway on the north side. Inside are remarkable seated statues (13th century) of Otto I and his wife Edith.

Though around 90 percent of Magdeburg, including part of the cathedral itself, was destroyed by Allied bombing in World War II, its central areas have been rebuilt and elegantly laid out with boulevards and shops, and many of the historic buildings have been carefully reconstructed or restored.

The Monastery of Our Lady, north of the Domplatz, now houses a collection of medieval wood sculptures and also the national collection of contemporary small-scale sculptures. A wine cellar in the Buttergasse dates from 1200 and was discovered only by chance during rebuilding operations.

In the old market square, the former heart of the city, is a baroque town hall and the Eulenspiegel Fountain, a modern tribute to the famous medieval folk hero and prankster Till Eulenspiegel. The baroque composer Georg Philipp Telemann (1671–1767) was born in Magdeburg, and the present-day concert hall bears his name.

Links between the River Elbe and the Mittellandkanal made in the 1930s allowed river traffic from the Ruhr to reach the Elbe, and Magdeburg as a result became an important inland port, increasing its trading and industrial importance. Cruise boats of the Weisse Flotte now operate from and through the city between Hamburg and Dresden.

►► **The Mecklenburgische Seenplatte and Muritz National Park**

The Mecklenburgische Seenplatte (Mecklenburg Lake Plateau) consists of over a thousand lakes, residue from the last Ice Age, when retreating glaciers left great moraines—banks of sand and pebblelike detritus. The ice also carved out channels and basins through which escaping water formed rivulets and waterfalls. Storms carried loose sand into hilly dunes, which, as the climate warmed, became carpeted with woodland to create an undulating landscape patterned with small lakes.

The 120-square-mile Müritz National Park was founded in October 1990 from Germany's largest nature reserve. It extends from Waren to beyond Neustrelitz and from the Müritzsee's eastern shore to the source of the Havel. Sixty-five percent of the area is forest, 25 percent moorland, and water, 6 percent meadow and grazing land, and around 4 percent currently under cultivation. About 200 years ago the River Elbe was widened and deepened, causing the water level of the Müritzsee to sink by 6 feet, so that the low-lying eastern banks of the lake dried out, with consequent changes to the natural flora.

The Müritzsee, or Morcze (small sea), as it was known by the Slavs, is one of 117 lakes in the national park. It is 20 feet deep and 17 miles long and is Germany's second-largest lake. Conditions on the lake area can be very severe, particularly in February, when blocks of floating ice are a common occurrence; heavy thunderstorms and impenetrable mist can also be a hazard at other times of the year. Carpets of beautiful white water lilies cover stretches of water in the

Relics of the past
Archeological remains indicate that the Mecklenburgische Seenplatte was already settled by Mesolithic (Middle Stone Age) times. Neolithic stone graves, pottery and flint axes, Bronze Age jewelry, a Roman import of a richly decorated silver bowl in Iron Age times, and 7th-century evidence of Slavic settlement bear witness to the area's complex history of settlement and resettlement. Among especially attractive townships in the area, many of them of Slav origin, are Neustrelitz, Feldberg, Mirow, and Weserberg.

Neubrandenburg
On the eastern edge of the lake district is this ancient fortified town. Its Altstadt was largely destroyed in the war, but the 13th-century ramparts survive, with their four quaint brick Gothic gateways, nicely restored. One of these, the Treptower Tor, now houses a local history museum. And tiny half-timbered houses are built into the ramparts at some points: one is now a bookshop.

The sculpted doorway of the Monstery of Our Lady, founded in 1015 by Augustinian monks. The cloister is superb

EASTERN GERMANY

At Meissen's porcelain factory, visitors taking the guided tour can watch skilled craftsmen and -women at work

summer months. The lake boasts 700 varieties of plants and grasses, 800 varieties of butterfly, and countless varieties of insects it is noted particularly for its orchids, gentians, sundew, and rare grasses, especially in the area known as the Spukloch (the Ghost's Hole). Only Scandinavian Fjallrinder (white unhorned cattle), sheep, and horses are allowed to graze in this very vulnerable area. Rare birds such as cranes, white-tailed eagles, and black storks enjoy the strictly protected habitat. The shore woodland consists of alders, birches, oaks, beeches, and firs. The wild deer in the forest can at times cause problems by overgrazing.

Despite the emphasis on nature protection, there are plenty of well-marked paths for walkers, riders, and cyclists to enjoy. The lake is also available for boating and sailing, though parts of the lake and its shore are restricted to exclude boats so that the breeding of the most vulnerable bird species will not be affected.

▶▶ Meissen

Meissen's castle—the Albrechtsburg, which stands on a rock rising above the broad River Elbe—was the birthplace in 1710 of the European porcelain industry, using local china clay deposits. Ever since, the town's name has been closely linked with the finest decorative tableware. The factory, at 9 Talstrasse, offers a demonstration workshop and showroom (closed Mondays), but the town's main attractions are on and around the **Albrechtsburg▶**. The castle itself (closed Monday) dates back to 929 and is a showpiece of late Gothic architecture. The rooms inside have richly decorated ceilings and vaulting. The neighboring Dom (cathedral), which shares the triangular hilltop site, is older still, dating from the mid- 12th century, though its soaring twin spires, which dominate the whole area, are early 20th century. Down in the town center, around the picturesque market square, you'll find numerous medieval town houses and a Renaissance brewery.

About 10 miles east, standing in pleasant informal parkland, is **Moritzburg Castle▶** (closed Mondays), an outstandingly well-preserved 16th-century hunting lodge containing a collection of baroque furniture and exhibits on the history of hunting. Two rooms are devoted to the radical artist Käthe Kollwitz, who came here to escape the Nazis in 1944–5.

▶ **Mühlhausen**

Mühlhausen's old town is quiet and remarkably well preserved, encircled by town walls that you can still walk around; they're punctuated by towers and gateways leading to murky cobbled streets lined with ancient houses. In the center are several impressive churches, including the enormous hall church of St. Marien (the second largest in Thuringia, after Erfurt Cathedral), as well as Renaissance mansions. The part-Gothic town hall has an attractive inner courtyard and incorporates a 16th-century church.

The town is associated with Thomas Müntzer, a leader of the Peasants' Revolt that was organized from here in 1524–5; he was seen by the former East German regime as an early revolutionary (though Martin Luther warned against him!). The town has several monuments and memorials, including one to Müntzer himself in the St. Marien church and one to the Peasants' Revolt in the Barfüsser Monastery church.

Scholtheim (10 miles east) has half-timbered houses, a baroque castle and a Romanesque church.

▶ **Nordhausen**

Nordhausen lies on a sloping site above the River Zorge and forms the southern terminus of the narrow-gauge railway crossing the Harz (the Harzquerbahn), which is partly operated by steam trains. Dating back over 1,000 years, the town center is still partly encircled by walls. The pleasant, irregularly shaped market square is lined with half-timbered houses and overlooked by the twin towers of St. Basil's parish church, an imposing and spacious late 15th-century Gothic building. A few blocks away, the modest Dom zum Heiligen Kreuz (Cathedral of the Holy Cross) dates back to the 13th century, with a Romanesque crypt and a 14th-century nave lined with massive octagonal pillars.

Parts of the center were damaged by heavy air strikes late in World War II, but numerous half-timbered houses survive, notably along the Barfüsser Strasse, at the top of which stands the Flohburg, a large black-and-white structure dating back to 1500. The large stone Renaissance town hall bears a colorful figure of Roland, a long-established symbol of the town.

To the southeast of Nordhausen (about 12 miles) lies the **Kyffhäuser Nature Park**, an area of modest but very striking wooded hills rising to 1,565 feet on the Kulpenberg, topped with a TV transmitter. The slightly lower Kyffhäuser (1,486 feet) bears a 262-foot monument to Kaiser Wilhelm. Legend has it that one of his predecessors, Friedrich I, dreamed of German unity on this site and would sleep until the day it came—but there have so far been no reports of his waking up. On the western edge of Kyffhäuser, there's bathing at the Kelbra reservoir, and the ruins of nearby Rothenburg castle lie in a secluded woodland setting. To the south is the small town of **Bad Frankenhausen**, which has mineral springs, a spectacularly leaning church (more precarious than the Leaning Tower of Pisa) and a gigantic mural▶ completed in 1990 by the Leipzig artist Werner Tübke. Measuring 410 foot by 46 foot, it depicts the decisive battle of the Peasants' Revolt in 1525.

The Iron Curtain Mühlhausen and Nordhausen lie near the old Iron Curtain, where twin electrified fences, with mines, guard dogs and watchtowers, kept citizens from escaping west. In some cases, the border cut villages in half, and people in the west had to make long detours, and get special passes to see friends or relatives. Today, the fortifications have vanished, but some bitterness remains.

Modern problems
In August 1992 refugee hostel residents in Rostock's bleak Lichtenhagen housing project came under attack from neo-Nazi rioters, cheered on by local residents. Faced with West Germans' questions about the ability and willingness of easterners to pull their economic weight, easterners in their turn have sought someone to blame for post-unification unemployment and inflation. The collapse of the wall brought an influx of refugees to the new Germany, many fleeing racial intolerance. The extreme right wing has found them an easy scapegoat for the east's fall from economic grace.

Warnemünde
This old fishing-port-cum-resort near Rostock has much appeal. the huge ex-GDR hotel on its broad sandy beach is no beauty: but at the east end of the promenade is a lively old quarter of fishermen's cottages, now full of cafés and bistros. Fishing boats line the quay and car ferries arrive from Denmark, in this post-Communist Baltic, buzzing with tourist activity.

▶▶   **Rostock**

The city of Rostock has a long history. Originally a Slavonic coastal fortress, after being sacked in 1161 by King Waldemar of Denmark, it was settled and developed in the 13th century by German merchants and soon became a prosperous port, part of the famous Hanseatic trading league. In 1419 one of the first universities in northern Europe was founded in Rostock, and the city became a center for learning and culture, though from the 17th century onward its economic importance declined compared with the rapidly growing rival ports of Hamburg and Kiel.

Sadly, much of the older part of this strategically situated Baltic port was destroyed in World War II—only four of the 22 former ancient city gateways remain, but these include the handsome 177-foot Kröpeliner Gate, dating from the 13th century. Several of the city's medieval churches have been restored, and there are some attractive gabled merchants' houses.

The city grew rapidly in importance during the postwar years, being developed into a major Eastern-bloc shipbuilding and industrial center and becoming East Germany's main seaport. The port was particularly significant in terms of trade to and from the former Soviet Union. But this traffic has now almost vanished: the port is in decline, and some shipyards have closed. There are, however, impressive museums of shipbuilding and shipping, and a large zoological garden and botanic gardens.

Excursions

Rostock is a conveniently situated base from which to visit a number of small but attractive seaside resorts along the Baltic coast. It's worth making the trip to the graceful old spa town of **Bad Doberan**, with its celebrated 14th-century Cistercian monastery, if only to take the narrow-gauge steam railway with the charming nickname of "Molli." This links Bad Doberan with **Ostseebad Heiligendamm**, Germany's oldest seaside resort, which was founded in 1793. It is celebrated for its charming period cottages, which resulted in it being known as "the white town by the sea." There is a lovely neo-classical spa building, or Kurhaus, in the center of town. Nearby is the Conventer Lake Nature Reserve, a wildlife sanctuary.

Kühlungsborn, also linked to Bad Doberan by "Molli," is a far newer seaside resort, developed from three villages linked together during the 1930s. As well as a heated seawater bathing pool, the town has 2½ miles of sandy beach. Notable features are an early Gothic church with a wooden tower, and a 19th-century windmill.

▶   **Rudolstadt**

Rudolstadt nestles in the pretty valley of the River Saale, on the eastern fringes of the Thüringian Forest. Its wide, pleasant main square, flanked on one side by an imposing medieval town hall and clock tower, is thankfully bypassed by the traffic that thunders through this town; from here it's a short, steep climb up to Schloss Heidecksburg, a graceful baroque hilltop palace

New private initiative in the east: a Rostock beer stand

ranged around three sides of a courtyard. It houses collections of furniture, painting and weapons, and hosts baroque music concerts in summer.

Further cultural attractions are provided by the small Thüringian Landestheater (provincial theater), which was founded by Goethe, a frequent visitor to the town (as was Schiller, who met his wife, Charlotte, here).

Across the river from the castle and historic center is the Thüringian Farm Museum (Volkskundemuseum), where two fine half-timbered farmhouses stand in a parkland setting.

Excursions
About 5 miles to the northeast of Rudolstadt lies **Kochberg (Grosskochberg)** which has a castle owned by the von Stein family, whom Goethe often visited. Many of its rooms have been restored to what they were in Goethe's time. **Paulinzella** (14 miles west) has romantic 12th-century monastic ruins in a wooded setting.

▶▶▶ Sächsische Schweiz
A short way upstream along the Elbe from the outskirts of Dresden, between the city and the Czech border, lies some of Germany's most dramatic scenery: Saxon Switzerland National Park, also known as the Elbe Sandstone District.

High sandstone cliffs and crags, forming a deep gorge through which the River Elbe flows, have been exposed, weathered and worn over millennia by frost, wind and rain into a series of fantastic sculptured shapes—pillars, towers, arches, and stacks towering some 984 feet above the river. In places they are exposed as bleak, bare crags, a kind of Central European Grand Canyon. In other parts trees and shrubs twist out of cracks, cling to crevices, crowd onto summits and form the kind of fantastic landscape that inspired such painters as the great 19th-century Romantic Caspar David Friedrich. Ancient woodlands—pine, beech, oak, maple, fir— flourish around and between the craggy rocks, forming a dense green backdrop to the sculptured formations.

Between the crags wind deep, narrow gorges, some of them only a few feet wide, cool and shady on even the hottest summer day, many of them penetrated by winding footpaths that suddenly emerge into full daylight at thrilling viewpoints. Narrow tributary valleys of the Elbe, especially the Polenz, the Sebnitz, and the Kirnitz, also create dramatic features within this unique area of natural beauty.

At **Bastei▶** (road access and parking lot), a footbridge was built from stone in the 1850s, 636 feet above the Elbe, creating a remarkable viewpoint. It is linked to a series of pedestrian walkways across the crag summits, all with safety rails.

Across the river at Königstein, a massive crag has been used as the base of a great medieval fortress, strategically placed to defend the valley and dating back to the 14th century.

Although the area is now strictly protected as a national park and nature reserve, access is easy from Dresden by road along the B172 or by suburban railroad, a series of ferries crossing the river to such small riverside resorts as Stadt Wehlen, Kurort Rathen, Schmilka, and Bad Schandau. In the summer months, the Weisse Flotte boat services operate a regular public passenger service along the river from Dresden.

Schwerin lies on a big lake, stretching to the gardens of its great castle

157

Wismar and Güstrow
The old Hanseatic seaport of Wismar belonged to Sweden from 1648 to 1803 and retains traces of that influence. The finest of the old buildings around the market square is the 14th-century *Alter Schwede* (Old Swede), with a striking stepped-gable façade. Güstrow, to the east, has an ornate Gothic cathedral and a superb Renaissance palace.

►► Schwerin

The old city of Schwerin in Mecklenburg has some lovely half-timbered houses in its center, and an imposing cathedral, founded in 1171. The town hall in the market square has a medieval core, though with a neo-Gothic façade of 1835. The early 18th-century Nikolaikirche, also called the Schelfkirche, is the finest of Mecklenburg's baroque churches, while the imposing Kollegiengebäude in Schloss Strasse is the administrative headquarters of the state government. Boat trips operate from the town center across the Schweriner See to Zippendorf, where the 453-foot television tower provides panoramic views of lake, city, and countryside.

Schwerin's spectacularly beautiful **castle**► is set on an island, joined to the mainland by twin bridges. Reminiscent of a Loire château, it was built for the Dukes of Mecklenburg in the 1840s in a mix of mock-Gothic and mock-Renaissance styles, one of the architects being Gottfried Semper, who designed Dresden's Semper Opera House. The castle now houses the Mecklenburg-Vorpommern State Parliament. You can visit the restored throne room and other dark-paneled state rooms. In the north wing there is a beautiful church. To the south of the castle are baroque pleasure gardens, with canals, groves, and paths in formal geometric patterning. To the northwest, in the former castle garden, is the state theater and the art gallery, with a collection of important Dutch and Flemish masters. Muess, near Schwerin, has a Freilichtmuseum in the form of a reconstructed village.

The Sorbs

The Sorbs are a Slavic people who have kept their own language and culture in two regions in Germany: in Lower Lusatia, around the Spreewald, and in Upper Lusatia, in the southeast of Saxony east of Dresden. Signposts and official notices in both areas are in two languages—German and Sorbian—and Catholic churches use the Sorbian language in their liturgy. Ortenburg, a castle in the beautiful 1,000-year-old town of Bautzen, is said to be the place where their tribal fortress used to stand. Today Bautzen, with its baroque- and Renaissance-style buildings, is the center of Sorbian culture and tradition, and the seat of the Sorbian national organization, the Domowina. There is also a Sorbian publishing house, a regular newspaper, a school and a Sorbian-German folk theater. Many Sorbian customs are preserved, such as Easter Riding, a mixture of the pagan and the Christian. During Lent young people go from house to house playing bagpipes and fiddles, asking for eggs and bacon, and money. Straw brooms are burned like the witches of old, and Easter eggs are decorated with beautiful, intricate designs. Sorbian national costume is now generally worn only for festivals and holidays; it is extremely colorful with intricate embroidery.

►►► The Spreewald

The River Spree southeast of Berlin, between Berlin and Cottbus, flows through an area of low-lying countryside, splitting into countless minor tributaries and creating the complex area of lakes, ponds, marsh, wetland, and riverine woodland known as the Spreewald. There are also areas of low-lying farmland drained by a network of small canals and dikes.

This area has a unique beauty, due to the effects of light both in early spring, when the birch trees lining its water channels are reflected in the water, and again in late summer and fall, when the luxurious vegetation and vivid colors turn the shortest excursion into an adventure. Much of the area is now a Biosphere Reserve, reflecting both the natural beauty and wildlife interest of the area and its rich cultural associations, particularly linked with the Sorbian settlements in the area. The region is divided into the **Unterspreewald**, north of Lübben, and the larger and better-known **Oberspreewald**, north of Lübbenau. The whole of the Spreewald teems with game, such as wild boar, deer, partridges and pheasants; white storks and herons can also be seen in abundance.

The area also had its own highly characteristic form of local transportation, with narrow barges or punts carrying both people and goods along the myriad channels between villages and outlying farms in the forest. A favorite summer activity for visitors is to be punted along the various canals and canalized rivers and streams, though motors have replaced muscle power in most instances.

The Lower Spreewald, around the Lübben area, is a large enclosed forest region with alder, birch, and beech

interspersed with areas of open, low-lying meadowland and water meadows, which provide an ideal habitat for numerous plants and animals, and biotopes for amphibians, water-loving insects, rare dragonflies, kingfishers, and cranes.

The attractive Sorbian township of **Lübben** was founded in 1150, but its history goes back as far as mid-Stone Age times. Its castle, with richly decorated rooms, was built in the latter stages of the Renaissance and became the seat and capital of the Lower Lusatian government. The town is also the gateway to both Upper and Lower areas of the Spreewald, with motorized punt services into the forest.

From **Lübbenau**, a small tourist resort, there are splendid walks into the Oberspreewald along well-signposted paths over old canal-side dikes that go deep into the forest. In nearby **Lehde**, a fascinating open-air museum has traditional Sorbian farmhouses with their own distinctive waterside architecture—a kind of miniature Venice in the forest. In the summer months motorized barges link Lübbenau with Lehde. The soil for the pleasure grounds of Lübbenau's early 19th-century castle had to be brought by barge. In the building itself is the old locomotive and carriage of the narrow-gauge train the Spreewaldguste, which ran for the last time in 1970.

The Oberspreewald has the historic town of **Burg** as its eastern gateway. There is another Biosphere Reserve here, where eels, pike, and flounder are available in abundance, while woodruff (used to color the Berlin Weissbier bright green) also flourishes. Labyrinths of water channels are crossed by high wooden bridges, there being at least 300 around the town of Burg and its satellite parishes alone. Water lilies bloom along quieter stretches of water; the whole area, with several nature reserves, is a paradise for the naturalist.

The textile-making town of **Cottbus**, near the Polish border, has a fine altarpiece of Jonah and the Whale in the Oberkirche.

Above and left: a favorite summer outing for Berliners is to be taken on a punt along the canals of the Spreewald

Spreewald produce
Market gardens in the area provide produce for nearby Berlin, Spreewald pickles being a much-prized delicacy. Plant extracts are also produced, used in a variety of homeopathic remedies.

▶▶ Stralsund

Stralsund occupies a defensive position on a small hillock between the Strelasund, the narrow strait that divides the Isle of Rügen from the mainland, and two attractive small lakes, the Knieper- and Frankenteichs.

Like Rostock, this was a Hanseatic town, but between 1648 and 1815 it became part of Sweden before being reclaimed by Prussia. The old town and small harbor boast particularly fine architecture, including impressive merchants' houses. In the Alt Markt is the remarkable reddish-brick town hall dating from the 13th century, with its high elegant façade. The Marienkirche dates from 1298, and two surviving towers are both 15th century in origin. The town center has an attractive pedestrianized market area, and scheduled passenger boats from the harbor link the mainland with the island of Hiddensee and with the Darss peninsula. The rail and road bridge linking Stralsund with the Isle of Rügen was built only in 1936.

Stralsund is a good base from which to explore the **Vorpommersche Boddenlandschaft National Park**—a national park consisting of a long, mainly wooded coastline along the Baltic, close to such small fishing villages and quiet seaside resorts as **Pramont**, **Prerow**, **Zingst,** and **Wiek**. This is an area of sand dunes, winding sandbanks, mudflats, and shallow seas, rich in birdlife, including many waders and coastal birds, and for that reason strictly protected. The area also offers sanctuary for thousands of birds of passage, including some of the largest colonies of marine birds in northern Europe. The coast itself is famous for its ancient coastal woodlands, including rare shrubs and grasses.

Rügen▶ The whole of the Isle of Rügen is fascinating. Putbus is a sleepy little inland resort deliberately planned by a local prince early last century to be like an English spa town, with elegant houses around a green "circus" in the style of Bath. There is a fine neoclassical theater,

Stralsund, on its hill overlooking the Strelasund

Along the coast
There are fine stretches of virtually tideless beach with clean sand around the small Stralsund resorts. A special feature of the area is the many attractive thatched cottages and farmhouses along the Darss peninsula and in many of the villages, giving the area an "English feel," though the style is markedly different.
The coastal road from Stralsund via Barth to Ribnitz Damgarten is a particularly attractive drive (there is also a bus service from Barth station). It follows the narrow peninsula between Darss and Fischland, the peninsula enclosing areas of quiet inland sea and saltwater marsh known as Bodden, with their spectacular birdlife. There are well-posted bike paths and walkways along the coast, especially along the raised defensive embankments, partially enclosed by woodland.

while the former Kurhaus in "English" parkland is the parish church. A narrow-gauge steam railway, known as "Rasender Roland" (Rushing Roland), links Putbus with the seaside resort of Göhren. It puffs its way through an idyllic landscape of old meadows, scattered woodlands, small lakes, and storks' nests to the seaside resorts of Binz and Göhren, with their fine sandy beaches.

The narrow peninsula to the south, known as **Mönchgut**, is also a protected landscape, this time a Biosphere Reserve, safeguarded as much for its cultural qualities as its landscape. It has old farmhouses and thatched fishermen's cottages, ancient meadows crowded with brilliant wildflowers, many of them rare, and low coastal cliffs and pebbly beaches overlooking a distant coastline stretching to Usedom and the Polish border. In the little museum in Göhren you'll find examples of 19th-century Staffordshire ware, traded and brought back from England by sailors.

Sassnitz is an old port and ferry terminal on Rügen, where train and car ferries leave for Trelleborg in Sweden. Originally a small fishing port and quarry town, it later became a resort, and handsome 19th-century villas are still to be seen around the older part of the town. Immediately to the north of Sassnitz lies Jasmund National Park, with some of the most impressive coastal scenery in Germany. High chalk cliffs crowned by dense beechwoods overlook the quiet Baltic. Though thousands of tourists crowd the Kaiserstuhl, a tall chalk cliff and impressive viewpoint, a few hundred yards away along the coastal path all is quiet, with impressive views. At Wissower Klinken, weather-carved chalk cliffs provide a dramatic feature that became the subject of one of the most famous of Caspar David Friedrich's Romantic paintings. The beechwoods, as well as the meadows and the heathland, provide a habitat for a rich flora, especially orchids. Fauna include small reptiles and rare butterflies.

EASTERN GERMANY

Modern troubles
Despite the Thüringer Wald's many charms, it also has its sad side. Emissions from nearby open-cast brown-coal mines have caused dreadful air pollution in many parts, and a survey in 1989 showed that more than half the trees were affected. Some of the area's towns have suffered, too, from ramshackle industrial installations and aggressive modern development.

Meiningen's theater
This little town in southern Thüringia is the home of one of Germany's grandest theaters, built in 1908 in the style of a Greek temple. Meiningen was the capital of a duchy in 1680–1918, and Duke Georg II, married to a famous actress, created its theater, which still flourishes under a dynamic manager. He draws top Euopean companies and orchestras, which play to packed audiences from the larger nearby towns.

► ► **Thüringer Wald (Thüringian Forest)**

The Thüringer Wald covers an area of ancient hills stretching for about 60 miles southeastward from Eisenach, and averaging about 20 miles wide. By German standards, the hills are not especially high—the highest point is the Grosser Beerberg at 3,221 feet—but the area is crossed by numerous narrow valleys and is quite densely settled with old-fashioned villages and small industrial towns. The area is heavily forested, as its name implies, mostly with fir and beech trees, but the woodlands are interspersed with meadows and orchards, and there's plenty of variety from one square mile to the next.

Because of its small scale and varied scenery, the Thüringer Wald is excellent walking country, and has long been popular for quiet country vacations and excursions, as well as for cross-country skiing in winter. A long-distance path—the Rennsteig—runs southeastward from the Wartburg for 100 miles within the Thüringer Wald. Even for those not inclined to tackle its full length, it offers lots of opportunities to get into the countryside. Like many of the shorter paths that crisscross the area, it's well marked ("R" symbols on trees and signposts) and easy to follow.

Today the Thüringer Wald offers a reasonably good variety of accommodations. Proximity to western Germany has encouraged many local people to try their

hand at catering for tourists, and you'll find plenty of small pensions and *Zimmer frei* (rooms to let) signs even in the villages, together with family-run restaurants and bars. There's plenty of Thüringer bratwurst to go around, often purchased from roadside barbecues. Thüringia has many of its own folk songs and folk dances. These were discouraged under the centralized GDR regime, but are now being revived.

What to see The best of the forest scenery in the Thüringer Wald lies along a line fairly close to the Rennsteig, and you will have to come off the main roads to see it—see page 165 for a suggested route.

Of the smaller places toward the center of the forest, it's worth making for **Schmalkalden** for its fine half-timbered houses grouped around an imposing irregular market square; nearby Schloss Wilhelmsburg dates back to the 1580s and is one of Thüringia's most important Renaissance buildings. **Bad Liebenstein** has dignified spa buildings lining its leafy avenues; there are extensive views from the ruins of medieval Liebenstein castle, while nearby 18th-century Schloss Altenstein is set in an English-style park. **Wasungen**, set in the wooded Upper Werra Valley, has numerous half-timbered buildings (including a fine three-story town hall dating from 1533) in its specially protected town center. **Friedrichroda** (see also page 144) is a relaxed forest

In the Thüringer Wald, the well-tended villages have red roofs and gray slate façades. In some parts there is skiing

163

Tanks used to patrol the Thüringer Wald, so close to the old border with West Germany

resort with fine parks, an open-air swimming pool, a lake and a large early 19th-century castle, Reihhardsbrunn, once reserved for high party officials and now a hotel. The nearby Marienglashöhle caves (open daily) boast unusual gypsum crystal formations. **Oberhof** is an important local winter-sports center, dominated by the strikingly modern Hotel Panorama, built in the form of two ski jumps. An alpine garden contains 1,500 specimens collected from all over the world (open from May to October).

A number of larger towns of historical and architectural interest ring the edge of the main forest area. **Suhl** was the capital of the whole region when this was part of the GDR, and gained high-rises and an egg-box-style shopping precinct. Famous since medieval times as a home of gun making, the town also has a weapons museum (open Tuesday–Sunday) in the 17th-century malthouse building. The nearby old main street, the Steinweg, has been pedestrianized and has several fine 18th-century houses.

Ilmenau, a glass- and porcelain-making town, was a favorite retreat of Goethe's and has several places associated with him: the Amtshaus (official's house), the Gabelbach hunting lodge, and the Goethe hut and Kickelhahn—all linked by a footpath called Auf Goethes Spuren (in Goethe's footsteps). **Arnstadt** gave J. S. Bach his first job as an organist, in the baroque church that now bears his name; a jaunty statue of the great man watches over the small market square of this very well preserved small town. The baroque Neues Palais has a remarkable collection of 400 dolls made locally in the 18th century. The surrounding landscape of lush, gentle hills is exceptionally pretty and is known for its botanical rarities, including German gentians. Lauscha, to the south, long a glassblowing center, invented Christmas tree decorations in 1848 and still produces them.

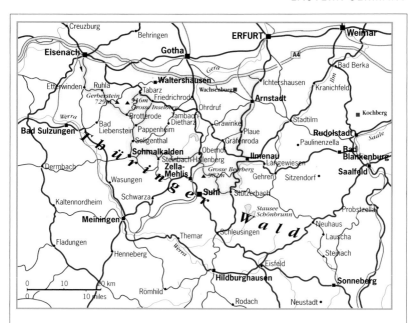

Drive Thüringer Wald

This 117-mile tour starts from Eisenach.

7½ miles out of Eisenach on the D19 Meiningen road, turn left at Etterwinden on an unclassified road to Ruhla and Brotterode. Here, turn left toward Tabarz.
After 2½ miles you can park in the large parking lot on the right, to climb the Grosser Inselberg (approximately half an hour each way, on an easy path) for the mountaintop café and a great view.

Continue to Tabarz, then right on the D88 road to Friedrichroda; leave by a minor road to Schmalkalden, then take minor roads to Steinbach-Hallenberg and Oberhof. Turn right onto the D247; then half a mile south, turn left on a minor road. This follows the Rennsteig and passes the Grosser Beerberg.

Continue to the main D4 road, turn left and return through Ilmenau and Arnstadt, to take the E40 highway back to Eisenach.

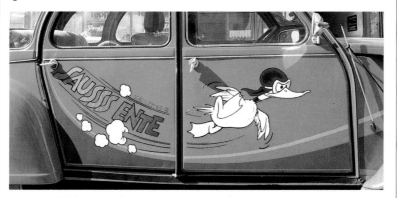

► **Vogtland**

This hilly region of forests, steep-sided valleys, isolated rocks, lakes and dams extends along the southern frontier of the former GDR, up as far as the Erzgebirge on the Czech border (see page 142). The area is dotted with small industrial towns—some of which are famous for making musical instruments—and with modest spas based on mineral-rich springs. The area's relaxed character and varied scenery make it a good choice for simple, open-air pursuits, notably walking on the many well-marked paths; there's some sailing on the lakes and reservoirs, too.

Some of the best scenery is around **Klingenthal**, a straggling semi-industrial village right up against the Czech frontier and famous for its manufacture of harmonicas. Three miles to the north lies **Schneckenstein**, the only place in Europe where topaz can be found—there are still some isolated rock formations in the area. **Schoeneck**, 7 miles northwest, marks the southern end of the dramatic, deeply cut valley of the Steinicht River. About 12 miles north of the town, around Schnarrtanne and Beerheide, you'll find some of the Vogtland's prettiest woodland scenery.

The biggest of the reservoirs is **Stausee Poehl**, near the region's main town, Plauen, but there are lots of attractive small lakes in the area stretching south from here to Markneukirchen and Bad Elster.

Markneukirchen has been Germany's leading musical instrument–producing town since the early 19th century; it has a small baroque castle, the Paulusschloessel. A collection of 1,000 musical instruments is housed in the Musikinstrumentenmuseum, Biensgarten 2 (closed Mondays). **Bad Elster**, in a quiet wooded valley off the main road, has spa buildings dating from the mid-19th century. At **Landwuest**, 4 miles to the east, there's a small open-air folk museum with farm implements and local history collections (closed Mondays). It is easy to make day excursions to the famous Czech spa towns of Karlovy Vary and Mariánské Lázně

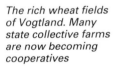

The rich wheat fields of Vogtland. Many state collective farms are now becoming cooperatives

▶▶▶ Weimar

Although only a modest-size town, Weimar is one of Germany's greatest cultural treasures. With its fine public buildings, parks, squares and boulevards, it feels like a small capital city—which indeed it was, of Sachsen-Weimar from 1547 to 1870. Following a meeting of the German parliament in the city in 1919, it gave its name to the ill-fated democratic republic that preceded the Hitler years, and was capital of Thüringia from 1919 to 1949. The city was lucky enough to be spared wartime destruction, and for 40 years after World War II it was spared the effects of mass international tourism. Now it's catching up fast, acquiring a Hilton hotel and plenty of bars and restaurants. Many of the fine buildings have been expensively restored.

Weimar's catalog of cultural connections is almost limitless: Goethe spent most of his working life here, and his influence on the life of the city was immense; the writers Friedrich von Schiller and Johann Gottfried von Herder lived here; musical residents included Franz Liszt and Richard Strauss, who were both masters of music at the court; the writer Nietzsche spent his final years here (his house contains a small museum); in the 20th century, Walter Gropius founded the Bauhaus movement here.

There are lots of sights, many associated with Weimar's famous residents. Provided you can dodge the seemingly endless construction sites, it can be a relaxing city, helped by its manageable size, neat squares, outdoor cafés, and above all by the huge park that extends along the River Ilm almost to the town center.

The **Goethehaus▶▶** on the Frauenplan (closed Mondays) will be at the top of most people's lists. This combines Goethe's own family house—still complete with his study, books, furniture and collections of coins, minerals and art—with an imposing museum explaining

Weimar: the Wittumspalais (top) and a flower stall in the market (above)

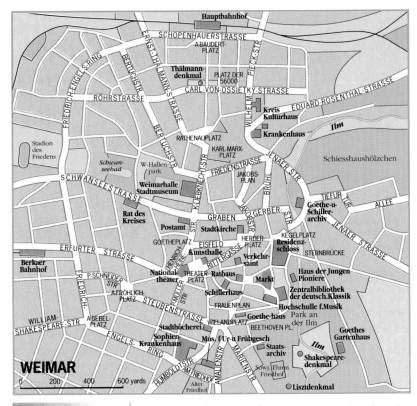

WEIMAR

Buchenwald camp
On a hill near Weimar lies the largest Nazi concentration camp on German soil: 56,000 died here, many from torture or starvation. A memorial and museum (closed Mondays) movingly give the details. The GDR regime firmly put the accent on the sufferings of the German Communist and Russian prisoners, and ignored the Jews. This shocking bias has now been corrected, and there is a new Jewish memorial—also a new museum about the cruel Soviet prison camp on the site in 1945–49, where 7,000 died.

the writer's life and influence (most explanations in German only). There's a charming small garden at the back. A few hundred yards away, in the Ilm Park, you can also visit **Goethe's Gartenhaus▶**, an idyllic rural retreat in which he lived for six years. The renovated **Schillerhaus▶** (closed Tuesdays), on Schillerstrasse, was lived in by Schiller for the last three years of his life and incorporates many of his and his family's possessions; a modern museum annex documents his work. The **Liszthaus▶** (closed Mondays), by the west entrance to the Ilm Park, was used by the composer as a summer residence for 17 years and sets out his living and working quarters with many of his possessions, documents, pictures and mementos.

Note: the Goethehaus and Schillerhaus were due to be closed in 1996–8, in preparation for the European Cultural Year of 1999 (see panel, opposite page).

Of the city's many palaces and castles, the **Wittumspalais** stands on the Theaterplatz, immediately opposite the National Theater, with its famous double statue of Goethe and Schiller holding hands. The small baroque palace itself (closed Mondays) was built for Duchess Anna Amalia in the 1770s when the main city palace burned down. It has been furnished in baroque style and has the atmosphere of a typical prosperous town house of the period. One room—the Tafelrundenzimmer (round-table room)—was a popular meeting point for artists friendly with the court. In one wing of the palace there's a museum commemorating another famous Weimar resident, the writer Herder. Beside the palace is a small new museum devoted to the Bauhaus movement. The main **Weimar Castle**, rebuilt in 1803, is an inspiring neo-baroque structure overlooking the Sternbrücke (Star Bridge) and River Ilm. It houses a collection of local paintings and fine arts (closed Monday). The nearby **Herzogin Anna Amalia Bibliothek** houses the 900,000 volumes of the Library of the German Classics, many of which are extremely ancient. The best pieces are kept in the large Rococo Room, decorated with busts of Weimar's literary giants.

Out of Town It's a very pleasant 20-minute walk along the River Ilm to the south of the town, through a large relaxed park, to the "**Roman House**," a classical pavilion built in the 1790s, which enjoys a beautiful setting overlooking the river; inside there's a collection of local works of art (closed Tuesdays). A further 3 miles out of town in the same direction brings you to **Schloss Belvedere**, a modest but charming country retreat and hunting lodge built in the 1730s and flanked by two delightful single-story pavilions (closed Mondays and all winter); the surrounding park was landscaped in the early 19th century, when it acquired a large exotic-plant collection kept in the Orangery and neighboring greenhouses. About 3 miles northeast of the town, **Schloss Tiefurt**, built in 1760, became a major cultural center in the late 18th century; the castle contains furniture, busts, porcelain and a collection of paintings and fine arts of the period, and stands in a finely landscaped park stretching down to the banks of the Ilm.

The Duchess Anna Amalia lived in this small yellow baroque palace (above) after the death of her husband in 1767. Here she held intellectual salons attended by Goethe, Schiller, Herder, and Wieland

Old and new allies
In 1346 a group of six towns from the Oberlausitz (Bautzen, Görlitz, Lobau, Laubau, Kamenz, and Zittau), with imperial permission, banded together to further the development of cloth making and linen weaving and to protect each other against attacks from robber knights and their followers. It has recently been decided to reconstitute this union as an aid to economic survival, an example of history partly repeating itself.

▶▶ **Wernigerode**

Wernigerode, strategically situated on the northern fringe of the Harz Mountains, is famed for its richly colored half-timbered houses and its elaborately carved, twin-spired, late Gothic town hall. Wernigerode was granted its town charter in 1229 and in 1449 became the seat of the powerful counts of Stolberg, and a prosperous trading center. Its decline in later years perhaps helped to keep its medieval character. Inevitably the town suffered a number of fires in earlier periods, but miraculously its town hall, most of its charming streets and part of its defensive walls (with impressive gates) were spared. In the 18th century a number of baroque buildings were added. Overlooking the town, Wernigerode's castle, largely rebuilt in the mid-19th century, stands on the site of a much older fortress dating from 1121. It is rapidly being rediscovered as a tourist center for the Harz, with several rebuilt and restored hotels. The town lies at the northern terminus of the Harzquerbahn narrow-gauge steam railway to Nordhausen, close to superb walking country.

It's worth traveling just 30 miles east of Wernigerode to **Quedlinburg**▶ (see also page 123), designated a UNESCO World Heritage Site because of its astonishing wealth of half-timbered houses along narrow streets and courtyards, with groups dating from the late Gothic (15th century) time onward. One example, in Wordgasse, dating from the first half of the 14th century, is the oldest house in central Germany. With its narrow windows and uneven floors, it has been restored as a museum. The castle, built between the 16th and 17th centuries, also houses a museum. The Renaissance Town Hall, with a statue of Roland dating from 1426 symbolizing citizens' rights, overlooks a handsome pedestrianized square fringed by old inns, cafés and attractive shops.

The countryside surrounding Wittenberg

▶ **Wittenberg**

Lutherstadt Wittenberg is forever associated with Martin Luther, the great Protestant reformer, and his criticism of contemporary clergy and particularly of the sale of indulgences or pardons. As was then customary, in 1517 his 95 theses were nailed up on the town's church door. His ideas gained further prominence at Wittenberg's university (founded 1502), then spread throughout Europe. Luther's house is a museum, and on the site of Luther's Oak, in front of which a Papal Bull condemning him was burned, a (later) oak tree stands. Close by is the

The Stadtkirche of St. Mary in Wittenberg, where Luther often preached

Lutherhalle, the world's largest collection of exhibited material devoted to the Reformation. Famous Wittenberg contemporaries of Luther included court painter Lucas Cranach the Elder and theologian Philipp Melanchthon, whose 16th-century dwelling is also a museum. The 450th anniversary of Luther's death is being marked by many special events in the town in 1996.

▶ Zittau

Zittau lies in the extreme southeast of Germany in the area known as Dreiländereck, where lakes and heather predominate. The town dates from the 13th century, when it became an important trade center under the protection of the Bohemian kings.

The town's former fortifications have now been replaced with green spaces and a flower clock, which in winter is decorated with moss, pinecones and branches instead of flowering plants. The town has a market square with a Mars fountain dating from 1585 and an Italian-style town hall. The Marstall (stables) of 1511 dominates the Salzmarkt while the Dornsprachhaus is a lovely Renaissance building. The church of St. Petri and St. Pauli was originally an old Franciscan monastery church; the buildings now house the town's museum.

The 7-mile Zittauer narrow-gauge steam railway, opened in 1890 to the spa towns of Oybin and Jonsdorf, passes beautiful rocky landscape in the Zittau Mountains, a paradise for walkers and climbers. Oybin has a medieval castle, churches and monastery ruins; Jonsdorf, a former weavers' village, has fine examples of the typical Oberlausitz Umbindehaus, a characteristic style of vernacular architecture with wooden arches over the house front to support the weight of looms.

The Beer Puddle
Zittau's relationship with its neighbors wasn't always peaceful. In the 15th century the town actually went to war over beer when townsmen of nearby Görlitz spilled several barrels of Zittau's celebrated beer at a place still known as the Beer Puddle.

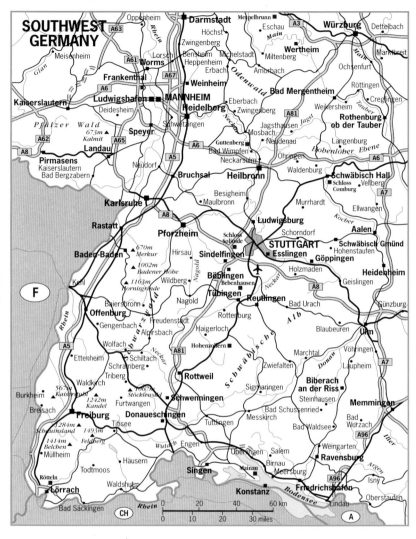

The southwest is an appealing region for gentle rural exploration, with plenty of peace and quiet, charming countryside, deep forests, wooden farmhouses and swanky village resorts. There is excellent potential for walking, and sports facilities are plentiful. A wide range of accommodations exists, offering higher standards than in much of the rest of the country.

The region defined here incorporates **Baden-Württemberg**, one of the youngest of the German *Länder*—it was formed only in 1952 and still has two distinct sides to its character. The people of Baden, most of them Catholic, are known for their friendly and relaxed dispositions, as opposed to their neighbors in Württemberg (or Swabia), who take life more seriously and are reputed to be careful how and when they spend their money and to spend much of their spare time spring-cleaning their houses.

The southwest is dominated by several upland masses, principally the **Schwarzwald** (Black Forest), which rises to over 3,936 feet. The **Danube** rises in the Schwarzwald and follows a course east, forming a deep gorge as it approaches the **Schwäbische Alb** (Swabian Jura), a less elevated and far less well known area of limestone ridges with cliff-top castles, half-timbered villages and gushing waterfalls. The Rhine defines the western border with France. Germany's largest lake, the **Bodensee**, shared with Austria and Switzerland (and also known by its other name, Lake Constance), is like an inland sea and has a string of pretty resorts on its shores. Another river, the **Neckar**, is Swabia's main waterway. Flowing through a country of vineyards and fruit trees in its upper course, and through wooded valleys in its lower course, it passes through the lovely university towns of **Tübingen** and **Heidelberg**. More commercial and industrial centers, such as **Stuttgart, Mannheim** and **Karlsruhe**, constitute the modern face of Baden-Württemberg. The region's charms may be well known—Heidelberg and the main resorts of the Black Forest and Bodensee are the principal draws—but its attractions are widespread.

Spectacular views from above Baden-Baden

▶▶ Baden-Baden

Stylish Baden-Baden, within the Upper Rhine plain, draws visitors from all over the world to its renowned spa and its casino, Germany's oldest. Its position in the lush valley of the River Oos, on the western slopes of the northern part of the Black Forest, adds much to its attraction

Though its heyday may be over, it remains a handsome place, with elegant 19th-century hotels, a Jugendstil (art-nouveau) Trinkhalle (drink hall) where you can test the saline waters, a white neoclassical **Kurhaus▶** (spa building) and a long park that looks as carefully and expensively manicured as most of the visitors.

Baden-Baden's mild climate makes it a pleasant place to visit all year round, but it is best known for its thermal springs, Europe's hottest, which gush out at 156° F. The Roman emperor Caracalla bathed here in AD 213 in the

Baden-Baden—still a fashionable and popular spa town

"Beautiful casino"
The casino at Baden-Baden can accommodate 2,500 gamblers at 35 tables. According to Marlene Dietrich, "The most beautiful casino in the world is at Baden-Baden—and I have seen them all."

hope of finding a cure for his rheumatism. The remains of the Imperial Baths (open all year round) can be found beneath the Stiftskirche.

The Lichtentaler Allee runs from the Kurgarten, site of both the Trinkhalle and the Kurhaus, to the old Cistercian monastery at Lichtental, passing on its way the Theater, the International Club, and the Kunsthalle (art gallery), where important temporary exhibitions are held throughout the year.

Baden-Baden suffered a calamitous fire in 1689, which destroyed most of the old town. The Stiftskirche survived; inside is the tomb of Margrave Ludwig Wilhelm and a huge sandstone crucifix, a masterpiece carved in 1467 by Nikolaus von Leyden.

The Renaissance/baroque Neues Schloss (guided tours May to September) stands at the top of steep steps and gives excellent views over the rooftops of the town to the Black Forest. It is still the residence of the Zähringen family, who were once the margraves—and for a time, grand dukes—of Baden. You can reward yourself after the climb by relaxing in the sumptuous Friedrichsbad or the modern (and less expensive) Caracalla Therm.

Excursion
The town of **Rastatt**, north of Baden-Baden, was rebuilt on uniform lines in the 18th century by Margrave Ludwig Wilhelm of Baden (nicknamed Louis the Turk because of his role in the anti-Turkish wars). Its massive red sandstone Schloss is Germany's first example of a palace in the style of Louis XIV's Versailles. It houses both the national Army Museum (with many of Ludwig Wilhelm's war trophies) and the Museum of Liberation (with displays on the evolution of German Liberalism). Ludwig's widow, Sibylla, was responsible for the small-scale and deliciously ornate Schloss Favorite, 3 miles outside of town.

► **The Bergstrasse (Mountain Road)**

This long-established route (the Strata Montana of the Romans and today's B3) runs through the orchards at the foot of the forested Odenwald hills for 36 miles from Darmstadt to Heidelberg. The fruit trees and almonds come into blossom here earlier than anywhere else in Germany, making a spectacular display in late March/mid-April, while a string of picturesque little towns offers a welcome at all seasons.

South of Darmstadt is half-timbered **Zwingenberg**, the oldest place along the route, with steep alleyways and a pretty little market square overlooked by the 13th-century church. Near **Bensheim** is the Schloss at **Auerbach**, with the first of many viewpoints over the wide plain of the Rhine.

Fürstenlager Park was laid out in the 18th century with pavilions and garden monuments in the taste of the time. A trail is laid out among the exotic trees which flourish in the mild climate.

Heppenheim is dominated by the ruins of Schloss Starkenberg, which contains an observatory and a youth hostel. The place has the cheerful air of a center of wine production, with fine timber-framed buildings in the market square, including an ancient apothecary's shop. The square is overlooked by the massive neo-Gothic church that is known as the "Cathedral of the Bergstrasse."

Weinheim has picturesque streets, an old tanners' quarter, and a friendly marketplace. The town's inviting Schlosspark has many rare trees, and nearby, up in the valley of the Weschnitz, is the restored castle of Wachenburg, with a fine panorama stretching west toward Mannheim and the Rhine.

Windeck Castle, on the Bergstrasse

Pioneering casino
Baden-Baden has long been a playground for the rich and famous—Brahms, Dostoevsky and Queen Victoria were among its many visitors. Following the construction of the Kurhaus in the 1820s, the French impresario Jacques Benazet opened a casino, the first in Germany. The famous Iffezheim races began here in 1858, further enhancing Baden-Baden's prestige. The Lichtentaler Allee is the most glamorous thoroughfare, scene of many a historic event.

Ancient Torhalle
A great Benedictine abbey once stood at Lorsch. Of it there remains the delightful little structure known as the Torhalle, Germany's oldest intact building, dating from the late 8th century and probably erected as a triumphal gateway for the emperor Charlemagne.

SOUTHWEST GERMANY

Lake wine
Seewein (lake wine) is a good reason for visiting the Bodensee. On the shores of the lake, Meersburg holds a wine festival every September, which is a good introduction to the region's wines.

▶▶ **Bodensee (Lake Constance)**

Fed by the Rhine and shared with Austria and Switzerland, the Bodensee is the second largest (after Lake Geneva) of the great Alpine lakes. Sometimes called the "Swabian Ocean" for its sheer size (roughly 40 miles by 7 miles), it has something of the character of an inland sea; this, together with the distant backdrop of the Alps and a mild climate which allows exotic vegetation to thrive, has made it a popular place for German vacationers, who flock to the chain of pretty resorts along the north shore.

The historic town of **konstanz▶** stands at the end of a peninsula astride the channel linking the main body of the lake—the Obersee—to the smaller Untersee, with its attractively varied shoreline. The lakeside at Konstanz is attractive enough, with steamers tied up in the harbor, a verdant park (the Stadtgarten), old defensive towers, and the venerable warehouse of 1388 known as the Konzil. In summer the traffic-free Altstadt (old town) has a bustling, almost Mediterranean atmosphere; there is a cathedral— the Münster—and a fine Renaissance Rathaus. The Rosgarten Museum exhibits finds dating back to prehistoric times. Now an elegant lakeside hotel, the town's 13th-century Dominican monastery was also the birthplace of Graf Zeppelin, the airship pioneer.

Mainau▶, reached by road and footbridge or by lake steamer, is a paradise island of tropical plants with a fairy-tale castle. Laid out by Grand Duke Friedrich I of Baden in the mid-19th century, it is now owned by the flamboyant Swedish count Bernadotte.

Reichenau Island▶ is accessible along its causeway or by boat. Less overcrowded than Mainau, it is of exceptional interest because of its Romanesque churches—testimony to an important monastic past. Look particularly for the 11th-century frescoes at Oberzell church. Mitterzell abbey dates from the 10th century and has Gothic reliquaries in its treasury. **Singen**, farther west, is dominated by the biggest castle ruin in Germany, Hohentwiel; the castle was razed by the French in 1801 but the ruins still offer a terrific panorama of lake and Alp.

One-thousand-year-old **Meersburg▶**, easily reached by car ferry from Konstanz, is perhaps the prettiest place

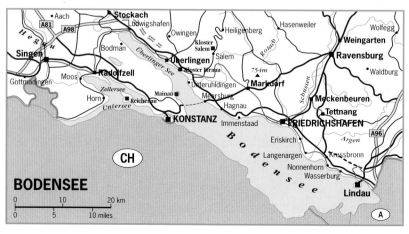

BODENSEE

CH

0   10   20 km
0   5   10 miles

A

along the lake, with a formidable feudal castle, the Altes Schloss, and a baroque palace, the Neues Schloss, built for the bishops of Konstanz, who fled here when that town turned Protestant. The clifflike shoreline between the Oberstadt (upper town), with its delightful Marktplatz (market square) and the Unterstadt (lower town), with its busy lakeside promenade, provides excellent growing conditions for the vines that stretch southward to Hagnau.

North of Meersburg the shore of the Überlingersee continues steep and rugged in places. At **Unteruhldingen** the prehistoric lake dwellers' village has been imaginatively reconstructed. A short distance inland lies Schloss Salem, its Gothic church complemented by baroque abbey buildings. Since 1922 this has been Germany's most famous boarding school, numbering among its alumni Britain's Duke of Edinburgh. One of the most appealing of all Germany's baroque buildings, the

Konstanz is the main town on the Bodensee (Lake Constance), which is very popular with tourists but has not been spoiled by high-rise construction

pilgrimage church at **Birnau▶** stands in a romantic setting among the vineyards overlooking the lake. Inside is a famous little figurine, a honey-stealing cherub licking his fingers.

Medieval **Überlingen**, clinging to its steep lakeside site, has retained most of its fortifications and is dominated by its richly furnished, five-aisled late Gothic Münster.

From Meersburg to Lindau Southeast of Immenstaad the lakeside becomes flatter and the main points of interest are the lakeside settlements, such as **Friedrichshafen**, where Zeppelin based his great airships; little **Wasserburg** on its peninsula; and, above all, **Lindau▶**. Built on the lake's largest island and connected to the mainland by two bridges, this ancient city is the southernmost in Germany, priding itself on its mild climate, its spectacular setting against the backdrop of the Alps and its high reputation as a summer resort. The monumental harbor entrance is guarded by the Lion of Bavaria and a lighthouse, the quayside by another lighthouse, the 13th-century Mangturm. Behind its traffic-free promenades, the Altstadt is full of interest, not least because of its happy blend of architectural styles, medieval painted houses, 15th-century Rathaus, baroque Cavazzen House (with a fine local museum) and Jugendstil train station.

Loved by yachtsmen, the big Bodensee is sometimes called "the Swabian ocean"

▶ Donaueschingen

High up among the rich farmlands of the Baar plateau between the Black Forest and Swabian Jura, little Donaueschingen owes its name to its position at the source of the Danube. The great river's starting point is marked by the monumental fountain standing in Donaueschingen's Schlosspark, though the name Danube really only applies downstream from the confluence of two streams (the Breg and Brigach) just outside the town.

From 1723 Donaueschingen was the seat of the princes of Furstenberg. Their Schloss (open April to October, closed Tuesdays) was rebuilt twice, in 1772 and 1893. It houses a sumptuous collection of porcelain, gold and silver plate, as well as Brussels tapestries. The princes' rich art collections can be viewed in the Karlsbau. They include paintings by both Cranachs and by the Master of Messkirch, as well as by a number of 15th- and 16th-century Swabian masters.

Music festival
Apart from brewing, Donaueschingen prides itself on its annual music festival—the Donaueschinger Musiktage—featuring works by contemporary composers.
The Donau (Danube) is Europe's second-largest river after the Volga. It travels 1,787 miles from its source at Donauquelle to the Black Sea, and on its course runs through three capital cities: Vienna, Budapest, and Belgrade.

▶▶ Freiburg

Known as the capital of the Black Forest, Freiburg has a lovely setting amid green hills and vineyards, and a sunny climate. It is a city where foreigners love to live. It is famous for its cathedral, while for many Germans it also conjures up images of youth: some 27,000 students are housed here, giving the town an unusually lively atmosphere all year round. The Albert Ludwig University was founded in 1457; the College of Education, State Music College, and five technical colleges are more recent additions.

What to see A walk through the squares and arcaded streets of the old town is delightful, but the real glory of Freiburg is its red sandstone **Münster**▶▶, with a soaring tower that dominates the city. Colorful medieval and baroque-style houses (many being careful postwar reconstructions) fringe the cathedral square.

Begun as a ducal burial place by Bertold V of Zähringen, whose family founded the city in 1118–20, the Münster passed into the hands of the citizenry after the last of the Zähringens died in 1218. To the late Romanesque east end were added the Gothic nave and the incomparable west tower. The desire of rich families for their own burial chapels determined the form of the late Gothic choir, begun in 1354. Its consecration in 1513 marked the completion of the minster. Since 1827 it has been the seat of an archbishop. The rich interior bears witness to the generosity and civic pride of local families: stained-glass windows with coats of arms of patricians and guilds; the magnificent high altar triptych by Hans Baldung Grien; and the splendid furnishings of the choir chapels with their 16th-century windows and

Top: a street in Freiburg leading to the 13th-century Swabian gate, part of the old ramparts. Above: the glorious Münster

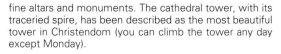

fine altars and monuments. The cathedral tower, with its traceried spire, has been described as the most beautiful tower in Christendom (you can climb the tower any day except Monday).

Augustinermuseum▶ This owes its name to the former monastery of the Augustinian Hermits, going back to about 1300. Since 1923 the church and cloisters of the monastery buildings have housed the attractively displayed collections of the museum, which specializes in Upper Rhenish art from the Middle Ages to the baroque. Besides the medieval art treasures, there is a special section for southwest German baroque sculpture and a rich collection of *objets d'art*. The Augustiner also has a folk-art section holding a collection of clocks, local costumes and folk art of the Black Forest. In the 19th century, artists became aware of the beauty of the Freiburg area and the Black Forest, and some of their canvases can be seen in the section devoted to Baden painters.

Remnants of the medieval town walls can still be seen south of the Augustinermuseum, while the old fishermen's quarter, known as the Insel (Island), has sensitively restored old buildings.

Other sights The colorful Münsterplatz (cathedral square) is graced by the Gothic/Renaissance Kaufhaus (merchants' hall), with an arcaded façade that contains statues of Habsburg rulers; the baroque Erzbischöfliches Palais (Archbishop's Palace); the 18th-century Wenzingerhaus; and the restored 15th-century Kornhaus (the original was destroyed during World War II).

A short distance away is Rathausplatz (town hall square), pleasantly shaded by chestnut trees. It contains the Neues Rathaus (the present town hall), once the university's main building.

Excursions

If you have time, there are some worthwhile side trips to be made to nearby places such as the fortified town of **Breisach**, which towers immediately above the Rhine and the French frontier; the **Kaiserstuhl**, a volcanic, vine-clad hill standing isolated in the plain; and the wine town of **Burkheim**—all less than 15 miles west of Freiburg.

▶▶ Haigerloch

This is one of southwestern Germany's most delightful small towns, a perfect synthesis of buildings and landscape at a point where the River Eyach has carved a deep double loop in the limestone of the Swabian Jura. The best panoramas of the town in its setting are to be obtained from the Kapf viewpoint, from the rococo St. Anne's pilgrimage church, and from the tower known as the Römerturm. The Hohenzollern Schloss dominates the place; its Gothic church has a resplendent rococo interior.

A curiosity in this remote place is the Atommuseum, where German scientists tinkered (thankfully unsuccessfully) with a nuclear reactor in the last stages of World War II.

Wine festivals
A showcase for Baden wines, the Freiburger Weintage (Freiburg Wine Festival) is held in Münsterplatz in late June. Another city celebration with wine associations is the Fastnet (carnival) in February, when masks traditionally ward off evil spirits from the vines.

▶▶▶ **Heidelberg**

For people the world over, friendly Heidelberg is the very image of romantic Germany. The River Neckar flows through its deep wooded valley past ancient towers and bridges; the red sandstone castle ruin rises majestically over the roofs of the old town. This, and the sheer exuberance of the life led by the students of Germany's oldest and most tradition-bound university (immortalized in the ditties of Sigmund Romberg's operetta *The Student Prince*), all combine to make the place quite irresistible to countless visitors. One big draw are the boisterous student pubs of the old town, former haunts of the exclusive Verbindungen (fraternities). Here giant mugs of beer, shaped like a boot or horn, are passed around the tables.

There are good views of Heidelberg as a whole from the graceful Alte Brücke (old bridge) spanning the fast-flowing waters. The bridge's gateway, its twin towers topped by spiky helmets, has long been one of the city's landmarks. It has been a favorite source of inspiration for poets and painters, among them J. M. W. Turner, who came in 1836 and left many oils and watercolors of the city in its changing moods. If time permits, there are breathtaking views from the **Philosophenweg▶** above the quayside, the "philosophers' path" trod by many wishing to contemplate the incomparable panorama to the south.

Scientific powers
Despite the romantic image of the city, Heidelberg is a major exporter of scientific know-how to countries throughout the world. Today "Made in Heidelberg" is proof of excellent quality for a number of famous products. Research institutes include the European Molecular Biology Laboratory, the German Cancer Research Center and the Max Planck Institutes. There is also a vigorous cultural life in Heidelberg, with more than 10 museums, several theaters, galleries, and an annual theater festival that takes place in the castle in August.

Heidelberg's great 17th-century castle above the river Neckar

SOUTHWEST GERMANY

Giant wine vat

The Grosses Fass (great vat) in the Fassbau in Heidelberg's castle is a wine barrel with a capacity of 58,000 gallons, built in the 18th century to hold the tithe of Palatinate wines. On top of it is a platform used as a dance floor.

"Fill me the beaker!
Now, Rhine and Nekkar,
Health to ye both, ye noble
streams!
Yours is a power,
To bring the hour
High above Wisdom's heavy
dreams."—Walter Savage
Landor, "Gardens at
Heidelberg."

Student duels

A generation or two ago, the caricature of a German male would show a reddened, almost bald pate with perhaps a few bristles adorning the roll of fat overlapping the collar, a monocle framing a glaring eye, and a scar or two adorning a cheek. Worn with pride, and known as a *Schmiss,* such a facial scar would have been acquired in the course of the fencing bouts that were a feature of upper-class student life in the more tradition-bound universities. The contestants, wearing goggles and padding to protect their vital parts, would face each other in the company of their supporters and attendant medics. The liberal-minded students of the postwar generation were eager to put such behavior, with all its associations of fanaticism and militarism, behind them. But the tradition persisted among certain student associations and has recently come into prominence again.

The Schloss▶▶▶ High above the city's alleyways are the majestic ruins of the castle (guided tours daily), graced with fine terraced gardens, the creation of Friedrich V between 1616 and 1619. The princes of Pfalz (the Palatinate) lived here for 500 years; they included Friedrich V, who married the English princess Elizabeth Stuart, daughter of James I. It was for her that he built the Englischer Bau (English building), near the Dicker Turm (fat tower), and the Elisabethentor (Elizabeth Gate), in the form of a classical triumphal arch. It was as a 17-year-old bride that Elizabeth came to the court over which she presided for five years before she was forced to flee to Prague when Friedrich V, who was a Protestant, failed in an attempt to oust the Catholic Habsburgs from their supreme position. He was eventually stripped of his titles, and his machinations contributed to the outbreak of the Thirty Years' War. Later, the Schloss, and the city itself, suffered badly when Louis XIV attacked the Palatinate, to which he laid claim, in 1689 (four years later, a disastrous fire destroyed the old town). The castle fabric was much restored in the 19th century by Count de Graimberg, but numerous earlier features survive.

The Well House contains Roman pillars brought from Charlemagne's palace at Ingelheim. Look, too, for the 16th-century Dicker Turm and the Glockenturm (bell tower), built for defense but with six subsequent residential floors added. The Deutsches Apotheken-Museum (German apothecary museum) within the castle complex provides a fascinating look into baroque and rococo workshops of German pharmacists from the early 17th century.

The University Heidelberg's is the oldest university in Germany, founded by Elector Ruprecht I von der Pfalz in 1386. It was badly neglected during the 18th century, but in 1803 Grand Duke Karl Friedrich declared it the first state university of Baden. One part of Universitätsplatz, dating back to the 18th century, is devoted to the Alte Universität (old university) while the rest of the square is taken up by university buildings of the 1930s. The Studentenkarzer (students' jail; open daily except Sundays and holidays), in use from 1712 to 1914, was built for unruly students, whose graffiti are still in evidence. In the library (open daily except Sunday), the *Codex Manesse▶*, a 14th-century collection of Middle High German poetry, is illuminated with 137 exquisite miniatures. Here, too, is *Des Knaben Wunderhorn* (*The Boy's Magic Horn*), a collection of folk poetry that inspired the German Romantic poets and also the composer Gustav Mahler.

Excursion

About 8 miles west, **Schwetzingen** is known for its Schlosspark▶ (closed Monday), a wonderfully fanciful 18th-century dreamland of romantic follies and eye-catching sites. Beyond the formal French garden lie a Temple of Apollo, a statue of Pan playing the flute in a grotto, mock ruins, tricks of perspective, and more. Mozart conducted an orchestral concert of his own works in the theater here.

▶▶ Karlsruhe

Karlsruhe is the youngest of German cities. In 1715, tired of living in a medieval castle that had seen better days, at nearby Durlach, Margrave Karl Wilhelm of Baden Durlach began building a new residence deep in the hunting forests of the Rhine plain. A city soon grew up, laid out in the shape of a fan, with the palace at its center. This unusual pattern persists today, enhanced by the sober civic buildings in neoclassical style by Friedrich Weinbrenner. On his Marktplatz stands the famous pyramid where the town's founder is buried.

What to see Standing smack dab in its formal gardens facing the city center, the Schloss is now the home of the **Badisches Landesmuseum▶**, where the rich and beautifully presented collections include the unique Türkenbeute, the booty won by Louis the Turk (see page 174) from his Ottoman opponents. Nearby are the excellent galleries of the Kunsthalle (an array of superb old masters, including Grünewald's intensely moving *Crucifixion*, together with fine examples of German 19th-century painting) and of the Orangery. The latter has works by the 19th-century German artist Hans Thoma, who died in Karlsruhe, as well as German and French Impressionists (Monet, Cézanne, etc.) and Cubist-inspired pictures by Delaunay and Léger.

Excursions

There are superb views of the surrounding area from the **Turmberg**, high above the margrave's old castle at Durlach. Karlsruhe's sleek tramway system will whisk you out beyond the city to delightful half-timbered **Ettlingen**, also with a Schloss, or even farther into the Black Forest itself, to the upland resort of **Bad Herrenalb**.

Hertz and Benz
Students of Karlsruhe's School of Technology (1825), have included such illustrious names as Hertz, the discoverer of electromagnetic waves; Benz, inventor of the automobile; and Karl von Drais, said to have invented the bicycle.

183

Constitutional Court
Karlsruhe (Karl's rest) is no longer the capital of Baden, but its importance was confirmed by the siting here of Germany's Federal Constitutional Court.

The Schloss (ducal palace) in Karlsruhe built by the Margave Karl Wilhelm

■ **Intellectuals enjoy high status in Germany, and many universities boast hundreds of years of tradition. Before World War II they tended to be elitist, conservative bastions—many German students and professors supported Hitler's rise to power ...■**

Students performing for passersby in Tübingen, an ancient university town with a lively cultural scene

184

The student movement and after Following the subdued period of the Wirtschaftswunder (economic miracle) in the 1950s, a generation of postwar German youth began questioning the establishment—and the university system—in the student movement that exploded in 1968. Student self-governing committees were formed and curricula opened to all qualified high-school graduates. Universities became vastly overcrowded, and the quality of teaching—already affected by the civil service status of professors and the bureaucratic administration—fell. In addition, students extend their studies well into their 30s—supported by generous government grants.

In German universities campus life, such as is found in Britain or the United States, hardly exists. Students rarely live on campus, although they eat together in a student *Mensa*, or cafeteria. Pressure to succeed is relatively low in German universities, with only a few exams before finals. In addition, as western German universities do not require compulsory attendance, many students do not take their studies very seriously. However, this may be changing: proposals for more rigorous, "elite" universities are gaining ground, and a new generation of competitive Germans has appeared.

Stasi suspect
Involvement by the west since unification has had some negative consequences. For example, in Berlin, western authorities dismissed the popular head of Humboldt University, the theologian Heinrich Fink, because of suspicions of secret police (Stasi) contacts under the Communist regime. This unleashed a storm of student protest, particularly since it was suspected that many western academics were after positions in the better-known universities of eastern Germany.

In the east Under the Communists, East German universities established their own traditions, with student admissions based on political criteria. The peaceful revolution in 1989 threw the universities into chaos, with large-scale firings of professors and restructuring of departments according to western standards.

▶ Mannheim

The second-largest river port in Europe and an important industrial center, Mannheim is situated at the meeting point of the Rhine and the Neckar. Like Karlsruhe, it is an 18th-century planned town focused on its Schloss, a huge edifice that is now the seat of Mannheim's university. Laid out on a grid pattern, the streets define 144 city blocks, each of which is designated by a letter and a number, a logical system without parallel in Germany.

Mannheim is proud of its former eminence in the world of music and theater, but little of its original 18th-century architectural elegance survives. The most striking part of the town is the Jugendstil Friedrichsplatz, laid out around a monster water tower. Here is the Kunsthalle▶, with one of Germany's leading displays of 19th- and 20th-century art. In the Zeughaus (arsenal) is the Reiss Museum, where the local collections evoke the look of the city before its industrialization.

French art
Mannheim's Städtische Kunsthalle has an excellent collection of 19th-century French art, including Manet's *Execution of the Emperor Maximilian of Mexico,* a work exemplifying the artist's realism and the influence of Spanish painting on his style.

185

▶ Maulbronn

Maulbronn has one of the earliest Cistercian monasteries (founded in 1147) to survive—a superb and almost untouched example. As the locals tell it, a group of monks stopped by here to let their mules drink (the name means "mule well"), and they stayed on forever. This story is depicted in sketches for a fresco on a wall of the Brunnenkapelle (well house). The monastery church—consecrated in 1178—is basically Romanesque with later Gothic additions. You can also see the cloisters with refectory and chapter house, early 15th-century chapels, and a crucifix of 1473.

▶▶ Neckartal (Neckar Valley) and Odenwald

The Neckar rises in the Black Forest and runs for nearly 250 miles before entering the Rhine at Mannheim. Downstream from **Bad Wimpfen** it flows through charming countryside of orchards and vineyards before cutting its way through the Odenwald uplands in a deep wooded trench. The best way of enjoying its varied

The lovely Neckar river flows past numerous old castles and fortified medieval towns

Picturesque Bad Wimpfen (right) is not a spa town, but gets its name from the big local saltworks.
Odenwald natural park (below) is gently pastoral in some parts, forested in others

186

Siegfried's spring
Taken on a hunting trip to the Odenwald, Siegfried, the hero of the *Nibelungenlied,* was speared in the back by Hagen at a spring. Several springs in the area claim to be the Siegfriedsquellen.

landscapes, attractive towns and castles is from a steamer (the river has been "improved" for shipping up to Stuttgart), but road (the signposted touring route called the Burgenstrasse) and rail closely follow its winding course.

To the east of Heidelberg the road passes beneath the 2,158-foot **Königstuhl** (King's Seat), crowned by a TV tower offering a panorama of the Neckar Valley and the Rhine Plain beyond. Equally dramatic views can be enjoyed from the castle ruins of **Dilsberg**, while Neckarsteinach is overlooked by no fewer than four castles. **Eberbach** has quaint inns and pubs, including the Wirtshaus Kraabbenstein, as well as Germany's oldest bathhouse (the 13th-century Altes Badhaus). The little resort of **Zwingenberg** has a splendid medieval castle; the Wolfsschlucht ravine inspired Weber's opera *Der Freischütz.* Just off the main valley, **Mosbach** is well known for its fine collection of half-timbered buildings. Back on the Neckar again, **Burg Hornberg** (open daily April to October) dates back to 1148, while **Burg Guttenberg** (open daily March to November) is famous today for its birds of prey, which are flown in public demonstrations.

Bad Wimpfen►► is the highlight of the valley. This fortified medieval town was once the imperial residence of the Hohenstaufens and retains an appealing mélange of half-timbering, narrow streets, and stepped gables.

The tall tower known as the Blauer Turm stands squarely among the steep-pitched roofs and gives the best views over town and river.

Odenwald Stretching northward from the Neckar, this wooded upland of beech and spruce contrasts strongly with the fertile landscapes of the Bergstrasse, running along its western rim. It is traversed from west to east by the Niebelungenstrasse on its way from Worms to Wurzburg, an attractive touring route that passes through delightful **Michelstadt**. The little town's Rathaus, with its stout oak columns and its corner turrets, is almost too picturesque to be true. Michelstadt makes a good center for visiting several of the Odenwald's other attractions: **Eulbach Park**, with ornamental hunting grounds dating from the 18th century; Renaissance **Schloss Fürstenau**, in a pretty countryside setting; and **Erbach**, also with a Schloss, plus a unique museum of ivory carving, or the nearby Einhardsbasilika—like the Torhalle at Lorsch, a striking example of Carolingian architecture, completed in the year 827.

187

▶ Ravensburg

This old town thrived in the Middle Ages, with its position on a great trade route connecting northern Europe to Italy. Before the rise of the Fuggers of Augsburg, the Ravensburger Handelsgesellschaft was southern Germany's most important trading company.

Ravensburg grew up at the foot of the Veitsburg, the fortified hill where Henry the Lion was born. The town walls are still mostly intact, with several gates and towers, including the Mehlsack (flour-sack tower), originally erected so the citizens could keep an eye on the Veitsburg. The Marienplatz is full of character, with another tall tower, the Blaserturm; a 15th-century Rathaus; and the Waaghaus, the focus of trading activity. Its hall once rang with the cries of foreign merchants promoting their wares while weights and measures were checked on the main floor.

▶ Rottweil

Rottweil enjoys a dramatic setting on a spur overlooking a bend in the upper Neckar. Its streets are a delight of fine old houses, mostly Renaissance and baroque, with such features as elaborate oriel windows and exuberant carving.

A further contribution to the townscape is made by four Renaissance fountains—the Marktbrunnen is the most splendid. The town's churches include the Kapellenkirche, baroquified inside but with a richly decorated Gothic tower, and the Heiligkreuz Minster, with a *Crucifixion* above its high altar attributed to Veit Stoss. The Lorenzkapelle houses a fine array of medieval sculpture.

The interesting local museum (Stadtmuseum) recalls the Roman presence here with a 2nd-century mosaic of Orpheus and also displays some of the weird and wonderful wooden masks worn at carnival time. Fastnet (carnival) spans six days; the climax is the Narrensprung (Fools' Dance) on the Monday before Shrove Tuesday and on Shrove Tuesday itself.

Ravensburg, once a Guelph bastion, is a fine old town of towers and painted gateways

SCHWÄBISCHE ALB

[Map of the Schwäbische Alb region showing towns including Metzingen, Dettingen, Westerheim, Bad Urach, Reutlingen, Pfullingen, Laichingen, Rottenburg, Neckar, Nehelhöhle, Münsingen, Blaubeuren, Bad Imnau, Mössingen, Lichtenstein, Engstingen, Gomadingen, Schelklingen, Haigerloch, Hechingen, Kornbühl, Buttenhausen, Schmiech, Rosenfeld, Hohenzollern, Trochtelfingen, Ehingen, Balingen, Raichberg 956m, Burladingen, Pfronstetten, Hayingen, Donau, Tailfingen, Gammertingen, Wimsener Höhle, Riss, Neufra, Zwiefalten, Obermachtal, Munderkingen, Albstadt, Hettingen, Winterlingen, Oberstadion, Messstetten, Veringenstadt, Riedlingen, Stetten a.Kalten, Langenenslingen, Dürmentingen, Biberach, Naturpark, Hausen, Sigmaringen, Federsee, Spaichingen, Wildenstein, Donau, Herbertingen, Bad Buchau, Obere Donau, Beuron, Mengen, Steinhausen, Mühlheim, Fridingen, Messkirch, Krauchenwies, Saulgau, Bad Schussenried, Tuttlingen, Lemberg 1015m, Wehingen, Grosser Heuberg, Nusplingen, Schömberg 963m, Lauchert, Schmeie, Gr. Lauter)]

Beuron monastery
The village of Beuron, west of Sigmaringen, clusters around its huge abbey. Founded by the Augustinians in the 11th century, Kloster Beuron now belongs to the Benedictines. It is celebrated for the monks' singing of the Gregorian chant (which can be heard by visitors at high mass and vespers) and for the Nazarenes, an early 19th-century group of artists who came here and adopted an early Christian art style (later known as the Beuron School). Male visitors might find accommodations in the abbey.

► **Schwäbische Alb (Swabian Jura)**

The Schwäbische Alb is a range of limestone hills to the east of the Black Forest, about 35 miles wide and 95 miles long. The young River Danube flows romantically through part of the region in a landscape of wooded limestone cliffs, crag-top castles and green meadows. The southwest part of the Schwäbische Alb has been designated the Naturpark Obere Donau (Upper Danube Nature Park).

The name of Hohenzollern is closely associated with this part of Germany—forged by the marriage of the Zollerns, originally Swabian overlords, to the Burgraves of Nuremberg. From the early 1700s, the family, as rulers of Brandenburg and Prussia, fought to establish a German empire and finally achieved this in 1871 under Wilhelm I. In 1918, after defeat in World War I, Wilhelm II abdicated, but the family name and tradition continue. The present head of the family, who would have the title of kaiser if the empire had continued, is Prince Ludwig Ferdinand of Prussia, grandson of Wilhelm II.

In **Sigmaringen**, at the mouth of the Upper Danube gap, the Swabian Catholic branch of the family managed to hold on to its **castle►**, which today is the product of several periods, most prominently of 19th-century Romanticism. There are guided tours from February to November; you have to leave your car at the Rathaus and walk from there. During the height of the tourist season there are vast crowds, but it is worth the wait. For those with an avid interest in European royalty this is a treasure trove, and there is perhaps the largest collection of armory and weapons in Europe, with more than 3,000 items in one hoard. In the neo-Gothic hall a splendid collection of south German art of the 15th and 16th centuries includes works by the Master of Sigmaringen—actually two brothers, Hans and Jacob

Strüb. The Johanniskirche, on the castle rock, is decorated with elaborate rococo stuccowork and houses the shrine of St. Fidelio, a local martyr.

Between Sigmaringen and Tuttlingen the Danube flows through a superb gorge dominated by crags and lofty castles, including Burg Wildenstein (now a youth hostel), giving a spectacular view of the river, and the Knopfermacherfelsen, a magnificent viewpoint from a chaos of cliffs.

In a valley at the edge of the Schwäbische Alb lies **Zwiefalten**. The great Münster here rivals its Bavarian counterparts in splendor. The abbey church is largely the work of the south German 18th-century architect J. M. Fischer. Its spacious interior is lavishly decorated in a whirl of white and gold, with stucco masquerading as marble; the sculptures and large figures on the altar, set between pink and white columns, are by J. J. Christian. Among the many caves hollowed out in the soft limestone of the Alb, the **Wimsener Höhle** is perhaps the finest. It can be entered by boat. The church at **Obermachtal**, built 1686, displays stucco decoration and is an early example of wall-pillar construction, where a wall of internal buttresses represents a refinement to the medieval approach of using external flying buttresses.

Cherry spirit
Dettingen in the Schwäbisch Alb is famous for its Kirschgeist (cherry spirit). Selected cherries are cropped to make this strong, clear pick-me-up, which is drunk from thimble-size glasses.

189

Broom-pubs
Amid the vine-clad hills east of Stuttgart, you'll find delightful wine pubs in the cozy villages—Stetten and Kernen, Uhlbach with its wine museum, and Strumpfelbach whose tiny quaint Rathaus stands in the middle of the road. One old tradition in this area is that of the *Besenwirtschaft* (broom pub): from November to March, many wine growers put a broom outside their houses to show that their new wine is ready, and they run an impromptu pub. You can sit among the locals in a chummy ambience, drinking the semi-fermented wine at well below pub prices.

In Schwäbish Hall, St. Michael's church is noted for its high vaulted ceiling and fine 16th-century altarpiece

SOUTHWEST GERMANY

Jurassic fossils
At Holzmaden, near Kirchheim, the remarkable Hauff museum displays fossilized skeletons of Ichthyosaurs 160–180 million years old. The Hauff family have long owned stone quarries here in the Swabian Jura, and they unearthed these crocodile-like Jurassic relics buried in the schist. Their museum includes big fossilized sea lilies looking like sea urchins, and a saurian mother with five embryos in her womb.

Hohenstaufen
Schwäbisch Gmünd was once the possession of the Hohenstaufen family, which ruled the Holy Roman Empire from 1138 to 1254. When the family fell from power, Schwäbisch Gmünd became a Free Imperial City.

Burg Hohenzollern►, the original seat of the Hohenzollern family, presents a spectacular outline, sited on a peak 2,788 feet above sea level near the town of Hechingen. There are guided tours and the castle is open all year round. The castle was largely rebuilt in the mid-19th century, but the 12th-century Catholic chapel of St. Michael, with beautiful stained glass, the oldest in Germany, remains. The Protestant chapel held the tomb of Frederick the Great until the mighty monarch's mortal remains were reburied at Potsdam in 1991 (see panel page 45). Many of his possessions, such as his uniforms and military decorations, can still be seen here.

Schloss Lichtenstein (open daily; weekends only November to March), a formidable 19th-century fortress, caps a craggy peak. Close by are several worthwhile caves, including the Nebelhöhle and the Bärenhöhle. Farther west, Rossberg (2,850 feet) gives a vast panorama of the region from its viewing tower.

Bad Urach is a pleasant small resort sited in a narrow valley and endowed with a pleasing half-timbered square. Out of town to the west, **Urach Waterfall** is attractively set only a short walk away from the main road.

►   Schwäbisch Gmünd

This attractive town set in good walking country, just north of the Schwäbische Alb, is famous for its jewelry and silver tableware. The 14th-century master builder Peter Parler was born here. One of the main works of the Parler family is the Heiligkreuzmünster (Cathedral of the Holy Cross). The attractive exterior includes fine tracery, pinnacles and a depiction of the Last Judgment in the south portal. The interior conforms to the Cistercian hall plan. Notice the magnificent vaulting, the Tree of Jesse altar in the Baptistery, and the carved choir stalls. The local museum (Johannisplatz 3) concentrates on late Gothic and baroque sculpture. The town maintains its craft traditions with its well-known college of gold- and silversmithing.

A short distance south of Schwäbisch Gmünd are the **Kaiserberge**, three wooded hills once topped by castles. One of these, Hohenstaufen, was the original seat of the great imperial family. There are wide-ranging views from ruined **Hohenrechberg**, which also has a baroque pilgrimage church.

►►   Schwäbisch Hall

One of the treasures of southwest Germany, this medieval town nestles in the heart of the Swabian forests, on the banks of the River Kocher, a tributary of the Neckar. Many of the houses and buildings are neatly arranged in tiers that overlook the ancient wooden bridges over the river. The site was already known for its saltwater springs in the 3rd century BC, and these encouraged a permanent Celtic settlement. During the Middle Ages, Schwäbisch Hall began to mint silver coins, first known as the Häller and then later renamed Heller (the name derives from Hall, meaning "place of salt"). In the 13th century the town became a Free Imperial City.

Its charming, sloping **Marktplatz►** is often reckoned to be among the most stunning in Germany. It is used for theatrical performances (June to August). The baroque **Rathaus►**, built 1730–35, has a palatial appearance and is architecturally one of the most important buildings of its time. It was rebuilt after war damage. The roof proudly displays a decorative clock and imperial eagle. The central part of the square is dominated by the

Timbered buildings above the river Kocher in Schwäbisch Hall

Marktbrunnen, a 16th-century fountain adorned with statues of St. Michael with St. George and Samson. The old pillory forms part of the fountain's structure. The Pfarrkirche (St. Michael's) adjoins the Marktplatz and you can reach it by mounting a wide flight of stairs. The church has hardly been touched since 1573, and besides the tombs in the chapels, there are interesting furnishings in the choir stalls, tabernacle, and altars.

The Keckenburg, once an aristocratic mansion, houses the Hällisch Fränkisches Museum (open daily except Monday), explaining the town's history.

About 18 miles north, the quiet countryside between the Swabian Forest and the Tauber Valley is known as the Hohenloher Ebene, after the princely German family, the House of Hohenlohe; here the most common language is the Schwäbish (Swabian) dialect, which even other Germans find difficult to understand.

At **Jagsthausen** is the much restored Götzenburg castle (now a hotel), which in 1480 was the birthplace of the knight Götz von Berlichingen—the Knight with the Iron Hand. Goethe wrote a drama about him, and every summer a drama festival including Goethe's play is held in the courtyard of the castle. About 4 miles on is the Cistercian abbey of **Schöntal** in the Jagst Valley (guided tours daily April to October). The church is famed for its 17th-century alabaster altarpieces.

At **Öhringen** the late Gothic Stiftskirche (dedicated to St. Peter and St. Paul), on the Marktplatz, contains tombs of members of the house of Hohenlohe. Note the monument to Philip of Hohenlohe, son-in-law of William the Silent, with detailed reliefs of battles from the Netherlands' War of Independence. Foremost among the furnishings is the high altar from around 1500.

The Schloss at **Neuenstein** (with an interesting collection of weapons) has been Hohenlohe family property since the 13th century and displays a variety of styles, including Renaissance, Romanesque and Gothic. **Waldenburg** was a fortified town, from which the princely family overlooked the plain and protected their empire.

Salt heroes
Schwäbisch Hall's annual Whit Week festival recalls an occasion when salt workers saved the town's mill from fire, and is called the Kuchen und Brunn en Fest de Haller Salzsieder—the Cake and Fountain Festival of the Salt Miners of Hall.

At Schwäbisch Hall in summer, a drama festival is held in the sloping Marktplatz

▶▶▶ Schwarzwald (Black Forest)

The highest land in southwest Germany, the Black Forest is a rewarding area for gentle exploration. Only in the gloom of its most inaccessible stands of spruce does the term "black" seem appropriate, and by no means all of it is woodland. Picturesque wooden farmhouses and pleasantly unassuming villages nestling in green valleys are distinctive elements of the landscape; the terrain gets more open as you travel south into the orchards and farmlands of the Markgräfliches Land. The western slopes are dominated by vineyards; the **Badische Weinstrasse** (Baden Wine Road) winds through the Black Forest foothills. Development across the region is mostly low-key and small-scale, with few big resorts.

Beneath all this is a thriving and well-organized tourist industry, mostly catering to the Germans themselves, who come for short breaks and nonmedical "cures." Newish hotels in traditional style are found on the edges of many villages and are scattered around the country areas. Sports facilities (mostly one-on-one activities,

The Schwarzwald is noted for its special rural architecture, as well as traditional industries and local costumes, still worn for Sunday church and festivals

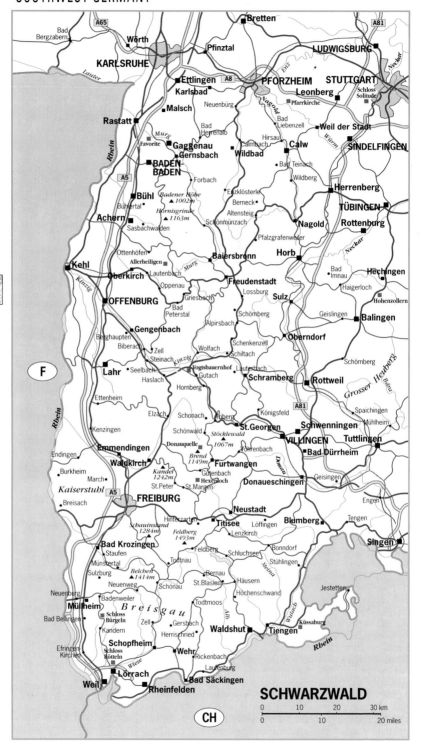

SCHWARZWALD

Huge ornamental clocks are typical of the Schwarzwald. One cuckoo-clock at Schönach forms the entire side of a chalet

such as tennis and squash) have been developed to an impressive degree, even in many smaller villages. The region excels as an area for outdoor pursuits, above all for walking; marked paths of varying degrees of difficulty (including many very easy ones) abound; signposting and tourist information are excellent. A useful tourist-board scheme is *Wandern ohne Gepäck* (walking without luggage), where you can walk from village to village, to prebooked guest houses, and have your luggage transported by car. In winter, many come here for cross-country skiing.

Black Forest specialties are prolific. Most famous are undoubtedly the Schwarzwälder Kirschtorte (of which the ubiquitous factory-made Black Forest cake is a pale imitation), and the cuckoo clocks on sale in every souvenir shop. Zwiebelkuchen (onion cake) is often served accompanied by a young white wine. Black Forest smoked ham is best eaten sliced thinly on locally made bread. In season, white asparagus, plums, and cherries appear on the menu. Local drinks include the Baden wines and Kirschwasser, an unsweetened type of cherry brandy.

The heart of Black Forest clock making is centered around the industrial town and spa of **Triberg** (see pages 196–7). **Furtwangen** is the home of the Deutsches Uhrenmuseum (German clock museum), a must even for non-enthusiasts. There are also factories and workshops in the area, which will be only too pleased to give you a firsthand glimpse of local clock production in this region.

Southern Schwarzwald You will find this region one of the sunniest in Germany. The cherry trees display their blossoms in the early spring while the mountains are still topped with snow from the previous winter. Four of the region's tallest hills lie close to **Freiburg**—the Feldberg, Schauinsland, Kandel, and the Belchen. All are easily reached from the road, but the Belchen has the best views; and just north of it is **Münstertal▶**, a deep and especially pretty valley, steep-sided and graced with the

Clock making
The tradition of Black Forest clock making goes back to 1667, when the wooden clock with foliot (weighted arm) was made for the first time in Waldau. Metal for the mechanisms was imported until 1787, when Leopold Hofmayer set up his brass foundry in Neustadt. Since then numerous variations have been produced, among them musical clocks with trumpeters or flutes, clocks with painted or lacquered shields, clocks to control watchmen, all leading to regulators, alarm clocks, even modern quartz-crystal clocks and radio clocks. As early as 1840, subsidiaries of the Black Forest clock traders existed in four continents and 23 countries. In 1845, 600,000 clocks were produced in the Black Forest—today the figure stands at 60 million a year!

baroque church of St. Trudpert. East of the Feldberg is one of the main resort areas; many come for the two lakes, the **Titisee** and the **Schluchsee**. Of these, the Titisee is the prettier, set among gentle woodlands, but the modern village on its northern side partly spoils the effect; the Schluchsee attracts older people and is less commercialized. More peaceful is **Hinterzarten**, an upmarket family resort.

The views are breathtaking in this area, whichever way you decide to travel. If it fits in with your plans, you might want to take a train ride from Freiburg to **Feldberg Bärental**, following a steep and winding route through the Höllental (Hell Valley) Gorge. The station at Feldberg Bärental is proud of its special location, at 3,200 feet the highest train station in Germany. If you prefer to put on your hiking boots, the nearby **Feldbergsee** lies at the end of an unspoiled romantic road available only to walkers.

Farther south, the terrain is lower and less spectacular, but the country is more open—typically consisting of orchards, meadows, and rounded hills of small-scale charm. There is less tourist development, and plenty of old-fashioned farmhouses have survived. Of the resorts, **Todtmoos** is especially pleasant, nicely placed amid gentle hills.

Not far from the Swiss border, halfway between Freiburg and Basel, is **Badenweiler▶**, a popular tourist attraction not only because of its spa, but also because of its fine views over the Rhine plain. The thermal springs here, well preserved since their rediscovery in 1784, have been flowing since Roman times. Today's inhabitants are intent on keeping things as clean and intact as possible, and you have to leave your car on the edge of town and walk in. There are open-air pavilions where numerous musical events are held throughout the summer months.

About 5 miles to the south of Badenweiler is **Schloss Bürgeln**, built in 1764 on the orders of the abbot of the Benedictine abbey of St. Blasien. From here you can obtain a spectacular view of the surroundings as far as the Swiss Alps.

Gutach and Kinzig valleys: the central Schwarzwald

A journey north through some fine towns and villages will bring you into the Gutach and Kinzig valleys. Here you will see examples of the distinctive Black Forest farmhouses with their low-hanging roofs, deep eaves and animal quarters under the roof, usually approached by an earth ramp. This is the heartland of Black Forest folk costume, such as the wide-brimmed hats with red pom-poms worn by local girls. The **Schwarzwaldbahn** (Black Forest railway), with its 45 tunnels, crosses this landscape.

The highest waterfall in Germany (531 feet) is at **Triberg▶** (the Gutach falls). Cuckoo-clock skeptics may be surprised that the business launched by Josef Weisser in 1824 in Triberg, called the "Haus der 1000 Uhren" (House of 1,000 Clocks), is still thriving. Triberg is not just clocks, however. It is a year-round spa, a winter-sports resort and a relaxed sort of town. The forest at Triberg acts as a dust filter, and visitors to the

Fruit cakes
As well as Schwarzwälder Kirschtorte (cherry cake), Black Foresters have other delicacies to tempt the sweet tooth at coffee time. Zwetschenkuchen (blue plums on a pastry base), Käsesahnekuchen (a rich cheesecake) and Johannisbeerenkuchen (a sponge cake covered with red currants) are just a few.

spa and health resort often remark on the purity of the air. In Triberg's **Schwarzwald Museum►** you'll find a wide array of local costumes on display, as well as wood carvings, ceramics and—of course—clock-making memorabilia, which will give you an idea of the rural culture. **Gutach** is known for the Vogtsbauernhof, an imaginatively arranged open-air museum with an absorbing collection of reconstructed and traditionally furnished thatched farmhouses, complete with farm implements; in its country setting, the whole place has the feel of a real village.

Freudenstadt► was badly damaged in World War II and has little ancient character, but it has been carefully reconstructed and is now second only to Baden-Baden as a health resort. The town sits high on a plateau at the meeting point of all the main routes in the northern Schwarzwald. The arcaded market square, which is Germany's largest, has neatly laid out sidewalks and lawns. The unusual 17th-century Stadtkirche has aisles set at right-angles, each with its own green-domed tower, and a glorious 12th-century carved lectern.

To the south, **Schiltach** and **Wolfach**, both close to main roads, are among the prettiest Black Forest villages and boast half-timbered market squares.

The northern Schwarzwald The B500 Schwarzwald Hochstrasse linking Freudenstadt with Baden-Baden is

Dark green trees, reflected in dark water, give the "Black" forest its name

Dying trees
Dying and diseased trees with yellowing needles and peeling bark are widespread in the forests. Acid rain is thought to be the main culprit, and government pollution controls have been increased to curb the *Waldsterben*—Dying Forest Syndrome.

SOUTHWEST GERMANY

Frolicking fools
The folklore frivolity of winter carnival, known as Fastnacht in the Black Forest, Fasching in Bavaria, is eagerly pursued in Catholic areas. The fun starts on the "Elfte Elfte Elfte Elfte" (11:11 AM on November 11), to reach a climax before Lent. At Elzach,masked fools clad in red scourge people with blown-up hogs' bladders; at Wolfach, fools scour the town in nightgowns and nightcaps; at Uberlingen they crack long whips.

a popular road. It runs along almost the entire spine of the Black Forest. There are numerous roadside stopping places that will enable you to picnic alfresco—if the weather allows—and to admire the view. Alternatively, there are plenty of villages or hamlets for a meal or perhaps an overnight stay. At romantic **Allerheiligen▶**, the ruins of a 13th-century church stand next to three 18th-century ornamental fishponds.

The drive along the Nagold Valley from Freudenstadt (part of the Schwarzwald Bäderstrasse) brings you to **Pforzheim**, at the northern extremity of the Schwarzwald, some 18 miles north of Calw, with its half-timbered houses. At Pforzheim, the River Nagold joins the River Enz. As a center of the jewelry trade, the town likes to think of itself as wealthy and has christened itself "Goldstadt" (town of gold). The Schmuckmuseum (jewelry museum) is in the Reuchlinhaus in Jahnstrasse. Pforzheim is also the starting point for hikes into the northern tip of the Schwarzwald (see **Walks**, below, for possible walking routes).

Walks Black Forest footpaths

The Black Forest offers an excellent range of long-distance walks, taking in viewpoints, unspoiled farmland, villages and wetlands. Signposting (look for diamond-shaped signs) and path maintenance are of a high standard; there are plenty of good-quality accommodations on the way, and there's no shortage of refreshment facilities.
Long tracks divide into Hohenwege (hill paths), which take north–south courses along the footpaths, and Querwege (linking paths), which lead west–east. Of the four Hohenwege, the longest is the 220-mile Pforzheim-to-Basel Westweg. The Querwege range from the 102-mile Freiburg-to-Bodensee Querwege to short expeditions such as the 30-mile Rheinfelden-to-Albbruck path.

Boats at Titisee

►► Speyer

The Rhine town of Speyer possesses, in its cathedral►►, one of Europe's great Romanesque churches. Founded in 1030, it was remodeled at the end of the 11th century with four towers and two domes. Located in front is the Domnapf (cathedral bowl) of 1490, where wine is traditionally poured at the induction of a new bishop or for other special occasions, such as the 2,000th anniversary of the city in 1990. At the entrance to the vault of the emperors, or **Kaisergruft►**, the name given to the huge 11th-century crypt► (the largest of its period in Germany) where eight rulers were buried, is the 13th-century tomb of Rudolph of Habsburg. From the cathedral's west front the broad Maximilianstrasse leads to the massive Altpörtel, the only city gateway to have survived.

At the Historisches Museum der Pfalz (Palatinate Museum, open daily) the Bronze Age "Golden Hat" of Schifferstadt is the highlight of the collection, which includes paintings and porcelain from ancient through to modern times. The Weinmuseum (Wine Museum) in the same building houses wine-making equipment with, amazingly, a 3rd-century bottle of wine (complete with contents).

The synagogue that once existed in Speyer has been destroyed, but 33 feet below ground level in Judenbadgasse is the Judenbad, a fine example of the ritual baths used by Jews for cleansing on important religious holidays and by brides prior to their wedding.

Heavy diet
Speyer hosted 50 imperial diets (assemblies) in the course of the Holy Roman Empire's history. As well as the emperor and the six electors, the diet was made up of 30 lay princes, 140 counts and lords, 120 bishops and archbishops, and the representatives of 200 cities.

199

Of the baroque churches of upper Swabia, one of the finest is the Wallfahrtskirche in the village of Steinhausen, near Biberach

► Steinhausen

Steinhausen's Wallfahrtskirche (pilgrimage church), built between 1728 and 1733, is the work of two brothers—Dominikus and Johann Baptist Zimmermann—who perfected the baroque style in the churches they designed and decorated. Dominikus designed the building and Johann was the painter; both were involved in the stucco work. The airy oval nave with an encircling gallery above has been left as the brothers decorated it. Stucco flowers, insects, birds, and squirrels form part of the composition. Not all the work originally intended was completed, as the building cost four times as much as was estimated in 1727. Work ceased in 1733.

Daimler and Benz
Stuttgart's prosperity is built on the work of Gottlieb Daimler, who developed the gasoline engine and produced one of the world's first automobiles in the city in the 1880s. In 1926 the Daimler company merged with that of Carl Benz (another automobile pioneer) to form Daimler-Benz.

In central Stuttgart, a café facing the elegant Schlossplatz

▶▶ Stuttgart

Capital of the *Land* of Baden-Württemberg, Stuttgart has an enviable valley setting among green hills. Home of charismatic names like Mercedes, Porsche, Bosch and Zeiss, the city is one of the most glittering jewels in the crown of industrial Germany, its standard of living one of the highest in the country. Cultural and environmental standards are high, too, with splendid galleries and a park system that is a model of its kind.

Stuttgart's evolution was closely tied to the fortunes of the house of Württemberg, who made the city their seat in the 14th century. Under Napoleon, who made Württemberg a kingdom, the city became a royal capital, and though this lasted only a century, something of the feeling of royal splendor has persisted to the present. Stuttgart takes its name from a stud farm (Stutengarten) established in the 10th century by the duke of Swabia, and a horse features in the city's coat of arms. In spite of being the focus of a metropolitan region of some 2 million people, the city has a relaxed air about it, possibly something to do with the abundance of vineyards within the municipal boundary; grapes grow within throwing distance of the central station.

Car museum
Both the Porsche Museum and the splendid Daimler-Benz museum are outside Stuttgart center but easily accessible by the S-Bahn rapid transit system. Porsche features racing cars, Daimler-Benz all kinds of stars from the Mercedes stable, right down to the first "Popemobile."

A good way of starting your tour of Stuttgart is to ascend the 723-foot TV Tower (Fernsehturm), completed in 1956 and the first of its kind in Germany. It rises above the woods in the south of the city. The viewing platform offers a magnificent panorama.

What to see The traffic-free main street, Königstrasse, runs south from the monumental train station to the vast Schlossplatz. Here are some of Stuttgart's great civic buildings, such as the baroque Neues Schloss, last home of the Württemberg kings and now used for government purposes; the shop-lined neoclassical

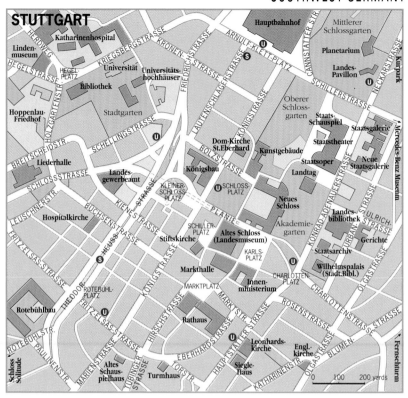

STUTTGART

(Map labels:) Katharinenhospital, Linden-museum, HERWEG, HEGELSTRASSE, HEGEL-PLATZ, KRIEGSBERGSTRASSE, KRONENSTR., Universität, Universitäts-hochhäuser, Bibliothek, ARNULF-KLETT-PLATZ, Hauptbahnhof, Mittlerer Schlossgarten, Planetarium, Landes-Pavillon, CANNSTATTER STR., SCHILLERSTRASSE, Kurpark, NECKARSTRASSE, Hoppenlau-Friedhof, Stadtgarten, HOLZGARTENSTR., SCHELLINGSTRASSE, LAUTENSCHLAGERSTRASSE, KÖNIGSTRASSE, Oberer Schloss-garten, Staats-Schauspiel, Staatsgalerie, Mercedes-Benz Museum, Liederhalle, BREITSCHEIDSTR., SCHLOSSSTRASSE, Landes-gewerbeamt, KLEINER SCHLOSS-PLATZ, Dom-Kirche St.Eberhard, BOLZSTRASSE, Königsbau, Kunstgebäude, Staatstheater, Staatsoper, Landtag, Neue Staatsgalerie, LEUSCHNERSTR., Hospitalkirche, BUCHSENSTRASSE, KIENESTRASSE, HEUSSSTRASSE, SCHLOSS-PLATZ, PLANIE, Stiftskirche, SCHILLER-PLATZ, Altes Schloss (Landesmuseum), Akademie-garten, Neues Schloss, Landes-bibliothek, KONRAD-ADENAUERSTRASSE, URBANSTRASSE, ULRICHSTRASSE, Gerichte, FRITZ-ELSAS-STRASSE, KARLS-PLATZ, Staatsarchiv, Markthalle, THEODOR-HEUSS-STRASSE, ROTEBÜHL-PLATZ, KÖNIGSTRASSE, MARKTPLATZ, Innen-ministerium, CHARLOTTEN-PLATZ, Wilhelmspalais (Städt.Bibl.), CHARLOTTENSTRASSE, OLGASTRASSE, Rotebühlbau, FRITZ-ELSAS-STRASSE, HIRSCHSTRASSE, MARKTSTR., Rathaus, ROSENSTRASSE, ROTEBÜHLSTR., PAULINENSTR., MARIENSTRASSE, TÜBINGER STRASSE, Altes Schaus-pielhaus, Turmhaus, TORSTR., EBERHARDSTRASSE, HAUPTSTÄTTER STRASSE, Leonhards-kirche, Engl.-kirche, Siegle-Haus, KATHARINENSTR., BLUMENSTRASSE, Fernsehturm, Schloss Solitude, 0 100 200 yards, 201

Königsbau; and the City Art Gallery. Linking the much more atmospheric Schillerplatz is the **Altes Schloss▶**, part medieval castle, part Renaissance palace, home of the Landesmuseum with its memorabilia of the House of Württemberg as well as an excellent collection of Swabian religious sculpture. Beyond the expressway is one of Europe's great modern art galleries, the **Staatsgalerie▶▶▶** (see page 202).

It is possible to walk from the city center via parks and gardens to the far bank of the Neckar and Bad Cannstatt, Stuttgart's spa, with its Kurhaus. The Canstatter Volksfest in September is one of Germany's largest beer festivals.

A good 10 miles from Stuttgart is **Schloss Solitude▶**, a fine example of 18th-century rococo and a glimpse of life under the Württemberg rulers, who used it as a summer residence (open daily except Monday).

Several places of interest lie close to the Neckar and other rivers. To the north are **Ludwigsburg**, with Germany's largest baroque **castle▶▶** (guided tours daily), where mechanical figures act out fairy tales in the Märchengarten (Fairy-tale Garden); **Marbach**, where Friedrich Schiller was born in 1759—his house (open daily) contains a few personal mementos—and where today the impressive **Schiller National Museum▶** (open daily) attracts literary pilgrims; and **Besigheim**, with its walls and towers. Felsengärten Hessigheim, a natural rock "garden," towers over a bend in the Neckar.

The Duke of Württemberg still inhabits Ludwigsburg's vast castle

■ **The Staatsgalerie was founded by Wilhelm I of Württemberg in 1843. Its famous extension, inaugurated in March 1984, was designed by a British architect, the late James Stirling. This new building put Stuttgart on the map in the world of art and architecture. Its varied forms and bold use of different materials have made it one of the landmarks of Postmodernism—and it is surprisingly popular with the public. Some 25 percent of the DM 70 million for its construction came from Lotto monies collected since 1958 ...■**

Modern collection The art is worthy of the building, with works by Henri Matisse and Oskar Schlemmer, Joseph Beuys and Alberto Giacometti, Franz Marc and Giorgio de Chirico. Modern German art is particularly well represented. The gallery also houses the largest Picasso collection in Germany.

The old gallery The mainstream collection of the Staatsgalerie provides an overview of the history of western European painting, with works from medieval times to the 19th century, from early altarpieces to French Impressionists. There is a particularly fine collection of works from the local 15th-century Swabian school; other German works include Cranach's *Judith with the Head of Holofernes* and Hans Baldung Grien's *Man of Sorrows*. One of the most important works is the Herrenberg Altar, with vivid scenes of Christ's Passion painted by Jörg Ratgeb in 1518–19 for the Herrenberg collegiate church; it was brought to Stuttgart in 1892. Almost every major 19th-century French painter is represented—including Manet, Monet, and Cézanne. One of the best-known works of German Romantic painting, Caspar David Friedrich's *The Cross in the Woods*, is in the Staatsgalerie. If you favor Romantic art, don't miss the eight scenes from *The Legend of Perseus* by English Pre-Raphaelite Edward Burne-Jones. The Dutch masters—Memling, Hals, Rubens and Rembrandt—are prominent, too.

Some of the best treasures are displayed in the basement—for security *and* to preserve the collection from environmental damage.

The gallery is located at Konrad Adenauerstrasse 30–32, tel: 2125050. *Open*: Wednesday, Friday–Sunday, 10–5, Tuesday and Thursday, 10–8.

Outside Tübingen's old Rathaus, farmers mix with students on market days

Küng dismissed
Founded on papal authority as a training center for Protestant ministers in the Reformation, Tübingen University has become the focus for religious controversy with the removal of Hans Küng, an academic theologian, for criticizing church dogma.

►► Tübingen

Situated on the tranquil upper reaches of the Neckar, Tübingen is one of Germany's oldest and most atmospheric university towns. Less plagued than Heidelberg by tourism, though quite its equal in charm, it has a castle, Hohentübingen, high above old color-washed houses, their gables turned to the river. The university, founded in 1477, has always been strong on philosophy, theology, and medicine. The philosopher Hegel was a pupil.

The best view of the town is from the Eberhardsbrücke over the Neckar. The bridge gives access to a long island between two arms of the river. The Platanenallee promenade, so called because it is lined with plane trees, is a favorite place for an evening stroll.

Schloss Hohentübingen is of Renaissance date, built on 11th-century foundations. Its entrance gateway bears the coat of arms of the house of Württemberg, together with the Order of the Garter awarded to one of the dukes by Queen Elizabeth I of England.

The Marktplatz, with its Neptune fountain, seems to be the hub of all the narrow winding streets and is still the focus of attention—particularly on market days (Monday, Wednesday, and Friday). On one side of the square is the 15th-century (but much restored) Rathaus►; a short distance east (in Münzgasse) is the Protestant collegiate church of St. Georg, which contains late Gothic features, including notably the rood screen, vaulting, and tracery.

Excursion

Reutlingen, 6 miles east of Tübingen, retains town walls and numerous fine buildings, despite war damage. In particular see the Marienkirche, a strikingly unified Gothic church of the 13th and 14th centuries.

The Cistercian monastery at Bebenhausen►, north of Tübingen, was founded 1185 and is encompassed by a double wall and centered on a late Gothic cloister (completed in 1496).

Famous writers
After the establishment of the "Cotta" publishing house—which published works by Goethe and Schiller—many distinguished writers and poets came to make their home in Tübingen. These included Friedrich Hölderlin, and the tower where he lived, insane, for 36 years is on the riverbank (it can be visited daily except Monday). The poets Eduard Mörike and Ludwig Uhland, as well as the philosophers Hegel and Schelling, also came to Tübingen.

*Ulm Münster (right)
boasts a set of 15th-
century carved choir
stalls (below)*

►► Ulm

Ulm's location at a significant crossing point of the Danube made it an important trading center in the late Middle Ages. The city suffered severe damage in a bombing raid in 1944, which virtually destroyed the old center, but much of the ancient edifices have now been restored. Ulm's most famous son was Albert Einstein, born here in 1879.

The best general view is from the Tahn Ufer, on the far side of the Danube. Look for the leaning gateway known as the Metzgerturm (butchers' tower). The Münster►► is one of the largest and most important religious buildings in Europe, and it was fortunately little damaged by the 1944 bombs. Construction began in 1377, and was completed, with the tower and steeple, in 1890. The latter, the tallest in the world, soars 528 feet above the rest of the city. You can climb almost to the top (768 steps) for a small charge and take in a view stretching from the Danube across the Black Forest to the Swiss Alps, if the weather is on your side. Above the doorway under the tower are carved details of the Book of Genesis, as well as figures of Mary and the Apostles. There is much to be seen in the massive interior, including a magnificent set of 15th-century carved choir stalls and a display of architectural plans by the various designers of the cathedral. The huge Ulmer Museum (closed Mondays) has 50 exhibition rooms, with a heavy accent on Gothic art in Upper Swabia, plus works by 20th-century artists. The baroque monastery at Ulm-Wiblingen is famous for its rococo library.

West of Ulm, the former abbey church at Blaubeuren► (open daily; afternoons only in winter) is charmingly reflected in a deep blue pool. The building contains an exceptional 15th-century late Gothic altarpiece, the work of a group of local craftsmen.

► Wertheim

At the meeting point of the Main and Tauber rivers, Wertheim is a town of delightful half-timbered houses neatly erected along narrow streets amid a setting of wooded hills. The ruined Altes Schloss, towering over the town, was built by the counts of Wertheim in the 12th century. There are wonderful views from here. A glass museum in Mühlenstrasse has collections of historic glass, while the 16th-century Rathaus contains an historical museum. The impressive Stiftskirche was built in the 14th century, and the Kilianscapelle (St. Kilian's chapel) in the 15th: its basement served as an ossuary. In the Marktplatz you will see half-timbered houses and the Engelsbrunnen (Angels' Well), dating from 1574, named after the stone angels bearing the Wertheim coat of arms. From the left bank of the Tauber there is a stunning view of part of the town.

► Worms

This cathedral city on the banks of the Rhine, one of the oldest in Germany, has a particularly eventful past. There was a Celtic settlement here, then a Roman garrison. According to the *Nibelungenlied* it was the seat of the Burgundian king. During medieval times over 100 imperial diets, or assemblies, were held in Worms, the most noted being the Reichstag of 1521 (Diet of Worms), which summoned Luther to stand before it. He refused to retract his doctrines and was banned from the empire.

Besides industry, Worms has a flourishing wine trade. The famous Liebfraumilch comes from here, taking its name from the Liebfrauenkirche (Church of Our Lady), standing proudly in the midst of a vineyard to the north of the city. It contains a 15th-century Madonna and tabernacle.

One of the supreme examples of Romanesque architecture in Germany is **Worms's cathedral**► ►, the Kaiserdom, with two domes and four corner towers. Despite other parts of the city being badly damaged as a result of a succession of wars, the cathedral has been carefully maintained. St. Martins Kirche, also Romanesque, has the same design as the cathedral.

Jewish cemetery
The synagogue of Worms—the oldest in Germany—and the Jewish cemetery date back to the 11th century. There was a large Jewish community here up to the 1930s. The Alte Synagoge was rebuilt in 1961, and the cemetery contains over 1,000 gravestones and pillars carved in Hebrew, amazingly untouched by the Nazis. After Prague's, this is the second-largest Jewish cemetery in Europe.

Worms's superb cathedral is Catholic, although the city itself is two-thirds Protestant

NORTHERN BAVARIA

206

Stretching from Aschaffenburg in the northwest to Passau on the Austrian border far to the southeast, this region offers some of Germany's most fascinating historical cities, including **Nürnberg, Regensburg**, and **Würzburg**, and stretches of unspoiled countryside. The world-famous **Romantische Strasse** (Romantic Road) links medieval towns, while backwaters of the Bavarian Forest are explored by the **Bayerische Ostmarkstrasse**.

The region's cultural riches are unsurpassed; in the late Middle Ages and Early Renaissance, some of the most characteristically German contributions to the arts were made by painters (Altdorfer, Cranach and Dürer) or by master craftsmen (Veit Stoss and Tilman Riemenschneider). Their work can be seen in museums such as the outstanding Germanisches Nationalmuseum at Nürnberg, or sometimes in the original settings—see

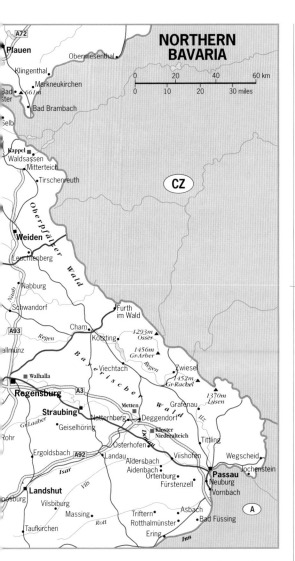

NORTHERN BAVARIA

0	20	40	60 km
0	10	20	30 miles

Riemenschneider's *Madonna in a Rose Garland* in the little church at Volkach. Architecture particularly worth noting includes a number of sumptuous 18th-century baroque and rococo edifices.

National parks offer unparalleled opportunities for exploring, on foot, by bike or by canoe along the rivers. Rural scenery ranges from the romantic **Altmühl Valley** to the mysterious depths of Europe's last remaining fragments of virgin forest in the **Bayerischer Wald**.

Enjoy the region for its food and drink. Hearty game dishes or spicy sausages from Nürnberg are complemented by famous beers (the world's oldest brewery is at **Freising**) or wines from Franconia, where Main Valley vineyards rival those of the Rhine and Mosel. This is a favorite vacation area, with bargains to be had in remoter places along the border with the Czech Republic.

Controversial canal
The lower reaches of the Ahtmül have become part of the new Main–Danube Canal. Completed in 1992, this gigantic and bitterly controversial project connects the waterways of western and central Europe, enabling large vessels to ply between the Rhine and the Black Sea. Nowhere else has a river landscape been so utterly transformed nor so conscientiously restored, a process best seen at Essing, just downstream from Prunn. Here the idyllic riverside scene of village, barbican, and ancient timber bridge seems untouched by time.

The Befreiungshalle (Liberation hall), built to celebrate "liberation" from Napoleon's rule

►► **Altmühltal (Altmühl Valley)**

This is one of Germany's most attractive river valleys, with unspoiled towns and villages, dramatic crags topped by castles, and the nation's largest nature park, **Altmühltal**. The river rises in the Frankenhöhe (Franconian Heights), near Rothenburg-ob-der-Tauber; crosses gently rolling countryside to the small spa town of Treuchtlingen; then twists deeply through the limestone of the Fränkische Alb (Franconian Jura), joining the Danube at Kelheim.

The meadowlands, rock pinnacles, and juniper-studded slopes are enjoyed by walkers and by cyclists on the riverside bike path.

Downstream is **Eichstatt►**, a superior little episcopal city of classic elegance, an architectural showpiece. Its 14th-century cathedral, a mix of Romanesque, Gothic and baroque, contains the famous Pappenheim Altar, an arresting late medieval depiction of the Crucifixion. Rococo mansions, neatly painted pale blue or yellow, line the Residenzplatz, crowned by a gilded statue of the Virgin. All is esthetically impressive, but almost too much like a stage set, with the Willibad fortress looming on a hill above. The town has a small private Catholic university. There are fine views from the Frauenberg pilgrimage chapel crowning a hilltop or from the chunky, chalk-white Willibaldsburg overlooking the river.

The valley's most extraordinary castle is 11th-century Prunn, perched precariously over the river.

► Amberg

Untouched by wars and heavy industry, Amberg has within its medieval walls a variety of buildings from its prosperous past, including four fine gateways and the ancient bridge—the Stadtbrille (City Spectacles—note the reflection of its twin arches in the waters of the River Vils).

Dominating the market square is the gabled and arcaded Gothic Rathaus, one of the finest town halls in Germany. The churches include the stately St. Martin's (1421), St. George's, its interior baroquified in the late 17th century, and the Deutsche Schulkirche, a rococo gem. Stations of the Cross lead uphill to the late Renaissance pilgrimage church of Mariahilf, with its fine views over the town and the countryside of the Oberpfalz (Upper Palatinate).

Amberg holds its Altstadtfest in June and its Bergfest in July, though the products of its 10 breweries can be sampled at any time!

► Ansbach

Administrative and cultural center of central Franconia, Ansbach is one of Germany's finest "Residenz towns," its history and townscape fashioned by its role as the seat of its rulers, the margraves of Brandenburg-Ansbach. Streets and squares feature many attractive buildings, from high-gabled medieval burghers' houses to the three-towered church of St. Gumbertus, redesigned in the 18th century to become an ideal "preaching church," dominated by the pulpit rather than the altar.

The **Residenz►** itself is a splendid Renaissance structure, incorporating parts of the original medieval moated stronghold. Its rococo interior contains the Bavarian state collection of Ansbach ceramics. Beyond is the palace's park, the Hofgarten, with stately avenues of lime trees, an impressive orangery, and a memorial to the enigmatic foundling Kaspar Hauser, mysteriously murdered here in 1833 and the subject of fascinated speculation ever since and of various books and films.

► Aschaffenburg

The first Bavarian town for visitors coming from the Frankfurt direction, Aschaffenburg is dominated by the huge red sandstone **Schloss►** standing foursquare on a bluff overlooking the River Main. Known as the Johannisburg, it was erected at the start of the 17th century by the bishop of Mainz, Aschaffenburg's overlord. The interior includes state apartments, fine paintings (including pictures by Cranach), and a range of glass and ceramics. Other master works including another Cranach and a Grünewald can be found in the town center's Stiftskirche, a church incorporating a variety of architectural styles from the Romanesque onward. Treasures of a different kind feature in the Automuseum, with its 200-odd classic racing cars and collection of automobile art.

The town's two parks, Schöntal (in the center) and Schönbusch (on the far bank of the Main), are excellent examples of German landscapers' attempts to imitate the "English Style" in garden design.

209

A golden baroque statue-fountain adorns Ansbach, once a royal town with a brilliant court

Aschaffenburg's Schloss above the River Main. Next door is a quiet quarter of old Fachwerk (half-timbered) houses down narrow alleys

Holbein and Luther
Augsburg's position meant that it was subject to the northward-moving influences of the Italian Renaissance. Churches, patrician houses, and public buildings were built or rebuilt, great artists including Holbein the Elder gave their best and metalworkers created masterpieces in gold and silver. Martin Luther's visits reflected the hold that Protestantism had here.

Excursions

The Spessart East of Aschaffenburg the River Main swings south then north again in a great bend, forming the southern boundary of the Spessart, one of Germany's finest areas of unspoiled uplands. Here are some of the country's most extensive woodlands, magnificent stands of beech and oak stretching away to distant horizons—an awesome prospect even when viewed from the great scenic highway, the Frankfurt–Nuremberg autobahn.

In the romantic setting of a deep forest valley lies **Schloss Mespelbrunn**, its picturesque silhouette reflected in the calm surface of its moat. Still inhabited, the castle's furnished interior is pleasingly evocative of the life of the provincial nobility.

The stretch of the Main upstream from Aschaffenburg forms part of the Franconian wine-growing area. It is a cheerful landscape of orchards, south-facing vineyards and pleasant little towns and villages, among them half-timbered **Miltenberg**—"the very essence of medieval Germany."

▶▶ Augsburg

With a population of 250,000, Augsburg is Bavaria's third-largest city (after Munich and Nürnberg) as well as its oldest, founded in Roman times and named after Emperor Augustus. Commanding the Alpine trade routes linking northern Europe to Italy, Augsburg enjoyed its heyday in the 15th and 16th centuries. Second only to London as a banking center, it became the base of great financial and commercial dynasties, such as the immensely rich Fuggers. Later names associated with Augsburg include Wolfgang Amadeus Mozart's father (who lived here in the 17th century, at no. 14 Mittleren Gasse), Rudolf Diesel (who invented his engine at the MAN works), Willy Messerschmitt (famous for his fighter planes), and the playwright Bertolt Brecht (who was born here but was no lover of the place).

What to see Augsburg has a big city center, focused on the Ludwigplatz. Here the imposing Renaissance Rathaus (1620) has a glorious Goldener Saal (golden hall), recently restored after wartime bombing. The landmark tower, the Perlachturm, offers good city views from its top. To the north stands the Domkirche St. Maria, originally Romanesque but much altered and added to subsequently. It has splendid 11th-century bronze doors, stained glass that is among the country's oldest, and a Holbein altarpiece.

Augsburg has a number of fine fountains. The Augustusbrunnen (1594), with its majestic figures of the emperor and river gods, stands in the Ludwigplatz, the Herkulesbrunnen (1596–1602) in the broad Maximilian-strasse to the south.

This stately city artery is lined with many splendid residences, including the Fuggerhaus and the rococo Schaezlerpalais, which has art collections and a Festsaal (banqueting hall). At the end of the street is the tall tower of the church of St. Ulric and St. Afra.

The Rathaus and Perlachturm in the Ludwigplatz at Augsburg

Excursion
Just east of Augsburg is the small town of **Friedberg**, rebuilt after being burned down in the Thirty Years' War. Its notable features include a castle, a pretty Rathaus, and above all Herrgottsruh, a pilgrimage church with an exuberant rococo interior.

Bad Kissingen

Located among parks and gardens along the banks of the River Saale, this is Bavaria's most popular spa.

The spa buildings include an 1838 arcade and the monumental 1913 Regentenbau, a complex of halls and public rooms linked to the Wandelhalle, a covered promenade. The Theater, completed in 1904, has a fine Jugendstil interior. On the far bank of the Saale from the Wandelhalle is the immaculate Kurpark with buildings housing spa and casino.

Crowning a hilltop south of town are the ruins of Bodenlauben Castle, once the residence of the medieval poet and keen crusader Otto von der Bodenlauben; his statue forms part of the fountain on the Rathausplatz.

The Rhön Bad Kissingen is one of the main "gateways" to this area of varied upland scenery that stretches northward to **Fulda**. Rising in places to over 2,952 feet, the rounded summits carry a covering of moorland and pasture rather than forest. This splendid walking country is also much favored by gliding enthusiasts. The most extensive views, both involving a short hike of half an hour or so, are from the **Wasserkuppe** (3,044 feet) and the **Kreuzberg** (3,116 feet). In the valleys are attractive little towns such as **Gersfeld**, with its three castles, and

An elegant Kurpark and Kurgarten are features of Bad Kissingen

Bad Brückenau, a spa with classical buildings inspired by the ubiquitous King Ludwig. **Bad Neustadt** has kept intact its ring of medieval fortifications; within the walls stands the former church of the Carmelites, dating from the 14th century but with an exceptionally fine baroque interior. On the far bank of the Saale are the spa facilities, including a Kurhotel comfortably installed within an 18th-century castle. **Münnerstadt**, too, has retained its walls, but its greatest treasure is the high altar by the great Riemenschneider in the parish church.

A favorite short excursion from Bad Kissingen is to **Bad Bocklet**, on the historic mail coach that plies between the two spas, passing the Renaissance castle at **Aschach**, its rooms filled with fine furniture and paintings and a collection of oriental art.

▶ Bad Mergentheim

Pleasantly situated in the friendly valley of the River Tauber, this is an important stopping place along the Romantische Strasse, as well as a spa. In contrast to the newer spa town, the old town has a picturesque market square, churches, high-gabled Rathaus and ancient fountain. The most prominent structure is the ocher mid-16th-century Deutschordensschloss (see also Ellingen, page 222). It is a fascinating assembly of high walls, gables, towers and turrets. Inside is a splendid Renaissance staircase. The baroque castle church has a light-filled interior with a magnificent ceiling painting; in the crypt are the tombs of long-dead grand masters.

Digestive waters
The waters of the three springs of Bad Mergentheim are used in the treatment of digestive complaints. Though the waters were discovered at the beginning of the 19th century, the spa only really developed in the interwar period, and its trim architecture reflects the taste of the time.

Excursion

The parish church at **Stuppach**, about 4 miles southwest, has a famous *Madonna and Child* by the great Grünewald, one of this tormented master's more spiritual paintings.

▶▶▶ Bamberg

Bamberg is perhaps the most perfect of all Germany's ancient cities, a wonderful synthesis of architecture of all periods in a harmonious setting of river vale and gentle hills. Since 1994 it has been named as part of UNESCO's World Cultural Heritage.

Founded in AD 973, the city was made a bishopric by King Henry II, and its division into two distinct districts is still apparent: the Bürgerstadt, or merchants' town, by the River Regnitz, and the Bischofsstadt, or ecclesiastical quarter, on the slopes above. Linking the two is the extraordinarily picturesque old **town hall▶**, an incongruous mixture of rustic half-timbering and rococo elegance perched on a tiny island in the Regnitz. Downstream is Bamburg's Little Venice, once the home of fishermen.

Higher up is the **Kaiserdom▶▶**, the city's great cathedral, with its four tall towers finding their echo in those of St. Michael's Church, crowning the hilltop in the middle distance. The cathedral is a triumph of the transitional period between late Romanesque and early

Bamburg's quaint old Rathaus was built on an island in the river, so as to serve the city's two rival parts

Hoffman's tales
One former resident of Bamberg was E.T.A. Hoffman (1776–1822), the versatile artist, musician, radical social critic, and writer of satiric fantasies and tales (Offenbach used some for his opera). His home is now a Hoffman museum: one room has a hole in the floor through which this intriguing eccentric would joke and quarrel with his wife in the room below.

Gothic. Its interior is enlivened by some of the most remarkable sculpture in Germany. The **Bamberger Reiter►** (Bamberg Knight) on his stone steed has come to represent the essence of medieval chivalry, while the **tomb of Henry II►** and his Queen Kunigunde is one of the masterpieces of the great Tilman Riemenschneider (*c* 1513). The royal pair appear again in the elaborately carved choir stalls, while the Marienaltar (1523) is by the Nürnberg wood-carver Veit Stoss.

The Domplatz (cathedral square) is overlooked on one side by the Neue Residenz, with its splendid baroque interior, and on the other by the Alte Hofhaltung. Beyond the Renaissance gateway the undulating cobbled courtyard is enclosed by a delightfully irregular sequence of late Gothic galleried buildings.

Bamberg offers much to the leisured explorer, including churches (from Gothic St. Jakob to the rococo interior of St. Gangolf), splendid town residences (the richly decorated Böttingerhaus or the riverside Concordiahaus) and museums (the Diocesan Museum, off the cathedral cloister, or the exemplary local history museum, in the Alte Hofhaltung). A close-up of the city can be seen from the Vierkirchenblick (four-church view), south of the cathedral, a more distant prospect from the old Bishops' castle, the Altenburg, 2 miles southwest.

Excursions
In **Pommersfelden**, 12 miles south, is Schloss Weissenstein, one of Germany's most grandiose baroque palaces, built (and, in part, designed) by Prince-Bishop Schönborn of Bamberg in 1711–18. There is a sumptuous interior and an English-style park beyond.

The **River Main** joins the Regnitz downstream from Bamberg. Along its course lie a number of pretty little places: Zeil-am-Main, half-timbered Königsberg (north of the river), and Hassfurt, graced by a parish church (with a Riemenschneider carving) and the Ritterkapelle (Knights' Chapel), a minor masterpiece of late Gothic.

►► Bayerischer Wald (Bavarian Forest)

Between the Danube and the Czech border stretch 2,300 square miles of upland country, forming, with the Sumava (Bohemian Forest) on the far side of the frontier, "Europe's Green Roof." Rising to 4,776 feet at the Grosser Arber, the area contains traces of primeval forest, ancient stands of spruce carefully preserved as part of Germany's first national park. Woodland is continuous on the higher land, interspersed elsewhere with attractive farming countryside and meticulously modernized villages. Churches with onion domes pierce the skyline; little streams channel through steeply sloping meadows to tributaries of the Danube. Though there are no large towns, impeccably engineered roads stitch the whole area together, and the occasional two-coach train still trundles the single tracks of the surviving branch lines. With an abundant variety of accommodations, this is one of the areas favored by Germans for their vacations. Attractions are plentiful, from relics of the metalworking industries that flourished until recently to castle ruins perched on rocks, or little medieval towns. Many places have their Heimatmuseum (local-history museum), and there are curiosities like the snuff museum at Grafenau.

So-called Klein Venedig (Little Venice) is a charming suburb of Bamberg, on the Regnitz River

Winter sports
Long winters provide the perfect conditions for winter sports in the Bayerischer Wald. As well as some provision for downhill skiing, there are more than 1,250 miles of cross-country trails.

Drive **Passau to Cham**

Climbing from the Danube, the B85, known as the Bayerische Ostmarkstrasse, is a splendid scenic highway linking Passau on the Austrian border with Bayreuth. Near **Tittling**, look around the Museumsdorf Bayerischer Wald, where old buildings have been renovated.

Continue on the Ostmarkstrasse to Cham via Regen, located on the Schwarzer Regen, and Viechtach with its 17th-century Rathaus, or detour on the indirect route around the Grosser Arber.

Just north of **Neuschönau**, the Hans-Eisenmann-Haus, the visitor center run by the Bavarian Forest National Park, has displays, leaflets (in English) and self-guided trails that tell you all about the origins of the great forest and its wildlife.

The road northwest to the Arber goes through country towns where the glass industry flourishes, though Spiegelau, Frauenau, and Zwiesel are more like resorts than manufacturing centers.

Some glassworks can be visited, while Frauenau has an excellent

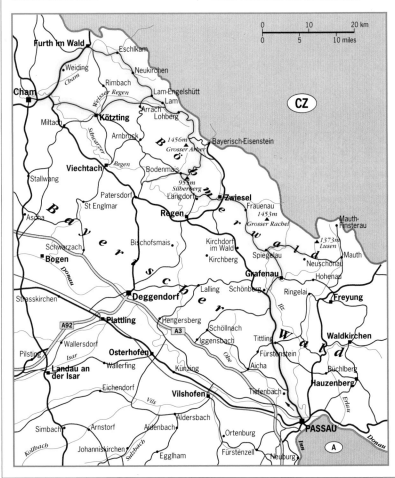

Open views across the Bayerischer Wald

Glasmuseum. **Bodenmais**, in the Bavarian Forest, deals in glass, but outside the town is the **Silberberg**, mined for its copper, tin and silver and now open to visitors (though no longer in production). To the north rises the Arber, with remnants of the inaccessible primeval forest. This is one of the most inhospitable areas in Germany. Frost occurs on 200 or more days a year, and deep snow lies well into spring. Solitude can be enjoyed here, though not around the chalets on the banks of the **Arbersee**.

An arduous ascent on foot (3½ hours there and back) will take you to the summit of the **Grosser Arber**—more easily reached by the skilift on the highway to **Lam**. This ridge-top road gives panoramic views of the mountains (notably from the Hindenburg viewpoint) before descending into gentler countryside around Lam.

The Ostmarkstrasse is rejoined at Cham, with its fine market square, via either Kötzting, rebuilt after a great fire in 1867, or Furth im Walde. Kötzting has a flamboyant Whit Monday procession (*Pfingstritt*) and Furth has the *Drachenstich*, a pageant in which a 59-foot animated dragon is spectacularly slain, with much jollity. Situated on the Regensburg–Plzen (Pilsen) road, Furth is a frontier town; the Skoda cars of Czech shoppers can be seen parked among the local cars on its stately little market square.

►► Bayreuth

Founded as long ago as the 11th century, Bayreuth first came into its own in the 18th century under the rule of Margrave Friedrich and his energetic and talented spouse, Wilhelmina, sister of Frederick the Great. A second flowering occurred in the late 19th century, when Richard Wagner made it the showcase for his innovative operas (see page 237). The operatic tradition persists, attracting fans in their thousands to the Bayreuth Festival, held annually in July and August.

Traces of Bayreuth's medieval past can still be seen, for example in narrow alleyways and the typically Bavarian elongated market square, as well as the Gothic Stadtkirche (city church). The original residence of the margraves, the Altes Schloss (old palace) goes back to the 14th century; its present appearance is due to 17th-century rebuilding.

The baroque age contributed most to Bayreuth's architectural character, again largely because of the energetic Wilhelmina. The Neues Schloss (new palace, 1754) has lighthearted rococo interiors, including grotto and garden rooms, and houses some of the town's museums. The grounds of the Hofgarten are an early example of Romantic landscape design.

To the north is the 18th-century Markgräfliches Opernhaus. Undistinguished outside, its galleried interior shows the baroque style at its most theatrical.

Connected to the Hofgarten by a gateway, erected in 1874 to celebrate the composer's 61st birthday, is Wagner's Bayreuth residence, the classical Villa Wahnfried, now the National Wagner Museum. In the gardens stands the grave of the great man. His wife Cosima, daughter of Franz Liszt, is buried beside him, his faithful hound Russ a short distance away.

Wagner's theater
Wagner's real monument is the bulky Festspielhaus, on rising ground north of the city center. Designed by Semper, but esthetically no rival to the Markgräfliches Opernhaus, it provides the optimum setting for the master's works. At intermission time during the festival the grounds fill with up to 1,800 people recovering from the operatic onslaught. Some admire the massive bust of Wagner by Arno Breker, one of the Third Reich's most successful sculptors, as well as representations of Cosima and of Liszt, who died during the 1886 festival.

Modern Bayreuth, much rebuilt since Wagner's day

Crops and caves
Marking the eastern extremity of the great limestone outcrop that begins far away in the Jura Mountains, Bayreuth is one of Germany's most romantically picturesque regions. The porous rock has been eroded to form some two dozen deep and narrow valleys through which flow clear trout streams that once powered ancient mills. Medieval castles cap many crags; look for the one perched above the tiny town of Pottenstein. Nearby Tüchersfeld has an even more bizarre setting, with fairy-tale houses wedged among the rock pinnacles. Below ground, equally strange landscapes can be seen in the caves known as the Teufelshöhle, with weirdly shaped concretions and the bones of prehistoric animals.

Excursions

The delectable grounds of the **Schloss Eremitage** (Hermitage Castle), 2 miles northeast of Bayreuth, go back to the 17th century, when the margraves would come here to escape court life in town. The original hermitage, the Altes Schloss, was built by the ruling margrave in 1715.

The **Fichtelgebirge** (Fichtel Mountains), ancient granite-littered uplands, form a horseshoe-shape massif enclosing eastward-facing lowlands, and are named after the extensive forests of *Fichte* (spruce) that clad their slopes. The area's abundant rainfall feeds rivers flowing to all points of the compass, the Eger east to the Elbe in the Czech Republic, the Naab south to the Danube, the Weisser Main west to the Rhine.

The Ochsenkopf summit (3,359 feet), with its TV tower (chairlift from Bishofsgrün), gives majestic views. In contrast is the tranquil scene by the banks of the little Fichtelsee, set deep among the dark conifers, or the Luisenberg labyrinth, a chaos of granite blocks eroded into strange shapes and much admired by Goethe. Here is Germany's oldest open-air theater, still the venue for summertime performances.

The towns in the sheltered lowland include the area's little capital, **Wunsiedel**, with the Fichtelgebirge museum, and busy **Marktredwitz**, on the route leading to the northwestern Czech Republic.

The **Frankenwald** (Franconian Forest) is Germany's smallest upland, with peaceful valleys, remote hamlets,

Above: Baroque sculptures reflect the golden age of 18th-century Bayreuth under Princess Wilhelmina

Sanspareil garden
The picturesque potential of rocky outcrop and eerie forest was appreciated by Margravine Wilhelmina. Around the crag-top ruin of Zwernitz Castle she laid out a romantic landscape to tickle the refined sensibilities of her contemporaries and called it Sanspareil, in the Francophile fashion. Beyond Morgenländischer Bau (an Asian hermitage), winding paths lead past strange rock formations to fanciful features like the theater conceived as a ruin and set in a grotto. The castle itself forms part of the artful composition; from its keep there is a wonderful panorama reaching far away to the Frankenwald and the Fichtelgebirge.

deep forest, and wild areas of heath bog. The highest point is the Döbraberg (2,604 feet) with a tower giving panoramic views to the Fichtelgebirge to the south and the Thüringian heights to the north. North from Bayreuth is **Kulmbach**, whose large breweries are known for their bitter dark beers and strong, sharp Pils. They lie below the **Plassenburg▶**, a splendid stronghold with a fine Renaissance courtyard. Once a prison, the castle now houses the Zinnfigurenmuseum, the national collection of 300,000 tin figurines. Kronach has beautifully preserved medieval houses, including the birthplace of Cranach (1472–1553), painter of rugged landscapes and courtly nudes. Above the town rises its great fortress, the Rosenberg. With its triple ring of walls pierced by a single entrance above ground, this is Germany's most extensive medieval stronghold to remain intact. Its picture gallery includes works by Cranach.

One of the prettiest valleys in **Fränkische Schweiz** (Franconian Switzerland) is the River Wiesent, best seen from the viewpoints in the little market town and resort of Gössweinstein, which is also famous for its pilgrimage church.

▶▶ **Coburg**

During Germany's division, Coburg was very much on the edge of things, in a cul-de-sac ending at the East German border. Its name, linked to half the dynasties that once ruled Europe, never lost its fame, and the place, busier now with the disappearance of the frontier, is still dominated by its two, very different, ducal castles.

High above the town, and visible from far across Coburg's attractive rural surroundings, broods the majestic **Veste▶** (fortress), called "the Crown of Franconia" because of its tower-studded outline. Founded in the 11th century and much rebuilt in Renaissance times by the vigorous Duke Johann Casimir, it ranks among the country's most splendid strongholds. Within its double ring of defensive walls are many treasures, including the 300,000-plus items of its print collection, paintings by a number of German masters (among them Cranach), arms, armor, furniture, and Johann Casimir's State Carriage (1560). Martin Luther stayed here in 1530, his visit commemorated by the room named after him.

Linking the Veste to town is the Hofgarten, its verdant slopes embracing a notable Natural History Museum. In the 16th century, the dukes moved down the hill into their new castle, the Ehrenburg. Remodeled externally to suit the 19th-century taste for the Gothic, the palace retains much of its original interior, including its resplendent chapel and the Riesensaal (Giants' Room), so called because of the 28 plaster heavies holding up the painted ceiling.

While the burghers built their fine half-timbered and high-gabled town houses, the dukes gave the town a Renaissance touch. Johann Casimir was responsible for the academy known as the Casimirianum and for the Stadthaus, facing the rococo town hall across the cobbled market square. The ducal imprint can be seen, too, in the Gothic Church of St. Moriz, with its incredibly elaborate 43-foot-high (five-story) memorial to Duke Johann Friedrich (d. 1598).

221

Coburg's massive Veste fortress, above the town, has a stark exterior but a pretty inner courtyard

Children's appeal
Dinkelsbühl has escaped the ravages of wars, though there was a close shave in the course of the Thirty Years' War, when the fury of the besieging Swedes was mollified by an appeal made to their commander by the town's children. The event is marked by the Kinderzeche, a colorful 10-day carnival held annually in July.

Oxcarts for tourists keep the medieval touch alive in delightful Dinkelsbühl, a town with watchtowers and ramparts

►►► Dinkelsbühl

More compact than Rothenburg-ob-der-Tauber, farther up the Romantische Strasse (Romantic Road—see page 230), Dinkelsbühl is one of Germany's most delightful medieval towns, perfectly preserved within its ring of walls, bastions, and 16 towers.

The best approach is across the causeway leading to the late 14th-century gateway known as the Rothenburger Tor. From the gate the broad Martin Luther Strasse curves down to the market square with its splendid early Renaissance town houses, among them the Deutsches Haus, with seven projecting stories reaching up into its high gable. The nearby Hezelhof has tiered flowerladen balconies in its lovely inner courtyard. The church of St. George still has its Romanesque tower; it is one of the grandest hall churches in southern Germany, with fan vaulting spanning the lofty interior and good carving and statuary.

Dinkelsbühl has many more delights; discover them on your own by wandering the narrow streets, or take the guided tour (in German) on foot that starts at St. George's. A walk around the ramparts at night is an atmospheric experience, especially in the company of the town's nightwatchman as he does his rounds.

A baroque gem
Ellingen was rebuilt following its destruction in the Thirty Years' War and is a little gem of baroque town planning, with a pretty Rathaus and several churches.

► Ellingen

Ellingen was for many years the headquarters of the Deutscher Orden (the Order of Teutonic Knights), a militant brotherhood of priests and soldiers founded around 1190 during the First Crusade but best remembered for their vigorous conversion to Christianity of the pagan population of the Baltic seaboard. Their somber castle, built 1708–21, rears clifflike over the town. Awkwardly approached from the side, it is enlivened by its main facade, a splendid staircase, rococo interiors, and an elaborately decorated church. The corridors are hung with portraits of the Hochund Deutschmeister, the order's leaders.

► Freising

Easily reached from the center of Munich by S-Bahn suburban train, Freising is a city in its own right, a bishopric from as early as 739. The dominant feature of the town is the Domberg, a bluff of higher land looking out over the interminable flatlands stretching southward to Munich. The chalk-white cathedral rises over a cluster of churches and other ecclesiastical buildings, including the Prince-Bishop's Residenz, now a museum, and the Gothic Johannes-Kapelle, with its baroque interior. The cathedral interior exults in baroque splendor, but a more somber era is evoked in the crypt, with its capitals and columns bearing strange figures of men and beasts.

► Ingolstadt

Strategically located on the upper reaches of the Danube, Ingolstadt is one of Bavaria's great cities, with a long history and a thriving present (oil refineries, Audi works). First mentioned in 806, Ingolstadt blossomed in the Middle Ages. Come into town via the brick Kreuztor gateway of 1385. Beyond is the minster, dedicated to Our Lady, its high west gable flanked by asymmetrical towers. There are fine old houses, including the Ickstatt-Haus of 1740, a rococo confection in yellow with white stucco icing. From the same period is the interior of the church of Maria de Victoria, its painted ceiling a masterpiece of perspective effects.

Excursions

Weltenburg Abbey (28 miles east via Neustadt) is sited on the Danube at the entrance to the Donaudurchbruch, a spectacular gorge cut by the river en route to its confluence with the Altmühl at Kelheim. "The Danube in Flames," a floodlit lighting of the gorge, takes place on the first Saturday in July. A high point of German 18th-century baroque, the abbey church's oval interior verges on high kitsch, with a tableau of St. George smiting the dragon and cherubs flying around in chunky clouds. It certainly draws the crowds, whom you can join for beer (the abbey's own) in the courtyard.

Weihenstephan
On a wooded bluff west of Friesing is Weihenstephan, famous for beer (the world's oldest brewery–1040) and the prestigious Technical University of Munich.

Military museum
Ingolstadt's importance as a fortress and garrison town was enhanced in the 19th century with the construction of massive fortifications. Most have been razed, but some severely classical gateways remain, including the Kavalier Heydeck. The Gothic Herzogschloss, a relic of earlier defenses, is an appropriate setting for the Bavarian Military Museum.

223

Neuburg an der Donau
Neuburg an der Donau is an old Residenz town 16 miles up the Danube from Ingolstadt. The place is dominated by the Renaissance palace built by Protestant Prince Ottheinrich, whose hope of making the town's Hofkirche a beacon of Protestantism in Catholic Bavaria was frustrated by the Counter-Reformation.

The 14th-century Kreuztor gateway, hexagonal, with six pointed turrets, stands at the entrance to Ingolstadt's old town

Lavish pageant
In 1475, at the peak of its prosperity and prestige, Landshut marked the wedding of its Duke George to a Polish princess with celebrations the lavishness of which became a byword all over Europe. These great days are recalled every three years by contemporary Germany's most extravagant pageant, the Landshuter Fürstenhochzeit, when revelers in period costume perform against the splendid stage set of Landshut's historic townscape.

"Daniel" tower
Nördlingen's massive gray stone parish church of St. George has a lofty white interior and a 292-ft tower nicknamed "Daniel." It is worth the climb for the view over the red roofs of the oval-shaped town. From here, an inner oval of streets can clearly be picked out, marking the course of an older ring of fortifications, long since demolished.

► Landshut

On the banks of the River Isar at the foot of Trausnitz Castle, Landshut has kept much of the appearance and atmosphere of the important provincial capital it once was. This old city is centered on two fine market streets lined with late medieval town houses, many with stepped gables and arcaded courtyards. The gently curving Altstadt (old town) dates to the founding of the city in 1204, and the Neustadt (new town) was laid out a century later.

The Altstadt is closed off by the church of St. Martin, a bold Gothic brick building. Its slender tower rises to 436 feet, higher than the castle behind it and the tallest structure of its kind in the world. Among the treasures of the light and airy interior is a huge Madonna and Child, carved in 1520 by a local man, Hans Leinberger.

In 1543, Duke Ludwig X moved from the castle into the Stadtresidenz, which has a splendidly decorated interior, part of which houses Landshut's museum. Not long afterward, the castle itself was refurbished for the lavish court life of Prince William of Bavaria. He kept the 13th-century chapel, with its superb Romanesque statuary, adding a fine galleried courtyard in Renaissance style, and had the famous Narrentreppe staircase painted with robust figures from the Italian comic theater. The castle balcony gives a spectacular panorama over the town.

Excursion

A sixth of the world's hops are grown in the **Hallertau** area around Mainburg. This is pretty, hilly countryside, the hops alternating with other crops against dark woodlands. Pickers no longer camp in the fields to help with the harvest, but the season is still celebrated by the election of a Hop Queen in the village of Wolnzach.

Nürnberg's huge Schöner Brunnen ("beautiful fountain") contains 40 different figures arranged in a pyramid

► ▓▓▓ Nördlingen

Nördlingen's heyday came between the 14th and 16th centuries, when its great Whitsun Fair drew traders from all over Germany. Its subsequent stagnation may have been tough on the townsfolk but helped preserve its townscape, much to the delight of today's many visitors, for whom it is one of the principal stops along the Romantische Strasse. The town's ramparts, still intact after some 500 years, have 16 towers and five gateways, from which five main streets converge on the Marktplatz, with its 13th- to 14th-century Rathaus.

Excursions

Two fine churches are close to Nördlingen. In spite of its baroque furnishings, the former abbey church at **Kaisheim** (4 miles northeast of Donauwörth) evokes the severe lives of its 14th-century Cistercian founders.

Neresheim (12 miles southwest) has a fine abbey church, too. The last work of Balthasar Neumann, it is a fitting conclusion to the career of this foremost architect of the South German baroque. Under its three domes, the interior is unusually light and spacious, with fine ceiling paintings by the Tirolean Martin Knoller.

► ► ► Nürnberg (Nuremberg)

Crowning the outcrop of warm red sandstone from which much of Nürnberg is built, the **Burg►**, or castle, goes back to the city's founding years in the 11th century. Kings and emperors resided here for some 500 years, and the sprawling complex of buildings was added to, demolished and rebuilt throughout this time. Thus the tall five-sided tower dates from 1040, the two-tier Imperial Chapel from the 12th century and the stables (now the youth hostel) from the late 15th century. From windows, towers and terraces there are fine views over

Nürnberg's Hauptmarkt, the site of Germany's biggest pre-Christmas market, the Christkindelsmarkt

Medieval heyday
Before the devastation wrought by the terrible air raids of 1945, Nürnberg was Germany's greatest surviving medieval city. The destruction was not total, and sensitive rebuilding has respected the ancient street pattern, enabling the visitor to recapture the atmosphere of the city's heyday, in the 15th and 16th centuries, when it was the principal focus of Germany's politics, culture, trade, science, and technology.

the city, with its nearly complete ring of walls.

Directly below the castle are timber-framed and gabled houses crammed up against the ramparts. Albrecht Dürer lived in this quarter from 1509 until his death in 1528. The Dürer-Haus has good interiors and displays, though there are more copies than original works. In the Burgstrasse is the 16th-century Fenbohaus, now the city museum. Beyond it is the Rathausplatz, with the Altes Rathaus and, opposite it, the twin towers of the early Gothic St. Sebald's Church, with outstanding artwork in the interior by Kraft (*Christ Carrying the Cross*), Vischer (*Shrine of St. Sebald*), and Stoss (*Passion and Crucifixion*).

South is the Hauptmarkt—a daily market and site of the pre-Christmas Christkindelsmarkt. The Schöner Brunnen fountain competes with the gabled façade of the Gothic Frauenkirche (Church of Our Lady) and its 16th-century mechanical clock with automata that perform at noon.

Nürnberg's Altstadt is divided into roughly equal halves by the River Pegnitz. The combination of water, ancient buildings and bridges makes an atmospheric townscape. One arm of the river is bridged by the Heiliggeist-Spital, a hospital dating originally from the 14th century; downstream is the Weinstadl, a venerable wine store that, together with an old water tower, covered bridge, and weeping willows, makes the most idyllic scene.

Although the southern half of the Altstadt has a more modern air, it contains much of interest. The Gothic church of St. Lawrence has a cathedral-like west front. Inside are splendid works: Stoss's multicolored carving of the Annunciation is suspended from the vaulting; the

Toy Fair
In view of Nürnberg's long-standing role as the toy-manufacturing capital of Europe, it is fitting that the annual Toy Fair, the most important of its kind, is held here.

"The Nasty Girl"
Passau, an ultra-conservative town, has not digested Nazism. In the 1980s a local girl, Anja Rosmus, courageously examined the past of many respected burghers: she found that some had once been active Nazis, but had kept it hidden. For this she was victimized and physically attacked locally. But nationally she became a heroine. The famous film *The Nasty Girl* told her story.

These decorated steins (beer mugs) are typical of Passau, famous for its beer

Nazi rallies
Hitler chose Nürnberg for his biggest mass rallies, with fanatical crowds of up to 250,000 yelling *"Sieg Heil!."* The buildings erected for them in the suburbs are today preserved as grim memorials—the giant stadium designed by Albert Speer, the Congresshalle modeled on the Colosseum in Rome. The Palace of Justice, where Hitler issued many anti-Jewish decrees, was chosen as the site of the Nuremberg Trials in 1946.

tall tabernacle is carried by the sculpted figures of Adam Kraft and his apprentices. The Mauthalle of 1502 was built to store corn; its six-story roof is pierced by sinister hooded dormers, so characteristic of the city.

Nürnberg has an array of museums. Among the Verkehrsmuseum (Transport Museum) exhibits is the gleaming Adler, the locomotive that hauled the first-ever German train along the line from Nürnberg to nearby Fürth. The Spielzeugmuseum holds the largest and most varied toy collection in the world. At the outstanding **Germanisches Nationalmuseum►►**, founded in the 19th century, exhaustion is only avoided by concentrating on a fraction of the exhibits. Don't miss the works of the great painters who spanned the transition from Middle Ages to Renaissance (Altdorfer, Cranach, Dürer) or the carvings and sculptures of their contemporaries, including Kraft, Riemenschneider, and Stoss.

▶▶ Passau

On a long tongue of land at the confluence of the rivers Danube, Inn, and Ilz, Passau has one of the most spectacular settings of any German city. Wooded heights hem in the rivers and provide splendid sites for the pilgrimage church of Maria Hilf to the south and for the Veste to the north, the great fortress built by the city's prince-bishops to keep unruly townsfolk firmly under control.

Passau is still one of Germany's main gateways to Austria; steamers sail from here to Vienna and beyond, to Budapest and the Black Sea. Inland, the web of narrow streets leads eventually to the great **cathedral▶**, with its trio of helmeted towers. Founded originally in the 8th century, it owes much of its present appearance to a thoroughgoing baroque rebuilding (1680). Inside is the world's biggest church organ, installed in the 1920s and with a total of 17,330 pipes. It is played daily at noon in summer. Reconstruction spared the flamboyant Gothic east end of the cathedral, best viewed from the Residenzplatz, an irregular square flanked by fine Renaissance mansions. One of them houses a small museum of toys. Opposite the 14th-century Rathaus is a large museum of glass.

The city's splendid roofscape is best appreciated from the lofty tower of the Veste. The bishops began building the fortress in 1219 and added to it over the centuries, creating an extraordinary mixture of Gothic, Renaissance, and baroque architecture. It now houses a medley of museums and galleries, including a folk museum.

Baroque monasteries
To the west of Passau are delightful landscapes between the rivers Vils, Rott and Inn, dotted with baroque monasteries (Vornbach, Aldersbach and Fürstenzell, the last with a particularly splendid library), castles (Neuburg, looming over the Inn; Ortenburg, with one of the finest carved ceilings in Germany) and attractive small towns (Vilshofen, Aidenbach, and Rotthalmünster, with a fine parish church and pilgrimage chapel).

227

Passau, on the Danube, has a legacy of glorious buildings from its past as a Free Imperial City

Roman gate
Regensburg's history goes back much further than the Middle Ages. The Celts' name for it, Radaspona, survives in the city's French name of Ratisbonne. As Castra Regina, it guarded the frontier of the Roman empire at the northernmost point of the Danube. The remains of the Roman Praetorian Gate still stand in the strangely named street Unter den Schwibbogen (Under the Flying Buttress).

Happy angel
Regensburg cathedral's rich sculptural decoration includes the famous *Angel of the Annunciation*, positively bursting with enthusiasm at the good news he has to tell, while another note is struck by the figures popularly known as *The Devil and His Grandma*, housed in niches in the main portal.

►►► Regensburg

The capital of eastern Bavaria, this historic cathedral city on the Danube was one of the largest in Germany to escape wartime destruction. Its narrow streets and intimate squares evoke its medieval heyday, when its merchants were among the most prosperous in Europe.

Near the remains of the Roman Praetorian Gate rise the lacelike **cathedral**►► spires, added as late as 1869 to the great edifice begun in the 13th century. This is one of Germany's finest Gothic churches and has lovely cloisters and 14th-century stained glass. Note the comic statue on the roof of a man with a jug. The squares around the cathedral form the kernel of the city, with ancient buildings crowding together. The cathedral's parish church, the Niedermünsterkirche, is a mid-12th-century basilica built over the remains of three previous churches. The oldest (700) goes back to the mysterious Merovingian Age and was erected on top of Roman remains. Across the Alter Kornmarkt is the ancient Liebfraukirche (Church of Our Lady). Its sumptuous interior is about as far as you can get from the remote world of primitive Christianity, having been remodeled in rococo style to suit 18th-century tastes.

Whole days could be spent wandering Regensburg's labyrinth of streets and alleyways lined by venerable houses in a style as much Italian as German. Like their counterparts in various Italian towns, the city's leading families built towers in competition with each other; in the 13th century there were 60 such structures, of which 20 survive to give the city its unique skyline. Among them is the Baumburger Turm, with its gallery, and the Goldener Turm in the Wahlenstrasse, the city's oldest street.

The broad Danube makes a pleasing contrast to this medieval inner city, best appreciated from the upper arches of the Steinerne Brücke (Old Stone Bridge), built in the 12th century and for 800 years the only river crossing hereabouts. To the left of the towered gateway guarding the bridgehead is the immense roof of the 17th-century salt store; at its side, Regensburg's oldest restaurant, the Historische Wurstküche.

Presiding over the far side of the city center is the mostly 19th-century palace of the princes of Thurn und Taxis. The palace incorporates the cloisters of the church of St. Emmeran, famous for its tombs. Among them is that of poor Queen Emma, who died in 876 and whose tomb bears a mournful expression.

The aristocratic air of an earlier era is captured in the Gothic Altes Rathaus, with splendid interiors redolent of the Imperial Diet which used to assemble here.

The Stadtmuseum (city museum), in the buildings of an old monastery, displays a wonderful scale model of the city as it used to be, and the works of members of the Danube School, including Albrecht Altdorfer.

Excursions

Kallmünz, about 19 miles northwest, is a self-conscious little place and a favorite subject for painters. The old stone bridge near the confluence of the contrastingly colored waters of the rivers Vils and Naab is overlooked by the castle, ruined in the Thirty Years' War but still a wonderful lookout point.

A view over the River Danube at Regensburg

Walhalla▶, a gleaming white copy of the Parthenon, sits incongruously in the utterly un-Grecian setting of wooded slopes running down to the Danube. Inspired by Ludwig I of Bavaria and completed in 1841, it houses busts of the great and good of Germanic history and was intended to foster national unity. The climb up its 358 steps may encourage an appropriately reverential mood; the splendid viewpoint over the Danube Valley and the ruins of Donaustauf Castle can be more easily reached from the back.

Thurn and Taxis
A far from mournful figure in Regensburg's life is that of Princess Gloria. Inheriting the Thurn und Taxis fortune (reputedly the biggest in Germany) from her husband, the late prince, this trend-setting doyenne of the international jet set features regularly in Germany's glossy magazines and is called "the pink princess."

Albrecht Altdorfer
Altdorfer raised landscape painting to a high pitch of emotional intensity—and also found time to serve his native Regensburg as city architect.

The statues on the main doorway are typical of the elaborate decoration of St. Peter's cathedral

Ries valley
Both Nördlingen and the little Residenz town of Wallerstein lie in the vast (12 miles across) fertile depression known as the Ries. Its origin was long a subject of controversy, but it is now known to have been created by the impact of a meteorite some 15 million years ago.

Würzburg, on the Main, lies amid vineyards. The people tend to be jovial and open-minded, as so often in wine-producing areas

▶▶ **Romantische Strasse**

Of all the named tourist highways spanning the country, Germany's renowned Romantische Strasse is the most popular. Linking Würzburg in the wine country of Franconia with the Alps at Füssen, and some 220 miles long, it is less remarkable for the tranquil scenery it traverses than for the string of historic towns through which it passes. Between them they encapsulate the essence of the country's past, from medieval *Gemütlichkeit*, or coziness (Rothenburg-ob-der-Tauber, Dinkelsbühl, Nördlingen), via the mercantile magnificence of the early Renaissance (Augsburg), to the splendors of the baroque (Würzburg). The major destinations on the way are described under their own headings, but others mentioned here should also be seen if possible.

The route strikes southwest from **Würzburg** (see page 235) to join the pretty valley of the Tauber at **Tauberbischofsheim,** an unspoiled medieval town with timberframed buildings and a good local history museum in the old princely palace. Beyond **Bad Mergentheim** (see page 213) is **Weikersheim,** the home of the Hohenlohe family (splendid Knights Hall and formal park). **Creglingen** and **Detwang** have churches that feature fine altarpieces by Tilman Riemenschneider, while **Feuchtwangen** boasts Romanesque cloisters that serve as an open-air theater in summer.

On the far side of the Ries (see panel), boldly standing out above the countryside, **Harburg Castle** no longer bars the way since the road tunnels straight under it.

On either side of **Augsburg** (see page 210) the road runs across the broad Bavarian plain. To the south of the city is the **Lechfeld**, today a NATO base and redolent of military memories. In 955 it was the site of one of the most decisive battles in European history, when Otto the Great finally put an end to the heathen Hungarians' incursions into western Europe and drove them back down the Danube.

Beyond **Landsberg** (see page 251) lie the Alps, a spectacular barrier when seen from the town walls of **Schöngau** on a clear day. Easily reached from the Romantische Strasse as it nears its end at **Füssen** (see page 245) are some of Bavaria's greatest architectural treasures, the glorious rococo church at **Wies** (see page 265) and the royal castles at **Höhenschwangau** and **Neuschwanstein** (see page 246).

▶▶▶ Rothenburg-ob-der-Tauber

Rothenburg is among Germany's best-preserved and most picturesque medieval towns, but *very* touristy. Once more important than Nürnberg, Rothenburg stagnated after the Thirty Years' War before being discovered by Romantic artists and writers in the 19th century as the "epitome of Germanic medievalism."

Completely ringed by ramparts, the town overlooks the winding valley of the Tauber. A succession of charming pictures unfolds as you stroll the cobbled streets or pace the sentry walk along the walls. A sea of red roofs rises above the half-timbered, high-gabled houses, no two quite alike, crowded together along the crooked streets. The highest roof is the Gothic St. Jakobs-Kirche. Its cool interior holds a meticulously carved 1505 altarpiece by the great Riemenschneider. The focal point of the town is the Marktplatz, dominated by the **Rathaus▶**, half Gothic,

Bibulous savior
Rothenburg's perfect state of preservation is in part due to its having survived the Thirty Years' War intact. The threat by General Tilly to raze the town was averted when Mayor Nusch proved himself able to drain a six-pint-plus measure of wine in one go. This feat—the so-called *Meistertrunk*—is commemorated by the mechanical figures on the clock attached to the Ratstrinkstube and also by a colorful pageant.

half Renaissance, with a splendid Imperial Hall inside. Enjoy the view from the top of the 197-foot bell tower.

Another excellent viewpoint is from the Burggarten, the little park on the promontory once occupied by the castle of the Hohenstaufens. Spanning the river below is the strange Doppelbrücke (Double Bridge), and not far away the even stranger Topplerschlösschen, a defensive tower on which an ordinary little house is perched.

Picturesque highlights of Rothenburg's townscape include the Plönlein, where changing street levels enhance the scene around the 1385 Siebersturm gateway; the patrician mansions along the Herrengasse; the Rodertor gateway, flanked by twin little tollhouses; or the Gerlach Schmiede (smithy) nearby, with its impossibly exaggerated gable.

Rothenburg-ob-der Tauber retains its old-world quaintness

► **Staffelstein**

Staffelstein, with its fine Rathaus, is one of a number of half-timbered small towns and villages on the fertile floor of the broad and tranquil valley of the Main, north of Bamberg. Just upstream is Lichtenfels, the country's basket-making center. Attractive enough in themselves, these places are visited less for their own sake than for their proximity to two great works of baroque architecture facing each other across the tranquil vale.

Crowning the wooded height to the west is the massive **Kloster Banz►**, a monastery founded by the Benedictines in 1069 and completely rebuilt between 1695 and 1768. The imposing domestic buildings (with collections that include a famous ichthyosaurus) are dominated by the twin spires of the great church, the work of Johann Dientzenhofer. The interior is outstanding, with splendid stuccos, colorful frescoes, and vigorous altarpieces. From the terrace are sweeping views across the valley toward the pilgrimage church of Vierzehnheiligen.

Vierzehnheiligen Pilgrimage Church►► is one of the key buildings of the 18th century in Germany. It is a place of pilgrimage not only for the faithful but for anyone prepared to be persuaded that the German spirit is capable of the most sublime flights of fancy.

The Benedictine monastery of Kloster Banz, not far from Staffelstein

A stiff uphill walk from the large parking lot leads to a bevy of booths selling every kind of souvenir. The church's conventional exterior, in rough-looking ocher sandstone, is grand enough, with two tall towers, but gives little hint of the delights that lie beyond. Inside, the mood changes; all semblance of convention disappears in the abundant light that illuminates an extravagant interior in a froth of pink, gold and white decoration. The focal point is less the main altar at the east end than the central confection, "half coral reef, half fairy sedan chair" (Nikolaus Pevsner), adorned with figures of the 14 saints who gave the church its name. This ecstatic creation is the work of the great Balthasar Neumann. His patron was the ambitious prince-bishop of Bamberg, Friedrich Carl von Schönborn.

► **Straubing**

Once one of Bavaria's most important cities, Straubing is still the center for the rich arable region known as the Gäuboden and has kept much of the air of a prosperous provincial city of the late Middle Ages.

The Romans built a fort here to guard their Danube frontier; spectacular evidence of their presence is provided by the rich hoard of gold masks and other objects that is the pride of the town museum. The wealth of a later age is expressed in a heritage of fine buildings, including such churches as Romanesque St. Peter's, with its atmospheric walled graveyard; the tall-towered Jakobskirche; and the little baroque jewel of the Ursuline church. Straubing's main landmark, however, is its 14th-century tower dividing the elongated market square into two parts; its corner turrets enabled an all-around watch to be kept for intruders or for the fires that could easily devastate the timber-built towns of the time.

Straubing's main festival, the biggest in Bavaria after Munich's Bierfest, is the annual Gäuboden Fair, held each August.

Excursions

Deggendorf, Some 21 miles southeast, resembles Straubing on a smaller scale, with a fine market square dominated by the town tower.

Nearby are two splendid baroque monasteries: **Metten**, with a particularly fine library, and **Nieder-alteich**, the first foundation of its kind in Bavaria. Built as a Gothic hall church, it was remodeled in baroque style. The unusual lantern windows in the galleries offer a good view of the vaulting.

The rich agricultural land around Straubing was settled at an early date and is well endowed with old churches, including the picturesquely sited Romanesque church at **Rankam**. Of later date are the Benedictine buildings of the monastery at **Oberalteich**, completed in 1630, though the interior had to wait another 100 years before being decorated with its spectacular frescoes.

Agnes Bernauer

Straubing's most famous figure was Agnes Bernauer, a barber's daughter whose beauty so impressed Duke Ernst's son that he married her in spite of her humble origins. This so enraged the duke that in 1435 he had Agnes tried on a trumped-up charge of witchcraft, then executed by drowning in the Danube. The tragic tale is reenacted in the courtyard of the ducal castle every four years.

Straubing, always lively, is most boisterous during the Gäuboden festival in August

►► Waldsassen

In the Middle Ages, many monasteries were established in the densely wooded uplands along the ancient border between Bavaria and Bohemia. Monks toiled to convert the forest to farmland and bring Christianity to the few inhabitants. Waldsassen (1133) is one of the greatest of these centers of medieval civilization. It stood alone for centuries until the little town to which it gave its name began to develop in the early 17th century.

The monastery buildings date from 1681 to 1704. The long, narrow church is one of the masterpieces of the great Bavarian baroque architect Georg Dientzenhofer, who worked with a cosmopolitan team including the Italian Carleone, who embellished the interior with 200 stucco angels. Attracting special reverence is a battered figure of Christ, found hanging on the border barrier with Czechoslovakia in 1951 at the height of the cold war.

In the monastery itself is the library. Karl Stopl, the master carver responsible for this extraordinary interior, took as his theme everything that goes into the production of a book; the sequence of 10 figures supporting the upper level includes the humble rag collector (gathering raw materials for paper), the author, the critic (his bound hands symbolizing his unproductive vocation), and the reader (a portrait of the artist).

Excursions

The gentle hills and vales of Waldsassen have always attracted admirers, including Goethe. **Tirscheneuth**, to the south, is the area's market center. The Renaissance Rathaus survived a great fire in 1814. All around are pools and ponds, breeding carp and trout.

On a hill to the northwest of Waldsassen stands one of the most unusual buildings in Bavaria, the pilgrimage church of **Kappel**. Commissioned by the abbot of Waldsassen, Dientzenhofer designed a church to honor the Holy Trinity, linking together three rounded apses, each topped with a bulbous tower. Seen across the fields, the church's exotic outline is more reminiscent of Orthodox Russia than Catholic Bavaria.

The Sudetenland
On the Czechs' side of their frontier with northern Bavaria and Saxony is the much-contested Sudetenland. Because of its large German minority, Hitler siezed it in 1938: then the Czechs won it back in 1945, and in reprisal expelled most of the Germans. Many of them settled in Bavaria, and during the Communist era felt deeply bitter. Even with today's open borders, hard feelings linger.

Waldsassen dates largely from the early 17th century

▶▶▶ Würzburg

This university city, the ancient seat of powerful prince-bishops, is situated among vineyards on the steep banks of the River Main. Celtic tribesmen first fortified the strategic height occupied by the massive Marienberg fortress, but Würzburg's history really begins with the martyrdom here in 689 of an Irish missionary, St. Kilian, whose mission was to convert the locals to Christianity. His gravestone is in the cathedral named after him, in the center of the old city on the far bank of the river.

Würzburg is notable for its many churches. One of the oldest is the round, thick-walled Marienkirche, in the fortress courtyard. The **Marienberg▶** itself was rebuilt and extended over the years to become a most formidable stronghold. Occupied for nearly 500 years by the prince-bishops, it now houses the splendid collections of the regional **museum▶** (Mainfränkisches Museum); its greatest treasures are the tenderly sculpted sandstone figures of Adam and Eve, by the great Tilman Riemenschneider (1460–1531), who was both artist and mayor.

By the 18th century, the Marienberg had become too cramped for the bishops' lifestyle, and they moved to purpose-built quarters on the far side of the city. Their new address, the **Würzburg Residenz▶▶**, designed by Balthasar Neumann, is the greatest baroque building of its kind in Germany, dominating the vast cobbled square linking it to the town. Its interior spaces are staggering, in both sheer size and lavishness of decoration. They include the grand staircase, covered by the largest

The Marienberg fortress overlooks the river at Würzburg

Augsburg's almshouses
One of Bavaria's major oddities is the Fuggerei in Augsburg, a collection of neat almshouses built in 1519 by Jakob Fugger "the Rich," a philanthropic banker. Here he housed some of the city's poor families, virtually for free. The snug kitchens must have seemed ultramodern then. Some 300 poorer people still live there, and the Fugger family still runs the place.

ceiling painting in the world (by the Venetian Tiepolo), the oval Kaisersaal (with *trompe-l'oeil* painting, also by Tiepolo) and the sumptuous Gartensaal, the great ground-floor room linking the palace to the gardens beyond. These form a perfect example of rococo garden art and make an ideal backdrop for the summer Mozart Festival. Neumann's palace chapel, the gorgeous Hofkirche, is a favorite place for weddings.

Würzburg suffered almost as grievously as Dresden in World War II, when an air raid left most of the city center in ruins. Bravely rebuilt, it is a cheerful and lively place, with plenty of wine taverns and a buzz of student life. Its restored churches include the splendidly severe Romanesque **Cathedral**▶, with the gravestones of the prince-bishops, among them two wonderful examples by Riemenschneider.

Opposite the cathedral is the Neumünster, built over St. Kilian's grave and given a fine baroque façade in the early 18th century. It also has a garden with the grave of Germany's medieval troubadour Walter von der Vogelweide. In the market square stands the Gothic Marienkapelle, with Neumann's tombstone at its portal. Nearby is the fine rococo façade of the Haus zum Falken, meticulously restored after the bombing. Spared destruction were the two great charitable institutions founded to house the city's senior citizens, the Bürgerspital of 1319 and the Johannesspital of 1576. Both derive part of their income from their vineyards; their produce is dispensed in their atmospheric wine taverns.

Würzburg's only church to survive the war unscathed was the Kappelle pilgrimage chapel. Owing its good fortune to its isolated position above the wooded ravine separating it from the Marienberg, it is yet another dazzling display of baroque virtuosity by Neumann.

Excursions

On either side of Würzburg, the deep valley of the Main forms one of Germany's most distinctive wine-growing regions. Its excellent wines are relatively dry and come in stumpy flasks, quite different from the elegant bottles of Rhine and Mosel vintages.

Upstream from the city, one delightful little place succeeds another: **Sommerhausen**, favored by artists; half-timbered **Ochsenfurt** ("Oxford") within its ramparts; **Frickenhausen**, accessible only through one of its four gateways; **Marktbreit**; **Sulzfeld**... Walled **Volkach** has many picturesque houses, a 16th-century Rathaus, and a local museum in the baroque Schelfenhaus. Crowning the hilly vineyards outside the town is Maria im Weingarten (Our Lady of the Vineyard), a late Gothic pilgrimage church, housing one of Riemenschneider's most delicate works, *Madonna in a Rose Garland*.

The summer palace of the prince-bishops of Würzburg, **Veitschöhheim** (4 miles northwest), has an exquisite rococo garden, a delight of hedged enclosures, playful statuary, and the Grosser See, an artificial lake with an even more artificial Mt. Parnassus rising from it. This jewel of landscape architecture was rescued from neglect by the indefatigable King Ludwig I of Bavaria, who restored it to its former glory.

Würzburg's splendid Residenz was intended to symbolize the wealth and power of the ruling prince-bishops

Wagner

■ **Revolutionary, exile, focus of scandal, writer and composer Richard Wagner's life at times matched the more dramatic passages of his titanic operas. Certainly, in works such as *Tristan und Isolde*, the themes of his own eventful life found most eloquent musical expression** ...■

In 1834, at the age of 21, Wagner was appointed director of the Magdeburg opera. Here he wrote his first operas, and married a singer, Minna Plater, with whom he lived for 25 years in a largely unhappy marriage. To escape his private life he composed increasingly, including *Rienzi* (1840) and *Der fliegende Holländer* (*The Flying Dutchman*, 1842). In the latter, the romantic idea of redemption through love—a theme recurring in Wagner's operas but absent from his marriage—is first expressed. Mixed receptions of his next, less conventional, works, including *Tannhäuser*, reinforced his belief in his own ability; this period of musical innovation even saw him as a political revolutionary, manning barricades during the Dresden uprising.

New rules Wagner abandoned the traditional "rules" of recitative and aria for a continuous musical dialogue, and used the leitmotiv, a representation of symbols and characters in musical terms, to perfection.

With the help of his friend Liszt, *Lohengrin* (1850) was triumphantly performed in Weimar—despite Wagner's enforced exile in Zürich due to the failure of the uprising. In Zürich he began a passionate affair with the wife of a Swiss benefactor and conceived the idea for *Tristan und Isolde*, while also working on his masterwork, *Der Ring des Nibelungen*, a cycle of four epic operas based on German mythology.

Scandal erupted again when Cosima, Liszt's daughter and the wife of composer Hans von Bülow, bore Wagner a child. She obtained a divorce and, after Minna's death in 1866, Cosima married Wagner in 1870.

In his later years, Wagner turned his attention to the foundation of the ideal opera house; in 1876 the Bayreuth Festspielhaus was opened with a complete performance of the *Ring* cycle. (The opera house is now the venue for the annual Bayreuth Festival.) After a full life, which among other things saw him writing on a variety of subjects, including vegetarianism and hygiene, Wagner died in 1883. He is buried at Wahnfried, his Bayreuth villa.

Above: Spy's impression of Wagner, from Vanity Fair, *1877*
Top: Richard and Cosima Wagner

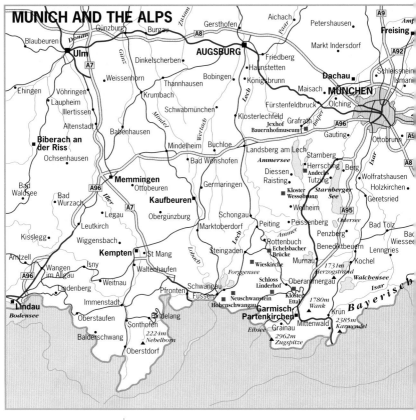

The panorama from Munich's Olympic tower makes this region appear remarkably compact. The easygoing, cosmopolitan Bavarian capital lies on a fertile plain that extends southward toward the snowy peaks of the Alps, Germany's highest and most dramatic mountains. In between are neat, clustered villages, pine forests, sparkling lakes and gently rolling pastures. It is a rewarding area for exploration, with a host of entertainment and cultural offerings in Munich itself, magnificent scenic variety and (particularly away from the Alps) a number of historic small towns. All over the area are examples of Bavarian baroque churches and castles, many of them spectacular compositions with ornate stuccowork and frescoed ceilings.

While the German Alps comprise only a thin strip (the bulk of the great range lies in Italy, Austria, Switzerland and France), the mountains form a backdrop that is the key to much of the charm of the low-lying hinterland. The scenery immediately around Munich is rather flat, but farther south are several lakes, popular for walks, boat trips and sailing. The Alps themselves can be enjoyed by driving along the **Deutsche Alpenstrasse** (German Alpine Road), a scenic theme road threading its way from **Lindau** to **Berchtesgaden** and passing close to the four remarkable 19th-century castles of Ludwig II, Bavaria's mad king, whose extravagant fantasies now provide

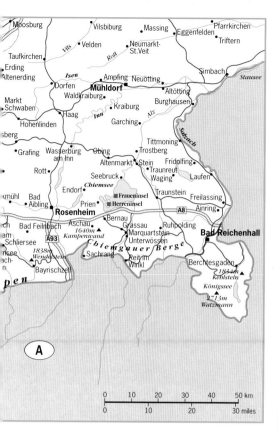

Bavaria with its top tourist attractions. Tourism is big business, with numerous resorts geared to winter sports and medical and nonmedical "cures." For most of the year, many Alpine summits can be reached by cable cars and chairlifts; at the top there's often a strategically sited restaurant. Walking is by no means confined to arduous mountain ascents; easy paths, meticulously signposted, give gentle strolls through woods, along gorges, around lakes and up to viewpoints. The mountain resort towns are not especially interesting, however.

Southern Bavaria—with the notable exception of liberal Munich—is staunchly conservative, both politically and in general outlook. You will see men wearing Bavarian hats and *Lederhosen* (leather trousers), and women in embroidered dirndl dresses; festivals are celebrated with gusto, particularly May Day, when huge maypoles are erected and decorated. The tradition of painting murals (and the family name in old Gothic lettering) on house exteriors is widespread. Food is hearty and traditional—quantities of pork, dumplings, potatoes and sauerkraut are *de rigueur* in country areas. The region is strongly Catholic: "*Grüss Gott*" (God's greeting) is the standard greeting (never "*Guten Tag*"—good day), and churches have a prosperous look. Much of the region is accessible within a day trip from Munich, but beware of crowds and traffic jams at peak times at the main sights and resorts.

Wessobrunn Abbey
Wessobrunn Abbey, west of the Ammersee, is famous for the "Wessobrunner Gebet" (Wessobrunn Prayer), a poetic fragment of nine lines that dates from the last 30 years of the 8th century. Although written in a Bavarian dialect, the "Wessobrunn Prayer" is often considered the oldest-known text written in the German language.

Ammersee: popular with weekenders

▶ Ammersee and Andechs

Ammersee, a 22-mile lake situated west of Munich, is a popular weekend retreat, with small, quiet resorts, reedy shores and pleasant, low hills. Boat trips and yacht rentals are on offer, and swimming is quite feasible in the warmer months. The west side is more congested, but Herrsching, on the east shore, is the main resort and a starting point for gentle lakeside walks.

The pilgrimage church of the Benedictine monastery of Andechs▶, close to Herrsching, is one of the rococo masterpieces of Bavaria, with frescoes and stuccowork by J. B. Zimmermann. Carl Orff (1895–1982), the composer best known for his *Carmina Burana*, is buried here. The tower offers a good view of the lake. Next door, the monastery *Bräustüberl* (beer hall) does a roaring trade in the excellent beer produced by the monks and dispensed straight from the barrel. The monastery shop sells a Klosterlikör (monastery liqueur) and its own bottled beer.

Höher Peissenberg, southwest of the lake and accessible by road from Höhenpeissenberg village, has been a place of pilgrimage since the 16th century, when peasants erected a chapel on this lofty site, with its magnificent panorama of the German Alps (on a clear day you can even discern the restaurant on top of the Zugspitze). The church has been expanded and given the ubiquitous rococo treatment; note the organ loft's elaborate parquetry. Railings on the roof of the adjacent house mark the site of the world's first weather station (1781). Observations were made first by Augustinian monks and then by priests and teachers; in 1937 an official weather station was set up here.

The huge satellite dishes at **Raisting**, just south of the Ammersee, that dominate the area constitute the world's largest telecommunications center. A visitor center (open Monday–Friday, 8:30–noon, 1:45–5; weekends, noon–4; admission free) is located within the huge white sphere.

Tables with a view at a Berchtesgaden mountaintop café

▶▶ Berchtesgadener Land

Jutting into Austria, Germany's southeastern corner offers glorious Alpine scenery; **Salzburg** is within close reach just across the border. The vicinity of **Schonau** and **Berchtesgaden** is ideal as a base for exploration.

Berchtesgaden▶▶ itself is a comfortable medium-sized resort with an active town center; turn-of-the-century villas full of character perch on the hillside. The menacing form of the Watzmann (8,899 feet) looms high to the south; not surprisingly, the mountain inspired many artists and is the subject of local legends. The town is the place for bad-weather days. Particularly enjoyable are the still-functioning **Salt Mines▶** (open Easter and May to October, 8:30–5; rest of year, daily except Sunday, 12:30–5:30), where visitors don miners' clothes, travel on mine wagons, slide down a slope (heavy-duty pants are issued for the purpose) and raft across a subterranean lake; miner guides explain the salt-extraction process.

In the town center are the Heimatmuseum (open Monday to Saturday, 10–3), with a display of local wood crafts, and the Residenz (open 10–1, 2–5; closed Saturday, also Sunday in winter), formerly an Augustinian priory, then from 1810 a Wittelsbach palace and now a museum housing a collection of weapons and paintings.

For details of guided walks (May to October) visit the national park offices in Berchtesgaden (tel: 08652–64343) or Königsee (tel: 08652–62222).

As with much of Bavaria, the area has many baroque churches. The most photographed are probably **Ramsau** and the idyllically sited **Maria Gern**.

Three magi
Many Bavarian doorways bear the chalked legend "C+M+B" (plus the year of inscription) over them, an age-old device to bring blessing on the building. The initials stand for Caspar, Melchior, and Balthasar, the three Magi, or wise men, known in medieval legends as the three kings of Cologne.

BERCHTESGADENER LAND

Weissbach · Karlstein · **Bad Reichenhall**

Saalach-see

Schneizlreuth

Predigtstuhl ▲ 1613m

Markt Schellenberg ▲ 1973m

A l p e n -

Unterjettenberg · Hintergern · Almbachklamm

Deutsche Alpenstrasse

Bischofswiesen · Maria Gern · Oberau

p a r k

R e i t e r A l p e

Schwarzbachpass 868m

Obersalzberg

Berchtesgaden

Ramsau · **Schönau** · Kehlstein 1834m

Hintersee

Wimbachklamm · Königssee

Hober Göll ▲ 2523m

Nationalpark

Hochkalter 2608m ▲

Jenner ▲ 1874m

Watzmann ▲ 2713m

Königssee

St.Bartholomä

Berchtesgaden

Gr.Hundstod 2594m ▲

Obersee

Grünsee

Funtensee

Steinernes Meer

0 — 5 — 10 km
0 — 5 miles

Left: Berchtesgaden, an active resort set on the hillside, and an ideal base for exploring the Berchtesgadener Land mountains

The road up to the 5,970-foot summit of the **Kehlstein►**, situated southeast of the town, takes a zigzag course with plenty of views all the way. The road is closed to motor vehicles but a bus operates from Obersalzberg-Hintereck to a point near the top. From here, between May and mid-October, a lift built into the mountain ascends to the Kehlsteinhaus (Eagle's Nest), which is now a restaurant. Hitler used to come here, for it is near his former Berghof retreat (see page 244). There are wide views down over the Salzburg plain. Connecting buses leave from the Berchtesgaden post office.

Often likened to a Norwegian fjord, the much-visited **Königsee►►** stretches over 5 miles below the mighty slopes of the Watzmann, its depths plummeting over 623 feet. At the lake's northern end, from the village of Königsee (a tourist trap of kitschy souvenir shops, fortunately invisible from the lake itself), boat trips are available over the length of the water, with breathtaking vistas all the way. The round-trip takes an hour and three quarters and operates all year, weather permitting. Attractions near the far end include short walks to the chapels of St. Johann and St. Paul, and a more ambitious ascent to an ice "chapel," which even the summer heat fails to melt (allow an hour each way).

A pleasant 75-minute circular walk, the Malerwinkel Rundweg, starts to the left of the main boat pier (at the

lake's north end), taking an easily managed gravel track up into the trees. The crowds disappear and you are soon rewarded with views over the Königsee.

Also from Königsee you can take the cable lift up the **Jenner** (6,147 feet), where the mountaintop restaurant gives views of the lake on one side and of nearby Austria on the other.

The Almbachklamm, a gloomy chasm with dramatic rock overhangs and swirling waterfalls, can be explored between May and October by a gently rising path (admission charge), which can be followed for an hour and a half to the Theresienklause Dam; the best of the gorge is seen at the beginning. The parking lot is signposted from highway 305, northeast of Berchtesgaden at the 5½-mile post.

Bad Reichenhall is a spa reputed to have the most powerful saline springs in Europe; look for the Quellenbau (guided tours daily, April to October; Tuesday and Thursday only, rest of year), a curious saltworks built by Ludwig I in grandiose medieval style in 1834. If driving here from Berchtesgaden, you are advised to take highway 305 westward for the splendid scenery of the Schwarzbach Pass.

243

Walk The Hintersee

This small lake nestles beneath the wooded lower slopes of the Schottmalhorn (6,708 feet) and the Hochkalter (8,551 feet). The walk around takes about 45 minutes, with an optional climb of the Wartstein (15 minutes).

Start at the Seeklause car park at the 15½-mile post on the Ramsau–Weissbach road, west of Berchtesgaden. Turn left out of the parking lot, along the road, which soon crosses a stream; immediately turn right on a broad path with wooden railings. Ignore turns to the right, and walk through the **Zauberwald** (magic wood). After following the shore, reach an intersection and turn left, signposted Fussweg am See. After 30 yards or so, detour right to the **Wartstein** (signposted), keeping right at subsequent intersections until the summit, with its fine view and tiny cave shrine. Return the same way to the bottom, turn right and continue the signposted Fussweg am See, which passes in front of the hotels and branches off left. The final section leads left along the footpath by the road.

Walk The Wimbachtal

The **Wimbachklamm**, west of Berchtesgaden on highway 305 at the 12-mile post, is a pretty gorge and a starting point for walks along the Wimbachtal (Wimbach River valley): from the parking lot, take the rising road (closed to cars) called Wimbachweg; after the road becomes unsurfaced, fork left into the gorge. Two-and-a-half hours' gentle ascent leads you to the Wimbachgrieshütte, sited in a majestic postglacial valley below the Watzmann and the Hochkalter. There is a restaurant (Wimbach Schloss) midway. Return the same way.

Fraueninsel
On the intimate little Fraueninsel (women's island on the Chiemsee), Benedictines have had a monastery since AD 780, and their nuns still live there (hence the name). They run a girls' boarding school, and still brew their *Klostergeist* liqueur ("convent spirit"), to be tasted in their Klostercafé. Behind the altar of the tiny 13th-century church are charmingly naive ex-votos, some by local fishermen giving thanks to the island's saint.

The landing stage of Fraueninsel, a lushly fertile little island, full of apple trees, birdsong, and religious peace

Hitler's eyrie
On the heights above Berchtesgaden (see page 242) Hitler built a grandiose mountain retreat, where he welcomed many top-rank visitors. It was razed to the ground in 1945 (only some stone slabs now remain); and it is not signposted, so as to deter Neo-Nazi pilgrims from using it as a shrine. But a nearby museum in the air-raid shelter shows photos of Adolf and Eva Braun.

►► **Chiemsee**

Bavaria's largest lake looks best from the northern side, particularly from the little resort of Gstadt; the Alpine foothills form part of a distinguished backdrop. It makes a good base for walks, with easy ones in the vicinity of the lake itself and more energetic rambles in the hills to the south. Boating is the other main attraction, with yachts for rent in many of the resorts, and a passenger boat service making stops around the lake. Try to see both of the principal islands. On **Herreninsel**, the larger, stands Herrenchiemsee, an unfinished palace of Ludwig II. The king decided to make a replica of Versailles, but only built the central portion before funds ran out. What exists is impressive, with formal French gardens, a hall of mirrors, and a state room where classical concerts are held by candlelight. This would have been the largest of Ludwig's castles. Nearby is lovely Fraueninsel (see left). From Prien, on the west side of the lake, a steam train pulls 19th-century wooden carriages 1¼ miles to the pier for boats to the

islands. The old village of Breitbrunn is a haunt of writers and artists from Munich.

Local tourist offices stock booklets detailing the annual classical music festival held in several venues in the area between May and July.

To the south lie the Alpine foothills, a fine area for medium to energetic walks without the daunting scale of the Alps proper. The **Kampenwand** (5,458 feet) is a popular objective and has cable lifts to get you up to the high ground. **Reit im Winkl** is an Alpine resort of considerable charm.

►► **Dachau**

A few places in the world cause a frisson at the mention of their very names. Dachau, a small commuter town near Munich, cannot forget the traumas of its notorious past as the site of the Third Reich's first concentration camp, established in 1933 in a former munitions factory. The camp has become a memorial museum (open daily except Monday, 9–5; admission free).

Although Dachau was not an extermination camp, torture, disease and death were commonplace. The barracks have gone, but accurate reconstructions give an idea of the cramped conditions prisoners had to endure. Around the perimeter fence, watchtowers still stand. The Jourhaus (guardhouse), formerly the camp entrance, still displays the chillingly inappropriate legend *Arbeit macht frei* (work makes freedom). The gas chambers, disguised as shower rooms, were never used for extermination, but hanging by the stake, a common punishment, was carried out within them; adjacent are the cremation ovens, which were kept burning day and night. A museum now occupies one side of the site, with a disturbing account of the camp and a half-hour film (in English at 11:30 and 3:30).

As an antidote to the bleakness of the visit to the camp, walk into **Dachau town**, perched above the River Amper. Despite its proximity to Munich, its center has an unspoiled small-town atmosphere, with a pretty Hofgarten (castle garden), a nicely laid out local museum and a Gemäldegalerie (picture gallery) of works by a colony of artists who were attracted to the area because of the unique light of the Dachauer Moos, an area of heathland. Both the museum and the gallery are open Wednesday and Friday, 10–4; Thursday, 2–6; Saturday, 11–5; and Sunday, 1–5.

Dachau camp is easily visited from Munich; take the S-Bahn 2 (direction Petershausen) to Dachau, from where, outside the station, bus 722 takes you to the Kozentrationslager (KZ) Gedenkstätte (concentration camp memorial).

▶▶▶ Füssen, Neuschwanstein and Höhenschwangau

Füssen abuts the Forggensee, a popular sailing area, and has its back to the Alps. Among several scenes of picturesque charm is the cobbled main street, the Reichenstrasse, with a trio of the town's most distinguished buildings at its far end—church, abbey, and Höhenschloss. Close by, an archway gives onto a riverside park by the Lech.

The Benedictine abbey of St. Mang now operates as a local museum (open daily except Monday from 11–4; from 2–4 from November to March), with a violin maker's workshop among the displays; above all, the abbey is an enjoyable place to wander around, with a host of well-preserved baroque rooms, including a delicious oval library. Within the Höhenschloss (open Monday to Saturday, 10–noon, 2–4; Sunday, 10–noon; December to March, Thursday, 2–4 only) is an exhibition of medieval religious art from the Allgäu and Swabia.

Königschlösser (royal castles) Despite unavoidable monstrous tourist crowds for most of the year, the wonderfully spectacular castles of Ludwig II—Linderhof (see page 261), Herrenchiemsee (see page 244), Hohenschwangau, and Neuschwanstein—are very seldom disappointing. Fair-weather timing assists an appreciation of the mountain setting, but may bring out the crowds. There is quite a lot of walking involved, particularly a fairly steep haul up from the parking lot by Höhenschwangau to Neuschwanstein; alternatively, you may prefer to make use of the horse-and-carriage service. It is best to make Höhenschwangau your first stop in order to avoid a sense of anticlimax (see also **Walk** on page 248).

Dachau: grim snapshots

● Over 206,000 prisoners were registered between 1933 and 1945; numerous other internees were never registered. Jews, religious and political dissenters and other "undesirables," were brought here.

● 31,591 died in the camp; thousands more were executed.

● In addition to camp work, many prisoners were victims of human experimentation, which included infection with malaria and experiments on tolerance of high pressure.

245

● Punishment, including hanging from the stake and lashing, was dispensed for the most trivial offense, such as not making beds correctly.

● S.S. men during 1940–1 executed many Jews by removing the prisoners' caps and hurling them into the neutral zone, ordering the Jews to retrieve them; when they did they were shot "for trying to escape."

● Roll call often lasted hours when not all the prisoners could be found. They would stand absolutely still, even in freezing conditions, as the slightest movement would be severely punished. Many of the sick simply collapsed on the spot.

Linderhof, one of Ludwig II's castles, was built in a mix of baroque and Renaissance styles. The gardens include a Moorish pavilion with bronze peacocks

Höhenschwangau►, on a forested hill, is the older of the two castles, built in the 12th century, but destroyed by Napoleon and restored by Crown Prince Maximilian (later Maximilian II) in the 1830s. Ludwig spent his early years here. The decor is troubadour style, with wall paintings of Bavarian knights and folk heroes; Ludwig's bedroom is decorated with stars that were illuminated in the evening. The music room evokes his love of Wagner.

Neuschwanstein►► stands high and mighty, bristling with turrets and mock-medievalism, its interior styles ranging from Byzantine through Romanesque to Gothic. This fairy-tale fantasy come true was built between 1869 and 1886 for Ludwig II; the king spent less than six months here before being certified insane and drowning mysteriously in the Starnberger See. Only about a third of the building was actually completed; the unfinished feeling is manifest everywhere—the second floor is a mere shell, doorways lead to nothing but suicidal drops, and steps in the throne room lead to a throneless stage. The 15 rooms you do see on the tour show astonishing craftsmanship and richness of detail, which extend to the lamp fittings and elaborate central heating system. The wood carving in Ludwig's bedroom took 14 carpenters four and a half years to complete. Wagner's operas are referred to everywhere, in murals and even in a mini-grotto recalling the Venusberg in *Tannhäuser.*

The best view of the castle is from the nearby **Marienbrücke** (Mary's Bridge), which spans a deep gorge. On the path between here and the castle is a splendid vista of Höhenschwangau and the Alpsee. (Both castles: open daily April to October, 8:30–5:30; November to March, 10–4.)

A recommended extra to the visit is the cable-car ascent of the **Tegelberg** (5,642 feet), signposted between Höhenschwangau and Schwangau. It operates all year (until 5 in summer and 4:30 in winter) and has a summit restaurant.

Map labels:
Böbing, Bernbeuren, Rottenbuch, Wildsteig, Uffing, Penzberg, Lechbruck, Steingaden, Bayersoien, Staffelsee, Riegsee, Benediktbeuern, Wieskirche, Saulgrub, Murnau, Grossweil, Rosshaupten, Halblech-Trauchgau 1638m, Bad Kohlgrub, Schlendorf, Glentleiten Freilichtmuseum, Kochel, Kochelsee, Forggensee, Bannwaldsee, Unterammergau, Ohlstadt, Walchensee, Ammergebirge, Oberammergau, Herzogstand 1731m, Füssen, Schwangau, Schloss Linderhof, Graswang, Kochel-Walchensee, Neuschwanstein, Hohenschwangau, Deutsche Alpenstrasse, Ettal, Oberau, Loisach, Bayerische Alpen, Isar, Kreuzspitze 2185m, Garmisch-Partenkirchen, Estergebirge, Wallgau, Reutte, Klais, Krün, Soiernspitze 2257m, Plansee, Grainau, Elmau, Eibsee, Mittenwald, 2385m, Lech, Zugspitze 2962m

A

0 5 10 km
0 5 miles

𝒟rive The Deutsche Alpenstrasse

A tour around and into the heart of the German Alps, using the Alpine Road for much of the way.

From the attractive town of Füssen, the road heads northeast past the turning for Höhenschwangau and Neuschwanstein—the famous castles of Ludwig II—and skirts the Bannwaldsee before reaching Steingaden. Head east.

Detour south at the signpost for the sumptuous baroque **Wieskirche**. Between the low-lying lakes, the **Staffelsee** and **Kochelsee**, is the turnoff for the **Glentleiten Freilichtmuseum** (open-air museum).

From Kochel, the road climbs into the Alps, passing the prettily set Walchensee, best seen by taking the cable car up the Wendelstein. Detour to the village of **Mittenwald** before continuing to **Ettal Abbey** and past **Linderhof**, a Ludwig II castle.

Cross the Austrian border to reach Reutte and continue on to Füssen.

The deep-blue Walchensee, one of the loveliest Bavarian lakes

Walk Höhenschwangau and Neuschwanstein

A good way of seeing castles and the Marienbrücke, and avoiding the crowds. Allow one hour for walking and at least two for sight-seeing.

Park at either of the first two parking lots (on the left) for the castles. Cross the road and take the steps to the left of the information center to Höhenschwangau. After seeing the castle, retrace your steps for a few yards, then, just after the end of the castle building, keep right at a fork, to drop down to hotels and restaurants. Cross the road and take steps to the left of the Schloss Hotel, up to reach the road. Cross over and take the stony path opposite, which ascends steadily. At the top, there is a surfaced track near a wooden shelter; detour right and immediately left to the Marienbrücke; return to the shelter and turn right to Neuschwanstein (don't miss the viewpoint over Höhenschwangau that shortly appears on the left). After leaving the castle, follow the main driveway down, forking right after 500 yards down steps (signposted Cafe Kainz) to reach the parking lots.

Schwangau, the village close to Höhenschwangau, is famed for its Colomansfest, on October 13, when the thanksgiving for horses and cattle takes place. With a grand procession of horse-drawn carriages, the festival marks the return of the cattle from the summer pastures and of the workhorses from the forests.

Höhenschwangau, set among the mountain crags

As well as ski resort, Garmisch is a center of Bavarian folklore, with a major Heimatmuseum

249

▶▶ Garmisch Partenkirchen

Garmisch Partenkirchen is really two towns, joined together but different in character. Garmisch has village origins and retains some old-world rusticity in Frühlingstrasse (in the northern outskirts) and surroundings, with quaint whitewashed, gabled houses and the village fountain. Partenkirchen has been a town for much longer, and has lively, narrow main streets. Both towns have expanded for tourism, above all for the winter-sports industry, together becoming the largest German Alpine resort. As the site of the 1936 Winter Olympics and the 1978 alpine skiing world championships, the town is endowed with an Olympic ice stadium and ski jump. It is not a very good place to get away from the crowds, but nearby villages make good bases.

The towering **Zugspitze▶▶▶** (9,715 feet), Germany's highest mountain, dominates the area and can be reached effortlessly by rack railway from Garmisch; clear-weather views justify the substantial fee, and there is a restaurant at the top. A quicker but less

Germany's leading ski resort is quite a glamorous place. It is also a leading U.S. Army center

Zugspitze, towering over Garmisch Partenkirchen

Badersee
Near the peaceful village of Grainau, west of Garmisch, the tiny Badersee is sited secretively among the trees. For a few marks you can rent a boat and view an endearingly ludicrous statue of Nixe, a nymph, placed at the bottom of the lake by Ludwig II.

exciting way up is by cable car from the **Eibsee**, itself a lovely lake encircled by a 4-mile footpath. Other mountains where you can ascend by chairlift from town and walk down gently graded paths include the **Wank** (5,838 feet) and the **Eckbauer** (4,057 feet); both have summit restaurants.

Whatever the weather, be sure to visit the famous **Partnachklamm►►**. From the Olympic ski stadium, walk or take a horse and carriage along a traffic-free road 1¼ miles to the entrance to the gorge. The path is one of the wonders of the Alps, snaking near the bottom of the immensely deep chasm past spraying water and remarkable rock formations. A cable car runs from the gorge entrance to the Hotel Graseck; from the hotel, follow the track up the valley, enter the gorge at its far end, and walk back down. Less crowded owing to its relative inaccessibility is the **Höllentalklamm**, sandwiched between the bases of the Alpspitze and the Waxenstein; allow at least two hours each way; start from Hammersbach, southwest of Garmisch.

Walk **Eckbauer and the Partnachklamm**

A route taking the chairlift up the Eckbauer, a superlative viewing platform, with close-ups of the Alpspitze. The Gasthof on the summit serves excellent fresh buttermilk. An easy ascent zigzags into a valley of Alpine meadows before the finale along the Partnachklamm, a magnificent gorge.

Take the Eckbauerbahn (chairlift) from the ski stadium in Garmisch. At the top, walk past the Berg Gasthof Eckbauer and follow signs for the

Partnachklamm, down through woods, later forking right to reach a track near the Hotel Graseck. Turn left (a detour is possible soon after this, to Hohe Brücke, a high bridge over the gorge), return to the main route to reach the top entrance to the gorge, which you follow downstream; if this is closed, follow the track the other way, past the Graseck to the bottom entrance, from which you either walk along the traffic-free road or take a horse and carriage.

► **Kaufbeuren**

The unspoiled town center, with its twisting, cobbled streets, merits exploration; the tourist information office (in the Rathaus) publishes a walk about town, in English. A walk along the town walls to Kaufbeuren's northwest corner leads past the Fünfknopfturm (five-spired tower) to the 15th-century church of St. Blasien. The church's greatly treasured high altar by the master Bavarian woodcarver Jörg Lederer (1518) features golden-robed figures of the Virgin and Child, St. John the Baptist, and St. Anne. The Stadtmuseum in Kaisergässchen (open daily except Monday and first Tuesday in month, 9–11, 1–4; Sunday 9–noon) features an impressive collection of crucifixes. In Ludwigstrasse, the Puppenmuseum (open Thursday to Saturday, 10–noon, 2:30–5; Sunday, 10–noon) displays puppets from Europe and the Far East.

The town's big event is in July, when the Tänzelfest takes place. This medieval-style pageant is played out by as many as 1,600 children and is accompanied by processions and re-enactments of scenes from the town's history.

► **Kempten**

A busy commercial center rather than a tourist destination, Kempten nevertheless has some good museums (all open Tuesday to Sunday, 10–4; closed at Christmas). These are the Alpenländische Galerie (Alpine arts gallery), Alpinmuseum (museum of the people and mountains of the Alps), the Museum für Kunst und Kulturgeschichte (sadly closed for the foreseeable future), the Allgäuer Heimatmuseum (regional museum for the Allgäu), and the Römisches Museum (Roman museum). East of the town center, across the River Iller, the Archäologischer Park (open Tuesday to Sunday, 10–5, November to April, 10–4:30; closed January and February; guided tours on Sunday at 11) occupies the former site of the Roman town of Cambodunum. The complex includes a partial reconstruction of a Roman-Celtic temple as well as many archeological finds from the vicinity.

► **Landsberg-am-Lech**

On the Romantische Strasse (Romantic Road, see page 230) and quickly reached by public transportation from Munich, the hillside town of Landsberg has retained an authentic old-world atmosphere without losing its workaday spirit. The signposted Stadtrundgang (circular town walk) takes in the best of Landsberg, weaving down crooked alleys and beneath arches, and climbing onto the largely intact town ramparts, with its series of gateways and views of red roofs huddled by the River Lech. Since the route is complicated, collect a free town map showing the walk from the tourist office; this is situated in the Rathaus, whose rich stucco exterior by Dominikus Zimmermann graces the Hauptplatz. Zimmermann was also responsible for the Johanniskirche, which he designed using the plans for the more famous Wieskirche (see page 265). Of the town's towers and gateways, the Bayertor is the most renowned and is one of the largest Gothic fortifications in southern

Hitler in prison
Chosen by Henry the Lion as a castle site in the 12th century, Landsberg became a regional center in the Middle Ages and gained prosperity, particularly as a trading town for salt mined in southeast Bavaria and sold to Swabian merchants. In this century, Adolf Hitler was imprisoned here following his unsuccessful *putsch* of 1923, and wrote *Mein Kampf* while incarcerated.

Kaufbeuren is an old-world town of narrow streets and tall churches

High rocky peaks, the Karwendel and Wetterstein, rise above Mittenwald

Germany. The Neues Stadtmuseum has a fair miscellany, including medieval religious art. In Hintere Salzgasse, between the Rathaus and the river, is the more modest Puppenstuben Museum (open Saturday and Sunday, 2–5), which displays a fun collection of antique toys.

►► Mittenwald

In a beautiful Alpine setting close to the Austrian border, the village has expanded as a tourist resort but retains much charm and numerous corners of old-world rusticity, with a photogenic array of houses with whitewashed walls, wooden balconies, and green or brown shutters. The best houses are in the Obermarkt and the Gries quarter. The baroque church has fine frescoes. Outside stands a statue of violin maker Matthias Klotz; the craft continues to be carried out here by Anton Maller, who can be seen working behind his shop window. The Geigenbau Museum close by (open 10–11:45, 2–4:45; mornings only on weekends and feast days; closed November 1 to December 20) has a collection of old violins and other string instruments, and exhibits detailing their history and manufacture.

Excursions

Cable-car and chairlift excursions include the **Karwendel** (7,820 feet) by Mittenwald and, farther north, the **Herzogstand** (5,678 feet), majestically placed above the attractive **Walchensee**.

Klotz's violins
Matthias Klotz (1653–1743) brought the violin-making tradition to Mittenwald. He is thought to have been a pupil of the great Amati of Cremona. This industry may have saved Mittenwald from economic oblivion after Venetian merchants, who had brought prosperity to the village, returned to Italy. Mittenwald violins are highly regarded by musicians and fetch good prices. Today's souvenir spin-offs include miniature violins and liqueurs sold in violin-shaped bottles.

Monument to a music maker: the statue of violin maker Matthias Klotz, in Mittenwald

▶ ▶ ▶ München (Munich)

Germany's third-largest city contrasts sharply with the cozy conformism of much of the rest of southern Bavaria. With its exuberant atmosphere and vitality, it is one of the great cultural centers of Europe. Despite wartime devastation the city has a seductive flavor—blue-and-cream trams, tree-lined boulevards, fountains, parks, pavement cafés, beer halls and beer gardens. Its array of museums is unrivaled in the country.

Central Munich is easy to see on foot. East of the main train station, from **Karlstor**, one of the surviving city gateways, runs the principal pedestrianized street, busy with shoppers, street performers and tourists. At its eastern end, the **Marienplatz▶** is at the heart of Munich; the square is dominated by the somewhat sinister-looking Gothic Neues Rathaus, its exterior jollified by the famous carillon whose mechanical musicians, jousting knights and dancing coopers perform at 11 AM and at other times posted below the clock. Close by are the **Frauenkirche▶**, the symbol of Munich, with huge twin onion-domed towers that dominate views from all around, and the Renaissance **St. Michael's Church**, with Wittelsbach tombs (see page 258) in the crypt. Immediately south of the Marienplatz, the **Viktualienmarkt▶** is a cheerful food market, excellent for regional cheeses and prepared hams in particular; the high quality is matched by the high prices.

A short distance southwest are two of the finest churches, the **Damenstiftskirche**, high baroque and thick with incense, and the astonishing **Asamkirche**, the ultimate statement in rococo, with no square inch unadorned in its dark, compact interior.

In the north-central area lie some of Munich's most impressive streetscapes. **Max-Joseph Platz** is presided

The tower of the Gothic Neues Rathaus (1867–1908) offers a good view over the town

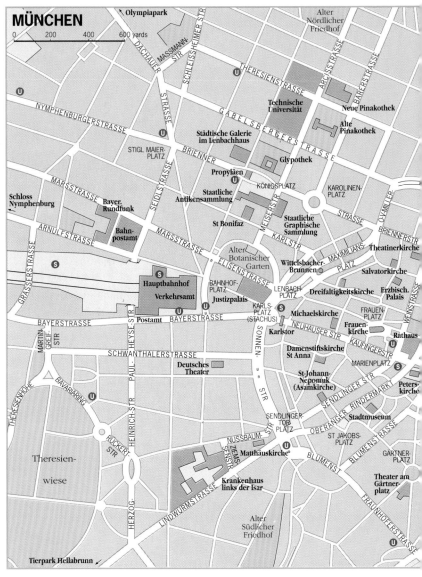

MÜNCHEN

0   200   400   600 yards

Olympiapark

Alter Nördlicher Friedhof

DACHAUER STRASSE

MASSMANN STR

SCHLEISSHEIMER STR

THERESIENSTRASSE

ARCISSTRASSE

BARERSTRASSE

Technische Universität

Neue Pinakothek

NYMPHENBURGERSTRASSE

GABELSBERGERSTRASSE

Alte Pinakothek

Städtische Galerie im Lenbachhaus

STIGL MAIER-PLATZ

BRIENNER STRASSE

Glypothek

Propyläen

MARSSTRASSE

SEIDLSTRASSE

Staatliche Antikensammlung

KÖNIGSPLATZ

KAROLINEN-PLATZ

Schloss Nymphenburg

Bayer. Rundfunk

MEISERSTR

St Bonifaz

Staatliche Graphische Sammlung

OXMILLER STRASSE

ARNULFSTRASSE

MARSSTRASSE

Bahn-postamt

KARLSTR

BRIENNERSTR

Theatinerkirche

Alter Botanischer Garten

Wittelsbacher-Brunnen

MAXIMILIANS-PLATZ

Salvatorkirche

GRASSERSTRASSE

ELISENSTRASSE

LENBACH-PLATZ

Dreifaltigkeitskirche

WEINSTR

Erzbisch. Palais

Hauptbahnhof Verkehrsamt

BAHNHOF-PLATZ

Justizpalais

KARLS-PLATZ (STACHUS)

Michaelskirche

FRAUEN-PLATZ

Frauen-kirche

Rathaus

BAYERSTRASSE

Postamt

BAYERSTRASSE

Karlstor

NEUHAUSER STR

KAUFINGERSTR

HEYSE-STR

MARTIN GREF-STR

SONNEN-STR

SCHWANTHALERSTRASSE

Damenstiftskirche St Anna

MARIENPLATZ

Deutsches Theater

St-Johann-Nepomuk (Asamkirche)

SENDLINGER STR

RINDERMARKT

Peters-kirche

BAVARIARING

PAUL HEINRICH-STR

SENDLINGER-TOR-PLATZ

OBERANGER

Stadtmuseum

THERESIENHÖHE

RÜCKERT STR

NUSSBAUM-STR

ST JAKOBS-PLATZ

BLUMENST

GÄRTNER-PLATZ

Theresien-wiese

HERZOG-STR

ZIEMS-SENSTR

Matthäuskirche

BLUMENST

Theater am Gärtner-platz

LINDWURMSTRASSE

Krankenhaus links der Isar

FRAUNHOFERSTRASSE

Alter Südlicher Friedhof

Tierpark Hellabrunn

254

over by the massive Corinthian columns of the National-theater and the southern end of the huge Residenz, which marks the western end of **Maximilianstrasse▶**. This is a tree-lined thoroughfare known for its high-class boutiques and galleries and punctuated at its far end by the towering Maximilaneum (1874), the Bavarian parliament and senate. **Odeonsplatz▶**, full of students on bicycles, has a reconstructed look, but the regularity of the composition is pleasing. Adjacent is the massive dome of the baroque Theatinerkirche (1677), whose bright yellow façade contrasts with an intricate gray stone interior. Across the road, the Hofgarten offers a peaceful retreat from the city bustle.

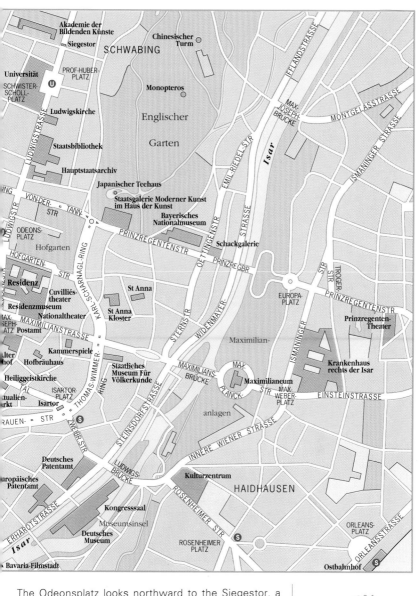

The Odeonsplatz looks northward to the Siegestor, a triumphal gateway close to the university; beyond it lies Leopoldstrasse, the main axis of the district of **Schwabing▶**, which offers numerous bars, outdoor cafés, theaters, cabarets, and other entertainment venues. Around Münchener Freiheit, just east of Leopoldstrasse, is good territory for browsing in secondhand shops.

Northwest of the center are **Ottostrasse**, packed with pricey antiques shops, and the main **museum quarter**.

The **Englischer Garten▶▶** (English garden) extends along the banks of the River Isar for roughly 4 miles and is one of the largest city parks in the world. The

Quick history

- The city's name means "monks," a reminder of a monastic settlement established here in the 9th century. The Münchener Kindl (little monk) is the city's emblem even today.

- Munich became the ducal residence of the Wittelsbachs in 1255, and the Bavarian capital in 1503. During the Thirty Years' War (1618–48) the city was a stronghold of German Catholicism.

- The city was enriched by the Wittelsbachs in the 18th century, when churches and two palaces were built. In the 19th century, Ludwig I endowed the city with its university and its great collections of art and antiquities.

- In 1920 Adolf Hitler launched his National Socialist Party's program at a meeting at the Hofbräuhaus.

- Postwar years have brought great prosperity. BMW is among the many companies with headquarters here.

"garden" resembles parkland landscaped in the English manner, with informal areas of grass and mature woodlands, and is the haunt of strollers, cyclists, joggers, picnickers, sunbathers, and the occasional nudist. The Chinesischer Turm (Chinese tower), with its beer garden, is a popular rendezvous.

Less countrified in character, but equally popular, is the **Olympia Park▶**, north of the center, the site of the ill-fated 1972 Olympic games, when Israeli athletes were taken hostage and died in a tragic shoot-out. Today people come for walking, jogging and boating, and for the range of sports facilities, which include the Olympic swimming pool. You can walk into the strange tentlike structure of the Olympic stadium. On clear days thousands take the lift up to the top of the Olympic Tower for a panorama of Munich and the Alps. The tower is open daily until midnight.

City tours in English Panorama Tours (tel: 089/1204–418) runs bus tours around the city; **Radius Touristik** (tel: 089/596113) offers personal guided tours by tram or bicycle and on foot.

Museums and galleries

Alte Pinakothek▶▶▶ *Bärenstrasse 27*. This great art museum will be closed for renovation until 1997 and meanwhile many of its main works are being shown in the **Neue Pinakothek** across the street. The Alte Pinakothek specializes in paintings up to the 18th century and is famed for works by Dürer (*Self Portrait, The Four Apostles, The Baumgärtner Altar*, etc.) and for its Spanish, Dutch and Italian collections. The Neue Pinakothek exhibits late 18th- and 19th-century art, from Turner and Friedrich to the French and German Impressionists.

Open: daily except Mondays, 10–5; till 8 Tuesday, Thursday.

Street musicians are a familiar sight in cosmopolitan, studenty Munich

Munich's Marienplatz

Antikensammlungen *Königsplatz 1* Adjacent to the Glyptothek (see page 258), the state collection of classical art owes its origins to the collecting endeavors of Ludwig I and boasts some superb Etruscan gold jewelry and a renowned set of Greek decorated vases.
Open: Tuesday and Thursday–Sunday, 10–4:30; Wednesday, noon–8:30.

Bavaria Film Studio▶ *Bavariafilmplatz* Guided tours (lasting 1½ hours) of the largest movie studios in Europe.
Open: March to October, daily.

Bayerisches Nationalmuseum▶ *Prinzregentenstrasse 3* Three floors of Bavarian arts and crafts. Highlights include wooden sculptures by Tilman Riemenschneider and a wonderful collection (the world's largest) of nativity tableaux.
Open: daily except Monday, 9:30–5.

Deutsches Museum▶▶▶ *Museumsinsel 1* Rated the world's foremost museum of science and technology, this has something for everyone, from do-it-yourself chemistry experiments and complicated models of hydraulics and bridges, to areas of more mainstream

Trains and buses
Munich's public transport system works admirably well but can confuse the newcomer. You can buy tickets individually or in blue strips (which works out cheaper); if choosing the latter, you need to use one ticket for short journeys (five bus or tram stops, or three train or subway stops) or two tickets for longer journeys. You are allowed to transfer among different modes of transport as long as you don't double back on your direction of travel; short journeys must be completed within one hour, long journeys within two hours. If you are doing a lot of traveling or are in a group, buy a *Tageskarte* (day pass).

As soon as you are about to use whichever ticket you have opted for, validate it in one of the automatic stamping machines. Day passes must be validated only the first time you travel. Travelers without validated tickets may be fined on the spot.

Plays and music
Munich is well endowed with theaters and concert halls. The Münchener Kammerspiel is one of the most famous theatrical companies; the Cuvilliés-Theater makes an evening out just for the architecture. The Nationaltheater in Max-Joseph Platz is a venue for opera and ballet. Munich has a number of resident orchestras, including the Bayerisches Rundfunk Sinfonie Orchester and the Münchener Philharmonie. For details of events contact the tourist offices at the train station or near the Rathaus.

appeal, such as historic cars, locomotives, musical instruments, space travel and aircraft.
Open: daily, 9–5.
Glyptothek *Königsplatz 3* Greek and Roman statuary, nearly all collected by Ludwig I, housed in an aptly classical building designed by Leo von Klenze.
Open: daily except Monday, 10–4:30; Thursday, noon–8:30.
Lenbachhaus► *Luisenstrasse 33* Of interest for the Italianate villa, complete with 19th-century furnishings, and for the Kandinsky collection of works by the Blauer Reiter group of Expressionist painters.
Open: daily except Monday, 10–6. Admission fee.
Nymphenburg►► In the western suburbs stands this great summer residence of the Wittelsbachs, former rulers of Bavaria. Although built and added to over many centuries, the palace has a strikingly unified symmetry. The best-known feature of its splendid baroque interior is the Schönheitsgalerie, 36 beauties of the day painted between 1827 and 1850 for the pleasure of Ludwig I.

Some beer houses take pride in their collection of decorated beer mugs

Adjacent to the house is the Marstallmuseum, with a grand array of royal carriages and sleighs, and rooms of Nymphenburg porcelain.
  Behind the palace lies perhaps its chief glory: a park with canals, a lake, and a series of whimsical hunting lodges and pavilions. Of these, the Amalienburg steals the show, a neat essay in rococo, with a hall of shimmering mirrors: from the center you see yourself reflected in all 10 of these. The Magdelenklause was built as a mock-hermitage, complete with a bizarre grotto chamber.
  Next door, the fine Botanical Garden has an alpinum, rhododendrons, and greenhouses.
Open: palace, daily except Monday, 9–12:30, 1:30–5; October to March, 10–12:30, 1:30–5. Botanical Garden, daily, 9–7; greenhouses are closed between 11:45 and 1.
Residenzmuseum► *Max-Joseph Platz 3* The vast baroque palace of the Wittelsbachs, painstakingly restored after extensive wartime damage; different parts of the building are open in the morning and evening, since there is far too much to see at once. In addition to

the state rooms, do not miss the magnificent vaulted Antiquarium (begun 1568), housing statues collected from the classical world, a dazzling treasury of pristine jewel-encrusted riches dating from the 11th century onward, and the enchanting Cuvilliés-Theater (separate admission), a rococo creation by François de Cuvilliés, still used for performances. Within the same complex, but requiring separate admission, are museums of coins and Egyptian art.

Open: daily except Monday, 10–4:30. Theater open Monday to Saturday, 2–5; Sunday and feast days, 10–5.

Spielzeug Museum *Marienplatz* In the tower of the old town hall is this most appealing (and nostalgic) treasure trove of retired dolls, vintage model cars, and prewar teddy bears. Also toys from as long ago as the 2nd century.

Open: daily, 10–5:30.

Staatsgalerie Moderner Kunst *Prinzregentenstrasse 1* Gallery of 20th-century art and sculpture, particularly strong on German modern art.

Open: daily except Monday, 10–5 (Thursday until 8).

Stadtsmuseum *Jakobsplatz* In a former arsenal, this is more than just the city local history museum, with floors devoted to brewing, the early days of photography, a film museum, a worldwide collection of musical instruments, and a splendidly entertaining puppet and fairground museum.

Open: daily except Monday, 10–5 (Wednesday until 8:30).

ZAM *Westenriedstrasse 26* Seven quaintly unrelated museums in one: pedal cars, memorabilia relating to Empress Elisabeth of Austria, *bourdalous* (fancy china containers), corkscrews, padlocks, chamber pots, and even Easter bunnies.

Open: daily, 10–6.

Munich is famed for its beer and beer halls

Here for the beer
Munich is one of Europe's foremost beer-producing cities, famous for its annual Oktoberfest (lasting 16 days up to the first Sunday in October) on the Theresienwiese fairground on the west side of the city. The Oktoberfest is a binge of beer guzzling, barbecues, processions, and general merrymaking.

Equally famous are the beer halls: huge, high-ceilinged affairs with noisy Bavarian brass band music. The Hofbräuhaus, northeast of Marienplatz, is the most touristy; the Mathüser Stadt, in Bayer Strasse near the station, is the largest, while the Forschungsbrauerei serves some of the most obscure beer varieties.

►► Oberammergau and area

The Passion play at Oberammergau
The Passion play was first performed in 1633, after villagers had been spared the ravages of the plague; the play now takes place every 10 years, the next occasion being in 2000. Some 100 daylong performances are given to aggregate audiences of over 500,000 by a cast of 1,700. Competition among the locals for the major parts is keen; traditionally Mary is played by a virgin. Male performers grow long hair and beards for the event. The 1674 text mentions the use of trumpets, but this music has been lost; this music now used is by Rochus Dedler (1779–1822). Versions of the text written in 1750 and 1850 created controversy recently for their allegedly anti-Semitic message, but this has now been altered in a new text.

Known the world over for its Passion play (see panel), Oberammergau is physically dominated by a rock pinnacle known as the Ettaler Mandl. The village has a number of painted houses and a pretty baroque church , but gets completely overridden with visitors at peak times. Its main streets cater to the mass tourist trade, notably with its plethora of shops selling locally produced wood carvings (mostly on religious themes). The Heimatsmuseum has a display of antique wooden artifacts.

In the Passiontheater (open daily, 10–noon, 1:30–4:30) you can see the monumental-style stage set used for the Passion play and can take a look backstage at an exhibition of costumes, props and models of former sets.

Ettal, the next village to the south, has two claims to fame. One is Ettaler, a sweet herbal liqueur originally made by monks. The other is the great Benedictine **abbey church►**, with an unusual 12-sided nave beneath a huge dome, modeled on the Church of the Holy Sepulcher in Jerusalem; though the foundation is 14th century, the church interior is high baroque, with a painted ceiling by Johann-Jakob Zeiller.

Westward from Ettal, the valley drive toward Reutte in Austria is a fine one, passing the peaceful village of

Painted buildings at Oberammergau, internationally known for its Passion play

■ **Born in 1845 in Nymphenburg Castle, near Munich, Ludwig II was a member of the Wittelsbach dynasty and became king of Bavaria at the age of 18. Within two years of his accession to the throne he became involved in a war with Prince Otto von Bismarck of Prussia; Bavaria was defeated, and the Prussians took over the Bavarian army ...■**

In 1870, under Bismarck's influence, Bavaria was drawn into the war between Prussia and France that was to be the catalyst in the formation of the German Empire, of which Bavaria became a part. Bismarck now had Ludwig under his thumb and ordered the Bavarian king to send a letter naming Wilhelm I of Prussia as the emperor of Germany. Disillusioned, Ludwig lost interest in politics and became increasingly eccentric. He built a trio of castles—Linderhof, Neuschwanstein, and Herrenchiemsee— at huge expense. A stage-set designer drew the first sketches for Neuschwanstein, the most theatrical of the three; Ludwig watched the progress of building through his telescope from Höhenschwangau. Linderhof, the only one of Ludwig's royal castles to be completed, was his favorite.

Louis XIV became Ludwig's inspiration: his dream was of absolute rule. He gave financial aid to Richard Wagner, whose operas fired his imagination. But the funds ran out; Ludwig's extravagance, homosexuality and near or actual insanity worried the Bavarian government, which colluded with Luitpold (his uncle and successor) to depose him. Ludwig was certified insane in his bedroom at Neuschwanstein; a few days later, on June 13, 1886, he and his physician were found drowned in the Starnberger See. It has never been ascertained whether this was an accident or an assassination.

Graswang and the entrance to **Schloss Linderhof▶** (open daily except Christmas and New Year's Day, summer 9–12:15, 12:45–5:30, winter 10–12:15, 12:45–4; guided tours in English), completed in 1878 for Ludwig II and modeled on the Petit Trianon at Versailles. Its interior, though nothing as spectacularly bizarre as Neuschwanstein (see page 246), is characteristically lavish, full of mirrors, painted ceilings and gilded cherubs, in a mixture of Renaissance and baroque styles. The grounds have some wonderfully offbeat features, including a grand cascade, a water jet that shoots higher than the Schloss itself, a grotto modeled on the Venusberg of Wagner's opera *Tannhäuser,* and a Moorish kiosk resplendent with a "peacock throne."

Locally produced wood carvings are sold in several Oberammergau shops

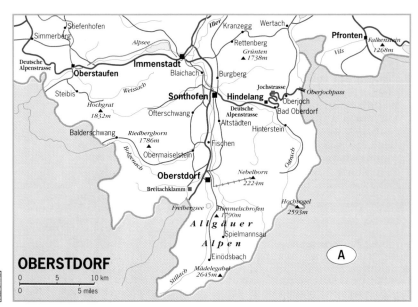

OBERSTDORF

0   5   10 km

0   5 miles

A

The Oberstdorf valley offers gentle walks as well as rock climbing

► **Oberstdorf and area**

Oberstdorf is a busy valley resort, excellently placed for exploring the Allgäuer Alps; it flourishes as a winter-sports (top-class skiing and skating facilities), climbing and hiking center. More peaceful bases include **Fischen**, on the valley floor but bypassed by the road, remote **Balderschwang**, high up a lonely side valley, **Oberstaufen**, large and neatly tended, **Altestädten**, with its characteristic wooden Allgäuer houses, and **Hindelang**, nestling in green countryside.

From Oberstdorf, horse-drawn carriages leave every day for the **Stillachtal**, the southernmost valley in Germany, with Einödsbach as its southernmost village. The road is closed to motor traffic and affords magnificent mountain views. Southwest of Oberstdorf, the **Kleines Walsertal►**, an enclave of Austria, can only be reached from Germany and has typical wooden farms and modest family hotels within a dramatic Alpine setting. The walk along the **Brietachklamm**, west of Oberstdorf, squeezes through a magnificent gorge and beneath unlikely looking overhangs (closed during the spring thaw). Cable cars from the east side of town whisk you up to the **Nebelhorn** upper station for a chairlift to the summit (7,295 feet), which is graced with a summit restaurant and a superb panorama.

►► **Ottobeuren**

The mighty Benedictine abbey church of Ottobeuren dwarfs the adjacent town. Founded in 764, the abbey prospered under the patronage of Charlemagne, and the complex was rebuilt in the 18th century by Johann-Michael Fischer. It is Germany's largest baroque church, and the proportions are quite cathedral-like, with a nave 300 feet long and a transept 200 feet across. Its interior is wonderfully light, and adorned with frescoes

by Amigoni, J. B. Zimmermann, and J. J. Zeiller, and stuccowork by J. M. Feuchtmayr. The Trinity organ, built by K. J. Riepp, is one of the most splendid in Europe. *Open*: daily 10–noon, 4–5.

► Starnberger See

The largest lake close to Munich is served by a suburban train service, which makes it a good out-of-town base for the Bavarian capital. It is well suited for yachting (boat rental available), strolls and relaxation; the scenery is undramatic but pleasant. A boat sails around the lakes; stops include the Votive Chapel at Berg, in memory of Ludwig II, who drowned here in 1886 and whose body was recovered at Possenhofen, the lake's main beach. The best views are had from the Bismarckturm (Bismarck tower), south of Berg, and from Ilkahöhe, a modest hill southwest of Tutzing, the main resort.

Just to the south lies the peaceful and unspoiled **Ostersee**, part of a complex of over 20 small lakes, with reedy shores and wooded isles. The 5-mile Rundweg Ostersee, a circular path, is an easy two-hour walk; the parking lot is between Seeshaupt and Penzburg.

At **Kochel**, the Franz Marc Museum exhibits a collection of work by the great 20th-century Bavarian artist.

Memmingen
Northwest of Ottobeuren, Memmingen has an attractive town center of arcaded buildings and patrician houses, with the irregular Marktplatz dominated by the Gothic tower of the Nikolaikirche (fine murals and stalls within). Parishaus, a pink-and-white building north of the Rathaus, houses the tourist office, which issues a leaflet detailing a walk around town. The Hermansbau (1766) is the town's finest house, and now contains the local museum (open daily except Saturday and Monday, 10–noon, 2–4), worth a look for its oak staircase and stucco ceilings; exhibits include porcelain, dolls' houses, clocks, medieval religious art, and an 1825 model of Memmingen.

𝒲𝒶𝓁𝓀 The Heini-Klopfer Ski Jump and the Freibergsee

A varied walk (1–2 hours) that begins with a gentle riverside path; you can either ascend on foot or take the ski lift up; the routes conjoin at the Eibersee, a small lake encompassed by wooded slopes, before the final descent.

Start at the parking lot northeast of the Freibergsee, in the Stillachtal. From the west side of Oberstdorf, drive southward (signposted Fellhornbarn and Schiflugschanze), the parking lot is seen in the trees after 2½ miles, on the right.

Walk to the rear of the parking lot and cross the footbridge; turn left, and follow the river 1 mile to reach the ski jump. Either take the ski lift to the top and turn right at the path above the lift; or continue forward, on a rising traffic-free road, forking right at the top and following signs to Freibergsee, past Gasthof Schwand, then forking right just before the ski jump. At the next major fork bear right downhill, then right again (signposted Parkplatz) to the river, then right to cross the footbridge into the parking lot.

The Schliersee (above) is one of the loveliest Alpine lakes

Wangen's Rathaus rules over a town of painted gateways and quirky modern sculptures

▶ Tegernsee, Schliersee, and Spitzingsee

Two lakes in beautiful settings. The **Tegernsee**, encompassed by wooded hills, can be enjoyed from a 1¾ hour boat trip and from the 5,648-foot summit of **Wallberg**, reached by cable car from just above the south end of the lake. The shores are somewhat crowded with weekend villas and a string of fashionable but unremarkable resorts. The **Schliersee** feels more Alpine. The town of Schliersee has boat rental, a swimming pool, and a surfing school. Higher up is the smaller **Spitzingsee**, finely set and well developed with winter-sports facilities; lake swimming is best at the southern end. In summer it is excellent for walking: the hills have Alpine character without being as daunting as the larger-scale mountains farther south; cable cars and chairlifts ascending Taubenstein (5,553 feet) and Stümpfling (4,940 feet) operate most of the year and offer a good basis for high-level walks.

▶ Wangen im Allgäu

An appealing Swabian town with a wealth of painted houses. Its old town is a simple crossroads, centered on the Marktplatz and entered by two frescoed gateways, the Frauentor (Ravensburg Gate) of 1608, the symbol of Wangen, and the St. Martin Tor (Lindau Gate), with its pyramidal roof and intriguing array of gargoyles. A local museum within a half-timbered building devotes itself to cheese making and folk art in the Allgäu.

The rolling hills around Wangen make good walking and cycling country, with quiet roads, forests and sleepy villages. **Isny**, to the east, is another unspoiled old town, with 13th-century ramparts, a pretty corner by the church of St. Jakob and St. Georg, and 17th-century monastery buildings (now a hospital). A signposted Stadtrundweg (town walk) takes in the best of it.

▶ **Wasserburg am Inn**

Wasserburg occupies a naturally fortified site all but surrounded by a tight meander of the turbulent Inn River, itself lined with white cliffs. This was one of the most prosperous towns in Bavaria during the Middle Ages, when it became a river port for Munich on a salt trading route and was allowed to levy tax on the salt that passed through town. Wasserburg's fortunes slumped after 1504, when the salt trade route was moved, and later suffered the ravages of war and plague. Its heyday gone, Wasserburg nevertheless retains a legacy of old merchants' houses and characterful winding streets. Opposite the Rathaus, the façade of the Kernhaus displays outstanding 18th-century stuccowork by J. B. Zimmermann. Behind the Rathaus, the local museum has items relating to the town's past, farm furnishings, and a collection of carriages. The main town gateway dates from 1374 and displays wall paintings of two warriors bearing the banners of Wasserburg and Bavaria; within it, the Erstes Imaginäres Museum houses a collection of old masters from all over the world, with a difference: all of them are fakes. Through the gateway, continue on over the bridge over the Inn River, then turn left into Kellerstrasse for a path up to a fine viewpoint over the town.

At Wasserburg even some of the modern buildings by the Inn River have stepped gable façades

265

▶▶ **Wieskirche**

Set amid quiet, green meadows, the famous Wieskirche stands almost by itself. It was built as a pilgrimage church to house a figure of the Scourging of Christ, which had allegedly shed miraculous tears. The architect, Dominikus Zimmermann, gave it a wonderfully light, frothy interior, with an outstanding frescoed dome depicting the Gate to Paradise. His composition was a personal masterpiece (so much so that he spent the rest of his life in a house close by) and is one of the great rococo buildings of Europe.

Arriving

A valid passport is required when entering Germany, but visitors from the U.S.A. on a tourist/business visit of up to three months will not need a visa (provided they do not intend to take up employment in Germany).

By air

The main international airports are Frankfurt, Düsseldorf, Cologne, Munich, and Berlin. Domestic flights connect these and other airports within Germany. The Lufthansa Airport Express Train also links certain airports and major city centers (see **Public transportation**). There is a regular airport bus transfer that runs between Berlin's Tegel and Schönefeld airports. All German airports connect efficiently with the local urban transportation network. In some cases there is a connecting bus service; other airports tie in with the metro system.

There are three types of flights: nonstop—no changes, no stops; direct—no changes, but one or more stops; and connecting— two or more planes, one or more stops.

Fly at night if you're able to sleep on a plane. Because the air aboard a plane is dry, drink plenty of beverages while aloft; remember that drinking alcohol contributes to jet lag, as do heavy meals. Since feet swell at high altitudes, remove your shoes before takeoff. Sleepers usually prefer window seats to curl up against; restless passengers ask to be on the aisle. Bulkhead seats, in the front row of each cabin, have more legroom, but since there's no seat ahead, trays attach awkwardly to the arms of your seat, and you must stow all possessions overhead. Bulkhead seats are usually reserved for the disabled, the elderly, or people traveling with babies.

Cutting Flight Costs

The Sunday travel section of most newspapers is often a good source of charters, consolidators, and discount travel services. When booking these flights, particularly through a lesser known company, always consider trip cancellation insurance.

Advance Purchases

If you can deal with the restrictions, you can save money. You must buy these tickets, called APEX, in advance (usually 21 days), they restrict your travel (usually to a minimum of seven days and a maximum of one month), and they penalize you for any changes in your travel plans (up to 100%). If you can live with this, they are excellent value. Various excursion and instant purchase fares are also on offer, at reduced prices: consult the airlines.

Flying as a Courier

A courier is someone who accompanies shipments between designated points. **Now Voyager** (74 Varick St., Suite 307, New York, NY 10013, tel. 212/431–1616) places couriers on flights to various destinations.

Charter Flights

Charters have the lowest fares and the most restrictions. Departures are limited and seldom on time, and you can lose all or most of your money if you cancel. Find out the packager's refund policy, and don't sign up for a charter flight before checking its reputation. One reliable charter operator to Europe is **Council Charter** (205 E. 42nd St., New York, NY 10017, tel. 212/661–0311 or 800/800–8222), a division of the Council on International Educational Exchange (CIEE). Others include:
DER Tours:
9501 W. Devon Rd., Suite 400, Rosemont, IL 60018, tel. 800/782-2424
TRAVAC:
tel. 212/563–3303 or 800/872– 8800)
Travel Charter:
1301 W. Long Lake Rd., Suite 270, Troy, MI 48098, tel. 810/641–9600 or 800/521–5267)
Travel CUTS:
(187 College St., Toronto, Ont. M5T 1P7, tel. 416/977–3703).

Consolidators

Companies buy blocks of tickets on scheduled airlines and sell them at wholesale prices. Fares are not as cheap as for charters but still cost

TRAVEL FACTS

less than APEX tickets. Tickets are subject to availability, so you must be flexible, and you can lose all or most of your money if your plans change, but at least you'll be on a regularly scheduled flight with little risk of cancellation. Once you've made your reservation, call the airline to confirm it. Good consolidators include:

UniTravel:
1177 N. Warson Rd., St. Louis, MO 63132, tel. 314/569–0900 or 800/325–2222.

1-800-TAKE-OFF:
3020 NW 33rd Ave., Ft. Lauderdale, FL 33311, tel. 800/825–3633.

Discount Travel Clubs and Agencies

Organizations include:

Moment's Notice:
425 Madison Ave, New York, NY 10017, tel. 212/980–9550.

Travel Management International:
TMI, 18 Prescott St., Suite 4, Cambridge, MA 02138, tel. 800/ 245–3672.

Traveler's Advantage:
CUC Travel Service, 49 Music Square West, Nashville, TN 37203, tel. 800/648–4037.

Worldwide Discount Travel Club:
1674 Meridian Ave, Suite 206, Miami Beach, FL 33139, tel. 305/534–2082.

Compare their prices before you buy your ticket.

Smoking

If cigarette smoke bothers you, book a seat far from the smoking section. If a U.S. airline representative tells you no non-smoking seats are available, insist on one: Department of Transportation regulations require U.S. flag carriers to find seats for all nonsmokers on the day of the flight, provided they check in within the required time.

Camping

Campgrounds abound in Germany—there are about 2,500 sprinkled liberally around the country. The standard is high and even the most basic of sites have toilet and washing facilities, plus an on-site shop. Top-class campgrounds feature swimming pools, super-

markets, discos and all the trimmings.

Campgrounds are located by a blue sign carrying the international camping symbol: a black tent on a white background. Most are open from Easter to October, with around 400 staying open all year. June to September is the busiest season, and as reservations are usually made on site, you must get there early to avoid disappointment, especially in popular places; better still, book in advance.

A list of campgrounds can be obtained free from the German National Tourist office (address under **Tourist offices**).

The German Camping Club (DCC) publishes a complete guide which is available from 28 Mandlstrasse, D–80802 Munich 40, while the German automobile association ADAC also produces a guide to over 1,000 campgrounds (address: 8, Am Westpark, D–81373 Munich).

If you prefer to pitch your tent outside official campgrounds, you must first ask the permission of the landowner or the local police.

Most of the major car rental firms will also rent out a trailer.

Children

If you're in need of a baby-sitter, enquire first at your hotel reception desk—they may well offer this service. Tourist offices in most towns and cities keep updated lists of recommended baby-sitters and details of local day-care facilities.

Under-fours travel free on mass transit, and children aged four to 11 go half price. Reduced rates are usually offered in hotels and guest houses for children, and it is the norm for attractions such as museums and historic buildings to offer discounts for their younger visitors.

Germanic theme parks tend to take the form of fairy-tale tableau lands, such as the Märchenwald, with its adventure playground, at Wolfratshausen near Bad Tolz in the Bavarian Alps, the Grimm "fairy tale park" at Ludwigsburg, near Stuttgart, and the Taunus Wonderland at

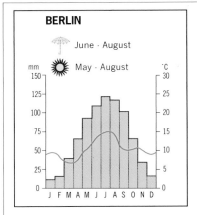

BERLIN

June · August

May · August

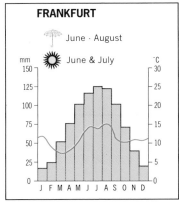

FRANKFURT

June · August

June & July

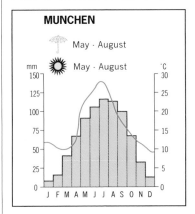

MUNCHEN

May · August

May · August

Wiesbaden. Attractions at Phantasieland at Brühl (halfway between Bonn and Cologne) include re-creations of the American Wild West, ancient China, and prewar Berlin, a massive roller coaster and an overhead monorail. Zoos and puppet theaters are popular features throughout the country.

Climate

Generally speaking, the weather in Germany is moderate, neither extremely hot nor cold, and sprinkled with rain.

The climate does not get dramatically warmer the farther south you go. Berlin has an average July temperature of between 59°F and 75°F, more southerly Munich of between 55°F and 75°F. This city also has an above-average summer rainfall. However, Hamburg in the north is consistently several degrees cooler than, for instance, Frankfurt in the center. Berlin is famous for its bracing air—the Berliner Luft—while south Bavaria has its Föhn, a mountain wind that can spring up at any season, causing a sudden change in temperature as it brings very warm conditions and a cloudless sky.

Summers are usually pleasantly hot and dry throughout the country. Toward the Alps they get shorter, starting around May and ending in warm autumns. May or October is a good time to visit Germany; the popular haunts can get crowded in the peak tourist months of June to September. Snows start around November, and winter can be very cold: the January temperature in Berlin and Munich, for example, can regularly dip below freezing.

Crime

Crime figures have risen sharply since unification, but violent crime remains less common in Germany than in many countries. Trouble spots, as in any other nation, are large cities, such as Hamburg, Frankfurt and Berlin, where the usual car theft and house robberies are a hazard of urban life. Late at night in eastern Berlin, be wary of empty areas or being alone in a train car.

As a tourist, it makes sense to avoid attracting unwanted attention: do not flaunt expensive jewelry or camera equipment, or leave baggage unattended, valuables on show in your car, or your vehicle

CONVERSION CHARTS

FROM	TO	MULTIPLY BY
Inches	Centimeters	2.54
Centimeters	Inches	0.3937
Feet	Meters	0.3048
Meters	Feet	3.2810
Yards	Meters	0.9144
Meters	Yards	1.0940
Miles	Kilometers	1.6090
Kilometers	Miles	0.6214
Acres	Hectares	0.4047
Hectares	Acres	2.4710
U.S. Gallons	Liters	3.7854
Liters	U.S. Gallons	0.2642
Ounces	Grams	28.35
Grams	Ounces	0.0353
Pounds	Grams	453.6
Grams	Pounds	0.0022
Pounds	Kilograms	0.4536
Kilograms	Pounds	2.205
U.S. Tons	Tonnes	0.9072
Tonnes	U.S. Tons	1.1023

MEN'S SUITS

U.S.	36	38	40	42	44	46	48
U.K.	36	38	40	42	44	46	48
Rest of Europe	46	48	50	52	54	56	58

DRESS SIZES

U.S.	6	8	10	12	14	16
U.K.	8	10	12	14	16	18
France	36	38	40	42	44	46
Italy	38	40	42	44	46	48
Rest of Europe	34	36	38	40	42	44

MEN'S SHIRTS

U.S.	14	14.5	15	15.5	16	16.5	17
U.K.	14	14.5	15	15.5	16	16.5	17
Rest of Europe	36	37	38	39/40	41	42	43

MEN'S SHOES

U.S.	8	8.5	9.5	10.5	11.5	12
U.K.	7	7.5	8.5	9.5	10.5	11
Rest of Europe	41	42	43	44	45	46

WOMEN'S SHOES

U.S.	6	6.5	7	7.5	8	8.5
U.K.	4.5	5	5.5	6	6.5	7
Rest of Europe	38	38	39	39	40	41

unlocked. Wear a shoulder bag on the side of you that is away from the street, or use a money belt for cash and traveler's checks. It is a good idea to have photocopies of important documents, including passport, driving license and traveler's checks, and to keep them in a safe place separate from the originals.

If you are unlucky enough to fall foul of thieves, register the theft right away with the police (Polizei). This is necessary if you wish to make a claim on your travel insurance. In an **emergency**, the number to call is **110**. When you arrive at the police station, make sure you have some form of identification (one instance when your photocopies could come in handy).

Do not inadvertently commit a crime yourself by, for instance, crossing the street before the green light for pedestrians shows. This may be acceptable at home, but it is illegal in Germany. Far more serious is being caught in possession of drugs of any sort—imprisonment or deportation is the penalty.

Customs

There are no restrictions on the import or export of German marks (DM) or any other foreign currency.

Duty-free allowances for taking goods into Germany from another E.U. country are as follows: 200 cigarettes; or 50 cigars; or 250g of tobacco. 4 liters of alcohol over 22% proof; or 2 liters below 22%; or 2 liters of sparkling wine and 2 liters of other wines.

Under the European single market, no duty is charged on goods brought into Germany from another E.U. country, as long as these goods are for personal use and not for resale. Alcohol and tobacco are only duty-free for people over 17 years old.

Disabled visitors

The German government agency involved in assisting travelers with disabilities has details of hotels with special facilities to meet their requirements. For information write to Help for the Handicapped (Hilfe für Behinderte) Kirchfeldstrasse 1 40215– Düsseldorf.

The wheelchair symbol (a wheelchair set in a box) indicates access for disabled tourists. Airports and rest stops on the autobahns are all equipped with toilet facilities, and at major train stations staff are specially briefed to help passengers in wheelchairs, etc.

Access guides produced in Germany by social services departments or groups of residents list hotels, restaurants, buses and other facilities accessible to visitors with disabilities.

Driving

The condition of autobahns and major and minor roads is excellent in the former West Germany, and has now greatly improved in former East Germany. The autobahns are toll-free.

Foreigners may drive a vehicle for up to one year in Germany with their own national or international driving license. Holders of U.S. licenses must carry an official translation. (Contact your embassy or nearest German National Tourist Office—see **Tourist offices**.)

Third-party insurance is compulsory. Check with your insurers, and they will issue a Green Card to show that they have extended your coverage to allow driving abroad.

Children under 12 are not allowed to travel in a front seat unless they are using special seats or safety belts suitable for children, or unless the rear seats are occupied by other children. It is compulsory for driver and passengers to wear seat belts in cars that are fitted with them.

Some drivers go very fast on autobahns. On these roads there is no official speed limit, though 130 k.p.h. (81 m.p.h.) is a recommended maximum (100 k.p.h./62 m.p.h. in some places: watch for the signs). There is a countrywide official limit on country roads of 80–100 k.p.h. (50–62 m.p.h.) and in urbanized areas of 50 k.p.h. (31 m.p.h.).

On-the-spot fines are levied for speeding and for other road offenses, such as using abusive

Mozart's house, Augsburg

language, making derogatory signs and running out of gasoline on the highway! The rule for drinking and driving is that the level of alcohol in the bloodstream must be under 80mg/100ml. Drivers are sometimes given breathalyzer tests if they seem to be driving incautiously, or after an accident.

In case of a **breakdown**, contact the ADAC (Allgemeiner Deutscher Automobil Club, 8, Am Westpark, D-81373 Munich 40). On autobahns emergency orange telephones are sited at regular intervals (follow the yellow marker arrows). Ask for "Strassenwachthilfe." On minor roads, dial 110. The ADAC does not charge you for labor, but only for materials (unless it's a serious problem, so check that your insurance covers this). Filling stations are regularly sited along autobahns and in urban areas off the main roads. Lead-free gasoline—*Bleifrei*— is available almost everywhere. Gas prices vary, tending to be higher on autobahns, cheaper at self-service— SB-Tanken—stations.

Car rentals

Prebooking a rental car from home can save time, and using a major company means you can pick up at one place and drop off at another for no extra charge.

Most airports, train stations and larger towns have booking offices if you prefer to arrange car rental (*Autovermietung*) in Germany. International firms include Hertz, Avis, and Sixt Budget. Ask at the local tourist office for German companies.

The minimum age at which you can rent a car is 21, and you need to have held a full driving license for one year.

Electricity
The current in Germany is 220 volts, 50 cycles. Sockets are the two-pin type.

U.S. Embassies
Within Germany:
Neustädtische Kirchstrasse 4–5, D–10117, Berlin; tel: 2385174.
At home:
4645 Reservoir Road N.W., Washington, DC 20007–1998; tel: 202/298 4000.

Emergency telephone numbers
Police: 110
Fire Department: 112
DZT (Deutsche Zentrale für Tourismus—German National Tourist Organization), Frankfurt (tel: 069 75720).
ADAC—Allgemeiner Deutscher Automobil Club (Germany's leading auto association)—emergency breakdown (tel: 01802 222222)

Etiquette
In Germany, never, *but never*, call anyone by his or her first name unless you are invited to do so.

Germans tend to be formal in business and in private, though the younger generation takes a more relaxed attitude to this rule. Always use the title *Herr* or *Frau*; it is considered an insult to address a woman as Fräulein until you know for sure that she is a Miss rather than a Mrs. You should also say, "Guten Morgen, meine Dame," as opposed to "meine Frau." When speaking to a professional person, such as a doctor, address him or her as Herr or Frau Doktor or with whatever other job title is appropriate. Holders of non-medical doctorates are also often addressed as Herr or Fran Doktor.

The distinction between *Sie* and *Du*—both meaning "you"—is comparable to the difference between the French *vous* and *tu*. You must wait to be told to use the familiar Du, although it's always safe to use it with children and animals.

Germans shake hands whenever they meet, even if it's only a casual encounter between neighbors on the stairs. Expect to offer to kiss a woman on both cheeks when greetings are conducted.

Another German custom is to bring a gift when invited to someone's home. The safest and most welcome item to take is a bunch of flowers.

As you will pick up pretty quickly if asked to a meal, Germans use their cutlery in a manner that may seem unusual to foreign visitors.

Health
Currently, no immunizations are required for entry into Germany. Health care is privatized; all Germans belong to a health insurance scheme. E.U. citizens are entitled to free medical treatment in Germany, on production of Form E111. If applicable, get one in advance, from post offices.

In addition, you should take out travel insurance to cover expenses connected with illness—such as a special flight home or a longer hotel stay—that are not covered by E111. And to be able to make a claim, remember to keep receipts of all

medical treatments, prescriptions and other expenses to give your insurers once home.

The number for emergency/ weekend doctors and dentists can be found in local telephone directories for German cities. If you want to ensure an English-speaking practitioner, contact the local consulate, which should have details.

Doctors

Consulting hours are usually 7 AM to 8 PM in hospital outpatient departments; in doctors' offices, about 10 AM to noon, 4 to 6 PM (times vary), closed Wednesday evening. (Hospital outpatient departments provide an emergency service outside these hours, too.)

Pharmacies

These are open during normal shop hours; in larger towns they display a list of pharmacies with late-night and Sunday hours (see **Pharmacies**).

Hitchhiking

Hitchhiking is not illegal, except on the autobahns and their feeder roads, although it is not encouraged. Since German unification and the increase in crime, drivers have generally become more suspicious of picking people up. Every major city has a Mitfahrzentrale, a useful alternative, in which drivers inform this office when and where they are traveling, and those wanting a lift—and willing to share the cost of gasoline—pay a fee to get the driver's name and telephone number. This is by far the cheapest way of traveling around the country by car, but again, it is not without hazards.

Lone travelers should always be aware of the inherent dangers of taking lifts with strangers. Some cities have Frauenmitfahrerzentrale, for women only.

Insurance

Make sure you take out travel insurance. It should cover you for accident or illness and also for the loss or theft of valuables while on vacation. This insurance is best taken out at home before departure. Speak to your insurers, travel agent or automobile association about it when planning your trip.

Language

There is one official standard German language, *Hochdeutsch*, which all the children are taught in school and which everyone in the country should be able to understand. However, regional dialects, with strong local accents, are widely spoken in many areas. Some cities, notably Berlin and Cologne, retain their own dialects which a visitor from a village even 20 miles away may find hard to follow; and the *Plattdeutsch* of Friesia is a distinct language with its own literature. Saxony, Bavaria and Swabia are regions with pronounced local dialects, which vary greatly. For example, "We have seen it" is "Wir haben es angesehen" in *Hochdeutsch*, "Mir hens a guckt" in Bavarian, "Mr hannet gesäh" in Swabian, and "Wir haben's angekiekt" in Berlin!

273

Pronunciation guide
Vowels (in Hochdeutsch)
a (short) as in hat, e.g., *Hand* (hand)
a (long) as in father, e.g., *sagen* (say)
e (short) as in bet, e.g., *Wetter* (weather)
e (long) as in day, e.g., *geben* (give)
i as in fit, e.g., *bitte* (please)
o (short) as in lost, e.g., *voll* (full)
o (long) as in coach, e.g., *Mond* (moon)
u as in boot, e.g., *gut* (good)
ä (short) as in wet, e.g., *Äpfel* (apple)
ä (long) as in wait, e.g., *spät* (late)
ö as in fur, e.g., *schön* (beautiful)
ü as in blue, e.g., *über* (over)
ai as in spy, e.g., the River *Main*
ei as in spy, e.g., *ein* (one)
au as in how, e.g., *Maus* (mouse)
ie as in tree, e.g., *Lied* (song)
eu as in boy, e.g., *treu* (true)
äu as in boy, e.g., *Fräulein* (miss)

Consonants
Most are pronounced as written. The following are exceptions.
ch is either a throaty sound as in Scottish *loch*, e.g., *Nacht* (night), or an unvoiced sh sound, e.g., *nicht* (not)

j is as y in yacht, e.g., *ja* (yes)
r is rolled
s is as z in zip, e.g., *sein* (his)
sch is as sh in shut, e.g., *scheinen* (to seem)
sp/st are pronounced shp/sht, e.g., *sprechen* (speak), *Stadt* (town)
v is as f in fit, e.g., *Vater* (father)
w is as v in very, e.g., *Wand* (wall)
z is as ts in bits, e.g., *Zeit* (time)

Words and phrases
Days of the week
Sunday	*Sonntag*
Monday	*Montag*
Tuesday	*Dienstag*
Wednesday	*Mittwoch*
Thursday	*Donnerstag*
Friday	*Freitag*
Saturday	*Samstag*
	or *Sonnabend*

274

Months of the year
Januar	*Juli*
Februar	*August*
März	*September*
April	*Oktober*
Mai	*November*
Juni	*Dezember*

Basics
yes/no	*ja/nein*
please	*bitte*
thank you	*danke*
	(can also mean "no, thank you")
hello	*Guten Tag; Grüss Gott* (in the south)
goodbye	*Auf Wiedersehen*
Do you speak English?	*Sprechen Sie Englisch?*
I don't understand	*Ich verstehe nicht*
Help!	*Zu Hilfe!*

Questions
Where is/are	*Wo ist/sind*
the bank?	*die Bank?*
the station?	*der Bahnhof?*
the airport?	*der Iughafen?*
the bus stop?	*die Bushaltestelle?*
the police station?	*as Polizeirevier?*
the nearest toilets?	*die nächsten Toiletten?*
right	*rechts*
left	*links*
straight ahead	*geradeaus*
How much is...	*Wieviel kostet...*

the fare?	*der Fahrpreis?*
the entrance fee?	*der Eintritt?*
When...	*Wann...*
does the museum open?	*wird das Museum geöffnet?*
does the train leave?	*fährt der Zug ab?*
at 10 o'clock	*um zehn Uhr*
at half past 10	*um halb elf*

Staying and eating
I'd like...	*Ich hätte gern...*
a single room	*ein Einzelzimmer*
a double room	*ein Doppelzimmer*
with bath	*mit Bad*
open	*Geöffnet*
closed	*Geschlossen*
Waiter!	*Herr Ober!*
May I see the menu, please?	*Die Speisekarte bitte?*
breakfast	*das Frühstück*
lunch	*das Mittagessen*
dinner	*das Abendessen*
bread	*das Brot*
butter	*die Butter*
egg	*das Ei*
cheese	*der Käse*
vegetables	*das Gemüse*
fruit	*das Obst*
coffee	*der Kaffee*
tea	*der Tee*
beer	*das Bier*
wine	*der Wein*

Numbers
0	*null*	18	*achtzehn*
1	*eins*	19	*neunzehn*
2	*zwei*	20	*zwanzig*
3	*drei*	21	*einund-zwanzig*
4	*vier*		
5	*fünf*	30	*dreissig*
6	*sechs*	32	*zweiund-dreissig*
7	*sieben*		
8	*acht*	40	*vierzig*
9	*neun*	50	*fünfzig*
10	*zehn*	60	*sechzig*
11	*elf*	70	*siebzig*
12	*zwölf*	80	*achtzig*
13	*dreizehn*	90	*neunzig*
14	*vierzehn*	100	*hundert*
15	*fünfzehn*	101	*hunderteins*
16	*sechzehn*	500	*fünfhundert*
17	*siebzehn*	1,000	*tausend*

Laundry
Most towns of any size in former West Germany have a laundromat—

Waschsalon—with prices ranging from DM5 for a wash (usually this will include the soap). Campgrounds have their own laundry facilities.

Lost property
All bus and train stations have lost-property offices; look in the telephone directory or inquire at the station for the Fundbüro.

It is very important to read carefully the instructions for loss issued with your traveler's checks. Make a separate note of the serial numbers of all checks (or take photocopies) and of the telephone number to call in case of emergency.

Major issuing companies will have refund facilities available. Contact their nearest office or, failing that, contact the nearest bank. Always register loss of checks with the police and, if you are stranded without money, contact your local consulate.

Follow similar procedure for the loss or theft of Eurocheques and credit cards. Lost passports should be reported to the police station, and you will have to contact your consulate if you need emergency travel papers.

Maps
Road atlases
The Grosse Shaell Atlas has detailed road maps of Germany (scale 1:400,000) with scenic routes, plus city plans, maps of the rest of Europe too, and a full index.

If you take a short ferry crossing from Britain, the British Automobile Association's 1:1,000,000 double-sided map of the whole of Germany could be a useful purhcase,as it extends to Channel ports from Dieppe.

Hallwag's three 1:500,000 maps of north, east and south Germany include useful plans showing approach and through roads in all big cities.

Hostelling
Mairs, *The Youth Hostels Map of Germany,* shows the location of hostels, plus a full list together with addresses and phone numbers, for the former West Germany (only East Berlin is covered in the East).

Walking
Special tourist maps of West Germany— *"Sonderkarte"*—showing footpaths and cycling routes for popular destinations are compiled by the German Topographic Society. A full list can be obtained from Stanford's, 12 Longacre, London WC2E 9LP U.K. (tel: 0171 836 1321).

Media
The leading German quality daily papers are the conservative *Frankfurter Allgemeine Zeitung* and the more liberal *Süddeutsche Zeitung* (Munich).

In addition, nearly every main city or area has its own daily, usually a morning paper. *Die Welt* and the mass-selling tabloid *Bild*, which tends to be sensational, are the two main dailies of the right-wing Springer group.

Some weeklies are also influential: the news magazines *Spiegel*, *Stern* and *Focus*, and women's weeklies such as *Brigitte*. In many towns, local publications will give you a run-down on what's on where: in Berlin, for instance, the best are *Tip*, *Zitty*, and the English-language *Checkpoint*.

The main German TV channels, run on a regional basis, are ARD and ZDF. There are also satellite and cable channels, and many radio networks. In many hotels, TV sets can get CNN, Super or Sky with news and other English-language programs.

Money matters
The Deutschmark (DM) is the official currency. DM1 equals 100 pfennig (pf). Coins are: 1, 2, 5, 10, and 50 pfennig; 1, 2, and 5 DM. Bills come in denominations of 5, 10, 20, 50, 100, 200, 500, and 1,000 DM.

There are money exchanges—Wechselstuben—at airports, border crossings, and major train stations, generally open 6 AM–10 PM daily.

Branches of the Deutsche Verkehrs-Kredit Bank, situated in train stations, can also be used for changing money, and they usually stay open until 6. Otherwise, normal banking hours are Monday to Friday, 8:30 or 9 AM to 12:30 or 1 PM, then

2:30–4 PM (5:30 PM on Thursdays). Banks are closed on Saturday and Sunday.

You can also change money at post offices, which are open Monday to Friday, 8 AM–6 PM, and Saturdays until noon. Money exchange is usually available in larger branches in main towns and cities only.

Traveler's checks can be cashed in banks, currency exchanges and post offices. Normally, they can only be used as direct payment in the classier shops in main cities.

Eurocheques, backed by the appropriate card, can be cashed in banks and exchanges. They can also be used in some shops and restaurants, but always take the precaution of checking first. Credit cards are less widely used in Germany than in other countries, so it is always sensible to check that they are acceptable before eating a meal or making a purchase.

National holidays

January 1: New Year's Day
January 6: Epiphany (only in Baden-Württemberg and Bavaria)
Good Friday
Easter Sunday/Easter Monday
May 1: Labor Day
Ascension Day (in May)
Whit Sunday and **Whit Monday** (May)
June 18: Corpus Christi (observed only in certain areas)
August 15: Maria Himmelfahrt (Assumption of the Blessed Virgin Mary, observed only in Bavaria and Saarland)
October 3: Day of German Unity
November 1: All Saints' Day (observed only in certain areas)
Day of Prayer and Repentence (in November, exact date changes annually)
December 25/26: Christmas

Opening hours

Shop hours are normally 9 AM to 6:30 PM, Monday to Friday, though some remain open until 8:30 PM on Thursday. (In addition, some close at noon for a couple of hours.) On Saturday, shops close at 2 PM, except for the first Saturday of each month, when they're allowed to stay open until 4 PM. Only flower shops and bakers can open on Sundays (between 11 AM and 3 PM), but train stations come to the rescue: shops in their vicinity are usually open late and on weekends. So are the modest shopping areas of larger gas stations. Time your arrival carefully at smaller out-of-the-way restaurants. They often serve meals only between noon and 2 PM, then from 5 to 8 PM.

Businesspeople are usually at their desks by 9 AM, often earlier, and government offices close punctually at 4 PM, or 2 PM on Fridays. For doctors' hours, see above under **Health**.

Evening entertainments—theater, concerts and so on—usually start at 8 PM, normally lasting about two hours.

Organized tours

Deutsche Touring runs a variety of coach tours, such as Bavaria's Romantic Road (Romantische Strasse) trip from Würzburg to Füssen, or vice versa. A variety of packages lasting from two to seven days is on offer. Details are available from the company at Am Romerhof 17, 60486-Frankfurt am Main.

See the German countryside afloat, on a river trip. The Köln–Düsseldorfer (KD) Line offers trips on the Rhine, Mosel, and Elbe. Trips range from five hours to five days, and discounts for children and senior citizens are a regular feature. KD Line is at Frankenwerf 15, 50667-Köln 1 (tel: 01221 208 80).

Sächsische Dampschiff Gesellschaft Weisse Flotte boat company makes tourist trips on the Havel, Elbe, Oder and Saale rivers, and the Baltic Sea. You can get in touch with them at Terrassenufer 1–2, 01067 Dresden.

Hiking is very popular in Germany, and the Jugendherbergswerk (German Youth Hostel Federation) publishes a useful list of guided walks with anything from two-day trips to cross-country treks. You can contact them at Hauptverband, Bismarckstrasse 8, D–32754 Detmold.

In addition, local tourist offices will be happy to suggest local tour opportunities.

Pharmacies

German pharmacists or their assistants are usually able to speak some English.

If you are taking a course of drugs and need to have a prescription filled while staying in Germany, get your doctor at home to write out a prescription using the generic rather than brand name. It's a good idea to have a letter from him or her to the effect that you need the drug for health purposes.

Check before leaving home that what you are taking with you is not illegal in Germany.

In larger towns, pharmacies—*Apotheken*—display late-night or 24-hour contact lists, or ask at your hotel reception or local police station where to find an open pharmacy. Apotheken trade in pharmaceuticals only—other items such as cosmetics must be purchased at a *Drogerie*.

Police

German police—*Polizei*—are well-mannered and expect members of the public to be equally correct in their behavior and forms of address.

Post offices

The main post office—*Hauptpostamt*—in any large town is usually located near the train station. Mail reaches the United States in about three days. Stamps for letters to E.U. countries cost from DM1, and stamps for postcards cost around 80pf.

To send a letter *Poste Restante* mark it "Postlagernde Briefe/Sendungen" and "Bitte Halten." As it will be filed alphabetically, according to last name, write that first on the address. Mail is kept, free of charge, for two weeks. When collecting it, take along some I.D.

Telegrams can be sent from post offices, or by telephone (see **Telephones**).

Public transportation

Domestic air services
Flights between cities are frequent and fast. Within Germany, check with Luftansa's central reservation service (tel: 01803 803 803) for information and advice on the many special ticket deals available. A smaller German airline, LTU, also offers intercity services, as does British Airways.

If you arrive at one airport and want to transfer to another, check with Lufthansa for onward train connections linking major cities.
German trains
These come in a variety of types, but all on time. The Deutsches Bundesbahn (AB) operates mainline trains.

S-Bahn trains are commuter types; the D and E trains are somewhat faster; FD trains really pick up speed, while the InterRegio (IR) trains, which link sizable towns, are fast and comfortable. Intercity trains are superquick, as are their border-crossing counterparts the Eurocity trains. InterCity Express (ICE) trains linking the cities of Munich and Hamburg don't quite break the sound barrier, but they do go very fast indeed.

A new BahnCard, for the frequent traveler to Germany, offers a 50 percent discount on standard fares for a whole year; details from European Rail, Tavistock House North, Tavistock Square, London WC1H 9HR.

If you are under 26 you may be eligible for a Eurail Youthpass. This lasts for one or two months, and offers unlimited second-class travel in Europe. Other Eurail passes exist for those who are over 26. You must buy your pass before you leave for Europe.

Buses

Buses link rural areas that railways cannot reach. Many are owned by the DB and are timed and routed to complement the train service. German towns operate their own local buses, and one ticket will often be transferable between these and other forms of city transportation, such as the S-Bahn, the Strassenbahn (trams), and the U-Bahn (subway).

On entering the bus, train or tram, passengers insert their tickets into a machine that validates them for that trip. Inspectors make frequent rounds to check that tickets are valid—and they are tough on fare dodgers.

Taxis
It is possible to hail a taxi in the street or pick one up from the many ranks at train stations, hotels, and so on.

They carry an illuminated roof sign, and fares are made up of a basic charge plus payment per kilometer (just over ½ mile) traveled. This varies from place to place, as do surcharges for carrying items of luggage, though this is usually somewhere in the region of 50pf per item.

Senior citizens
Certain discounts on public transportation systems for senior citizens are available, but since these benefits are regularly updated, it's best to get the latest information. This can be obtained from the Deutsches Zentrum für Altersfragen, M. von Richthofenstrasse 2, D–12101 Berlin.

German railways sell Senior Pass cards, which allow for half-price travel for part or whole weeks (ask any German National Tourist Office for details).

Student and youth travel
There are over 600 youth hostels in Germany that accept members of all associations affiliated with Hostelling International—USA, based at 733 15th St. N.W., Washington, DC 20005, tel. 202 783 6161.

Deutsches Jugendherbergswerk Hauptverband (the German youth hostel association) publishes a complete list of hostels; it is on sale (DM6.50) at tourist offices and hostels themselves.

It's wise, particularly in peak season, to prebook accommodations in hostels; officially, there's a three-day limit to your stay, though if the hostel is not full you may be able to remain longer. It is worth noting that in Bavaria priority is given to under-27s.

The DJH is at Bismarckstrasse 8, Postfach 1455, D–32704 Detmold (tel: 5231 74010).

If you are under 23, or a student under 27, inquire about the Tramper Monats Ticket, entitling holders to one month's unlimited travel on the DB system (except the ICE) and DB buses. Prices start at around DM290 (DM300+ for ICE).

Ask at train stations for further details (remember to take along some form of identification to prove your age).

Telephones
A few public phone booths take 10pf, DM1 and DM5 coins. Most also take phone cards—*Kartentelefone*—which you can buy at the post or tourist office for DM12 or DM50. Local calls cost 30pf for five minutes. You cannot make international calls from booths marked "National." You can also go to a post office, where the connection will be made for you and you pay after you have made the call.

For information, dial 1188 or, for Europe, 00118. For the operator, dial 010 (for Germany) or 0010 (for abroad). It is worth remembering that call rates are lower after 8 PM and on weekends. To call the United States or Canada, dial 001; Britain, 0044; Ireland, 00353; Australia, 0061; New Zealand, 0064.

Time
German time is one hour ahead of British time nearly all the year except for a few weeks in spring (when Germany is two hours ahead) and autumn (when the two times are the same): this is because the Continent changes its clocks sooner than Britain. German time is usually six hours ahead of New York and Toronto time, nine hours behind eastern Australian time, and 11 hours behind New Zealand.

Tourist offices
Staff are normally very helpful and will provide maps and literature on attractions in the area, plus a list of local hotels. Sometimes they may be willing to make a reservation for a room for you (for a small fee).

The head office of the German National Tourist Organization, the Deutsche Zentrale für Tourismus, is based at Beethovenstrasse 69, D–60325 Frankfurt am Main (tel: 069 75720).

In the **United States** the German National Tourist Office is at 122 East 42nd Street, New York, NY 10168–0072 (tel: 212/661 7200). **Canada** has the German National Tourist Office at 175 Bloor Street East, North Tower, 6th Floor, Toronto, Ontario, M4W 3R8 (tel: 416/968 1570). In the **United Kingdom** the GNTO is at 65 Curzon Street, London W1Y 7PE (tel: 0171 495 3990). In **Australia**, the office is at Lufthansa House, 9th Floor, 143 Macquarie Street, Sydney 2000 (tel: 00612 3673890). There is no office in **Ireland**. Enquiries can be dealt with by the London office. For **New Zealand**, the nearest tourist office is based in Australia.

Tourist offices in major German cities include:

Berlin
Europa-Center Budapester Strasse, 10787 Berlin (tel: 030 262 6031)

Bonn
Munsterstrasse 20, 53111 Bonn (tel: 0228 77 34 66)

Hamburg
Burchhardt-Strasse 14, 20095 Hamburg (tel: 040 30 05 10)

Köln
Verkehrsamt Am Dom, 50667 Köln (tel: 0221 3340)

Munich
Sendlinger Strasse 1, 80331 Munich (tel: 089 2330 300)

Taking in the fantastic view from Jenna Mountain, Berchtesgaden

Walking and hiking
There are more than 82,500 miles of walks in Germany. Detailed information can be obtained from the Verband Deutscher Gebirgs- und Wanderverein, Reichsstrasse 4, D–66111 Saarbrücken 3. The Deutsches Alpenverein, which is based at Praterinsel 5, D–80538 Munich 2, can give advice on hiking trips in the Alps and also organizes a number of mountaineering courses. So can the Summit-Club, Am Perlacher Forst 180, 81545 Munich, (tel: 089 6510 720).

HOTELS AND RESTAURANTS

Accommodations

These recommended hotels are divided into three price brackets, for a double bedroom with breakfast for two:

(B) **budget**: up to DM 160.
(M) **moderate**: from DM160 to DM280.
(E) **expensive**: over DM280.

BERLIN

Alsterhof Ringhotel
Augsburgerstrasse 5, D-10787 Berlin (tel: 212420). Set behind Berlin's big department store KaDeWe. Considerable style inside, despite ugly exterior. Well-equipped and practical bedrooms. Stylish restaurant. Conservatory annexe. (E)

Hotel Belvedere
Seebergsteig 4, 14193 Berlin (tel: 82 60 010). A gabled villa in a quiet garden, in the chic western suburb of Grünewald. A high-grade but homey *pension*, like a private home; period furnishings. (B)

Bristol Kempinski
Kurfürstendamm 27, D-10719 Berlin (tel: 88 43 40). Regards itself as the only place of its class in west Berlin. Highly traditional, rather staid furnishings. Restaurants with elaborate, ambitious and, of course, very expensive menu. (E)

Hecker's Hotel
Grolmanstrasse 35, 10623 Berlin (tel: 88 90 0). Just off Ku'damm in a quiet sidestreet. Bright, spacious bedrooms, good range of facilities. (E)

Hotel-Pension Dittberner
Wielandstrasse 26, 10707 Berlin (tel: 881 64 85). Charming and idiosyncratic. Frau Lange's *pension* is something of a cult. Classy art gallery on the main floor. The rooms may not be faultless, the facilities may be simple, but for these prices there is nowhere better in Berlin. (B)

Hotel-Pension Modena
Wielandstrasse 26, 10707 Berlin (tel: 8 85 70 10).

Directly below the Dittberner, on the second floor, and in its way just as recommendable for its good housekeeping. Pleasant and welcoming owners. Clean rooms. (B)

Hotel-Pension Schöneberg
Hauptstrasse 135, 10827 Berlin (tel: 7818830). This elegant and stylish building has comfortable rooms with a well-supplied buffet breakfast and a small bar. (B)

Hotel Residenz Berlin
Meinekestrasse 9, 10719 Berlin (tel: 88 44 30). Elegant building with captivating Jugendstil decoration. Ancient and rather terrifying elevator travels to upper bedrooms. High-ceilinged rooms give a sense of Berlin's prewar beauty. French cuisine in Grand Cru restaurant. (E)

Seehof Lietzensee-Ufer 11, 14057 Berlin (tel: 3 20 020). Situated beside a small lake in Charlottenburg. Fairly formal, but staff are friendly. Many rooms and dining room (good food) face the lake. Garden terrace; pool. (E)

NORTHWEST GERMANY

Abtei Abteistrasse 14, 20149 Hamburg (tel: 040 44 29 05). Small, elegant, and family run with a personal touch, in a wealthy residential area. Handsome furniture, lovely garden. Excellent cooking, for residents only. (E)

Atlantic Hotel An der Alster 72-79, 20099 Hamburg (tel: 040/28880). Elegant and famous hotel near lake. Swimming pool. (E)

Benen-Diken-Hof
Süderstrasse, 25980 Sylt Ost (tel: 04651 31035). In the pretty village of Keitum, an attractive bed-and-breakfast. (E)

Bergström Hotel Bei der Lüner Mühle, 21335 Lüneburg (tel: 04131/3080). Comfortable, well situated at the water's edge in the Wasserviertel. (M)

Friesenhof Hauptstrasse 16, 25996 Wenningstedt, Sylt (tel: 04651 41031). Former Friesen guest house turned into a modest modern hotel. (M)

Fürstenhof Celle
Hannoverschestrasse 55/56, 29221 Celle (tel: 05141 2010). Elegant former palace in center, with superb food. Swimming pool. (E)

Kaiserhof Kronsforder Allee 11-13, 23560 Lübeck (tel: 0451 791011). Bed-and-breakfast hotel in tastefully renovated old town houses. Swimming pool. (B)

Landhaus Louisenthal
28359 Leher Heerstrasse 105, (tel: 232076). In the suburb of Horn, this handsome 18th-century mansion is now an appealing family-run hotel, with a garden. Good food served in a half-timbered building. (M)

Maritim Grand
Friedrichswall 11, 30159 Hannover (tel: 0511 36770). Well located in the center of town, modern. (E)

Mövenpick 3300
Jöddenstrasse 3, Braunschweig (tel: 0531 48170). Part of the Swiss-owned Mövenpick chain; very central. Swimming pool. (M)

Niemeyer's Posthotel
Hauptstrasse 7, 29328 Fassberg-Müden (tel: 05053 10 77). Pleasantly rustic and *gemütlich*, but full of comfort. A half-timbered old building in a village on Lüneburg Heath. Superb local dishes.(M)

Romantikhotel Georgenhof
Herrenhauser Kirchweg 20, 30167 Hannover (tel: 0511 70 22 44). Small, elegant yet quite rustic, set in a large garden in the suburbs. Superb French and German regional cooking served in the chic Stern restaurant. (E)

Vier Jahreszeiten Neuer Jungfernstieg 9-14, 20354 Hamburg (tel: 040 34940). Ultraluxury and well-run hotel located by the Binnenalster. Excellent service. (E)

Waldersee
Walderseestrasse 39, 30177

Hannover – List (tel: 0511 909910). Northeast of center, in List, by park. Bed-and-breakfast hotel. Swimming pool. (M)
Am Wasserturm Blasberg 13, 24943 Flensburg (tel: 0461 36071). Quiet, at edge of Volkspark. Simple and tasteful in style. Swimming pool. (B)

RHINELAND

Breidenbacher Hof Heinrich-Heine-Alle 36, Düsseldorf (tel: 0211 13030). Luxury, with a bar where the "in" people meet. (E)
Brenner Rizzastrasse 20–22, 56068 Koblenz (tel: 0261 32060). Small, central bed-and-breakfast hotel with friendly and efficient service. Garden. (M)
Burghhotel auf Schönburg 55430 Oberwesel (tel: 06744 70 27). Perched high above the Rhine, a medieval castle converted into a hotel. Friendly family owners, beamed courtyards, four-poster beds and very good food. (M)
Esplanade Fürstenplatz 17, 40215 Düsseldorf (tel: 0211 375010). Modern bedrooms with cable TV. English-style restaurant. (E)
Eurener Hof Eurener Strasse 171, 542904 Trier – Euren (tel: 0651 88077). Rustic-style decor; rooms well furnished. Swimming pool. (B)
Favorite Parkhotel Karl Weiserstr 1, 55131 Mainz (tel: 06131 80150). Set in an attractive location amid trees at the edge of the city's Stadtpark. Comfortable, well-kept. (M)
Günnewig Bristol Prinz-Albertstrasse 1, 53113 Bonn (tel: 0228 26980). Luxury hotel, located near station. Swimming pool. (E)
Haus Lipman Marktplatz 3, 56814 Beilstein (tel: 02673 15 73). Picturesque and full of character, this old half-timbered inn beside the Mosel river serves good regional food on a flowery

terrace. You can drink with the locals in a vaulted pub. Rooms are quaint but comfortable. (B)
Petrisberg Sickingerstrasse 11–13, 54290 Trier (tel: 0651 41181). Modern bed-and-breakfast hotel in wonderful position on vine-clad hill above town (20-minute walk). (B)
Hotel Pfalzer Wald Kurtalstrasse 77, 76887 Bad Bergzabern (tel: 06343 10 56). A warm welcome and good food are offered at this family-run hotel beside a lake amid green hills, on the edge of a spa resort. (B)
Schlosshotel Kommende Ramersdorf Oberkasselerstrasse 10, Ramersdorf, 53227 Bonn (tel: 0228 440734). Elegant small hotel in grounds of castle with an Italian restaurant. (M)
Schloss Wilkinghege Steinfurterstrasse 374, 48159 Münster (tel: 0251/213045). 16th-century building in quiet rural setting. Atmospheric restaurant. (M)
Schnellenburg Rotterdamerstrasse 120, 40474 Düsseldorf (tel: 0211 43 41 33). Right beside the Rhine and close to the exhibition center, a small hotel of some character. River views from some rooms, and from the excellent restaurant. (M)
Hotel im Wasserturm Kaygasse 2, 50676 Köln (tel: 0221 20080). Declared a city historic site, in a former water tower. Spacious and comfortable, renovated at the end of 1989. Roof terrace with views. (E)

CENTRAL GERMANY

Altes Herrenhaus zum Bären Marktplatz 15, 56379 Holzappel (tel: 06439 70 14). In the village square, a half-timbered 17th-century house, now a small and stylish hotel. Good, food in a cozy room. (M)
Hotel Corum Rudolph-Breitscheidstrasse 3, 04105 Leipzig (tel: 0451 79 10 11).

HOTELS AND RESTAURANTS

Near the station, a newly modernized business hotel, fully up to western standards. Health club. Good food. (M)

Detmolder Hof Langestrasse 19, 32756 Detmold (tel: 05231 282 44). A much-gabled hotel in the main street, offering old-world charm. Friendly and efficient staff. Good modern cooking. (M)

Domus Erzbergerstrasse 1–5, 34117 Kassel (tel: 0561 72960). Elegant and charming, in *Jugendstil*. (B)

Dorint Hotel Kreuzeck Am Kreuzeck, 38644 Goslar (tel: 05325 74140). Located in an attractive part of the Upper Harz—at the spa of Hahnenklee. Swimming pool. (M)

Dornröschenschloss Saburg, 34369 Hofgeismar (tel: 05671 80 80). The Brothers Grimm stayed at this 14th-century former royal Schloss whilst on a hunting trip. It has been named after *The Sleeping Beauty* and is self-consciously "romantic," but appealing. Try the game dishes, when in season. (M)

Frankfurt Inter-Continental Wilhelm-Leuschnell-Strasse 43, 60329 Frankfurt am Main (tel: 069 26050). First-class international hotel near to the river. Swimming pool. (E)

Hardtwald Hotel Philosophenweg 31, 61350 Bad Homburg (tel: 06172 81026). Modern, in a quiet area. Attractive terrace. (M)

Hessischer Hof Friedrich Ebert Anlage 40, 60325 Frankfurt am Main (tel: 069 75400). Elegant town house furnished with antiques. (E)

Zum Löwen Markstrasse 30, 37115 Duderstadt (tel: 05527 3072). Built in the 16th century and renovated in 1988. Good cooking. (M)

Nassauer Hof Kaiser Friedrichplatz 3, 65183 Wiesbaden (tel: 0611 1330). Opposite the Kurhaus, ultra-elegant luxury hotel. Ample facilities, including swimming pool. (E)

Parkhotel Ropeter Kasseler Landstrasse 45, 37081 Göttingen (tel: 0551 9020). Extremely quiet, despite proximity to roads. Swimming pool. (B)

Westend Westendstrasse 15, 60325 Frankfurt am Main (tel: 069 746702). Old-fashioned bed-and-breakfast in private house in residential area, with atmosphere, garden. (M)

EASTERN GERMANY

Anna's Hof Haupstrasse 118, 01824 Gohrisch (tel: 035021 682 91). In a little resort by the Elbe, a neat villa now a small and friendly privately run hotel, of a kind still uncommon in the former GDR. Decent Saxon cooking. (B)

Bülow Residenz Rähnitzgasse 19, 01097 Dresden (tel: 0351 440 33). Quite central, a handsome 18th-century baroque mansion now a luxury hotel, elegant but friendly. Good Swabian cooking. (E)

Dresdner Hilton An der Frauenkirche 5, 01067 Dresden (tel: 0351 48410). Central. One of Dresden's well-known and overpriced hotels, built when the Communists were still in power. The hotel also boasts a swimming pool. (E)

Erfurter Hof Willy Brandt Platz 1, 99084 Erfurt (tel: 00361 5310). Near station; despite its dilapidated appearance, the interior is modern and fairly comfortable. (M)

Flamberg Hotel, Am Markt 19, 99423 Weimar (tel: 03643 8020). Established in the 17th century; one of Germany's most famous hotels, with a guest list to prove it. Large bedrooms. (E)

Gaststätte Grenzbaude Haupstrasse 161, 02799 Waltersdorf (tel: 035841 26 83). Situated in a ski-resort by the Czech border, a rustic-style place with beer garden and good food. Swimming pool. (B)

Intercontinental Gerbustrasse 15, Leipzig

04105 Leipzig (tel: 0341 9880). Very large; modern. Pool. (E)

Linderhof Strasse des Friedens 12, 99198 Erfurt-Linderbach (tel: 0361 421 19 20). Near Erfurt, this is a new building in a rural farm setting, well run by local couple. Restaurant. (M)

Maritim Bellevue Grosse Meissner Strasse 15, 01097 Dresden (tel: 0351 56620). Good service and plenty of facilities. Swimming pool. (E)

Martha Hospiz Nieritzstrasse 11, 01097 Dresden (tel: 0351 567 60). Founded by the Lutheran churches as a hostel, and still church-owned today, this building north of the Elbe offers discreet comfort. Inexpensive restaurant. (M)

Residenz Joop Jean-Burgerstrasse 16, 339112 Magdeburg (tel: 0391 626 20). The friendly Joop family, returned from exile in the west, have reclaimed their old gabled villa to form this elegant bed-and-breakfast hotel. (M)

Schloss Cecilienhof Neuer Garten, 14469 Potsdam (tel: 0331 370 50). This Tudor-style country house, situated in a park by the Havel lake, is worth visiting for its famous history (see page 45) and has decent food and comfort. (E)

THE SOUTHWEST

Alt Heidelberg Rohrbacherstrasse 29, 691158 Heidelberg (tel: 06221 9150). Near the old town, with excellent restaurant. (M)

Bad Hotel Otto Neidhart Allee 5, 75385 Teinach–Zavelstein (tel: 07053 290). A former royal residence, with a corridor linking the hotel directly to the spa facilities including swimming pool. (M)

Bayerischer Hof Am Bodensee, 8990 Lindau (tel: 08382 5055). On the island, near the port. Swimming pool. (M)

Brenner's Park-Hotel Schillerstrasse 6, 76530 Baden–Baden (tel: 07221 9000). One of Germany's most luxurious hotels (host to Queen Victoria, among others). Facilities include beauty center and swimming pool. (E)

Erbguth's Landhaus Nuegartenstrasse 39, 88709 Hagnau (tel: 07532 90 51). A sophisticated villa by Lake Constance, run with panache by the Erbguth family. Splendid comfort and cooking. (E)

Der Europäische Hof Hotel Europa, Friedrich Ebert Anlage 1, 69117 Heidelberg (tel: 06221 5150). Traditional, family owned, quiet inner courtyard, good cuisine. (E)

Heiligenstein Heiligensteinstrasse 19a, Neuweier (tel: 07223 520 25). Vineyards slope down to this modern chalet-style hotel in a Baden wine village. Charming staff, cozy atmosphere and excellent local cooking. Sauna. (M)

Hirschgasse Hirschgasse 3, 69120 Heidelberg (tel: 06221 4540). A historic inn dating from 1472, with beautifully and individually decorated bedrooms. The inn also has an excellent restaurant. (E)

Hohenlohe Weilertor 14, Schwäbisch Hall (tel: 0791 75870). Most of the rooms have large balconies. The hotel lies behind trees by a small lake. Swimming pool. (M)

Hohenried Zeppelinstrasse 5, 72250 Freudenstadt (tel: 07441 2414 16). Most rooms have private balconies, in peaceful hotel just outside this large Black Forest resort. Swimming pool. (M)

Kaiser's Tanne-Wirtshus Am Wirbstein 27, 79874 Breitnau (tel: 07652 120 10). This big chalet-style Black Forest hotel is stylishly folksy, full of warmth and charm. Swimming pool, garden. Splendid food. (M)

Krone Uhlandstrasse 1, 72072 Tübingen (tel: 07071 31036). Solid hotel with formal or rustic-style bedrooms. (M)

Löwen Marktplatz 2, 88709 Meersburg (tel: 07532 430 40). In the market square of a pretty town on Lake Constance, a picturesque vine-clad 15th-century building, full of heirlooms and antiques. Good local cooking in a cozy restaurant. (M)

Maritim Parkhotel Friedrichsplatz 2, 68165 Mannheim (tel: 0621 15880). Jugendstil, elegant, with formal atmosphere and good service. Swimming pool. (E)

Am Markt Marktplatz 18, 76530 Baden-Baden (tel: 07221 227 47). In the heart of this smart resort, yet modest and family run. Plentiful Baden cooking. (B)

Öschberghof Golfplatz 1, 78166 Donaueschingen (tel: 0771 840). On an 18-hole golf course, used more by companies arranging seminars. Swimming pool. (M)

Parkhotel Wehrle Marktplatz, 78098 Triberg (tel: 07722 860 20). In a small Black Forest town, a very stylish old hostelry with charming family owners. Swimming pools. Superb food. (M)

Das Pelikan Türlensteg 9, 73525 Schwäbisch Gmünd (tel: 07171 3590). In the middle of the old town, this old building has recently been renovated. (B)

Romantik Hotel Der Kleine Prinz Lichtentaler Strasse 36, 07221 Baden-Baden (tel: 76530 3464). Small, elegant and stylish family-run hotel in a pedestrian precinct. (M)

Romantik Hotel Spielweg Spielweg 61, 79244 Münstertal (tel: 07636 709 77). Luxuriously elegant yet warmly cozy, an old Black Forest hostelry amid hills, owned and run by the charming Fuchs family for five generations. Swimming pool, garden. Superb Baden cooking and buffet breakfasts. (E)

Zum Roten Bären Oberlinden 12, 79098 Frieburg (tel: 0761 387 870). In the old city, a 600-year-old inn of character with glorious painted façade. Sauna. Good food. (M)

Am Schelztor Schelztorstrasse 5, 73728 Esslingen (tel: 0711 353051). Comfortable, central—opened in 1986. (B)

Am Schlossgarten Schillerstrasse 23, 70173 Stuttgart (tel: 0711 20260). A luxury hotel facing the palace gardens. (E)

Zum Schwanen Uferstrasse 16, 69151 Neckargemünd (tel: 06223 70 70). You can dine deliciously under the trees by the river at this warm and charming little hotel on the Neckar. (M)

Schloss Döttingen Hubertusstrasse 2, 74542 Braunsbach (tel: 07906 1010). Former hunting lodge turned into a simple but comfortable hotel. Swimming pool. (B)

Schwarzwaldhof Hohenriederstrasse 74, 72250 Freudenstadt (tel: 07441 7421). Rustic hotel in a peaceful setting near a golf course. Swimming pool. (B)

Steigenberger Badischer Hof Lange Strasse 47, 76530 Baden-Baden (tel: 07221 9340). Comfortable, well-furnished rooms. Swimming pools and elegant restaurant. (E)

Steigenberger Inselhotel Auf der Insel 1, 78462 Konstanz (tel: 07531 81250). Formerly a monastery, now turned into a luxury lakeside hotel. Garden. (E)

Victoria Eisenbahnstrasse 54, 79098 Freiburg (tel: 0761 31881). Small and friendly; no restaurant. (M)

Weber Hotel Frankenthalerstrasse 85, 68307 Mannheim – 31-Sandhofen (tel: 0621 77010). Styled like an old farm-house, but with all modern comforts. (M)

NORTHERN BAVARIA

Anker Obertorstrasse 6–8, 97828 Marktheidenfeld (tel: 09391 60 04 0). In a wine town on the Main, a modern hotel with family ambience. Rich, much-praised cooking. (M)

283

HOTELS AND RESTAURANTS

Aschaffenburger Hof
Frohsinnstrasse 11, 63739
Aschaffenburg (tel:
06021 21441). Centrally
located, quiet, with good
range of modern facilities.
(M)
Bären Hofbronnengasse 9,
91541 Rothenburg-ob-der-
Tauber (tel: 09861 94410).
Quietly situated, recently
renovated. Good
cooking. (M)
Bavaria
Feldkirchenerstrasse 67,
85055 Ingolstadt (tel: 0841
95340). Tasteful small bed-
and-breakfast hotel.
Swimming pool. (B)
Bayerischer Hof
Bahnhofstrasse 14, 95444
Bayreuth (tel: 0921
78600). Modernized hotel
near station; fine
swimming pool and a
restaurant terrace. (B)
Bischofshof am Dom
Krautermarkt 3, 93047
Regensburg (tel: 0941
59086). Old inn with beer
garden and offering very
good food. (M)
Central Kulmbacherstrasse
4, 95030 Hof (tel: 09281
6050). Modern, rustic-style
interior; frequently used for
conferences. (M)
Residenz Heinz Winkler
Kirchplatz 1 (tel: 09052 17
99 0). This 15th-century
coaching inn contains one
of Germany's best
restaurants. Lovely
bedrooms. (E)
Landhotel Schindlerhof
Steinacherstrasse 6–8,
90427 Nürnberg-Boxdorf
(tel: 0911 93 020). On
the city's outskirts,
this big 17th-century
farmhouse is now an
unusual hotel. Rustic yet
sophisticated with stylish
bedrooms, superb food.
Sauna. (M)
Pflaums Posthotel
Nürnbergerstrasse 12–16,
91257 Pegnitz (tel: 09241
72 50). Stylishly civilized
old posthouse with a
musical flavor (Bayreuth
is nearby). Warm family
owners, the Plaums.
Some rooms traditional,
some daringly modern.
Stunning food. Swimming
pool and pleasant
garden. (E)

**Romantik Hotel
Augsburger Hof** Auf dem
Kreuz 2, 86152 Augsburg
(tel: 0821 31 40 83).
Gasthof Zur Rose
Dedlerstrasse 9, 82487
Oberammergau (tel: 08822
4706). Traditional little inn,
simple and friendly, with
good food. (B)
St Nepomuk Obere
Mühlbrücke 9, 96049
Bamberg (tel: 0951 251 83).
Built on stilts on the
rushing river, an old
millhouse stylishly
converted. Excellent food,
pleasant staff. (M)
Steigenberger Hotel Am
Kurwald 2, 94086 Bad
Griesbach (tel: 08532 7990).
A large and spacious spa
hotel with all the
appropriate facilities.
Swimming pool. (E)
Waldhotel Stein 95448
Bayreuth-Seulbitz (tel:
0921 90 01). In a village
near Bayreuth, excellent
modern hotel superbly run
by Stein family. Rooms
are in villas in the big
garden. Caring staff, good
food, (M)
Walfisch Am Pleidenturm 5,
97070 Würzburg (tel: 0931
50055). A family-run inn
with good home cooking.
(M)
Weinhaus Steichele
Knorrstrasse 2, 90402
Nürnberg (tel: 0911
204378). Central, old
fashioned family-run wine
tavern, with good
cooking. (B)
Wilder Mann Am
Rathausplatz, 94032 Passau
(tel: 0851 35071). Fine old
mansion with renowned
restaurant. (M)

MUNICH AND THE ALPS

Alpenhotel Kronprinz Am
Brandholz, 83471
Berchtesgaden (tel: 08652
6070). Spacious bedrooms
and elegantly furnished
dining areas. (M)
Biederstein Keferstrasse
18, 80802 München (tel:
089 395072). Stylish
bed-and-breakfast in a

residential part of
Schwabing. (B)
Englischer Garten
Liebergesellstrasse 8,
80802 München (tel: 089
392034). At the edge of
the Englischer Garten, in
Schwabing, a homey
bed-and-breakfast guest
house in converted water
mill. (B)
Garmischer Hof
Chamonixstrasse 10, 82467
Garmisch Partenkirchen
(tel: 08821 51091). Stylish
bed-and breakfast chalet in
center, with fine garden
and views. (B)
Krone Am Rad 5, 83471
Berchtesgaden (tel: 08652 6
20 51). Cozily furnished in
Bavarian rustic style, this
small hotel on a hill oin the
outskirts has a warm
ambience and good home
cooking. (B)
Müller Alpseestrasse 16,
87645 Schwangau (tel:
08362 8 19 90). Stylish and
well run. The great royal
castles are in full view.
Food in the winter garden
is excellent. (M)
An der Oper
Falkenturmstrasse 10,
80331 München (tel: 089
2900270). Simple, good-
value bed-and-breakfast
hotel near
the opera. (B)
Splendid
Maximilianstrasse 54,
80538 München (tel: 089
296606). Central bed-and-
breakfast hotel, with
elegant, traditional decor.
(M)
Staudacherhof
Höllentalstrasse 48, 82467
Garmisch Partenkirchen
(tel: 08821 55155). Large
chalet bed-and-
breakfast hotel, with
excellent views. Swimming
pools. (M)
Turmwirt Ettalerstrasse 2,
82487 Oberammergau (tel:
08822 3091). Popular old
hotel with lively folk
evenings. (B)
Vier Jahreszeiten
Maximilianstrasse 17,
80539 München (tel: 089
230390). Luxury hotel with
all facilities, including a
rooftop swimming pool
and highly rated
restaurants. (E)

Index

INDEX

INDEX/ACKNOWLEDGMENTS

288

Acknowledgments

The Automobile Association would like to thank the following photographers, libraries and associations for their assistance in the preparation of this book.
ALLSPORT UK LTD 23 Boris Becker MARY EVANS PICTURE LIBRARY 14 Beethoven, 24/5 French royalty, 25 French ruler, 26 German patricians, 27 Peasants co-opt leader, 27 Paul Rieth, 28/9 Nazi rally, 28 Treaty of Versailles, 29 Nazi Parteitag, Nürnberg, 32 Baccalaureate lecture, Luther 33 Friedrich Wilhelm Nietzsche, Hansel and Gretel, 75 Danzig, Ships – Hanseatic League, 120 Grimm's Red Riding Hood, 121 The Valiant Tailor, The Goose Girl, 147 Händel, 237a Wagner with Cosima, 237b Wagner, 261 Ludwig II FOOTBALL ASSOCIATION 17 L Matthaeus GERMAN NATIONAL TOURIST OFFICE 15 Berlin Philharmonic, 17 Skiing, 18 Courthouse, Bonn REX FEATURES LTD 23 Helmut Schmidt, Helmut Kohl SPECTRUM COLOUR LIBRARY LTD 14 Munich Oktoberfest, 20 Smoking chimneys, 21 BMW Black Forest, Car scrapyard, 259 Munich Oktoberfest THE BRIDGEMAN ART LIBRARY 35 *People by the Pool, The Garden Café* (Kirchner) 240b *Wings of Desire* TOPHAM PICTURE SOURCE 30 Breaking down the Berlin Wall ZEFA PICTURES LTD 19 Money, Hintergrund.
All remaining pictures are held in the AA's own photo library (© AA Photolibrary) with contributions from:
A BAKER 3, 4, 5, 6/7, 8b, 9a, 12, 16a, 20/1, 27c, 31b, 34, 38, 39, 42, 43, 44, 46, 47, 49, 50, 79, 80, 81, 82, 84, 88, 89, 90, 91, 92, 93, 95, 96, 98, 99, 100, 101, 106, 107, 112, 113, 114, 131, 133, 166, 173, 174, 175, 177, 178, 179, 181, 183, 184b, 185, 186, 187, 189, 191, 192, 193, 195, 196/7, 198, 199, 200, 201, 202, 203, 204, 205, 208, 209, 210, 211, 212, 213, 214, 215, 217, 218, 219, 221, 222, 223, 224, 225, 226, 227, 228/9, 229, 230, 231, 232, 233, 234, 235, 236, 240, 241, 242, 244, 246, 247, 248, 249a, 250, 251, 252, 253, 256, 257, 258, 260, 261, 262, 263, 264, 265, 267, 271, 279 P ENTICKNAP 13a, 83 R STRANGE 240b D TRAVERSO 7, 10, 13b, 15b, 31a, 35c, 40, 45, 48, 51, 54, 55, 56, 57, 60, 61, 62, 63, 64, 65, 67, 68, 69, 70, 71, 73, 74, 75, 77, 105, 109, 110, 111, 117, 118, 119, 122, 123, 124, 125, 126, 127, 128, 129, 130, 134, 136, 138, 139, 140, 141, 142, 143, 144, 145, 146, 147, 148, 149, 150, 151, 152, 155, 156, 157, 158, 159, 160, 161, 162/3, 164, 165, 167, 169, 170, 171, 184a, 270, 272

Contributors

Revision copy editor: Barbara Vesey
Original copy editor: Joan Miller